SPEECHES AND
DOCUMENTS ON
NEW ZEALAND
HISTORY

SPEECHES AND DOCUMENTS ON NEW ZEALAND HISTORY

EDITED BY

W. DAVID McINTYRE

AND

W. J. GARDNER

OXFORD
AT THE CLARENDON PRESS
1971

Oxford University Press, Ely House, London W. 1

GLASGOW NEW YORK TORONTO MELBOURNE WELLINGTON
CAPE TOWN SALISBURY IBADAN NAIROBI DAR ES SALAAM LUSAKA ADDIS ABABA
BOMBAY CALCUTTA MADRAS KARACHI LAHORE
DACCA KUALA LUMPUR HONG KONG TOKYO

© OXFORD UNIVERSITY PRESS 1971

PRINTED IN GREAT BRITAIN

PREFACE

THIS selection of 194 speeches and documents is designed primarily for use in general courses on New Zealand history. Although we hope that virtually all the 'basic' documents mentioned in such courses are represented, selection from so rich and varied a field presents serious problems. Certain themes were chosen; some topics rigorously excluded. The volume leans, in the main, towards the history of 'structure', particularly the constitutional evolution of New Zealand, the development of political parties, and certain aspects of reform legislation and external relations. Thus material of a social, descriptive or quantitative nature is only slightly represented. A partial remedy has been provided by a brief statistical appendix. Consideration of the pre-annexation period has been deliberately excluded.

It may appear that this selection permits an 'optimistic' interpretation of New Zealand history. The opening section on 'Colonization' begins with a letter of Edward Gibbon Wakefield and ends with Julius Vogel's public works and immigration scheme. To some this would suggest a line of progress from idealistic planning in Britain to bold development in New Zealand. To others it might suggest a descent from the Tory idealism of Godley to the 'maxims of the counter' as practised by Vogel. It is true that some of the British founders held quasi-utopian views about the colonies they were going to establish in New Zealand, and that many of their less lofty-minded followers professed such views, but the utopian approach to New Zealand history can lead to a *cul-de-sac* remote from the harsher realities of colonial life. There does, however, run through New Zealand history a firm strain of colonial initiative, summed up in the favourite word of William Pember Reeves: 'experiment'. This was by no means a New Zealand monopoly, but so impressed were such observers as Henry Demarest Lloyd and Frank Parsons that they wrote as if New Zealand were a utopian model for their own imperfect societies. Thus, in this selection, landmarks such as the Industrial Conciliation and Arbitration Act of 1894, the Social Security Act of 1938, New Zealand's attempt to reform the League of Nations in 1936 and to revise the United

Nations charter in 1945, and the National Party's promise, in its 1943 platform, to improve housing conditions and schools, in rural areas equally with the towns, receive more attention than do critiques of New Zealand culture and society. In spite of the economic set-backs of the 1880s, the 1930s, and the 1960s, the notion of a rather special destiny for New Zealand has remained. As a leading public servant said recently of a colleague: 'What he fails to realise is that we're trying to build a nation.' An historian expressed his indignation at the growing tendency among New Zealand academics to favour the idea of federation with Australia, with the words: '*I don't* want to lose my identity.'

A selection of documents to illustrate so elusive a concept as that 'identity', would require a very wide range of material. Three significant themes have been included in this volume. First, considerable attention is given to what may be termed the failure of socialism, even in the comparatively muted terms of Reeves's 'State Socialism' or the Labour programme of 1935. The State has certainly been granted immense powers in New Zealand to foster the interests of its inhabitants. Reeves proclaimed the death of 'individualism' in the early 1890s. But New Zealand experience has proved him wrong. New Zealanders have carried the use of collective means for individual ends to a high art, provided the ends are modest. This undiminished individualism is shown in the preponderance of the National Party in New Zealand politics in the 1950s and 1960s. Thus it might be argued that the 'Left' in New Zealand, gets a disproportionate amount of space in this volume, from William Pember Reeves's articles on Socialism and Communism in 1890, and the doctrinaire socialism of the Social Democratic Party and of Harry Holland, through to the radical attack on the Labour Party leadership at the end of the 1930s, and the Fabian attack on the effects of the wartime stabilization scheme in 1948. But the failure of this pressure from the 'Left' may help us understand how both the Labour and National Parties have come to espouse a pragmatic pursuit of the mixed economy and the welfare state.

The second element of the New Zealand identity to receive some emphasis is Maori affairs, particularly the resistance, and later adjustment, of the descendants of the ancient migrants who possessed New Zealand when British colonists arrived. Although this is the biggest single section of the book, it does not adequately represent the most dramatic events in New Zealand history—the

Anglo-Maori wars of the 1860s—for to do so would give too much credence to non-Maori sources. Until the interpretation of both Maori written sources and of Maori oral tradition reaches the stage where general students have access to, and an understanding of, tribal history, the picture of the conflicts of the 1860s will be incomplete. New Zealand studies in this respect have yet to reach the level which is now possible in certain areas of African history.

The third aspect of the national identity, and the one which receives the greatest treatment here, is the overriding reality that New Zealand developed as a British Colony and a Dominion, and that its parliamentary institutions, most of its foreign and defence policies, and even its citizenship laws have been shaped by this experience. Thus two sections are devoted specifically to New Zealand's constitutional relations with Britain. In this we are indebted to two collections of documents, long used by M.A. courses in New Zealand: 'Select Documents relative to the Development of Responsible Government in New Zealand, 1839–1865', compiled by James Rutherford and 'British Colonial Policy in Relation to New Zealand, 1871–1902' compiled by D. K. Fieldhouse.

Since so many documents belong to the exchange of correspondence between Government House, Wellington, and the Colonial Office in London, a word is necessary about the version of documents used. If a dispatch from the Governor to the Secretary of State for Colonies (or vice versa) is selected: there are at least four versions of such documents available. There will, in each case, be the final signed draft (either in London or Wellington). There will be the 'dispatched' document—sent either to London or Wellington. In many cases there is then a printed version, either in the *Appendices to the Journal of the House of Representatives* or in the British *Parliamentary Papers*. All would be well if these versions were identical. But copyists and printers took great liberties in Victorian times, and where we have checked printed versions against the manuscripts, either in the National Archives or in the Colonial Office 209 series, we have not found a single printed document free from error! Often it is merely printer's mistakes and punctuation, but sometimes words are incorrectly rendered ('nation' for 'native', for example) or lines left out. In these cases we have used the 'final' manuscript version, if it is available.

Finally, we wish to extend our warmest thanks to the following colleagues who have assisted with their advice: Professors Keith

PREFACE

Sinclair and M. P. K. Sorrenson and Associate Professor P. S. O'Connor, of Auckland University, Mrs. Mary Boyd, of Victoria University of Wellington, Professor W. H. Oliver of Massey University, Professors Angus Ross and W. P. Morrell, of Otago University, Mr. P. R. May, of Canterbury University, Mr. Ian Wards of the Government Historical Publication Branch, and Professor G. W. O. Woodward, head of the Canterbury history department, who supported the expenses of preparation from his departmental fund. The staffs of the General Assembly Library, the Hocken Library, the Canterbury Public Library, the Alexander Turnbull Library, the University of Canterbury Library, the Canterbury Museum, and the National Archives have given us unfailing help in hunting down material. We would also wish to thank several generations of Canterbury students, whose tutorial classes in the documents of New Zealand history have helped us to shape this volume. We trust their successors will enjoy the convenience of this book in the place of yet another sheaf of cyclostyled papers.

Christchurch 1970   W. D. McI.
                                                                      W. J. G.

CONTENTS

CONTENTS

2. CONSTITUTIONS, GOVERNMENT, AND POLITICS, 1840s TO 1870s

CONTENTS

CONTENTS

CONTENTS

CONTENTS

CONTENTS

CONTENTS

CONTENTS

CONTENTS

CONTENTS

xix

CONTENTS

CONTENTS

CONTENTS

CONTENTS

CONTENTS

CONTENTS

CONTENTS

APPENDIX

LIST OF MAPS

ABBREVIATIONS

N.Z.P.D.	*New Zealand Parliamentary Debates*
A.J.H.R.	*Appendices to the Journals of the House of Representatives*
C.O. 209	Colonial Office original Correspondence between the Secretary of State and the Governor of New Zealand from 1839, in the Public Record Office, London.
G.1.	Ordinary Dispatches from the Secretary of State 1840–99, in the National Archives, Wellington.

1

COLONIZATION 1830s TO 1870

1. THE THEORY OF SYSTEMATIC COLONIZATION —THE SUFFICIENT PRICE

In a letter of 2 June 1835 Edward Gibbon Wakefield outlines his idea that a high price for colonial land is necessary if 'civilization' is to be transplanted, but he refuses to commit himself on a 'sufficient' price.

. . . When each member of a society employs no more capital than his own hands will use, the labour of the whole society is necessarily cut up into separate fractions as numerous as the families; each family, necessarily, in order to live, cultivates the ground, and does scarcely anything else. As each family is occupied in the same mode of production, there is no motive for exchange between the different families; and as, in such a society, there is no co-operation, so there can be no division of employments. Without co-operation and division of employments, capital and labour are so weak, so unproductive, that surplus produce, either for foreign exchange or for accumulation at home, cannot be raised. This is the primitive or barbarous state of things, under which famine is the necessary consequence of one bad season: it is a state of things which all nations have suffered; and which, during the earlier stages of the world's progress, was, in every nation, succeeded by a state of slavery. . . . Slavery appears to have been the step by which nations have emerged from poverty and barbarism, and moved onwards towards wealth and civilization. . . .

. . . along with slavery came combination of labour, division of employments, surplus produce of different sorts, the power of exchanging, a great increase of capital, all the means, in short, to that better state of things in which slavery becomes an unmixed evil, and when, accordingly, it has generally been abolished. . . .

The process by which a colony goes to utter ruin, or is reduced to misery, and then gradually recovers, has been witnessed over and over again. The colonists proceeding from a civilized country, possessing capital, divided into classes, skilful, accustomed to law and order, bent on exertion and full of high hopes; such a body of people reach their destination, and then what happens? The society, which at the moment of its landing consists of two ranks, bearing towards each other the relation of master to servant, becomes instantly a dead level, without ranks, without either servants or masters. Every one obtains land of his own. From that moment no one can employ more capital than his own hands will use. The greater part, therefore, of the capital which has been taken out necessarily wastes away. . . .

An extensive and uninhabited country is a field where, unless something be done to counteract the influence of too much land, a small body of civilized people must inevitably fall back into what is called a primitive state. Hitherto, in young colonies, the influence of too much land has been counteracted no otherwise than by means of slavery. In this case, slave-labour of every sort, whether that of slaves, bondsmen, redemptionists, or convicts, is wholly out of the question. What we have to consider, therefore, is the other means by which to preserve civilization. . . . Hence the project of an undertaking, of which the object is to try whether, in countries where land is naturally superabundant, free or hired labour may be secured by means of rendering land dear enough for that purpose. . . .

. . . let it be clearly understood, that the object in putting a price on public land is not to prevent labourers for hire from ever becoming landowners. On the contrary, everyone wishes that all the labourers taken out should be able to obtain land and servants of their own, after, and by means of, a few years of labour for hire. . . . All the purchase-money of land shall be employed in taking labourers to the colony, so that as labourers become landowners others shall arrive, not only to take their place as labourers, but also to supply them with servants, who in their turn again may become landowners and masters. Consequently, such a price only is requisite, as will prevent the labourer from becoming a landowner until he shall have worked for hire during a few years. . . .

In whatever light . . . this question is viewed, it appears that you are bound to adopt from the outset that price which you consider sufficient.

2

Do I pretend to know what that price is? Certainly not. On the contrary, I acknowledge the impossibility of ascertaining before-hand what the price ought to be; but there are means of arriving at a probable price; at that price which, all things considered, would seem to be best. . . . This is one of those numerous cases in which what seems best is best. . . .

Why, then, it may be asked, do I not name a price? I answer, because that is not my business. . . .

Great Britain, *Parliamentary Papers: Reports from Committees*, 1841, iv, 119, Appendix to the Report of the Select Committee on South Australia, pp. 332–9

2. EXTENDING THE 'FRONTIER' OF NEW SOUTH WALES

Edward Gibbon Wakefield's plea that the colonization of New Zealand, which he saw as inevitable, should not be left to take place in a haphazard fashion. He was giving evidence before the Parliamentary Select Committee on the Disposal of Land in Colonies, 27 June 1836.

. . . [Question] 961. Are there any parts of the world, subject to our dominion now, in which you imagine that new colonies might be founded advantageously under this proposed system?
[Wakefield]—Many: I consider that in Australia at present there are no colonies; I look upon the settlements in New South Wales and Van Dieman's Land as mere gaols of peculiar kind. They call the keeper 'His Excellency', and the chaplain 'Right Reverend'; but the real truth is that they are nothing else but gaols. Then South Australia is not yet founded. There remains a large extent of country between South Australia and that which is called Western Australia; there is in extra-tropical Australia, a district of ground open to colonization of which the outline, touched by the sea, cannot be less than 4,000 miles. Very near to Australia there is a country, which all testimony concurs in describing as the fittest country in the world for colonization; as the most beautiful country, with the finest climate, and the most productive soil; I mean New Zealand. It will be said that New Zealand does not belong to the British Crown, and that is true; but Englishmen are beginning to colonize New Zealand. New Zealand is becoming under the dominion of the British Crown.

Adventurers go from New South Wales and Van Dieman's Land, and make a treaty with a native chief, a tripartite treaty, the poor chief not understanding a single word about it: they make a contract upon parchment with a great seal: for a few trinckets and a little gunpowder they obtain land. After a time, in these cases, after some persons have settled, the Government at home begins to receive hints that there is a regular settlement of English people formed in such a place; and then the Government at home generally has been actuated by a wish to appoint a governor, and says, 'This spot belongs to England; we will send out a governor'. The act of sending out a governor, according to our constitution, or law, or practice, constitutes the place to which a governor is sent a British province. We are, I think, going to colonize New Zealand, though we be doing so in a most slovenly, and scrambling, and disgraceful manner. The country appears to me to be open to colonization. . . .

> *Report of the Select Committee on the Disposal of Lands in the British Colonies*, 512, 1 August 1836, p. 108.

3. MISSIONARY OPPOSITION TO THE NEW ZEALAND COMPANY

Evidence of Dandeson Coates, Lay Secretary of the Church Missionary Society, before the House of Lords Committee on New Zealand, 14 May 1838, in which he opposes the plans of the New Zealand Company on the grounds that Britain had, through the Resident, James Busby, recognized the sovereignty and independence of the New Zealand chiefs.

(*To Mr. Coates.*) Have the Committee of the Church Missionary Society formed any Opinion on the Plan of the New Zealand Association for colonizing that Country? if so, what is that Opinion, and on what Considerations is it grounded?

The Committee of the Church Missionary Society formed an Opinion on the Plan of the New Zealand Association very soon after the Prospectus of the Association was made public. They adopted, in reference to it, these Resolutions, on the 6th of June 1837:—
'First. That the New Zealand Association appears to the Committee highly objectionable, on the Principle that it proposes to engage the British Legislature to sanction the Disposal of Portions of a foreign Country over which it has no Claim of Sovereignty or Jurisdiction whatever. Secondly. That the Association is further objectionable

from its involving the Colonization of New Zealand by Europeans; such Colonization of Countries inhabited by uncivilized Tribes having been found by universal Experience to lead to the Infliction upon the Aborigines of the greatest Wrongs and most severe Injuries. Thirdly. That the Committee consider the Execution of such a Scheme as that contemplated by the New Zealand Association especially to be deprecated in the present Case, from its unavoidable Tendency, in their Judgment, to interrupt, if not to defeat, those Measures for the Religious Improvement and Civilization of the Natives of New Zealand, which are now in favourable Progress through the Labours of the Missionaries. Fourthly. That, for the Reasons assigned in the preceding Resolutions, the Committee are of opinion, that all suitable Means should be employed to prevent the Plan of the New Zealand Association from being carried into execution.' At the recent annual Meeting of the Society held on the 1st of this Month, when the Proceedings of the Society for the Year were reported to the Members, this Paragraph formed a Part of that Report: —'Your Committee cannot close their Report of this Mission,' that is, the New Zealand Mission, 'without adverting to the peculiar Situation of New Zealand as it is regarded by the Public at large. What Events may await this fair Portion of the Globe; whether England will regard with a sisterly Eye so beautiful an Island, placed like herself in a commanding Position, well harboured, well wooded, and fertile in Resources; whether this Country will so stretch forth a friendly and vigorous Arm, as that New Zealand may with her native Population adorn the Page of future History as an industrious, well-ordered, and Christian Nation, it is not for the Committee of the Church Missionary Society to anticipate; but this Consolation they do possess,—they know that the Society has for Twenty Years done good to the Natives, hoping for nothing again; nothing save the Delight of promoting Glory to God and Goodwill among Men. The Society has sent its Heralds of Peace and Messengers of Salvation, and has thus contracted such an Obligation toward those whom it has sought to benefit; that your Committee are constrained to lift up their Voice on behalf of that Island, and to claim that no Measures shall be adopted toward that interesting Country which would involve any Violation of the Principles of Justice on our Part or of the Rights and Liberties of the Natives of New Zealand.' The Grounds on which the Committee of the Church Missionary Society have arrived at the Conclusions stated in the Resolutions which I have read are briefly these: that to acquire Sovereignty in that Country would be a Violation of the fundamental Principles of international Law, New Zealand being, to all Intents and Purposes, an independent State. That Fact is evident from what I may call diplomatic Acts on the Part of this Country; a British Agent has been appointed as the Representative of the British Government in New Zealand; the Natives of New Zealand have adopted a national Flag under the Sanction of that Agent, and there is a distinct Recognition of national Sovereignty. . . .

Under the Sanction, and probably under the Influence of the British Agent, a Declaration of the Independence of New Zealand was adopted by the confederate Chiefs on the 28th of October 1835; which is as follows:—

'1. We, the hereditary Chiefs and Heads of the Tribes of the Northern Parts of New Zealand, being assembled at Waitanga, in the Bay of Islands, on this 28th Day of October 1835, declare the Independence of our Country, which is hereby constituted and declared to be an independent State, under the Designation of "The United Tribes of New Zealand".

'2. All sovereign Power and Authority within the Territories of the United Tribes of New Zealand is hereby declared to reside entirely and exclusively in the hereditary Chiefs and Heads of Tribes in their collective Capacity, who also declare that they will not allow any legislative Authority separate from themselves in their collective Capacity to exist, nor any Function of Government to be exercised within the said Territories unless by Persons appointed by them, and acting under the Authority of Laws regularly enacted by them in Congress assembled.

'3. The hereditary Chiefs and Heads of Tribes agree to meet in Congress at Waitanga, in the Autumn of each Year, for the Purpose of framing Laws for the Dispensation of Justice, the Preservation of Peace and good Order, and the Regulation of Trade; and they cordially invite the Southern Tribes to lay aside their private Animosities, and to consult the Safety and Welfare of our common Country by joining the Confederation of the United Tribes.

'4. They also agree to send a Copy of this Declaration to His Majesty the King of England, to thank him for his Acknowledgment of their Flag; and in return for the Friendship and Protection they have shown and are prepared to show to such of His Subjects as have settled in their Country, or resorted to its Shores for the Purposes of Trade, they entreat that He will continue to be the Parent of their infant State, and that He will become its Protector from all Attempts upon its Independence.

'Agreed to unanimously on this 28th Day of October 1835, in the Presence of His Britannic Majesty's Resident. . . .'

[Signatures or Marks of 35 chiefs from the region, North Cape to the Thames, witnessed by Henry Williams, George Clarke, James Clendon, and Gilbert Moir, and signed by James Busby.]

If I may be permitted, I would argue, from this Document, that it clearly establishes the Position with which I set out; viz. that New Zealand is recognized by this Country as an independent and sovereign State; consequently any Act on the Part of the Government or Legislature of this Country which would infringe the acknowledged national Sovereignty is one which the British Government cannot warrantably adopt. If the British Government cannot, on the Grounds which I have ventured to lay down, adopt any Measure which would be a direct Violation of the independent Sovereignty of New Zealand, much more impossible is it, in my humble Opinion, that the British Legislature or Government should adopt any Measure which, without directly violating that Sovereignty and Independence, would do it in an indirect Manner. I refer especially to the Idea of locating British Colonies on the Shores of New Zealand on the ground of Contracts with the Natives for the Purchase of their Lands, it being avowed that those Purchases are to carry along with them a Cession of the Sovereignty of the Tribes who made such Sales of Land to the British Government. I apprehend such a Proceeding would be a Violation of moral Obligation, on this additional Ground; that in our advanced State of Civilization we should have a clear and distinct Understanding of all the Results and Consequences of such an Arrangement as that to which I refer, while I hold it to be utterly impossible that a Set of Barbarians, like the Natives of New Zealand, can by any Explanation, however honestly given, be made to comprehend the ultimate Consequences of the Transaction, and that therefore such an Arrangement is essentially inequitable, and such as the British Government could not with Propriety make themselves Parties to. . . .

Minutes of Evidence before Select Committee on the Islands of New Zealand, House of Lords, 1838, pp. 243–6

4. THE COLONIAL OFFICE AND THE NEW ZEALAND COMPANY

Minute dated 15 March 1839 by Sir James Stephen, Permanent Under-Secretary of State for Colonies, in which he assumes that colonization is inevitable and suggests the priorities which should guide British policy in New Zealand.

1st. I assume as an established principle that the Colonization of New Zealand is, if not an expedient, at least an inevitable measure. It is, in fact, Colonized already by British subjects of the worst possible character, who are doing the greatest possible amount of evil with the least possible amount of good, and who are living under no restraint of Law or Government.

2nd. I hold that the two Cardinal points to be kept in view in establishing a regular Colony in New Zealand are, first, the protection of the Aborigines, and secondly, the introduction among the Colonists of the principle of self Government, to the utmost extent in which that principle can be reconciled with allegiance to the Crown, and with the Colony moving in the same political orbit with parent state-participating that is, in the Commercial, Diplomatic, Belligerant or Pacific relations of the Parent State. Any restrictions which aim at more than this at the Antipodes will in my judgement be utterly futile.

3rd. I, therefore, adhere to the opinions communicated by Lord Glenelg to Lord Durham in the Spring of last year. They were in substance that a Colony should be formed on the model of the Old New England Constitutions, that is, as a Body Corporate with a joint stock, the management of that stock being the business of the Governing Body in England—the Settlement and Government of the Colony being the business of the Corporation abroad. To this were added various elaborate provisions for the defence of the Natives.

4th. The real difficulty of executing this project consisted and I think still consists in obtaining a List of Names of Directors &c. which would disarm the opposition of the Great Missionary Societies—an opposition which would be fatal to any project of Colonizing N[ew] Zealand. But if this difficulty can be overcome, I hold that Lord Normanby would pursue the best practicable course by adopting and executing Lord Glenelg's project of 1838, altho' in favor of a very different List of persons.

5th. If that arrangement is impracticable, then I hold that the next best course is that of executing Lord Glenelg's second, or substituted scheme. That scheme was shortly as follows. A British Consul was to be appointed. He was to be instructed to obtain from the Natives the Cession in Sovereignty to the British Crown of such Districts as might seem to him best adapted for the purpose. He was to be armed with a Commission to govern in Her Majesty's name whatever Territory he might so acquire. A Bill was to be brought into Parlt. enabling the Queen to nominate Five or Seven persons to make Laws as a Legislative Council for the Government of the proposed Colony. The Bill would have rendered amenable to the Tribunals of that Colony any British Subjects committing Crimes within any part of the Islands of New Zealand. The Bill would also have declared invalid any future acquisitions of Land by British Subjects within New Zealand from the Native Chiefs or people. This Constitution would of course have been provisional only, and of short continuance.

6th. Besides these two modes of Colonizing New Zealand, I know of none other except that of at once establishing a Governor, Council, and Assembly. Notwithstanding all that is said of the dangers of that system of Colonial Polity, all my information compels me to think that it is the best possible scheme for any Colonial Society of the Anglo Saxon Race who are exempt from the disaster of Caste. It is only because in New Zealand that calamity would prevail between the European and the Aboriginal Colonist that I should hesitate in at once convening an assembly, if I had any voice in such a decision.

7th. There are other questions of great difficulty behind. The most considerable is the following. Shall we aquire the Sovereignty of all the Islands and brave the discussion which must follow with the United States and with France with all the arduous responsibility of protecting the Inhabitants of so extensive a Dominion? Or, shall we take the Sovereignty of particular Districts only, and hazard the evils of a new unauthorized Colonization beyond our own limits. Or, shall we attempt the middle course of obtaining from the Chiefs an agreement to place under British protection so much of the Islands as are not to be placed under British Dominion? The distinction may perhaps truly be said to be verbal rather than substantial; but in this, as in other Cases, an unsubstantial verbal distinction may be of very great practical use.

8th. Then arises the question regarding Land. I fear that great disappointment awaits the Projectors here. Enormous Tracts are already claimed by British Subjects on Titles which it will be found impossible to get rid of. The Canadian mischiefs will reappear in a new form. The local Govt. will be undersold and thwarted to a great extent in its operations respecting Land by the present claimants of the soil. For example, there is one Body in London which possesses or claims no less than a Million Acres. If nothing is done to check this abuse New Zealand will ere long be like Prince Edward's Island, the property of some Forty or Fifty English Absentees.'

The preceding brief notes may serve the purpose of showing what the questions for discussion are. If I might hazard my advice as to the right way of bringing those questions to a conclusion, I would recommend that two or three persons on the part of the Govt., should be authorized to meet a joint Deputation from all the Different Bodies of Projectors, to ascertain distinctly their common views upon the right mode of proceeding, and to report the result to Lord Normanby for the decision of his Lordship and his Colleagues. This is on the assumption that the plan of a Colonial Corporation would be entertained by the Govt. On the opposite supposition there is I think nothing to be done but to select the Consul and future Governor, and to prepare the Instructions and other Instruments under which he is to act.

C.O. 209/4, pp. 326–31

5. ANNEXATION OF NEW ZEALAND TO NEW SOUTH WALES

Instructions from the Secretary of State for War and Colonies, Lord Normanby, to Captain Hobson, recently appointed H.M. Consul at New Zealand, concerning his duty as Lieutenant-Governor of New Zealand as a part of the Colony of New South Wales, dated 14 August 1839.

... a very considerable Body of Her Majesty's Subjects have already established their residence and effected Settlements there, and that many persons in this Kingdom have formed themselves into a Society, having for its object the acquisition of Land, and the removal of Emigrants, to those Islands.

Her Majesty's Government have watched these proceedings with attention and solicitude. We have not been insensible to the importance of New Zealand to the interests of Great Britain in

Australia, nor unaware of the great natural resources by which that Country is distinguished, or that its geographical position must in seasons, either of peace or of war, enable it, in the hands of Civilized men to exercise a paramount influence in that quarter of the globe. There is probably no part of the earth in which Colonization could be effected with a greater or surer prospect of national advantage.

On the other hand, the Ministers of the Crown have been restrained by still higher motives from engaging in such an enterprise. They have deferred to the advice of the Committee appointed by the House of Commons in the year 1836, to inquire into the state of the Aborigines residing in the vicinity of our Colonial Settlements; and have concurred with that Committee in thinking that the increase of national wealth and power promised by the acquisition of New Zealand, would be a most inadequate compensation for the injury which must be inflicted on this Kingdom itself, by embarking in a measure essentially unjust, and but too certainly fraught with calamity to a numerous and inoffensive people, whose title to the soil and to the Sovereignty of New Zealand is indisputable, and has been solemnly recognised by the British Gov[ernmen]t. We retain these opinions in unimpaired force; and though circumstances entirely beyond our control have at length compelled us to alter our course, I do not scruple to avow that we depart from it with extreme reluctance. . . .

The necessity for the interposition of the Gov[ernmen]t has however become too evident to admit of any further inaction. The reports which have reached this Office within the last few months establish the facts that, about the commencement of the year 1838, a Body of not less than two thousand British Subjects had become permanent inhabitants of New Zealand, that amongst them were many persons of bad or doubtful character—convicts who had fled from our penal Settlements, or Seamen who had deserted their Ships; and that these people, unrestrained by any Law, and amenable to no tribunals, were alternately the authors and the victims of every species of Crime and outrage. It further appears that extensive cessions of Land have been obtained from the Natives, and that several hundred persons have recently sailed from this Country to occupy and cultivate those Lands. The spirit of adventure having been thus effectually roused, it can no longer be doubted that an extensive Settlement of British Subjects will be rapidly established in New Zealand; and that, unless protected and restrained by

11

necessary Laws and Institutions, they will repeat, unchecked, in that corner of the Globe, the same process of War and spoliation, under which uncivilized Tribes have almost invariably disappeared as often as they have been brought into the immediate vicinity of Emigrants from the Nations of Christendom. To mitigate, and, if possible, to avert these disasters, and to rescue the Emigrants themselves from the evils of a lawless state of Society, it has been resolved to adopt the most effective measures for establishing amongst them a settled form of Civil Gov[ernmen]t. To accomplish this design is the principal object of your Mission.

I have already stated that we acknowledge New Zealand as a Sovereign and independent State, so far at least as it is possible to make that acknowledgement in favour of a people composed of numerous, dispersed, and petty Tribes, who possess few political relations to each other, and are incompetent to act, or even deliberate, in concert. But the admission of their rights, though inevitably qualified by this consideration, is binding on the faith of the British Crown. The Queen, in common with Her Majesty's immediate Predecessor, disclaims for herself and for her Subjects, every pretention to seize on the Islands of New Zealand, or to govern them as a part of the Dominion of Great Britain, unless the free and intelligent consent of the Natives, expressed according to their established usages, shall be first obtained. Believing however that their own welfare would, under the circumstances I have mentioned, be best promoted by the surrender to Her Majesty of a right now so precarious and little more than nominal and persuaded that the benefits of British protection, and of Laws administered by British Judges would far more than compensate for the sacrifice by the Natives of a National independence which they are no longer able to maintain, Her Majesty's Gov[ernmen]t have resolved to authorize you to treat with the Aborigines of New Zealand for the recognition of Her Majesty's Sovereign authority over the whole or any parts of those Islands which they may be willing to place under Her Majesty's Dominion. I am not unaware of the difficulty by which such a Treaty may be encountered. The motives by which it is recommended are of course open to suspicion. . . .

It is not however to the mere recognition of the sovereign authority of the Queen that your endeavours are to be confined, or your negociations directed. It is further necessary that the Chiefs should be induced, if possible, to contract with you, as representing Her

12

Majesty, that henceforward no Lands shall be Ceded either gratitu-
ously or otherwise, except to the Crown of Great Britain. Con-
templating the future growth and extension of a British Colony in
New Zealand, it is an object of the first importance that the alienation of the unsettled Lands within its limits should be conducted,
from its commencement, upon that system of Sale, of which experience has proved the wisdom, and the disregard of which has
been so fatal to the prosperity of other British Settlements. . . . You
will, therefore, immediately on your arrival announce by a Proclamation addressed to all the Queen's Subjects in New Zealand, that Her
Majesty will not acknowledge as valid any title to Land in that
Country which is not either derived from, or confirmed by, a Grant
to be made in Her Majesty's name, and on her behalf. You will
however at the same time take care to dispel any apprehensions
which may be created in the minds of the Settlers that it is intended
to dispossess the owners of any property which has been acquired
on equitable conditions, & which is not upon a scale which must
be prejudicial to the latent interests of the community. . . .

I shall in the sequel explain the relation in which the proposed
Colony will stand to the Gov[ernmen]t of New South Wales. From
that relation I propose to derive the resource necessary for en-
countering the difficulty I have mentioned. The Governor of that
Colony will, with the advice of the Legislative Council, be instructed
to appoint a legislative Commission, to investigate and ascertain,
what are the Lands in New Zealand held by British Subjects under
Grants from the Natives, how far such grants were lawfully acquired,
and ought to be respected,—and what may have been the price or
other valuable considerations given for them. The Commissioners
will make their Report to the Governor, and it will then be decided
by him, how far the Claimants or any of them may be entitled to
confirmatory Grants from the Crown; and on what conditions such
confirmations ought to be made.

Having by these methods obviated the dangers of the acquisition
of large tracts of Country by mere Landjobbers, it will be your duty
to obtain, by fair and equal contracts with the Natives, the Cession
to the Crown of such Waste Lands as may be progressively required
for the occupation of Settlers resorting to New Zealand. All such
contracts should be made by yourself, through the intervention of
an Officer expressly appointed to watch over the interests of the
Aborigines as their Protector. The resales of the first purchases that

may be made, will provide the Funds necessary for future acquisitions; and, beyond the original investment of a comparatively small sum of money, no other resource will be necessary for this purpose. I thus assume that the price to be paid to the Natives by the local Gov[ernmen]t will bear an exceedingly small proportion to the price for which the same Lands will be resold by the Gov[ernmen]t to the Settlers. Nor is there any real injustice in this inequality. To the Natives or their Chiefs much of the Land of the Country is of no actual use, and, in their hands, it possesses scarcely any exchangeable value. Much of it must long remain useless, even in the hands of the British Gov[ernmen]t also, but its value in exchange will be first created, and then progressively increased, by the introduction of Capital and of Settlers from this Country. In the benefits of that increase the Natives themselves will gradually participate.

All dealings with the Aborigines for their Lands must be conducted on the same principles of sincerity, justice, and good faith as must govern your transactions with them for the recognition of Her Majesty's Sovereignty in the Islands. Nor is this all. They must not be permitted to enter into any Contracts in which they might be the ignorant and unintentional authors of injuries to themselves. You will not, for example, purchase from them any Territory the retention of which by them would be essential, or highly conducive, to their own comfort, safety or subsistence. The acquisition of Land by the Crown for the future Settlement of British Subjects must be confined to such Districts as the Natives can alienate without distress or serious inconvenience to themselves. To secure the observance of this rule will be one of the first duties of their official protector.

There are yet other duties owing to the Aborigines of New Zealand, which may be all comprised in the comprehensive expression of promoting their Civilization,—understanding by that term whatever relates to the religious, intellectual and social advancement of mankind. For their religious instruction, liberal provision has already been made by the zeal of the Missionaries, and of the Missionary Societies in this Kingdom; and it will be at once the most important, and the most grateful of your duties to this ignorant Race of men, to afford the utmost encouragement, protection and support, to their Christian Teachers. I acknowledge also the obligation of rendering to the Missions such pecuniary aid as the local Gov[ernmen]t may be able to afford, and as their increased labours may reasonably entitle them to expect. The establishment of

Schools for the education of the Aborigines in the elements of Litera-
ture, will be another object of your solicitude; and until they can be
brought within the pale of Civilized life, and trained to the adoption
of its habits, these must be carefully defended in the observance of
their own customs, so far as they are compatible with the universal
maxims of humanity and morals. But the savage practices of
human sacrifice, & of Cannibalism, must be promptly and decisively
interdicted. Such atrocities, under whatever plea of Religion they
may take place, are not to be tolerated within any part of the
Dominions of the British Crown. . . .

It remains to consider in what manner provision is to be made for
carrying these instructions into effect, and for the establishment and
exercise of your authority over Her Majesty's Subjects who may
settle in New Zealand, or who are already resident there. Numerous
projects for the establishment of a Constitution for the proposed
Colony have at different times been suggested. . . . But the common
result of all inquiries, . . . was to show . . . the extreme difficulty of
establishing at New Zealand any Institutions, legislative, judicial, or
fiscal, without some more effective control than could be found
amongst the settlers themselves in the infancy of their Settlement. It
has, therefore, been resolved to place whatever Territories may be
acquired in Sovereignty by the Queen in New Zealand, in the relation of a Dependency of the Government of New South Wales. . . .

It is impossible to confide to an indiscriminate Body of persons
who have voluntarily settled themselves in the immediate vicinity of
the numerous Population of New Zealand, those large and irresponsible powers which belong to the representative system of Colonial
Government. Nor is that system adapted to a Colony struggling with
the first difficulties of their new situation. Whatever may be the
ultimate form of Government to which the British Settlers in New
Zealand are to be subject, it is essential to their own welfare, not less
than to that of the Aborigines, that they should at first be placed
under a rule, which is at once effective, and to a considerable degree
external. . . .

The proposed connection with New South Wales will not however
involve the extension to New Zealand of the character of a penal
Settlement. . . .

It is not for the present proposed to appoint any subordinate
Officers for your assistance. That such appointments will be indispensable is not indeed to be doubted. . . .

15

The selection of the Individuals by whom such Offices are to be borne must be made by yourself from the Colonists either of New South Wales or New Zealand, but upon the full and distinct understanding that their tenure of Office, and even the existence of the Offices which they are to hold must be provisional and dependent upon the future pleasure of the Crown.

Amongst the Officers thus to be created, the most evidently indispensable are those of a Judge, a Public Prosecutor, a Protector of Aborigines, a Colonial Secretary, a Treasurer, a Surveyor General of Lands, and a Superintendent of Police. Of these the Judge alone will require the enactment of a Law to create and define his functions. The Act now pending in Parl[iamen]t for the revival, with amendments, of the New South Wales Act, will, if passed into a Law, enable the Governor and Legislative Council to make all necessary provision for the establishment in New Zealand of a Court of Justice and a Judicial system separate from, and independent of, the existing Supreme Court. The other Functionaries I have mentioned can be appointed by the Governor in the unaided exercise of the delegated prerogative of the Crown.

Whatever Laws may be required for the Government of the new Colony will be enacted by the Governor and Legislative Council. It will be his duty to bring under their notice such recommendations as you may see cause to convey to him on subjects of this nature.

The absolute necessity of a Revenue being raised to defray the expenses of the government of the proposed Settlements in New Zealand, has not of course escaped my careful attention. Having consulted the Lords of the Treasury on this subject, I have arranged with their Lordships that, until the sources of such a Revenue shall have been set in action, you should be authorized to draw on the Gov[ernmen]t of New South Wales for your unavoidable expenditure. Separate accounts however will be kept of the public Revenue of New Zealand, and of the application of it, and, whatever Debt may be contracted to New South Wales, must be replaced by the earliest possible opportunity. Duties of import on Tobacco, Spirits, Wine, and Sugar, will probably supersede the necessity for any other Taxation, and such Duties, except on Spirits, will probably be of a very moderate amount.

The system at present established in New South Wales regarding Land, will be applied to all the Waste Lands which may be acquired by the Crown in New Zealand. Separate accounts must be kept of the Land Revenue. Subject to the necessary deductions for the expense of surveys & management, and for the improvement, by Roads & otherwise, of the unsold Territory, and subject to any deductions which may be required to meet the indispensable exigencies of the local Government, the Surplus of this Revenue will be applicable, as in New South Wales, to the charge of removing Emigrants from this Kingdom to the new Colony. . . .

. . . Your correspondence with myself will, as far as may be practicable, be carried on through the Governor of New South Wales. You will in fact be one of the Officers of that Gov[ernmen]t, and you will apply to the Head of it for instructions in all those cases in which he would himself address a similar reference to Her Majesty's Gov[ernmen]t in this Country. This rule however is not to be so strictly construed as to prevent your transmitting to me direct reports of every occurrence of which Her Majesty's Gov[ernmen]t should be informed, as often as opportunities may occur of communicating with this Country more rapidly than such communications could be made through Sydney, and whenever the occasion shall appear to you of sufficient importance to justify this deviation from the general rule. It will however be your duty to transmit to the Governor copies of all Dispatches which you may thus address directly to this Office. . . .

C.O. 209/4, pp. 251–81

6. CAPTAIN HOBSON'S SUPPLEMENTARY INSTRUCTIONS

Dispatch from Lord Normanby providing further explanations concerning his instructions, which had been requested by Captain Hobson, 15 August 1839. They include the admission that Hobson would not be provided with troops by the Government.

. . . 6. It is impossible for me to prescribe the course to be pursued for the prevention of cannibalism, human sacrifices, and warfare among the native Tribes. But I have no difficulty in stating that, if all the arts of persuasion and kindness should prove unavailing, practices so abhorrent from the first principles of morality, and so calamitous to those by whom they are pursued, should be repressed by authority, and, if necessary, by actual force, within any part of the Queen's dominions. I am, however, convinced that habits so repulsive to our common nature as cannibalism and human sacrifice, may be checked with little difficulty; because the opposition to them will be seconded by feelings which are too deeply rooted in the minds of all men, the most ignorant or barbarous not excepted, to be eradicated by any customs however inveterate, or by any errors of opinion however widely diffused. The New Zealanders will probably yield a willing assent to your admonitions, when taught to perceive with what abhorrence such usages are regarded by civilized men. . . .

Lastly, I am perfectly aware of the great advantage which you might derive from a military force, and of the inconvenience to which the want of it may expose you. This, however, is a difficulty which must be encountered. It is impossible, at the present time, to detach any of Her Majesty's troops to New Zealand, nor can I forsee any definite period at which it will be practicable to supply that deficiency. It will probably, therefore, be necessary to raise a militia, or to embody an armed police. But this also is amongst the questions which must be reserved for consideration after your arrival, and upon which it will be your duty to consult with the Governor of New South Wales.

Great Britain, *Parliamentary Papers*, 1840, xxxiii. 238, p. 45

7. AUCKLAND: CHOOSING THE SITE FOR THE CAPITAL

Dispatch from Captain Hobson to the Secretary of State, Lord John Russell, 15 October 1840, giving his reasons for siting the seat of government on the shore of the Waitemata.

. . . after mature consideration, I have decided upon forming the seat of government upon the south shore of the Waitemata, in the district of the Thames.

In the choice I have thus made, I have been informed by a combination of circumstances: 1st, by its central position; 2ndly, by the great facility of internal water communication by the Kaipara and its branches to the northward, and the Manakou and Waikato to the southward; 3rdly, from the facility and safety of its port, and the proximity of several smaller ports abounding with the most valuable timber; and finally, by the fertility of the soil, which is stated by persons capable of appreciating it, to be available for every agricultural purpose; the richest and most valuable land in the northern island being concentrated within a radius of 50 miles. . . . The Valley of the Thames and the Piako alone would furnish employment and support for any number of immigrants that we can reasonably expect for the next five years. . . .

Great Britain, *Parliamentary Papers*, 1841, xvii. 311, pp. 113–14

8. THE NEW ZEALAND COMPANY

After earlier attempts by the New Zealand Company of 1825, the New Zealand Association of 1837 and the New Zealand Colonization Company of 1839, the New Zealand Land Company published its Terms of Sale, 1 June 1839.

(a) From the *First Report* of the Directors.

'The object of the Company will be so to determine the place of their first Settlement, as to insure its becoming the commercial capital of New Zealand, and, therefore, the situation where land will soonest acquire the highest value by means of colonization. Within this district, the site of the Company's chief town will be carefully selected; after which, out of the whole territory there acquired, a further selection will be made of the most valuable portion as respects fertility, river frontage, and vicinity to the town. The site of the town will consist of 1100 acres, exclusive of portions marked out for general use, such as quays, streets, squares, and public gardens. The selected country lands will comprise 110,000 acres. The situation of the whole quantity of acres constituting the first settlement, will, accordingly, be determined by a double selection:—first, of the best position with reference to all the rest of New Zealand; and secondly, of the most valuable portion of the land acquired by the Company in that position, including the site of the first town. The lands of this first and principal settlement, therefore, if both selections are properly made, will be more valuable, and will sooner possess the highest value than any other like extent of land in the Islands.

'These doubly-selected lands will be divided into 1100 sections, each section comprising one town-acre, and 100 country-acres. 110 sections will be reserved by the Company, who intend to distribute the same as private property amongst the chief families of the tribe, from which the lands shall have been originally purchased. The

19

remainder, being 990 sections of 101 acres each, are now offered for sale in sections, at the price of £101 for each section, or £1 per acre.

'In return for the purchase-money, the Company will deliver to the purchaser of each section, an order on their officers in the settlement, which will entitle the holder thereof, or his agent, to select one town-acre, and a country section of 100 acres, according to a priority of choice, to be determined by lot, subject to the provisions hereinafter mentioned.

'The lots for priority of choice will be drawn at the Company's office in London, in the presence of the Directors, on a day of which public notice will be given.

'An officer of the Company will draw in the same manner for the 110 sections reserved and intended for the native chiefs; and the choice of these reserved sections will be made by an officer of the Company in the settlement, according to the priority so determined.

'The choice of sections, of which the priority has been so determined by lot in England, will take place in the settlement, as soon after the arrival of the first body of colonists as the requisite surveys and plans shall have been completed, and will be made under such regulations as an officer of the Company in the settlement, authorized in that behalf, may prescribe. Neglect, or refusal to comply with such regulations will occasion a forfeiture of the choice; and vest the right of selection in such officer as to the sections in regard to which the choice shall have been forfeited.

'The land-orders will be transferable at the pleasure of the holders; and a registry will be kept at the Company's offices in London, and in the settlement, as well of original land-orders, as of all transfers thereof.

'Of the £99,990 to be paid to the Company by purchasers, 25 per cent. only, or £24,997. 10s., will be reserved to meet the expenses of the Company. The remainder, being 75 per cent., or £74,992. 10s. will be laid out by the Company for the exclusive benefit of the purchasers, in giving value to the land sold by defraying the cost of emigration to this FIRST and PRINCIPAL SETTLEMENT.

'Purchasers of land-orders intending to emigrate with the first colony, (which it is proposed shall depart by the middle of August next), will be entitled to claim from the Company, out of the £74,992. 10s. set apart for emigration, an expenditure for their own passage, and that of their families and servants, equal to 75 per cent. of their purchase-money, according to regulations framed by the

Company with a view to confining the free passage to actual colonists. But unless this claim be made in London by written application to the Secretary, delivered at the office of the Company, on or before a day of which public notice will be given, it will be considered as waived.

'The remainder of the £74,992. 10s. set apart for emigration, will be laid out by the Company in providing a free passage for young persons of the labouring class, and as far as possible of the two sexes in equal proportion.'

It will be observed that the principle of colonization thus adopted by the Company is the sale of its lands at an uniform and sufficient price, and the employment of the greater portion of the purchase-money as an emigration fund.

(b) From a company advertisement.

The aim of the Directors is not confined to mere emigration, but is directed to colonization in its ancient and systematic form. Their object is to transplant English society with its various gradations in due proportions, carrying out our laws, customs, associations, habits, manners, feelings—everything of England, in short, but the soil. They desire so now to cast the foundations of the colony, that in a few generations New Zealand shall offer to the world a counterpart of our country, in all the most cherished peculiarities of our own social system and national character, as well as in wealth and power.

Great Britain, *Parliamentary Papers*, 1852, xxxv. 570, p. 18

9. THE NELSON LAND LOTTERY, 1841

An account of the method of choosing the first allotments in the New Zealand Company's second colony.

On one of the tables stood the four wheels in which were to be deposited the cards to be drawn, so made as to revolve for the purpose of mixing the cards properly. These wheels were severally marked 'Register Numbers,' 'Town Land,' 'Accommodation Land,' and 'Rural Land;' and an opening in the side, large enough to admit of a child's arm, was provided, in order to draw out the cards. The ballot had been announced to begin at eleven o'clock; and shortly after that hour, the Governor, Mr. Somes, accompanied by several

Directors, entered the room and took his seat in the chair. Four little boys were then stationed immediately behind the four wheels, and a Director took his place behind each of them, to call out the numbers as they were drawn. Silence having been obtained, the Governor briefly explained the course of proceeding which would be adopted so as to insure accuracy, and combine perfect fairness and equal chance to all the purchasers. . . .

. . . The cards were then produced, tied up in hundreds, and marked in the same manner as the wheels, and numbered consecutively; those numbers upon being drawn would denote the order of choice. Two of the Directors then proceeded to deposit the cards in their respective wheels; and the drawing commenced. One of the little boys, placing his hand in the wheel marked 'Register numbers,' drew out a card upon which was written the number on the Register of applications, with the name of the purchaser. This was called out by the Director immediately behind him; and a few moments having elapsed to give time to the check-clerks to find the number in the books, the second boy drew a card marked 'Town Land' with a number, which was likewise called out by a Director; and this proceeding having been repeated by the boys at the wheels marked 'Accommodation Land,' and 'Rural Land,' the four cards were passed to the Governor, and immediately filed. Thus the numbers on the cards respectively marked Town, Accommodation, and Rural Land, indicated the priority of choice which attached to a particular number on the Register of applications, as each was drawn, and consequently to the several purchasers.—This plan, although simple in its working, requires, in fact, perfect accuracy, as it is obvious any error would invalidate the whole of the numbers drawn, from the impossibility of deciding to whose purchase the error should attach. Fortunately, the little boys understood their work; and the Directors behind them calling loudly the numbers as they were drawn, allowed all present the opportunity of checking the whole proceeding.

The first card was drawn at about twelve o'clock; and the ballot proceeded with only the intermission of half an hour to rest the children, and occasional interruptions for the purpose of giving the wheels a turn round, until eight o'clock in the evening; when the whole was completed. The Directors having opened the wheels and turned them upside down, in order to insure that no cards remained undrawn, the check-books were examined for the same purpose; when the whole being properly filled up, and the numbers entered, the Governor declared the ballot concluded; and the meeting broke up, perfectly satisfied with the proceedings of the day. . . .

Altogether, the meeting was very satisfactory, and went off as well as could have been wished. A cheerful spirit reigned throughout the whole proceedings; and if an occasional good-humoured laugh marked the drawing of *high* numbers of choice, it was compensated by the universal expression of satisfaction which greeted the fortunate drawer of the better numbers; and every one appeared contented with the result which attended his particular lot. . . .

The New Zealand Journal, 4 Sept. 1841, p. 1

10. OTAGO: PLANS FOR A SCOTTISH FARMING COLONY

From the 'Address to Scotch Farmers', published in 1843, by George Rennie M.P., who has been called 'the father of the Otago settlement'.

. . . At a time when everybody is complaining, you are perhaps more severely pinched than any set of men above the mere class of labourers. There may be exceptions, but, as a body, you have not for many years been able to lay anything past. If you can, by pinching and sparing, make both ends meet at the end of the year, it is as much as any of you can do, and more, it is feared, than most of you have done. . . .

The truth is that there are more of you want farms than can get farms. . . . Every year adds to the number of farm wanters. . . . You have been bred Scotch farmers—accustomed all your lives to live among Scotchmen . . . you doubt whether you could feel happy if you cease to 'dwell among your own people'. . . .

The scheme of life you chalk out for yourselves, *if attainable*, is a wise and prudent one. *And it is attainable.*

If there are not farms enough for all *here*, there is land enough, and to spare in the colonies. Though any one of you, who was merely to cross the border and settle down there, would feel himself among a strange people and strange ways, that need not be the case if a number of us resolve to go together. . . . It is not our hills and glens alone that make Scotland. It is our Kirk, our schools, the *hamely* Scotch tongue, the bonspeil, the market, in short, all our

Scotch ways. In any climate nearly approaching to our own, a knot of us can make at any time a Scotland for ourselves. . . .

A party has been formed for the purpose of making a settlement in New Zealand. . . .

It is not my intention to hold out prospects of large fortunes rapidly acquired with little labour. There, as everywhere, prudence and industry will be required to make a man prosper. But the prudence and industry are at least certain of their reward. For £120, a property, consisting of 50 acres of rural land, 10 acres of suburban land, and a town lot of $\frac{1}{4}$ acre, can be had. The mere land is not all they get for their money: there is a labour market fairly supplied by means of immigration; roads, bridges, and other improvements; a church and school—a share in all these advantages is obtained for the money. . . . One hundred and fifty pounds would provide his outfit in indispensable furniture and stock, and suffice for his keep till he reaped his first harvest. Three hundred pounds would set an active and intelligent young man on his feet in the settlement. . . .

The New Zealand Journal, 5 August 1843, pp. 195–6

11. OTAGO: PLANS FOR A FREE CHURCH OF SCOTLAND COLONY

Captain William Cargill, in a letter of May 1847, outlines the purposes of the Lay Association of the Free Church of Scotland for settlement of a Scotch Colony at Otago.

. . . With respect to the classes of our people for whom these benefits are secured, and to whom they are now to be offered, I would at once disclaim the remotest idea of unsettling the mind, or exciting the ambition, of a single individual who is contentedly and usefully located at home. But, on the other hand, I would refer to the fact, that an annual average of 4,000 souls is actually oozing out of Scotland to the colonies; and a full portion of these being cabin passengers, it follows, that capital and labour amongst these emigrants are somewhat in proportion to each other. That they are also from the Free Church in some proportion to the number of her people, is witnessed by the number of her Scotch adherents in the colonies. But in what circumstances are they found by our ministerial deputations? Mixed, here and there, with all sorts of people, and so scattered that religious and educational appliances in an efficient form are perfectly hopeless. Now, what we desiderate is, to turn the existing current of Free Church emigration into a wholesome channel, and I believe that the provision now offered is barely sufficient to absorb it. . . .

But, whatever be the motive of those who emigrate, as heretofore, at so fearful a sacrifice to their own souls, and those of their children, it is manifest that the tendency is all too strong to be overcome; and it ought, therefore, to be an object, to guide this current into a course which shall be at once useful to themselves and to the cause of our Divine Master. . . .

. . . that there is a continual tendency of pressure of population upon subsistence is the everyday experience of all classes of society. The question then is, whether this tendency be a mere stimulus to action which shall have its reward, or the utterance of a stern law, by which the increase of population must be checked and arrested on the spot where it occurs, and by the *sole* means of 'moral restraint'? That none should marry, until in circumstances to maintain a family, is a simple and palpable truth. But I am inclined to think, that every one who desires the attainment of these circumstances, is not only warranted, but bound, to take an enlarged view of the means to that end which his Creator has put within his reach. And, when I consider the munificent arrangements of Providence for our teeming population, the vast amount of fertile lands which have been given to the empire, . . . I cannot but believe that the tendency referred to is, in very deed, but a stimulus to action—a pressure, not intended to consign to a hopeless and withering 'restraint', but, by means of which a healthy increase in the most gifted section of our race, shall be combined with the spread of civilization and the diffusion of the Gospel. . . .

The three elements of prosperity and comfort are labour, capital, and a profitable field for their joint employment. The field at home may have become narrow, in proportion to the accumulation of the two former, but the colonies assigned to the empire are just an extension of that field. . . . With respect to New Zealand it may be safely affirmed, that the labouring man, with economy and industry, does, within three or four years, become himself an owner of property, and independent of working for wages. . . .

But I desire to call very special attention to that which constitutes the most important feature of our plan, namely, a systematic and permanent provision for religious ordinances, and for schools and a college in the colony.

No similar provision has found a place in any British colony since the time of the 'Pilgrim Fathers'. . . .

> From the pamphlet *Free Church Colony at Otago in New Zealand. In a Letter from Capt. Cargill to Dr Aldcorn, of Oban*, London, 1847, pp. 7–9

12. BEGINNINGS OF PASTORALISM IN WELLINGTON AND NELSON

John Robert Godley, writing from Wellington, 8 July 1850, describes Frederick Weld's success with sheep farming—'a gentlemanlike pursuit'.

Mr. Weld . . . and his partner, Mr. Clifford (a Roman Catholic like himself,) are the largest sheep-owners in the colony, having about 16,000 . . . he has given me much valuable information . . . about this, the most important economically, of colonial topics—I mean, cattle & sheep-keeping. . . . Weld and others . . . agree that there is no field of investment now open in the world, at once so safe and so profitable as pastoral husbandry in N.Z. the only drawback to it is the want of a government. It is from men such as Weld that one hears the deepest and most earnest deprecations of the 'central' system, because as capitalists they want well-informed and stable legislation. At present there is literally no security except public opinion for a sheep-farmer; no title to his run; no law of trespass; no pasturage regulations; (for the attempts of the Colonial Office & the N.Z. Co. to frame regulations are laughed at, & are completely dead letters;) in short, he is a speculative squatter, trusting to the general fairness & good feeling of his neighbours not to be interfered with, & hoping (against hope,) that *before long* we shall have a change of system. In spite of all obstacles however, the profits of sheep-farming are very large—Mr. Weld says 'with decent management 30 per cent', & almost everybody else goes beyond him. . . .

Mr Weld considers that the gross profits of his 12000 sheep this year will be £6000, from which are to be deducted for expenses and contingencies £2000 leaving £4000 net profit on a flock which represents (at 15s. a sheep) a capital of £9000 only. He has, however, a peculiarly well-circumstanced run, & the average profits should, he thinks, be calculated at less. Neither he, nor any other sheep-farmer would consider 12 or 15 per cent a high rate of interest to pay for money, which they would invest in sheep, & make double on. Sheep-farming, also, is here a gentlemanlike pursuit, & involves no severe or unpleasant labour—merely a general superintendence and management—nor is it, as in N.S. Wales, a gambling & uncertain speculation (except for the political reasons above-men'td)—for there are no droughts, & no catarrh among sheep. Now droughts and catarrh are to N.S. Wales what the potato-rot is to Ireland, Hudson to the railway-world, etc. At present there are vast tracts of land lately discovered & still unoccupied which ignorance and want of government—i.e. of laws & titles—have prevented capital from flowing into —I repeat, that I believe this to be, for the first who are fortunate enough to occupy it, the best field of investment in the world. . . .

While here he received bad news from his station—namely, that the 'scab' had appeared in his flocks, which will involve him in considerable trouble and expense for 'dressing' every sheep, as a precaution. This is one of the 'contingencies' on wh. a man must calculate & on which *he* did calculate in making the above estimates. They (the estimates) are based on a price of 1*s*. 4*d*. for wool in the British market, which leaves about 1*s*. or 1*s*. 1*d*. clear to the grower, after paying freight & charges. Weld is not *particularly* well circumstanced, which makes his experience specially valuable for an average calculation. . . . He is obliged . . . to have a schooner of his own, & he reckons the expense of bringing his wool here [Wellington] at more than the freight from hence to London. Each sheep ought to produce 4 lbs of wool, & fat wethers bring about 15*s*. apiece; as yet the sheep-owners have not been driven to 'boil down', but expect to do so, as their stock increases, the market for meat remaining nearly stationary. The advantages of N.Z. over Australia for sheep-farming are manifold; they consist chiefly in the freedom from droughts & from catarrh; the abundance of water for washing, etc. the proximity of the whole country to the coast; & the general superiority of the pasturage. Add to this, *at present*, that in Australia all the best runs are occupied, whereas here there are vast tracts of available land almost unexplored. On the other hand, *it is said* by Australians that the wool produced in the warmer climate will always be finer & more valuable, which *our* sheep-farmers deny— N.Z. wool now brings a lower price, it is true, but this they attribute to the less careful & *knowledgeable* preparation of it; an inferiority which is only temporary, of course. I hear a better account than I expected of the young men who superintend the 'stations'—at least, in one particular; namely, that they do not *drink*, as almost all the bachelor settlers in the back woods of Canada do. . . .

It is customary here, & sometimes very profitable, to have sheep 'on thirds'; which means to send them to a station, & allow the owner of it half the wool, & ⅓d. of the increase for the trouble & expense of looking after them—the owner receives half the wool, & ⅔ds. of the increase, as profit on his capital. For instance, Mr Petre sent sheep for which he paid £300 to Mr Weld's station two years ago, & took no further trouble about them. At the end of 18 months he sold them to Weld, & received, on the whole transaction, £750. i.e. he made £450 profit on £300 in 18 months—but in this he was, as you may suppose, exceptionally fortunate. . . .

J. R. Godley to his father, 8 July 1850. Godley
Papers, Canterbury Museum

13. SKETCH PLAN FOR THE CANTERBURY SETTLEMENT

From the first outline plan published by the Canterbury Association, in which it announced the intention of transplanting all the elements of a 'good and right state of society' and indicated its appeal to 'uneasy classes' who feared pauperism and decline because of social change at home.

It has now become a truism to say that, as a nation, we do not take—indeed, never have taken—a proper view of our duties and responsibilities as the founders of Colonies. The ancients sent out a full representation of the parent state, a complete segment of society, to become the germ of a new nation. They carried with them their gods, their rites, their festivals; nothing was left behind that could be moved, of all that the heart and eye of an exile misses. Under the influence of such consolations for the loss of home, men of all classes yielded to the natural feeling of restlessness and desire for scope and room which is produced by the pressure of population in an old country, a feeling not only excusable but laudable, and evidently implanted by Providence for the purpose of carrying out the scheme by which the earth is replenished and subdued.

It is humiliating to reflect on the contrast which modern colonizing operations have exhibited; most of our emigrations have been composed almost entirely of one class, and that class the one which is least able to take care of itself, as regards the preservation of all the higher elements of civilization. Driven from their mother country by the difficulty of obtaining subsistence, they found themselves in the British colonies strangers in a strange land. They got comparatively rich, doubtless; at any rate they lived better, and provided for their families better, than they could have done at home; but at what price were these advantages purchased! If the institutions and arrangements of British society be (as we are in the habit of considering them) wholesome and desirable; or if, whether wholesome and desirable or not, they have become essential to the comfort and happiness of those who have grown up under their shadow, how painful and injurious must be the shock when the habits, feelings, and associations which are produced by them, and which have become so deeply rooted in the moral being of an English emigrant, are suddenly torn away! It is no wonder if we find that society in our colonies, originating as it did under such circumstances, has so often presented but a defaced resemblance to that of the parent state, while exhibiting, in an exaggerated form, some of the worst characteristics of our age and country. How could it be otherwise? Let us consider the position of the poor and uneducated emigrant, in his adopted country. He has been accustomed to seek from the affluent and cultivated class above him, relief in distress, and advice in difficulty; members of that class rarely emigrate under our present system. He has been used to go to the neighbouring church; in the new settlement he has access if at all, certainly with difficulty, to any place of worship. He has children old enough to go to school; he needs religious rites and consolations; the schoolmasters and clergymen are few in number, and widely dispersed. In short, no care has been taken to make due provision for the cravings of his moral nature; we have thought of our colonists chiefly as of so much flesh and blood requiring to be renewed by food, and covered with clothing; the food of the heart has received but secondary care. Hence have proceeded the materialism, the rudeness, above all, the neglect of religion, which have been too general in the new countries which we have peopled, but which we have been in the habit of regarding with indifference, if not with contempt. . . .

. . . Our present object is, therefore, to set an example of a colonial settlement, in which, from the first, all the elements, including the very highest, of a good and right state of society, shall find their proper place, and their active operation.

Such are the first principles of the design; the promoters of it have become convinced that men of station and character, of cultivation and refinement, moral and religious men, such as contribute by their influence to elevate and purify the tone of society, are in great measure deterred from emigrating, by a fear of those moral plagues which have been described as rife in new countries. Especially fathers of families, who see no prospect of providing for their children in their own station of life at home, must be quite aware of the opportunities which a colonial life affords of comfortable independence and advantageous settlement, but they consider, and justly, such benefits as too dearly purchased by the possible loss of the appliances of civilization and the ordinances of religion. They do not choose to expose their children to the danger of growing up without the means of education, and thus of relapsing into virtual atheism, or of joining, from a kind of necessity, the communion of the nearest sect which bears the Christian name. It is perceived, then, that adequate provision for man's moral and religious wants in the new country, contains the primary element of successful colonization, not only on account of the importance of such provision *per se*, but also because thereby alone can a really valuable class of men be induced to join in the foundation and settlement of colonies.

Upon this idea our plan is founded. We intend to form a Settlement, to be composed entirely of members of our own church, accompanied by an adequate supply of clergy, with all the appliances requisite for carrying out her discipline and ordinances, and with full provision for extending them in proportion to the increase of population. . . .

It is conceived by the promoters of the settlement now contemplated, that the present time is one peculiarly fitted for bringing the plan before the public. Extraordinary changes are taking place in the political and social system of Europe; the future is dark and troubled; 'men's hearts are failing them for fear;' and many persons who have been deterred hitherto by dread of change from entering upon the new career afforded by colonization, will now probably be impelled into it by the same motive acting in a different direction. There can be no doubt whatever that the 'uneasy classes' in this country are very numerous. They belong to all ranks of society; but we have one, more particularly, in view; we allude to clergymen and country gentlemen who began life, perhaps, with what was then a competency, but who have now to meet the demands produced by large and growing families, who foresee the necessity of descending to a lower station in life than that which they have hitherto occupied, and to whose children the crowd and pressure observable in every walk of life seem to close every reasonable chance of progress, or even subsistence. Such are especially the persons to whom a civilized and well-ordered colony, such as we propose to found, cannot but appear a welcome refuge. There is in a colonial life an absence of pretension, a universal plenty, a friendship of social intercourse, a continually increasing demand and reward for every kind of labour and exertion, which to those who have been suffering from the struggle between pride and penury, and whose minds are continually filled with anxiety about the future, is very pleasing and enjoyable. Supposing, even, that there be not opportunity for making large fortunes, the class of whom we speak do not aspire to make them; they would be satisfied with living in comfort and plenty, without care for what is to come, on a level, in point of income, with their friends and neighbours; looking upon each additional child as an additional blessing, instead of, as now, an additional burden; enjoying a quiet and happy life in a fine climate and a beautiful country, where want is unknown, and listening from afar, with interest, indeed, but without anxiety, to the din of war, to the tumult of revolutions, to the clamour of pauperism, to the struggle of classes, which wear out body and soul in our crowded and feverish Europe.

It would be easy to swell the list of those whom circumstances have predisposed to emigration, by describing the benefits which it holds out to the struggling yeoman, the small capitalist, the enterprizing trader; to these the prosperity promised by good colonization cannot fail to render our settlement specially attractive; but its peculiar feature consists in the benefits which it is intended to hold out to persons of refined habits and cultivated tastes, whom the moral evils inherent in our present modes of emigration have prevented from availing themselves of its material advantages.

Our settlement will be provided with a good college, good schools, churches, a bishop, clergy, all those moral necessaries, in short, which promiscuous emigration of all sects, though of one class, makes it utterly impossible to provide adequately.

It is hoped that nothing may be left undone which is required to fill the void (so far as it can be filled) which the loss of home presents to the imagination of a colonist,—to strengthen, instead of weakening, the ties of memory and affection which should connect him with England,—to save him, in short, from losing his old country while he gains a new one. . . .

Canterbury Papers, 1850, nos. 1 and 2, pp. 5–8

14. THEORY AND PRACTICE IN THE CANTERBURY SETTLEMENT

Comments on pasturage regulations for sheep runs and the effect of the operation of the 'sufficient price' on intending squatters from Australia by John Robert Godley, 4 June 1851.

The question of pasturage regulations becomes every day more pressing. Already the discouraging, indeed prohibitory, nature of those which we have published, taken in connection with the far more reasonable terms offered by Government, has had the most prejudicial effect on the prosperity of the Settlement. Several stockholders have come from Australia with a view of settling here, but not one of them admits the possibility of establishing a station, or taking an extensive run on the terms offered by the Association. If no better are offered, our district would soon apparently be, so far as stock is concerned, an unoccupied waste in the midst of pastures teeming with cattle and sheep. Mr. Rhodes has just driven 5000 of his sheep to a run immediately outside our block, and several of the Canterbury settlers who are going to invest in stock meditate following his example. The subject is felt by every one here to be so important that I will make no apology for once more endeavouring to make its difficulties and requirements clear to the Committee. The terms proposed by Government have now been made public; it will charge one penny per head for sheep, allowing, as I understand, a run sufficient for five years' increase. Thus, supposing a run to carry a sheep to every two acres, and supposing that a squatter intending to stock a run of 20,000 acres fully in five years put 2000 sheep upon it the first year, which is the ordinary calculation, he would only have to pay a rent of £8. 6s. 8d. at first, increasing gradually as his means of payment increased, until when his run should be fully stocked with 10,000 sheep he would pay about £40 a year. Under our regulations he would have to pay £200 a year from the first, a rent which no possible profit from his sheep in the early years would approach to defraying, and which would be far too heavy to the last. Besides this, the expenses of forming a station are very considerable, especially in a country where timber is excessively scarce, and there is no security whatever for his improvements without buying the land. The mere statement of these circumstances must, I should think, convince the Committee of the paramount necessity of altering the arrangements which have so unfortunately been introduced into the Act of Parliament, and, in the meantime, relaxing as far as possible the strict letter of the law in favour of intending squatters. . . .

> Godley's comment, Lyttelton, 4 June 1851.
> From *Writings and Speeches of John Robert Godley*, Christchurch, 1863, pp. 205–6

15. SYSTEMATIC COLONIZATION IN PRACTICE: CANTERBURY AFTER EIGHT YEARS

William Fox, a New Zealand Company settler who believed in systematic colonization, writes to Robert Godley (the former Resident Agent in Canterbury) on 31 December 1858, suggesting that, while some of the founders' intentions have failed, Canterbury, on the whole, flourished as a colony.

I have just returned from spending a month at Canterbury which I had not visited since your four first ships were discharging their first batch of Immigrants; when . . . Christchurch consisted of a surveyors pole stuck upright on the banks of the Avon. . . . I know nothing more exciting than to ride on good roads through the midst of colonial villages, farms, and gardens where less than ten years ago I 'explored' with blankets on my back, without meeting a living thing for fifty to a hundred miles at a stretch. It in some small degree rewards one for colonizing, and realizes something of the dreams one dreamt when one first formed the Robinson Crusoeish design of pitching a tent in the Pacific isles. . . .

On the whole I think the progress of Canterbury has been most satisfactory. . . . It is very true that many of the original plans of its founders have come to nothing; . . . but as a general success . . . it is complete. . . .

As regards its ecclesiastical aspect, I think it has failed altogether to realize the aspirations of its founders. In short, owing to causes not very far to seek the Church of England seems less popular, though it may have more adherents, than in the other provinces of New Zealand where it took its chance among all comers. Complaints were not few of the hardship of having to pay twice over for Church ministrations, once in the price of the Land and now in voluntary subscriptions, for Cathedrals, schools, maintenance of clergy, and so forth, from which the purchasers of three pound an acre land flattered themselves they had escaped for the rest of their natural lives. The individual clergy also with one or two exceptions are perhaps not considered very bright and shining examples of the efficacy of apostolic descent to qualify for the ecclesiastical leadership of the model Church Colony of the 19th century. . . .

Another thing which struck me as a curious departure from the intention of the founders was the ground on which the high price of land continues to be maintained. There is no doubt, I suppose, that the original intention was to carry out the Wakefield theory, and there is no doubt at all that the basis of that theory is a high price laid on for the avowed purpose of preventing the labouring man from acquiring land too quickly. Now, however, though the high price is maintained, it is to *enable* the working man to get land, and *he* is the loudest supporter it has. He has found out that if the price were low the whole would pass into the hands of large capitalists, speculating runholders etc., that the day labourer would not be able to get an acre. Therefore, the price is maintained for exactly the reverse reason to that for which it was imposed. If it were down to 10*s*. and 5*s*. I have no doubt that half the runs in the province would have been purchased by the sheep-farmers and half the flat land on the plains by speculators, before this; and the working man would have a perpetual serfdom before him not as the result of Wakefield's high price, but of the low price intended for his advantage. The more one sees of these Colonies however, the more I am satisfied of the absurdity of an *uniform price* for all. The characteristics of the different settlements are so various that what suits one is ruin to another. *Here* [Wellington] we have many thousand acres of rough bush land which I would gladly see given away to anyone who would undertake the task of clearing them.

There can be little doubt as to the future of Canterbury. . . . There are 5 million acres under pastoral license now. They are certainly capable of carrying from 2 to 3 million sheep at the lowest estimate. . . . There is a good deal of land speculation at present, but it is chiefly within a short distance of Christchurch, and though prices have run up pretty high I do not think there is anything wild in it. I feel sure that any one who could spare a few thousand pounds to invest them and wait say ten years, might make a very large fortune by land speculation at present. In fact that may be done in any of these colonies. . . .

> Fox to Godley, 31 Dec. 1858, Godley Papers,
> Canterbury Museum

16. UNPLANNED COLONIZATION: AUCKLAND AT THE END OF THE 1840s

Unfavourable comment from a New Zealand Company Agent, in which he suggests that Government expenditure has enabled Auckland to become the largest and most compact town in the Colony, but that its society exhibited weaknesses not found in the 'planned' settlements.

. . . The town of Auckland is the largest and most compact in the colony. It has one or two very good streets, but the lower parts are as filthy as 'Deptford and Wapping, navy-building towns'. Very little except shopkeeping was going on at Auckland when I was there. The amount of cultivation was very small, and consisted almost entirely of a few fields of grass, within four or five miles of the town, where newly imported stock were kept alive till the butcher was ready to wait upon them for the benefit of the troops and townsmen. In short, the settlement was a mere section of the town of Sydney transplanted to the shores of New Zealand, filled with tradesmen who were reaping a rich harvest from the expenditure of a regiment of soldiers, a parliamentary grant, missionary funds, and native trade. As an instance of colonization, it was altogether rotten, delusive, and Algerine. The population had no root in the soil, as was proved by some hundreds of them packing up their wooden houses and rushing away to California, as soon as the news of that land of gold arrived. In Cook's Straits not half a dozen persons were moved by that bait. If the government expenditure had ceased, and the troops been removed at that time, I believe Auckland would have melted away like a dream. The expenditure of British money by the government has been enormous in this part of the colony, and easily accounts for so large a town having so suddenly sprung up. . . .

... Nearly the whole population of Auckland has been imported from Sydney and Van Diemen's land. With the exception of the pensioners, I believe only one, or at most two regular emigrant ships —that is, vessels carrying bodies of men of the labouring class, ever proceeded from this country to that settlement. The returns of crime, compared with those of the southern settlements, exhibit fearful traces of the origin of its population, and display the great importance of colonizing on a regular system, which may ensure a pure origin for a colony.

William Fox, *The Six Colonies of New Zealand*, London, 1851, pp. 40-3

17. AUCKLAND'S PETITION FOR SEPARATION, 1855

Petition of Auckland Provincial Councillors, signed by the Speaker of the Provincial Council, T. H. Bartley, 18 May 1855, pointed out Auckland's interests as distinct from those of the New Zealand Company settlements, and demanding that their revenues should not be used in the interests of the southern majority.

... your Majesty's Petitioners would humbly represent, ...

4. That the Province of Auckland was founded by your Majesty's authority, and the City of Auckland chosen by your Majesty's Representative as the Capital of New Zealand and the Seat of Government. . . .

5. That the Settlements of the South were established by a trading company, not only without the sanction, but in defiance of the authority of her Majesty's Government, and without any guarantee or promise at any subsequent period that any of these Settlements should become the Seat of Government. . . .

7. That Auckland has no commercial relations with the Southern Settlements; that there is no interchange of commodities between it and them; that their exports and imports are the same, the same markets being open to both; and that in short the Province of Auckland is as little connected with those of the South and as little likely to become so, as with Canada or any other of your Majesty's Colonies in America. . . .

13. That while the extent of the Province of Auckland, the number of its inhabitants, both British and aboriginal (being greater

than that of all the other provinces in the aggregate), the amount of Revenue (being four-ninths of that of the whole six Provinces), and the circumstances of its first Settlement, entitles Auckland to be the Seat of the Government of New Zealand; and while your Majesty's Petitioners firmly protest against the injustice of subjecting its interests to a majority of Representatives from the Southern Provinces (those representing the South being twenty-five, while those representing Auckland are only twelve in number), they would equally deprecate the hardship of the Southern Provinces of being required to send Representatives to a General Legislature at Auckland....

Enclosed in Wynyard to Grey, no. 60, 18 May 1855, C.O. 209/129, p. 190

18. CHEAPER LAND: GOVERNOR GREY'S REGULATIONS, 1853

At the time of annexation both the New Zealand Company and the Government had adopted prices of not less than £1 per acre. By a proclamation of 4 March 1853 Grey published General Land Regulations which permitted the sale of rural lands outside Hundreds for 10s. per acre, or 5s. per acre where the land was of 'hilly or broken character'. Although land grants were still allowed for military settlers and the regulations did not apply to the land reserved for the Otago and Canterbury Associations the Lyttelton Times *attacked Grey's policy on 26 March 1853.*

... Without at present going into detailed criticism, we may say that we consider it a most ungracious act on the part of the Executive. It is the last act of an expiring despotism, and is evidently intended to gloss over the misdeeds which have attended the government of Sir George Grey. We have called it an ungracious act, for his Excellency has forestalled a question which must have been the first taken up by the General Assembly; which representing, as it will, the interests and opinions of the colonists would have dealt with the question in a spirit commensurate with its importance. As it is, the policy of Sir George will throw New Zealand into two hostile camps, and the land question, instead of being submitted to, and settled by, the Representatives of the people and thus acquiring the force of established law, will be regarded as a measure dictated by interested motives, and will, we clearly foresee, tend to much and bitter animosity.

Lyttelton Times, 26 March 1853, p. 7

19. PROVINCIALISM: THE SOCIAL CHARACTERISTICS OF THE EIGHT COLONIES

Dr. Arthur Saunders Thomson, the army doctor who wrote the Colony's first history, published in 1859, discusses the social contrasts between the settlements.

... In 1842, there were 10,992 white persons in the colony; Wellington, the largest settlement, had 3701 inhabitants; Auckland, 2895; Nelson, 2500; New Plymouth, 895; Russell, 380; Hokianga, 263; Wanganui, 200; and Akaroa, 198.

The northern settlers were chiefly derived from Australia; those in the south from Great Britain. The former were distinguished for colonial wisdom; the latter for education and good home connections. The Company's settlers, having come direct from a country where the people rule themselves, felt more keenly than the northern immigrants the irritation arising from living under irresponsible government. The male population exceeded the female in all the settlements, and this inequality was greater in Auckland than in Wellington. Few of the settlers were above fifty years of age. Crime was almost unknown. At the Bay of Islands the inhabitants gained their bread by trading with the whale ships; at Hokianga, in felling the giant Kauri trees for the Australian and English markets. At Auckland the people were living on the government expenditure, and awaited the arrival of immigrants to occupy the houses they had built, and re-purchase the town lots they had bought. The French at Akaroa were cultivating vines; and were settling down into idleness and happiness amidst their beautiful gardens and vineyards. At Wellington, Wanganui, New Plymouth, and Nelson, the settlers were living on their own resources, from not having got possession of their lands; some were frittering away their lives in idle pastimes, while torpor and drinking had taken possession of a few. There was little land under cultivation, farming implements were rusting for want of use, and money was spent in purchasing what labour should have supplied. . . . The Canterbury Association, . . . consisted of noblemen, archbishops, clergymen, and gentlemen, whose objects were to found a colony in New Zealand upon high social and ecclesiastical principles, to carry out the religious and refined element, to transport from England a section of the people, to plant the church of England in New Zealand, and make the colony look like home. . . .

. . . An old Australian squatter, who visited the Canterbury settlement in 1851, divided the inhabitants into pilgrims, shagruns, and prophets; the first were the original colonists, the second were people from other parts of New Zealand, and the last were settlers from Australia. At the first anniversary of the settlement it was admitted that the original scheme had failed, but the place was prospering; that the best shops were kept by Wellington settlers; that Australians had brought sheep and cattle, and that 6000 acres were under crops. . . .

. . . it is worthy of notice, that the colonists, soon after the formation of all the settlements, acquired distinguishing epithets; thus there was an Auckland cove, a Wellington swell, a Nelson snob, a Taranaki exquisite, an Otago cockney, and a Canterbury pilgrim. These epithets, almost already forgotten, are too characteristic to be buried in oblivion, as each originated in some peculiarity of the leading colonists. The Otago settlers derived theirs from their ignorance of the country in which they lived; the Auckland people from their extensive Sydney connexions; and the origin of the other names are sufficiently obvious without explanation.

Eight settlements were now progressing; six started on the principle of monopoly, and two on free trade: the former were Wellington, Wanganui, Taranaki, Nelson, Otago, and Canterbury; the latter were Auckland and Hawke's Bay. Otago and Canterbury were religious monopolies. . . .

New Zealand in 1856 was a widely different place from what it was in 1842. The child had become a man proud of his increasing strength, and confident of a splendid future. Self-government had already diffused a spirit of enterprise, . . . politics in New Zealand are very differently managed from politics in England. In the old country, men give and take; in New Zealand, politics tear the community asunder. . . .

Arthur S. Thomson, *The Story of New Zealand*, vol. ii, London, 1859, pp. 59–60, 183–4, 186–9, 238–9, 246

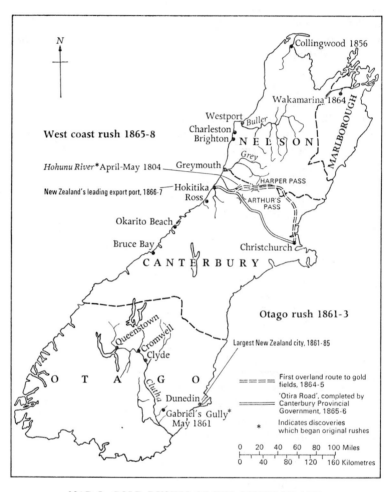

MAP I. GOLD RUSHES OF THE SOUTH ISLAND

20. GOVERNMENT IN THE GOLD FIELDS

*The colonization of the South Island received its biggest impetus
from the gold rushes, starting in Otago 1861 and the West Coast
1865. These gold rushes were not accompanied by the spread of
lawlessness, as in California. Administration was provided under the
Gold Fields Act of 1858, which was passed in response to the minor
Golden Bay, Nelson, gold rush and it followed Australian precedents.*

AN ACT to make provision for the management of Gold Fields in
the Colony of New Zealand. . . .

OCCUPATION OF GOLD FIELDS

II. It shall be lawful for the Governor from time to time by Proclamation to constitute and appoint any portion of the Colony, to be
a 'Gold Field'. . . .

III. It shall be lawful for the Governor to cause documents to
be issued, each of which shall be called "The Miner's Right" and
shall be granted to any person applying for the same upon payment
of the sum of One Pound. . . .

V. It shall be lawful for the Governor in Council, subject to the
provisions of this Act, and to such Rules and Regulations as he
may think fit to make for the purpose, to cause Licenses to be issued,
which shall be in force for the period of twelve months from the
date thereof respectively, authorising the Holder to occupy Waste
Lands of the Crown for the purpose of carrying on business upon
any Gold Fields, and the fees to be paid for every such License
shall be Five Pounds. . . .

VI. It shall be lawful for the Governor to License any person to
sell, or to License any house for the sale of spirituous liquors, wine,
ale, beer, or porter, in any quantity, in any Gold Field. . . .

VII. It shall be lawful for the Governor in Council to demise to
any person, for any term not exceeding fifteen years from the making
of the Lease, any auriferous Crown Land for mining purposes, and
also to grant water rights and other easements for such purposes,
and to fix the amount to be paid by way of Rent or Royalty for the
same respectively. . . .

LOCAL LEGISLATION

XII. Upon petition of not less than one hundred persons holding
Miner's Rights or Leases under this Act at any Gold Field, and
having held such rights, or leases for not less than three Calendar

Months, it shall be lawful for the Governor in Council, by proclamation, to declare such Gold Field or any part thereof, containing not less than one hundred persons holding Miner's Rights or leases to be a district for the purpose of forming a 'Mining Board', . . . and after the publication of any such proclamation the locality so described shall be and become a 'Mining District' for the purpose aforesaid. . . .

ADMINISTRATION OF JUSTICE

XV. It shall be lawful for the Governor, by Order in Council, from time to time to constitute for any Gold Field, or for any part thereof, Wardens' Courts for the administration of Justice therein, and to appoint Wardens as Judges of such Courts, with power to act alone or with Assessors or Juries, and in such manner, and to exercise all or any of the powers hereinafter mentioned as the Governor shall think fit to direct. . . .

XVI. It shall be lawful for every such Court, subject to the provisions of this Act, to hear and determine all complaints respecting boundaries of claims, or respecting any encroachments upon the same, to enquire into and decide upon breaches of Rules and Regulations of Mining Boards, or of any Laws Rules or Regulations relating to the Gold Fields in force for the time being, and to inflict the Penalties imposed by the same, to entertain Partnership questions, and generally to hear and determine all disputes between Miners relating to Gold mining, and to ascertain damages, and award compensation, as hereinafter more particularly provided. . . .

New Zealand Statutes, 1858, 21 and 22 Vict. no. 74, pp. 442–6

21. COLONIZATION BY PUBLIC WORKS AND IMMIGRATION

The third ministry of William Fox, a New Zealand Company colonist who had written a book about systematic colonization, began in 1869. He was still one who cherished 'the sacred fire of colonization' and he said the time had come to 'again recommence the great work of colonizing New Zealand . . . to re-illumine that sacred fire'. The public works and immigration scheme was outlined by Julius Vogel, the Treasurer, in his budget speech, 28 June 1870.

Last year we had in this Assembly many evidences that the colonizing spirit was reawakening. During the recess, from all parts of the country, those evidences have been repeated, in the anxious desires expressed for a renewal of immigration and of public works. I now ask you to recognize that the time has arrived when we must set ourselves afresh to the task of actively promoting the settlement of the country. . . .

I will, very briefly, trouble you with the principles which are at the base of these proposals. They are, 1stly, That both Islands should aid in the colonizing work; both be placed in a position to contribute to the general requirements; both share in the results obtained.

2ndly, That it is inexpedient to embarrass colonizing operations with unnecessary political changes, and that, therefore, it will be wise to adhere as closely as possible to the political institutions with the working of which we are familiar.

3rdly, That the conditions and circumstances of different parts of the Colony vary widely, though there is throughout the Colony the same necessity for colonizing operations. . . .

We recognize that the great wants of the Colony are—public works, in the shape of roads and railways; and immigration. I do not pretend to decide which is the more important, because the two are, or ought to be, inseparably united.

I will first refer to public works. One Island, we are aware, is tolerably well provided with ordinary roads, but is deficient in railways. The other Island is deficient in both railways and roads, and wants, moreover, the special means for constructing them, in the nature of a public estate. . . .

. . . We propose that, in a part or parts of the North Island, the Colony shall be at the cost of constructing a trunk road, to place it or them in communication with the rest of the Island. The expense of this we estimate to be £400,000, requiring an expenditure of about £100,000 per annum for four years. But if the Colony finds the money for these works, it is fair that it should contribute an equal amount to analogous works in the Middle Island. We propose that it should be so—that an equal amount should be placed to the credit of the Middle Island, to be spent on railways, each Province to be entitled to share, upon the basis of its receipts from the consolidated revenue. Such a sum will not, of course, be sufficient for the construction of railways, but it will be a valuable contribution towards their cost, and, as between the two Islands, the arrangement will be absolutely fair.

The opening of a road through the North Island will promote its real, and probably rapid settlement; and this brings us to the consideration of whether, in common prudence, we should not, when we improve the value of the North Island estate, endeavour to procure a portion of that estate to share in the profit of that improvement. Whilst we do not seek to disable private purchasers, we do seek, in the interest of both races, that the Government shall not be precluded from acquiring land. We propose that land for a public estate shall be purchased from time to time at its fair value; that such estate shall be subject to the land laws in force in the Province or Provinces within which it is situated; that the cost shall be a charge against the Provinces respectively, to be recouped in such manner as shall be agreed upon with the Provincial Government when the land is handed over; and that the land itself, or its proceeds, shall be exclusively devoted to immigration and railway purposes. We propose that, for the purchase of these lands, £200,000 shall be available. I may add that the Government intend to ask for power, under similar conditions for recouping the outstanding liability for treasury bills on their account, to hand over to the Provinces from time to time such portions of the confiscated lands as may be relinquished without fear of evil results following. The condition of such relinquishment would be, that the proceeds in excess of the repayments of liabilities should be set aside for railway and immigration purposes.

We are now to suppose the two Islands with a landed estate, and therefore possessed of some means for promoting settlement, with the inducement to encourage settlement which the consequent improvement in the value of the estate will afford. The position of the Islands is the position of the Provinces they comprise. We are to suppose that within those Provinces there will exist such a desire for public works in the shape of railways, and for immigration, as will be suitable to their several conditions. We propose that the Government shall be armed with power to conclude arrangements for the construction of certain railways within the different Provinces, as desired by their respective Governments. By 'certain railways', I mean that the Legislature should indicate the direction of the railways for which it is proposed to allow the General Government to contract; and I think that, speaking generally, railways should, in each Island, be designed and constructed as parts of a trunk line. According to the nature of present traffic [this] should be the immediate character of the respective railways. I hope the Provinces will recollect that the

44

colonial rate of interest on money is large, and that it is extravagant to lock up more capital than is necessary. . . .

Now, as to the mode of paying for these railways. It is essential, in order that we shall not proceed too fast and undertake more than our means will justify, that we should fix a very effectual limit to the liabilities to be incurred. Speaking broadly, I contend that during the next ten years the Colony will run no risk if it commits itself to an expenditure, or a proportionate liability for guarantee of interest, of ten millions for railways, and for the other purposes comprised in these proposals.

This would mean an expenditure, at the rate of present population, of £40 a head; or for interest, at $5\frac{1}{2}$ per cent., of about £2 per head per annum, supposing the whole amount was expended, or an average on the ten years of, say, £1. This supposes that the cost is all to be paid in cash, and that there are to be no returns to reduce cost or interest. If the railways are inexpensively constructed and worked, I contend that a considerable portion of them will soon be self-supporting, that is to say, will yield sufficient, beyond working expenses, to cover either interest or guarantee, according to the principle adopted for raising the money for their construction.

But there is another source from which to anticipate a reduction in the money cost—the land should be made to bear a considerable portion of the burden. We propose that authority should be given to contract for the railways by borrowing money, by guaranteeing a minimum rate of profit or interest, by payments in land, by subsidies, or by a union of any two or more of these plans. I am inclined to think that, judiciously combined, they will enable us to obtain our railways to the greatest advantage. The contractors may want some money, but they should be glad to receive some land to yield them a profit consequent upon the effects of the railway; and, similarly, if the routes be judiciously selected, the contractors should be glad to keep the railways with the security of a minimum guarantee. I will not dwell further on this part of the subject, because I am sure honorable members will see that almost every agreement must possess its own special features.

I now come to the question from what source the payments, if any, are to be made. We may at once concede that the Colony is to be primarily liable, but the question is, should the Colony find the money finally, or should the charge be made a local one? I do not submit an arbitrary rule on the subject. Two courses suggest themselves,—

45

1st. That any money paid should be charged at once to the Provinces; or

2nd. That if the Colony make the payments, it should, on contracting the liability, take possession of land of commensurate value....

There is much to be said in favour of the second plan—that of the Colony taking land as security; but, on the other hand, there may be urged against such a plan, that it would involve in each case, a duplication, so to speak, of Provincial Government.

I have already said it is desirable to avoid as much as possible mixing up organic political changes with the great colonizing question. I would not shrink from declaring that if the existence of the present institutions of the country are inconsistent with the promotion of public works and immigration, and a choice must be made, I would infinitely prefer the total remodelling of those institutions to abandoning that stimulating aid which, as I believe, the condition of the Colony absolutely demands. But violent political changes are much to be deprecated, and in the present case they would not answer the end in view. You might sweep away the Provinces and provincial institutions by legislation, but you could not destroy those feelings of separate and distinct interest which have grown up with the settlement of the Provinces. In the course of time, as the separate interests become blended, the distinctive sentiment will subside; but time and the progress of settlement and intercommunication must work their undemonstrative yet inevitable effects. To attempt to anticipate their action would be to induce an exciting political struggle, in the determination of which public attention would be so much absorbed as to lead to the neglect of the great colonizing question. We say that we attach far more importance to the progress of colonization than to the maintenance of any particular form of government, but we say, also, that we see that colonization can be best promoted by using, as far as they are capable of being used, those institutions which already exist, making only such changes from time to time as circumstances demand.

In the cases where railway construction can be carried out by the Provinces, we are of opinion that it is desirable the Provinces should be charged directly and immediately as already explained; but we are not willing to exclude the Colony from undertaking the primary liability, and in some cases, as proposed by the second plan we think it should accept, as a satisfaction of the liability, a fair equivalent in landed estate. Let the railways go on, we say, and from time to time the internal policy in reference to them can be adjusted. Supposing them to be commenced under Provincial and General Government auspices combined, there will be nothing to prevent their being, should it ever be found necessary, consolidated into one entity. . . .

. . . I am going to put before you a conjectural sketch of what might be the position, supposing the Colony sooner or later took the whole matter into its charge, or that it remained partly a colonial and partly a provincial matter. . . . I suppose that some 1,500 or 1,600 miles of railway will require to be constructed, and that this can be effected at a cost of £7,500,000 together with two and a half million acres of land, and that in addition about £1,000,000 will be required to carry out the other proposals I am making. I leave on one side the cost of immigration, because, as I have before remarked, that expenditure will be essentially and immediately reproductive. Suppose that this money is expended at the rate of £850,000 a year for ten years. . . .

We suppose that, during ten years, eight and a half millions are expended, and that the rate of interest is 5½ per cent. The following table will represent the yearly payments:—

	Interest, 12 months on £	Interest, 6 months on £	Total interest £
1st year		850,000	23,375
2nd year	850,000	850,000	70,125
3rd year	850,000	850,000	116,875
4th year	850,000	850,000	163,625
5th year	850,000	850,000	210,375
6th year	850,000	850,000	257,125
7th year	850,000	850,000	303,875
8th year	850,000	850,000	350,625
9th year	850,000	850,000	397,375
10th year	850,000	850,000	444,125

On the other side, merely as conjecture recollect, let us see to what desperate lengths this might drive the Colony. Is it extravagant to suppose that, in one way and another, six million acres of land will be devoted to railway purposes? Two and a half millions, we assume, will be directly employed in the way of payments, the other three and a half millions would be available in reduction of the capital cost or the yearly interest. Some of this three and a half millions of acres will be sold, some be let, some will remain in pastoral occupation until, in course of time, it has acquired position value. Is it unreasonable to estimate that, from all sources, of sale, letting, and licenses, during the ten years, such sums as the following will result, say—

1st year, £5,000	6th year, £55,000
2nd year, £10,000	7th year, £70,000
3rd year, £20,000	8th year, £90,000
4th year, £30,000	9th year, £110,000
5th year, £40,000	10th year, £130,000

Is it unreasonable to suppose that, at the end of the third year, a sum of £10,000 will be the result over and above working expenses, from the railways opened up to that time, by the expenditure of the two and a half millions, which our calculation supposes to be expended, and that the return will be from the

4th year, £20,000	7th year, £100,000
5th year, £50,000	8th year, £150,000
6th year, £75,000	9th year, £200,000
and the 10th year, £250,000	

Let us suppose, further, that half of the stamp duties are to be brought to aid, and that these should be made to yield as follows:—

1st year, £40,000	6th year, £65,000
2nd year, £45,000	7th year, £70,000
3rd year, £50,000	8th year, £75,000
4th year, £55,000	9th year, £80,000
5th year, £60,000	10th year, £85,000

Our totals will then be as follows:—

	$5\frac{1}{2}$ per cent		
	Interest, 12 months on	Interest, 6 months on	Total Interest
	£	£	£
1st Year		850,000	23,375
2nd „	850,000	850,000	70,125
3rd „	850,000	850,000	116,875
4th „	850,000	850,000	163,625
5th „	850,000	850,000	210,375
6th „	850,000	850,000	257,125
7th „	850,000	850,000	303,875
8th „	850,000	850,000	350,625
9th „	850,000	850,000	397,375
10th „	850,000	850,000	444,125

LESS

	Receipts over and above Working Expenses on Railways	Receipts from Railway Estate	Stamp Duties Estimated	Total
	£	£	£	£
1st Year		5,000	40,000	45,000
2nd „		10,000	45,000	55,000
3rd „	10,000	20,000	50,000	80,000
4th „	20,000	30,000	55,000	105,000
5th „	50,000	40,000	60,000	150,000
6th „	75,000	55,000	65,000	195,000
7th „	100,000	70,000	70,000	240,000
8th „	150,000	90,000	75,000	315,000
9th „	200,000	110,000	80,000	390,000
10th „	250,000	130,000	85,000	465,000

That is to say, expenditure and receipts each year as follow:—

	Expenditure	Receipts
	£	£
1st Year	23,375	45,000
2nd „	70,125	55,000
3rd „	116,875	80,000
4th „	163,625	105,000
5th „	210,375	150,000
6th „	257,125	195,000
7th „	303,875	240,000
8th „	350,625	315,000
9th „	397,375	390,000
10th „	444,125	465,000

. . . We ought, in dealing with this question, to recollect that it is regarded from opposite points by the country parting with, and that which is receiving, the population. In the one case, the desire is natural to part with the worst, in the other to obtain the best, portion of the population. A class of persons may be introduced to the Colony than which even the convict element would be scarcely more detrimental. I allude to the refuse population of large towns and cities, composed of beings hopelessly diseased in body and mind, deficient in all capacity for useful labour, vagrant and idle alike by habit and inclination, paupers by profession, and glorying in being so. You could not subject those beings to the discipline to which convicts might be subjected; they would be not only themselves burdens to the State, but they would be fruitful sources of corruption to others. It is painful to have to make reflections of this kind; but it is due to the colonists that they should be assured that the Government have their attention directed to the possible pernicious use to which the agitation at home for emigration may lead. . . .

If the Imperial Government are willing to expend money on emigration in conjunction with the colonies, then, to make the movement satisfactory, the colonies must absolutely have the charge of selection.

We put on one side the contingency of Imperial aid, and ask the House to concur with us in determining that the Colony must take into its own charge the conduct of immigration. . . .

From whatever point of view you regard it—whether from the highest social or the narrowest pecuniary view, immigration is a profit to the State, if the immigrants can settle down and support themselves. If many thousands of immigrants, introduced at once, could earn a livelihood in the Colony, I would not hesitate to ask you to vote the money to pay for their passages. Long before the money would have to be paid, supposing it to be borrowed, the immigrants would recoup the amount by contributions to the revenue. But it would be cruel to bring out immigrants if you do not see the way to their finding the means of self-support. As every immigrant who becomes a settler will be a profit, so every immigrant who leaves the Colony, or is unable to procure a livelihood in it, will be a loss. We therefore say that we will introduce immigrants only to those parts of the Colony which are prepared to receive them. What the nature of the preparation may be it would be impossible now to define. It might be land for settlement; it might be employment of an ordinary nature, or on public works; it might be that facilities for establishing manufactories, or aiding special or co-operative settlements, were offered. . . .

. . . Whatever the cost, we propose that the General and Provincial Governments shall share it, and we shall be quite willing that the Provinces should appoint agents to select suitable immigrants. The more immigration agents there are, the better, so long as they are properly qualified persons. I believe a great many immigrants may be introduced free, or at a small cost, in connection with public works, or land grants, or special or co-operative settlements. . . .

In the course of the remarks I have made on these various proposals, I have abundantly evidenced the desire of the Government to respect the integrity of provincial institutions, and to put them to their highest and most valuable uses; but I have not hesitated to declare that, inasmuch as the objects of Government are superior to a blind subserviency to particular forms, we must not shrink from making such alterations in the provincial system as the requirements of the country, and of a colonizing policy, demand. . . .

N.Z.P.D., 1870, vol. vii, pp. 102–8

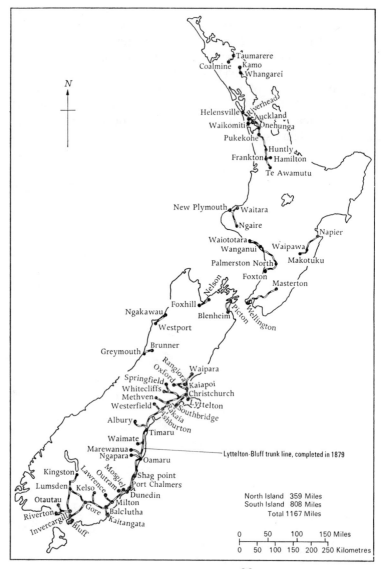

N

Taumarere
Coalmine · Kamo
Whangarei

Helensville
Riverhead
Auckland
Waikomiti
Onehunga
Pukekohe
Huntly
Frankton · Hamilton
Te Awamutu

New Plymouth · Waitara
Ngaire
Waiototara
Wanganui Waipawa
Palmerston North Makotuku
Foxton Masterton
Nelson Napier

Foxhill
Ngakawau
Blenheim Picton
Westport Wellington
Brunner
Greymouth
Waipara
Rangiora
Oxford
Springfield Kaiapoi
Whitecliffs Christchurch
Methven Lyttelton
Westerfield Southbridge
Albury Rakaia
Ashburton
Waimate Timaru
Marewanua
Ngapara Oamaru
Kingston Lawrence Mosgiel Shag point
Lumsden Kelso Outram Port Chalmers
Otautau Dunedin
Riverton Gore Milton
Invercargill Balclutha
Bluff Kaitangata

Lyttelton-Bluff trunk line, completed in 1879

North Island 359 Miles
South Island 808 Miles
Total 1167 Miles

0   50   100   150 Miles
0 50 100 150 200 250 Kilometres

MAP 2. RAILWAYS 1880

The railway construction of the 1870s brought the trunk and branch lines of
Otago and Canterbury to an advanced state, but elsewhere provincial systems
were fragmentary.

52

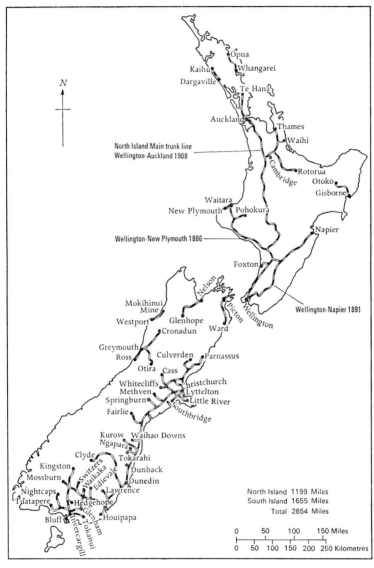

N

Opua
Kaihu
Dargaville
Whangarei
Te Han
Auckland
Thames
Waihi
North Island Main trunk line
Wellington-Auckland 1908
Cambridge
Rotorua
Otoko
Gisborne
Waitara
New Plymouth
Pohokura
Napier
Wellington-New Plymouth 1886
Foxton
Mokihinui
Mine
Nelson
Westport
Glenhope
Cronadun
Picton
Ward
Wellington
Wellington-Napier 1891
Greymouth
Ross
Culverden
Parnassus
Otira
Cass
Whitecliffs
Methven
Springburn
Fairlie
Christchurch
Lyttelton
Little River
Southbridge
Kurow
Waihao Downs
Ngapara
Clyde
Tokarahi
Kingston
Switzers
Waikaka
Edievale
Dunback
Mossburn
Nightcaps
Tuatapere
Lawrence
Dunedin
Bluff
Hedgehope
Glenham
Tokanui
Invercargill
Houipapa

North Island 1199 Miles
South Island 1655 Miles
Total 2854 Miles

0   50   100   150 Miles
0   50   100 150 200 250 Kilometres

RAILWAYS 1914
Though three North Island trunk railways were operating by 1914, some
trunk and much regional construction still remained incomplete.

53

2

CONSTITUTIONS, GOVERNMENT, AND POLITICS, 1840s TO 1870s

---

22. CROWN COLONY GOVERNMENT

Letters Patent issued on 16 November 1840 entitled 'Charter for erecting the Colony of New Zealand, and for creating and establishing a Legislative Council and an Executive Council'.

NOW KNOW YE that we, in pursuance of the said recited Act of Parliament, and in exercise of the powers thereby in us vested, of our especial grace, certain knowledge, and mere motion have thought fit to erect, and do hereby erect the said Islands of New Zealand, and all other Islands adjacent thereto, and lying between the 34th degree 30 minutes North,* to the 47th degree 10 minutes South Latitude, and between the 166th degree 5 minutes, to the 179th degree of East Longitude (reckoning from the Meridian of Greenwich) into a separate Colony, and the same are hereby erected into a separate Colony accordingly. And we do hereby declare, that from henceforth the said Islands shall be known and designated as the Colony of New Zealand, and the principal Islands, heretofore known as, or commonly called, the 'Northern Island,' the 'Middle Island,' and 'Stewart's Island,' shall henceforward be designated and known respectively as 'New Ulster,' 'New Munster,' and 'New Leinster.' . . .

NOW THEREFORE, in pursuance and further exercise of the powers so vested in us as aforesaid, in and by the said Act of Parliament, we do, by these our Letters Patent, authorize the Governor or the Lieutenant-Governor for the time being of the said Colony of New Zealand, and such other Persons, not less than six, as are herein-

---

* This should have read 'South'. The error, which was repeated in a number of documents in 1840, 1841, 1845, and 1846, implied that the colonial boundaries stretch to a point on the same latitude as Tokyo.

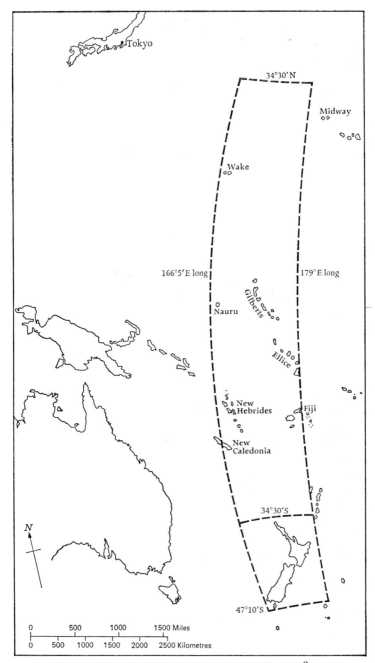

Tokyo

34°30′N

Midway

Wake

166°5′E long

179°E long

Gilberts

Nauru

Ellice

New
Hebrides

Fiji

New
Caledonia

N

34°30′S

47°10′S

| 0 | 500 | 1000 | 1500 Miles |
| 0 | 500 | 1000 | 1500 | 2000 | 2500 Kilometres |

MAP 3. BOUNDARIES IN THE CHARTER OF 1840

55

after designated, to constitute and be a Legislative Council for the said Colony; and, in further exercise of the powers aforesaid, we do hereby declare that, in addition to the said Governor or Lieutenant-Governor, the said Legislative Council shall be composed of such public officers within the said Colony, or of such other Persons as shall from time to time be named or designated for that purpose by us, by any Instruction or Instructions, or Warrant or Warrants to be by us for that purpose issued under our Signet and Sign Manual, and with the advice of our Privy Council, all of which Councillors shall hold their places in the said Council at our pleasure.

And we do hereby require and enjoin that such Legislative Council shall, in pursuance of the said Act of Parliament, make and ordain all such Laws and Ordinances as may be required for the Peace, Order, and good government of the said Colony of New Zealand, and that in the making all such Laws and Ordinances the said Legislative Council shall conform to and observe all such Instructions as we, with the advice of our Privy Council, shall from time to time make for their guidance therein.

And WHEREAS it is expedient that an Executive Council should be appointed to advise and assist the Governor of our said Colony of New Zealand for the time being in the administration of the Government thereof, we do therefore, by these our Letters Patent, authorize the Governor of our said Colony for the time being to summon as an Executive Council, such Persons as may from time to time be named or designated by us in any Instructions under our Signet and Sign Manual, addressed to him in that behalf. . . .

And we do hereby give and grant to the Governor of our said Colony of New Zealand for the time being, full power and authority, in our name and on our behalf, but subject nevertheless to such provisions as may be in that respect contained in any Instructions which may from time to time be addressed to him by us for that purpose, to make and execute, in our name and on our behalf, under the Public Seal of our said Colony, Grants of waste Land, to us belonging within the same, to private persons, for their own use and benefit, or to any persons, bodies politic or corporate, in trust for the public uses of our subjects there resident, or any of them.

PROVIDED ALWAYS, that nothing in these our Letters Patent contained shall affect or be construed to affect the rights of any aboriginal natives of the said Colony of New Zealand, to the actual occupation or enjoyment in their own persons, or in the persons of their descendants, of any Lands in the said Colony now actually occupied or enjoyed by such natives.

And we do hereby authorize and empower the Governor of our said Colony of New Zealand for the time being, to constitute and appoint Judges. . . .

> *The Ordinances of New Zealand passed in the first ten sessions of the General Legislative Council, A.D. 1841 to A.D. 1849.* Compiled by Alfred Domett, Wellington, 1850, pp. 4–8

23. REPRESENTATIVE GOVERNMENT—THE 1846 CONSTITUTION

Dispatch from the Secretary of State, Earl Grey, to the Governor, Sir George Grey, 23 December 1846, enclosing the 1846 Constitutional Act (9 & 10 Vict. Cap. 103), a new Charter, and these instructions for the gradual implementation of the new constitution. A land register is to be begun and the country temporarily divided into 'Provincial' and 'Aboriginal' districts.

For the institutions established under the Charter of November 1840, [it] contemplates the substitution of municipal corporations for the government of each separate District of New Zealand which is or which shall be settled by Colonists of European birth and origin. Every such district is to be erected into a Borough; every such Borough is to elect a Common Council, from which are to be chosen a Mayor and a Court of Aldermen; every such Common Council is to elect members to serve in a House of Representatives, forming one of the three estates of a Provincial Assembly. For this purpose the whole of New Zealand is to be divided into two or more provinces. In every such Provincial Assembly, laws will be made for the Province by the House of Representatives, by a Legislative Council, and by the Governor, who together will constitute the Provincial Legislature.

But as there are many topics of general concern to all the Inhabitants of New Zealand, respecting which some uniformity of legislation and of administration will be indispenable, it is further provided, that a General Assembly of the New Zealand Islands shall be holden by the Governor in Chief. That General Assembly will be composed of himself, and of a Legislative Council, and of a House

57

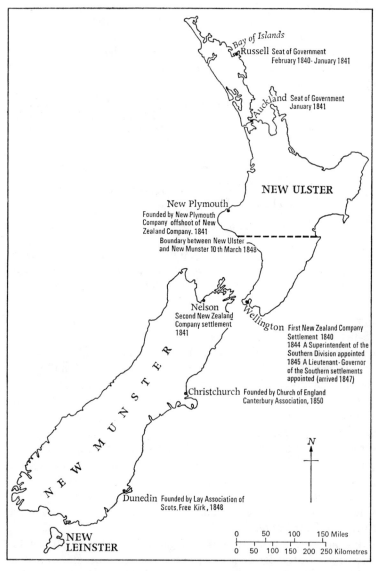

Bay of Islands
Russell Seat of Government
February 1840- January 1841

Auckland Seat of Government
January 1841

NEW ULSTER

New Plymouth
Founded by New Plymouth
Company offshoot of New
Zealand Company. 1841
Boundary between New Ulster
and New Munster 10 th March 1848

Nelson
Second New Zealand
Company settlement
1841

Wellington First New Zealand Company
Settlement 1840
1844 A Superintendent of the
Southern Division appointed
1845 A Lieutenant-Governor
of the Southern settlements
appointed (arrived 1847)

Christchurch Founded by Church of England
Canterbury Association, 1850

NEW MUNSTER

N

Dunedin Founded by Lay Association of
Scots.Free Kirk, 1848

NEW
LEINSTER

0   50   100   150 Miles
0   50   100 150 200 250 Kilometres

MAP 4. CROWN COLONY GOVERNMENT 1841-53

of Representatives. But no one will be a Member of the Legislative Council of the General Assembly who is not also a member of one of the Legislative Councils of the Provincial Assemblies; neither will any one be a Member of the House of Representatives of the General Assembly who is not a member of one of the Houses of Representatives of the Provincial Assemblies. . . .

In favour of this scheme of municipal, legislative, and executive polity, I rely on the following considerations: — It is framed with as close an adherence as circumstances would allow, to the model of our English institutions, an object which I regard as of the highest importance in every such design. It adheres, as nearly as practicable, to that scheme of colonial policy once diffused over the greater part of the North American Continent, and still surviving in our remaining Colonies there, and yet to be distinctly traced in the constitutions of the flourishing States now united into the Great American Commonwealth. It provides for the local self government of districts in a Country where the dispersion of the settlements is such as to render any one central authority incompetent to that task. But while public spirit, and a practical acquaintance with public affairs, will thus be cherished in every part of New Zealand, the erection of Provinces and Provincial Assemblies will, I trust, counteract the tendency which such Corporate Institutions must otherwise have to disunite, in interest and in feeling, the various remote districts from each other. Natural causes forbid the combination of all those Districts in the choice of Members to serve in a single Assembly for the whole of New Zealand; but two such Assemblies at present, and perhaps more than two such hereafter may be sufficient to consolidate and cement and protect the interests of the various separate Boroughs. To prevent those intercolonial contests, of such frequent occurrence elsewhere, and to watch over the general interest of the whole Country, the General Assembly is charged with the exclusive care of those interests, and with no other function. The circumstance that the General Assembly will consist of members chosen by the Provincial Assemblies out of their own number, will, I hope, prove an effectual security against the otherwise too probable conflicts between the local and the general Legislatures.

The Queen, as entitled in right of her Crown to any waste lands in the Colony, is free to make whatever rules Her Majesty may see fit on the subject. The accompanying Charter accordingly authorizes the Governor to alienate such lands. The accompanying instructions direct how that power is to be used. I proceed to explain the motives by which those instructions have been dictated.

The opinion assumed, rather than advocated, by a large class of writers on this and kindred subjects is, that the aboriginal inhabitants of any Country are the proprietors of every part of its soil of which they have been accustomed to make any use, or to which they have been accustomed to assert any title. This claim is represented as sacred, however ignorant such natives may be of the arts or of the habits of civilized life, however small the number of their tribes, however unsettled their abodes, and however imperfect or occasional the uses they make of the land. Whether they are nomadic tribes depasturing cattle, or hunters living by the chase, or fishermen frequenting the Sea-Coasts or the banks of rivers, the proprietary title in question is alike ascribed to them all.

From this doctrine, whether it be maintained on the grounds of religion, or of morality, or of expediency, I entirely dissent. . . .

The Islands of New Zealand are not much less extensive than the British Isles and capable probably of supporting as large a population, while that which they actually supported has been variously estimated, but never I believe so high as 200,000 souls. To contend that under such circumstances civilized men had not a right to step in and take possession of the vacant territory, but were bound to respect the supposed proprietary title of the savage tribes who dwelt in but were utterly unable to occupy the land, is to mistake the grounds upon which the right of property in land is founded. To that portion of the soil, whatever it might be, which they really occupied, the aboriginal inhabitants, barbarous as they were, had a clear and undoubted claim; to have attempted to deprive them of their patches of potato ground, even so to have occupied the Territory as not to leave them ample space for shifting, as was their habit, their cultivation from one spot to another, would have been in the highest degree unjust; but so long as this injustice was avoided, I must regard it a vain and unfounded scruple which would have acknowledged their right of property in land which remained unsubdued to the uses of man. But if the savage inhabitants of New Zealand had themselves no right of property in land which they did not occupy, it is obvious that they could not convey to others what they did not themselves possess, and that claims to vast tracts of waste land, founded on pretended sales from them are altogether untenable. From the moment that British dominion was proclaimed in New

Zealand, all lands not actually occupied in the sense in which alone occupation can give a right of possession, ought to have been considered as the property of the Crown in its capacity of Trustee for the whole community, and it should thenceforward have been regarded as the right and at the same time the duty of those duly authorized by the Crown, to determine in what manner and according to what rules the land hitherto waste should be assigned and appropriated to particular individuals. There is another consideration which leads to the same conclusion. It has never been pretended that the wide extent of unoccupied land, to which an exclusive right of property has been asserted on behalf of the native inhabitants of New Zealand, belonged to them as individuals; it was only as tribes, that they were supposed to possess it; and granting their title as such to have been good and valid, it was obviously a right which the tribes enjoyed as independent communities—an attribute of sovereignty, which, with the sovereignty naturally and necessarily was transferred to the British Crown. Had the New Zealanders been a civilized people, this would have been the case—if these islands, being inhabited by a civilized people, had been added either by conquest or by voluntary cession to the dominions of the Queen, it is clear that, according to the well known principles of public law, while the property of individuals would have to be respected, all public property, all rights of every description which had appertained to the previous Sovereigns, would have devolved, as a matter of course, to the new Sovereign who succeeded them. It can hardly be contended that these tribes, as such, possessed rights which civilized communities could not have claimed.

Such are the principles upon which, if the Colonization of New Zealand were only now about to begin, it would be my duty to instruct you to act; and though I am well aware that in point of fact you are not in a position to do so, and that from past transactions a state of things has arisen in which a strict application of these principles is impracticable, I have thought it right that they should be thus explicitly stated in this dispatch (as they are in the Royal instructions to which it refers), in order that you may clearly understand that although in many respects you may be compelled to depart from them, still you are to look to them as the foundation of the policy which, so far as is in your power, you are to pursue. . . .

The first and most important step which you will have to take with the view of introducing a regular system with respect to the disposal of land, will be to ascertain distinctly the ownership of all the land in the Colony. The extent and limits of all which is to be considered as the property either of individuals, of bodies politic or corporate, or of the native tribes, must in the first instance be determined, and the whole of the remainder of the territory will then be declared to be the royal demesne. The result of this inquiry must be carefully registered and a regular record henceforth preserved, showing to whom all the lands of New Zealand belong. . . .

Such being my general views regarding the settlement of the public lands in New Zealand, I return to the kindred topic of the state of the aborigines there. . . . The laws and customs of the native New Zealanders, even though repugnant to our own laws, ought, if not at variance with general principles of humanity, to be for the present maintained for their government in all their relations to and dealings with each other; and that particular districts should be set apart within which such customs should be so observed.

It will be your own duty to give effect to the general principle which would separate, by well defined lines of demarcation, those parts of New Zealand in which the native customs are to be maintained, from those in which they are to be superseded. For the sake of distinctness, the one may be called the aboriginal, and the other the provincial districts. The last, or provincial districts, will be entirely divided into the various municipalities already mentioned. With an increasing British population, and with the advance of the natives in the arts of civilized life, the provincial districts will progressively extend into the aboriginal, until, at length, the distinction shall have entirely disappeared. In the mean time the provincial districts, and they alone, will be the seats of courts and magistracies, and of other institutions requisite for the government of civilized men. The aboriginal districts will be governed by such methods as are in use among the native New Zealanders. The chiefs or others, according to their usages, should be allowed to interpret and to administer their own laws. . . . With the increase of Christian knowledge, of Civilization, of the use of the English tongue, and of mutual confidence between the two races, these distinctions of law and of legal customs will, I trust, become unnecessary and obsolete. . . .

. . . [Finally, I] do not scruple to observe, that the experience of our widely-extended empire has ascertained that the otherwise inestimable advantages of colonial self-government are attended with at least one serious danger. It is the danger that the powers conferred by this great franchise on the representatives of the people may be perverted into an instrument for the oppression of the less civilized and less powerful races of men inhabiting the same Colony. This abuse has arisen in our Colonies not because the wealthier and better-educated Classes of society there are in any respect inferior in character to the corresponding classes of society elsewhere, but because they are exposed to a temptation from which the greater number of imperial and independent legislatures are exempt. They live in a vicinity to which nothing parallel exists in the ancient States of Europe. Such a vicinity exists, and consequently such a temptation will arise in New Zealand. I therefore acquit myself of a duty involving no failure of respect to the future assemblies of that Colony, in thus unreservedly pointing out to you, and through you commending to their attention, the sacred duty which will be incumbent on them, of watching over the interests, protecting the persons, and, as far as may be, cultivating the minds of the aboriginal race among whom they and their constituents have settled. . . .

No. 23 received 30 June 1847. G1/17

24. THE 1846 CONSTITUTION—GREY'S REQUEST FOR POSTPONEMENT

Confidential dispatch from Governor Grey to the Secretary of State, Earl Grey, 3 May 1847, suggesting that self-government for the settlers would further excite Maori resistance.

. . . by the introduction of the proposed Constitution into the Province of New Ulster, Her Majesty will not confer, as is intended, upon Her subjects, the inestimable advantages of self-government; but she will give to a small fraction of Her subjects of one race, the power of governing the large majority of Her subjects of a different race. She will not give to her subjects the valuable privilege of appropriating, as they may think proper, the funds raised from themselves by taxation, but she will give to a small minority of one race, the power of appropriating as they think proper a large revenue raised by taxation from the great majority of Her subjects of another race. And these further difficulties attend this question, that the race which is in the majority is much the most powerful of the two,—the people belonging to it are well-armed, proud, and independent, and there is no reason that I am acquainted with, to think that they would be satisfied with, and submit to the rule of the minority, whilst there are many reasons to believe that they will resist it to the utmost;— And then it must further be remembered that the minority will not have to pay the expenses of the Naval and Military forces which will be required to compel the stronger and more numerous race to submit to their rule; but that, on the contrary, these expenses must be paid by Great Britain. . . .

. . . I think it proper to mention that Her Majesty's native subjects in this country will certainly be exceedingly indignant at finding that they are placed in a position of inferiority to the European population,—they will undoubtedly argue, as they now frequently do, that they not only cheerfully ceded the sovereignty of their country to the Queen, but that when attempts have been made by some discontented tribes to throw off the sovereignty of Great Britain, and that at a period when, from the smallness of the British force in the country, they had apparently some hopes of success, the principal Chiefs came forward and freely gave the services of themselves and their people, and shed their blood in assisting to maintain for Her Majesty that sovereignty, which they had yielded to Her. . . .

A great change has also recently taken place in their position, the mutual jealousies and animosities of the tribes have greatly disappeared, and a feeling of class or race is rapidly springing up, and has been greatly fomented by the efforts which have been made by designing Europeans to obtain their lands from them for a merely nominal consideration. This feeling of nationality has been extended by many other causes . . . so that their intercourse and power of forming extensive conspiracies, and of executing combined and simultaneous movements upon different points is daily increasing. . . .

It is, I think, doubtful, therefore, if it would be prudent to hazard the attempt to force upon a nation so circumstanced a form of Government which would at the same time irritate their feelings, and, I think, insult their pride, and which, there can be no doubt, would separate them from the Europeans, placing them in an inferior position as a race, and thus at once create this feeling of nationality, the consequence of which would, I fear, be so hurtful. . . .

Whatever form of Government it may however be determined ultimately to bestow upon the Northern Colony of New Zealand, I beg to suggest that it would be desirable in the first place that it should not be such as to render it doubtful, whether the large native population will submit to it, and secondly, that so long as the Governor has so formidable and numerous a race to control, it is necessary not only that he should have the power by his negative, of preventing any measures being passed which might result in rebellion, but that he also requires to be in possession of the active power of carrying such measures as are essential for the welfare, and pacification of the native race. . . .

At present, the natives are quite satisfied with the form of Government now existing, and as the Chiefs have always ready access to the Governor, and their representations are carefully heard and considered, they have practically a voice in the Government, and of this they are well aware; but under the proposed constitution they would lose their power, and the Governor would lose his influence over them, in fact the position of the two races would become wholly altered, and the Governor would, I fear, lose that power which I do not see how, he can well dispense with, in a country circumstanced as this.

The Natives are, at present, certainly not fitted to take a share in a representative form of Government, but each year they will become more fitted to do so, and each year the numerical difference between the two races will become less striking,—so that a great advantage would be gained by delaying even for a few years the introduction of the proposed constitution into the Northern parts of New Zealand. . . .

C.O. 209/52, pp. 247-63

25. GOVERNOR GREY PROPOSES A LOW PROPERTY QUALIFICATION FOR VOTERS

Dispatch from Governor George Grey to the Secretary of State, Earl Grey, 29 November 1848, in which he made suggestions for a representative constitution to replace the 1846 Act. He would grant the vote to all those with a modest property qualification on the ground that they had 'a stake in the Colony'.

. . . I would recommend that the right of voting at elections should be exercised by such European subjects of Her Majesty as can read and write, and who have either an estate of freehold in possession, in lands or tenements, situated within the district for which such vote is to be given, of the value of Thirty Pounds, or who are householders within such district occupying a dwelling within the limits of a

Town of the annual value of Ten pounds or in the Country of the Annual value of Five pounds.

And I would recommend that such right of voting should be exercised by such native subjects of Her Majesty as are possessed of property in Government Securities, in vessels, or in tenements within the district for which their vote is to be given, of the clear value of two hundred pounds, or who may be authorized to exercise such vote by a certificate granted to them for that purpose by the Governor-in-Chief. . . .

In proposing the low rate of franchise which I have named in this dispatch, I have been influenced by the desire of including among the voters all those persons who have acquired or are acquiring small properties on which they intend to reside themselves during the remainder of their lives and to settle them on their children.

Persons of this class have such a stake in the Colony, that they will sincerely desire its prosperity and welfare. They are also generally speaking an extremely religious, well conducted class of persons, and as owners of property are required to make themselves acquainted with a large class of subjects which are seldom brought under the notice of persons of their condition in England. I think therefore that the right of giving a vote may with great safety be left in their hands. . . .

No. 106. C.O. 209/63, pp. 369-70, 379-80

26. THE DEMAND FOR RESPONSIBLE GOVERNMENT—ROBERT GODLEY, 1850

In November 1850 Governor Grey published the draft of a new Provincial Councils Ordinance providing for a system of representative government through Provincial Legislative Councils (not less than nine members) one-third of whom would be nominated and two-thirds of whom would be elected by £50 freeholders, £10 urban householders, £5 rural householders, and £10 leaseholders. At a public meeting called by the Constitutional Association in Wellington on 15 November 1850, John Robert Godley pointed out that representative institutions did not give 'political power'.

. . . I want you to ask yourselves what this great political object is that you have been striving after, for many long and anxious years, and of which this measure professes to be the realization. There are some who will tell you that it is 'representative institutions', for it is the fashion to say that all colonial reformers want 'representative institutions'. If this be so, then I admit that the Bill ought to satisfy you, for it certainly gives you, in a measure, and after a sort, representative institutions. But I deny that representative institutions are what we have striven and prayed for; we have representative institutions enough already . . ., but the next question is, what we can do with them when we have them. There is no magic in the word 'representative'; no people was ever redeemed or regenerated by the mere election of delegates. No, sir, the object which the colonists of New Zealand have given their energies to obtain, and which they will obtain, if they be true to themselves, is something very different from the mere form of a constitution; it is the substance which all such forms are but methods of exercising; in a word, it is *political power;* the power of virtually administering their own affairs, appointing their own officers, disposing of their own revenues, and governing their own country. . . . never forget that the *end* we aim at is the power of self-government; representative institutions are merely the most convenient and desirable means of exercising it. To give us representative institutions without full powers, is worse than a mockery and a delusion: it is a careful and deliberate provision for keeping the machine of government at a perpetual deadlock; or, if that be avoided through the weakness of the Assembly, for constituting a political debating club of the worst kind, and investing it with the dignity and the claims of a National Legislature. I have insisted thus strongly upon this preliminary point, because it is clear to me that, if it were not for this juggle and word-play about representative institutions, nobody could have seriously proposed that you should accept such a measure as this of Sir George Grey's as the charter of your liberties. It is a measure for constituting Provincial debating-clubs; that is all. . . . it withholds from you the disposal of the greater part of the revenue, and consequently of all practical control over the Executive; that it compels you to conform your legislation to Colonial Office instructions; that it contains that ridiculous and inexplicable provision against making any law repugnant to the law of England; that it makes the pernicious element of nomineeism part and parcel of your Constitution; and that, besides all this, it gives a veto upon all local legislation to a Governor not responsible to yourselves. If you think that the privilege of electing representatives to do nothing be sufficent to compensate for such defects as these; if your ambition be to enjoy the name of a constitutional country, while the real power of governing you resides 16,000 miles off, then, I say, throw up your hats, and cheer for the Constitution. But if you think with me, that this Bill will be merely a stumbling-block and an obstacle in your way; if you believe as I do, that by accepting and sanctioning it, you will debar yourselves for an indefinite time from getting any thing better; that you will compromise every principle that you have been asserting, and make it evident to friends and foes that you have been fighting for names, and not for realities—above all, if you feel convinced, as I do, that if you refuse to be put off with the shadow, you will assuredly get the substance, then I ask you to assert those sentiments and views by an emphatic condemnation of the Bill. . . .

. . . Now, we want no provisional relaxation of arbitrary power, depending on the casual favor of the men who may happen to exercise it; we want the sanction of irrevocable laws for our own rights, and this we can only get from the fountain of law for the British Empire—the Imperial Parliament. Never forget, that the battle of our Constitution must be fought in London; it is by the influence which we can exercise, or the trouble we can give there alone, that we can hope to obtain our local independence; it is because as yet not one of the Australian colonies has taken a stand which entitles and enables it to be heard in London, that not one of them has got local independence yet. I trust that we shall set a brighter example; I trust that we shall shew New Zealand standing pre-eminent and alone among the colonies of England, proclaiming that her people will have nothing to do with counterfeits or half measures; that they will have things in New Zealand called by their proper names—real despotism or real liberty. For my own part, I would far rather live under the avowed despotism of one able and energetic man, acting on his own responsibility, according to his own pleasure, than under such a regimen as it is the fashion in Downing Street to call constitutional and representative; a regimen in which the people exercise no real power, and the Government incurs no effective responsibility; in which the utmost privilege granted to the colonists is that of obstructing the action of their own Government, and in which the right of perpetual agitation is dignified with the name of freedom. . . .

J. E. Fitzgerald (Ed.), A Selection of the Writings and Speeches of John Robert Godley, Christchurch, 1863, pp. 64–7

27. GOVERNOR GREY CALLS FOR PROVINCIAL INSTITUTIONS, 1851

In his celebrated 'constitution-making' dispatch to the Secretary of State of 30 August 1851, Governor Sir George Grey stresses separation of the settlements in New Zealand, and the obstacles in the way of a General Legislature. He also warns the Colonial Office about the military advantages possessed by the North Island Maoris but predicts a rapid fusion of 'the two races into one nation'.

. . . 11. The group of Colonies comprised in the New Zealand Islands are composed at present of what may be termed nine principal European settlements; besides smaller dependencies of these. The largest of these settlements contains about nine thousand (9,000) European inhabitants; and their total European population may be stated at about twenty six thousand souls. These settlements are scattered over a distance of about nine hundred miles of latitude; they are separated from each other by wide intervals, and communication, even for persons on horseback, exists only between three of them. Their inhabitants are chiefly British subjects, but there are amongst them many Americans, French, and Germans. The majority of them have never been trained to the use of arms. The settlers, both in the main colonies and the subordinate dependencies, have occupied the country in so scattered and irregular a manner, that it would be found impossible to afford them efficient protection. . . .

12. The wide intervals between these European colonies are occupied by a native race, estimated to consist of one hundred and twenty thousand (120,000) souls, a very large proportion of whom are males, capable of bearing arms. These Natives are generally armed with rifles or double barrelled guns; they are skilled in the use of their weapons, and take great care of them; they are addicted to war; have repeatedly, in encounters with our troops, been reported by our own officers to be equal to any European troops; and are such good tacticians that we have never yet succeeded in bringing them to a decisive encounter, they having always availed themselves of the advantage afforded by their wilds and fastnesses. Their armed bodies move without any baggage, and are attended by the women, who carry potatoes on their backs for the warriors, or subsist them by digging fernroot, so that they are wholly independent of supplies, and can move and subsist their forces in countries where our troops cannot live. . . .

14. These natives, from the positions which they occupy between all the settlements, can choose their own point of attack, and might even so mislead the most wary Government as to their intended operations as to render it extremely difficult to tell at what point they intended to strike a blow. They can move their forces with rapidity and secrecy from one point of the country to another; whilst, from the general absence of roads, the impassable nature of the country, and the utter want of supplies, it is impossible (except in the case of some of the settlements where good roads have been constructed) to move a European force more than a few miles into the interior from any settlement.

15. The natives, moreover, present no point at which they can be attacked, or against which operations can be carried on. Finding now that we can readily destroy their pas or fortifications, they no longer construct them, but live in scattered villages, round which they have their cultivations, and these they can abandon without difficulty or serious loss, being readily received and fed by any friendly tribe to whom they may repair. They thus present no vulnerable point. Amongst them are large numbers of lawless spirits, who are too ready, for the sake of excitement and the hope of plunder, to follow any predatory chief. To assist in any thing which might be regarded as a national war, there can be little doubt that almost every village would pour forth its chiefs and its population. . . .

16. With these characterisics of courage and warlike vagrancy, the Maories present however other remarkable traits of character. Nearly the whole nation has now been converted to Christianity. They are fond of agriculture, take great pleasure in cattle and horses; like the sea, and form good sailors; have now many coasting vessels of their own, manned with Maori crews; are attached to Europeans and admire their customs and manners; are extremely ambitious of rising in civilization and becoming skilled in European arts; they are apt at learning, in many respects extremely conscientious and observant of their word; are ambitious of honours, and are probably the most covetous race in the world. They are also agreeable in manners, and attachments of a lasting character readily and frequently spring up between them and the Europeans. Many of them have also now, from the value of their property, a large stake in the welfare of the country. One chief has, besides valuable property of various kinds, upwards of five hundred pounds (£500) invested in Government securities; several others have also sums of

from two to four hundred pounds (£200 to £400) invested in the same securities.

17. A consideration of these circumstances will, I think, lead to the conclusion that any attempt to form in those portions of these islands which are densely peopled by the natives, an ordinary European settlement, the inhabitants of which produced all they required and were wholly independent of the native race, must end in failure. The natives in the vicinity of such a settlement, finding themselves excluded from all community of prosperity with its inhabitants, would soon form lawless bands of borderers, who, if they did not speedily sweep away the settlement, would yet, by their constant incursions, so harass and impoverish its inhabitants, that they would certainly soon withdraw to the neighbouring Australian settlements, where they could lead a life of peace and freedom from such incursions. Upon the other hand, however, it would appear that a race such as has been described could be easily incorporated into any British settlement, with mutual advantage to both races; the natives supplying agricultural produce, poultry, pigs, and a constant supply of labour (although yet for the most part rude and unskilled); whilst upon the other hand, the Europeans would supply the various manufactured goods required by the natives, and provide for the manifold wants created by their increasing civilization. Such a class of settlements might easily grow into prosperous communities, into which the Natives, with characters softened by Christianity, civilization, and a taste for previously unknown luxuries, would readily be absorbed.

This process of the incorporation of the native population into the European settlements has, accordingly, for the last few years, been taking place with a rapidity unexampled in history. Unless some sudden and unforeseen cause of interruption should occur, it will still proceed, and a very few years of continued peace and prosperity would suffice for the entire fusion of the two races into one nation. . . .

25. In the two Islands there exist six principal Towns, five of which are situated on good harbors, and each of these form emporiums for considerable Colonies in their neighbourhood.

26. These five Colonies were settled at different times, each upon a totally distinct plan of colonization, and by persons who proceeded direct to their respective Colony, either from Great Britain or from the neighbouring Australian colonies, and who rarely passed

through any other New Zealand Settlement previously to reaching the Colony which they now inhabit; and who, except in a few instances, rarely travel from their own Colony to any neighbouring settlement.

27. Each of these chief towns carries on an independent trade with Great Britain, and with the neighbouring Australian Colonies, and hardly any interchange of commerce takes place between them, since they at present all produce nearly the same commodities, and require the same kind of supplies, which they naturally seek at the cheapest mart; whilst the cost of transport from a port in the Australian colonies, but in a triflling degree, if at all, exceeds the corresponding charges from a Port in New Zealand. There is indeed already a considerable and increasing coasting trade in New Zealand, which in some parts is chiefly carried on in vessels owned and manned by Maories; but it consists rather of a trade between various small Native and European settlements and that one of the principal European towns from which they derive their supplies, and with which they are immediately connected, than of any trade between the principal Colonies themselves.

28. I think it must be clear that between Colonies so constituted, little of what may be termed community of interest can be said to exist. There is no general Capital or mart to which all merchants and persons having extensive business, at all times resort. There is no one central Town for all the Islands in which the courts of Law hold their sittings. Individuals who inhabit one Colony rarely have property or agents in another. Personal acquaintance or intercourse between the inhabitants of the various settlements can be scarcely said to exist.

29. Any attempt therefore to form a General Legislature for such a group of Colonies which should at present annually or even frequently assemble, and which should be so composed as fairly to represent the various interests of all parts of this country, must, therefore, I think, fail; because there are as yet no persons in these Islands who have the means or leisure to enable them to abandon their own affairs each year for the purpose of resorting to another Colony, there to discharge their senatorial duties. . . .

No. 121, C.O. 209/93, pp. 10–11, 15–30

28. REPRESENTATIVE GOVERNMENT— THE 1852 CONSTITUTION ACT

An Act of the Westminster Parliament entitled 'An Act to grant a Representative Constitution to the Colony of New Zealand', 15 & 16 Vict. Cap. 72, 30 June 1852.

. . . whereas it is expedient that further and better Provision should be made for the Government of *New Zealand:* Be it therefore enacted. . . .

[I. Previous constitutional instruments are repealed; existing laws remain in effect except where they conflict with the Act.]

II. The following Provinces are hereby established in *New Zealand;* namely, *Auckland, New Plymouth, Wellington, Nelson, Canterbury,* and *Otago;* and the Limits of such several Provinces shall be fixed by Proclamation by the Governor as soon as conveniently may be after the Proclamation of this Act in *New Zealand.*

III. For each of the said Provinces hereby established, and for every Province hereafter to be established as herein-after provided, there shall be a Superintendent and a Provincial Council, and the Provincial Council of each of the said Provinces hereby established shall consist of such Number of Members, not less than Nine, as the Governor shall by Proclamation direct and appoint.

IV. Upon or before the Issue of Writs for the First Election of Members of the Provincial Council for any Province established by or under this Act, the Persons duly qualified in each of the said Provinces to elect Members for the Provincial Councils as hereinafter mentioned shall elect a Superintendent of such Province; and on the Termination of such Council by Expiration of the Period hereinafter fixed for its Continuance, or by the previous Dissolution thereof, the Persons qualified as aforesaid shall elect the same or some other Person to be Superintendent, and so on from Time to Time; and every such Superintendent shall hold his Office until the Election of his Successor: Provided always, that it shall be lawful for the Governor of *New Zealand,* on behalf of Her Majesty, to disallow any such Election. . . .

V. It shall be lawful for the Governor, by Proclamation, to constitute within each of the said Provinces hereby established convenient Electoral Districts. . . .

N

AUCKLAND

NEW PLYMOUTH
(re-named Taranaki 1st January 1859)

HAWKES BAY
(1st November 1858)

WELLINGTON

MARLBOROUGH
(1st November 1859)

NELSON

WESTLAND
Independent County (1st January 1868
Province 1st December 1873)

CANTERBURY

OTAGO

SOUTHLAND (25th March 1861
re-united with Otago
5th October 1870)

Original six provinces proclaimed
17th January 1853. Boundaries
gazetted 28th February 1853
New Provinces under act of 1858

0   50   100   150   Miles
0   50 100 150 200 250 Kilometres

MAP 5. THE 1852 CONSTITUTION 1853–76

VI. Every Person within any Province hereby established or here-after to be established who shall be legally qualified as an Elector, and duly registered as such, shall be qualified to be elected a Member of the Provincial Council thereof, or to be elected Superintendent thereof: Provided always, that it shall not be necessary that he reside or possess the Qualification in the particular District for which he may be elected to serve as a Member.

VII. The Members of every such Council shall be chosen by the Votes of the Inhabitants of the Province who may be qualified as herein-after mentioned; that is to say, every Man of the Age of Twenty-one Years or upwards having a Freehold Estate in pos-session situate within the District for which the Vote is to be given of the clear Value of Fifty Pounds above all Charges and Incum-brances, and of or to which he has been seised or entitled, either at Law or in Equity, for at least Six Calendar Months next before the last Registration of Electors, or having a Leasehold Estate in possession situate within such District, of the clear annual Value of Ten Pounds, held upon a Lease which at the Time of such Regi-stration shall have not less than Three Years to run, or having a Leasehold Estate so situate, and of such Value as aforesaid, of which he has been in possession for Three Years or upwards next before such Registration, or being a Householder within such District occu-pying a Tenement within the Limits of a Town (to be proclaimed as such by the Governor for the Purposes of this Act) of the clear annual Value of Ten Pounds, or without the Limits of a Town of the clear annual Value of Five Pounds, and having resided therein Six Calendar Months next before such Registration as aforesaid, shall, if duly registered, be entitled to vote at the Election of a Member or Members for the District.

VIII. Provided always, That no Person shall be entitled to vote at any such Election who is an Alien, or who at any Time theretofore shall have been attainted or convicted of any Treason, Felony, or infamous Offence within any Part of Her Majesty's Dominions, unless he shall have received a free Pardon, or shall have undergone the Sentence or Punishment to which he shall have been adjudged for such Offence. . . .

[IX–XII. Vacancies in Provincial Councils.]

XIII. Every Provincial Council shall continue for the Period of Four Years from the Day of the Return of the Writs for choosing the same, and no longer: Provided always, that it shall be lawful for the Governor, by Proclamation or otherwise, sooner to dissolve the same, whenever he shall deem it expedient so to do. . . .

[XIV–XVI. Writs for Elections to Provincial Councils. Meeting places and prorogation of Provincial Councils.]

XVII. Provided always, That there shall be a Session of every Provincial Council once at least in every Year, so that a greater Period than Twelve Calendar Months shall not intervene between the last Sitting of the Council in One Session and the First Sitting of the Council in the next Session.

XVIII. It shall be lawful for the Superintendent of each Province, with the Advice and Consent of the Provincial Council thereof, to make and ordain all such Laws and Ordinances (except and subject as herein-after mentioned) as may be required for the Peace, Order, and good Government of such Province, provided that the same be not repugnant to the Law of *England*. . . .

XIX. It shall not be lawful for the Superintendent and Provincial Council to make or ordain any Law or Ordinance for any of the Purposes herein-after mentioned; (that is to say,)

1. The Imposition or Regulation of Duties of Customs to be imposed on the Importation or Exportation of any Goods at any Port or Place in the Province:
2. The Establishment or Abolition of any Court of Judicature of Civil or Criminal Jurisdiction, except Courts for trying and punishing such Offences as by the Law of *New Zealand* are or may be made punishable in a summary Way, or altering the Constitution, Jurisdiction, or Practice of any such Court, except as aforesaid:
3. Regulating any of the current Coin, or the Issue of any Bills, Notes, or other Paper Currency:
4. Regulating the Weights and Measures to be used in the Province or in any Part thereof:
5. Regulating the Post Offices and the Carriage of Letters within the Province:
6. Establishing, altering, or repealing Laws relating to Bankruptcy or Insolvency:
7. The Erection and Maintenance of Beacons and Lighthouses on the Coast:

8. The Imposition of any Dues or other Charges on Shipping at any Port or Harbour in the Province:

9. Regulating Marriages:

10. Affecting Lands of the Crown, or Lands to which the Title of the aboriginal native Owners has never been extinguished:

11. Inflicting any Disabilities or Restrictions on Persons of the Native Race to which Persons of European Birth or Descent would not also be subjected:

12. Altering in any way the Criminal Law of *New Zealand,* except so far as relates to the Trial and Punishment of such Offences as are now or may by the Criminal Law of *New Zealand* be punishable in a summary Way as aforesaid:

13. Regulating the Course of Inheritance of Real or Personal Property, or affecting the Law relating to Wills.

XX. Every Provincial Council shall immediately on their First Meeting, and before proceeding to the Dispatch of any other Business, elect One of their Members to be the Speaker thereof, during the Continuance of such Council. . . .

[XXI–XXIV. Procedure of Provincial Councils relating to Speakers, Quorums, divisions and Standing Orders.]

XXV. It shall not be lawful for any Provincial Council to pass, or for the Superintendent to assent to, any Bill appropriating any Money to the Public Service, unless the Superintendent shall first have recommended to the Council to make Provision for the specific Service to which such Money is to be appropriated; and no such Money shall be issued or be made issuable, except by Warrants to be granted by the Superintendent.

XXVI. It shall be lawful for the Superintendent to transmit to the Provincial Council, for their Consideration, the Drafts of any such Laws or Ordinances as it may appear to him desirable to introduce. . . .

XXVII. Every Bill passed by the Provincial Council shall be presented to the Superintendent for the Governor's Assent, and the Superintendent shall declare, according to his Discretion, (but subject nevertheless to the Provisions herein contained and to such Instructions as may from Time to Time be given him by the Governor,) that he assents to such Bill on behalf of the Governor, or that he withholds the Assent of the Governor, or that he reserves such Bill for the Signification of the Governor's Pleasure thereon; provided always, that it shall and may be lawful for the Superintendent, before declaring his Pleasure in regard to any Bill so presented to him, to make such Amendments in such Bill as he thinks needful or expedient, and to return such Bill with such Amendments to such Council . . ., provided also, that all Bills altering or affecting the Extent of the several Electoral Districts which shall be represented in the Provincial Council, or establishing new or other such Electoral Districts, or altering the Number of the Members of such Council to be chosen by the said Districts respectively, or altering the Number of the Members of such Council, or altering the Limits of any Town or establishing any new Town, shall be so reserved as aforesaid.

XXVIII. Whenever any Bill shall have been assented to by the Superintendent as aforesaid, the Superintendent shall forthwith transmit to the Governor an authentic Copy thereof.

XXIX. It shall be lawful for the Governor at any Time within Three Months after any such Bill shall have been received by him to declare by Proclamation his Disallowance of such Bill, and such Disallowance shall make void and annul the same from and after the Day of the Date of such Proclamation or any subsequent Day to be named therein. . . .

[XXX–XXXI. Reservation of Provincial Bills.]

XXXII. There shall be within the Colony of *New Zealand* a General Assembly, to consist of the Governor, a Legislative Council, and House of Representatives.

XXXIII. For constituting the Legislative Council of *New Zealand* it shall be lawful for Her Majesty, before the Time to be appointed for the First Meeting of the General Assembly, by an Instrument under Her Royal Sign Manual, to authorize the Governor in Her Majesty's Name to summon to the said Legislative Council such Persons, being not less in Number than Ten, as Her Majesty shall think fit. . . .

. . . Provided always, that no Person shall be summoned to such Legislative Council who shall not be of the full Age of Twenty-one Years, and a natural born Subject of Her Majesty, or a Subject of Her Majesty naturalized by Act of Parliament, or by an Act of the Legislature of *New Zealand*.

XXXIV. Every Member of the Legislative Council of *New Zealand* shall hold his Seat therein for the Term of his Life, subject nevertheless to the Provisions herein-after contained for vacating the same. . . .

[XXXV–XXXIX. Procedure of the Legislative Council relating to vacancies and quorums.]

XL. For the Purpose of constituting the House of Representatives of *New Zealand* it shall be lawful for the Governor, . . . and . . . by Proclamation in Her Majesty's Name, to summon and call together a House of Representatives in and for *New Zealand,* such House of Representatives to consist of such Number of Members, not more than Forty-two nor less than Twenty-four, as the Governor shall by Proclamation in that Behalf direct and appoint; and every such House of Representatives shall, unless the General Assembly shall be sooner dissolved, continue for the Period of Five Years from the Day of the Return of the Writs for choosing such House, and no longer.

XLI. It shall be lawful for the Governor by Proclamation to constitute within *New Zealand* convenient Electoral Districts for the Election of Members of the said House of Representatives, and to appoint and declare the Number of such Members to be elected for each such District, . . .

[XLII–XLIII. Qualifications for electors to the General Assembly the same as for Provincial Councils. Writs for Elections.

XLIV–LII. Procedure of General Assembly relating to times and place of meetings, validity of elections, Oaths, affirmations, election of Speaker, vacant seats in House, Standing Orders.]

LIII. It shall be competent to the said General Assembly (except and subject as herein-after mentioned) to make Laws for the Peace, Order, and good Government of *New Zealand,* provided that no such Laws be repugnant to the Law of *England;* and the Laws so to be made by the said General Assembly shall control and supersede any Laws or Ordinances in anywise repugnant thereto which may have been made or ordained prior thereto by any Provincial Council; and any Law or Ordinance made or ordained by any Provincial Council in pursuance of the Authority hereby conferred upon it, and on any Subject whereon under such Authority as aforesaid it is entitled to legislate, shall, so far as the same is repugnant to or

79

inconsistent with any act passed by the General Assembly, be null and void. . . .

LIV. It shall not be lawful for the House of Representatives or the Legislative Council to pass, or for the Governor to assent to any Bill appropriating to the Public Service any Sum of Money from or out of Her Majesty's Revenue within *New Zealand*, unless the Governor on Her Majesty's Behalf shall first have recommended to the House of Representatives to make Provision for the specific Public Service towards which such Money is to be appropriated, and (save as herein otherwise provided) no Part of Her Majesty's Revenue within *New Zealand* shall be issued except in pursuance of Warrants under the Hand of the Governor directed to the public Treasurer thereof.

LV. It shall and may be lawful for the Governor to transmit by Message to either the said Legislative Council or the said House of Representatives for their Consideration the Drafts of any Laws which it may appear to him desirable to introduce. . . .

LVI. Whenever any Bill which has been passed by the said Legislative Council and House of Representatives shall be presented for Her Majesty's Assent to the Governor, he shall declare according to his Discretion, but subject nevertheless to the Provisions contained in this Act and to such Instructions as may from Time to Time be given in that Behalf by Her Majesty, Her Heirs or Successors, that he assents to such Bill in Her Majesty's Name, or that he refuses his Assent to such Bill, or that he reserves such Bill for the Signification of Her Majesty's Pleasure thereon; provided always, that it shall and may be lawful for the Governor, before declaring his Pleasure in regard to any Bill so presented to him, to make such Amendments in such Bill as he thinks needful or expedient, and by Message to return such Bill with such Amendments to the Legislative Council or the House of Representatives as he shall think the more fitting, . . .

LVII. It shall be lawful for Her Majesty, with the Advice of Her Privy Council, or under Her Majesty's Signet and Sign Manual, or through One of Her Principal Secretaries of State, from Time to Time to convey to the Governor of *New Zealand* such Instructions as to Her Majesty shall seem meet, for the Guidance of such Governor, for the Exercise of the Powers hereby vested in him of assenting to or dissenting from or for reserving for the Signification of Her Majesty's Pleasure Bills to be passed by the said Legislative Council and House of Representatives; and it shall be the Duty of such Governor to act in obedience to such Instructions.

LVIII. Whenever any Bill which shall have been presented for Her Majesty's Assent to the Governor shall by such Governor have been assented to in Her Majesty's Name, he shall by the first convenient Opportunity transmit to One of Her Majesty's Principal Secretaries of State an authentic Copy of such Bill so assented to; and it shall be lawful, at any Time within Two Years after such Bill shall have been received by the Secretary of State, for Her Majesty, by Order in Council, to declare Her Disallowance of such Bill; . . .

[LIX. Reserved Bills.

LX. Promulgation of Acts in Government Gazette.

LXI. Imports for HM Services exempted from taxes and foreign ships exempt from charges which are contrary to treaties.]

LXII. The Governor is hereby authorized and required to pay out of the Revenue arising from Taxes, Duties, Rates, and Imposts levied under any Act or Acts of the said General Assembly, and from the Disposal of Waste Lands of the Crown, all the Costs, Charges, and Expenses incident to the Collection, Management, and Receipt thereof; also to pay out of the said Revenue arising from the Disposal of Waste Lands of the Crown such Sums as may become payable under the Provisions herein-after contained for or on account of the Purchase of Land from aboriginal Natives, or the Release or Extinguishment of their Rights in any Land, and such Sums as may become payable to the *New Zealand* Company under the Provisions of this Act in respect of the Sale or Alienation of Land. . . .

[LXIII. Audits.

LXIV. Civil List, specified in Schedule to Act. Governor £2500, Chief Justice £1000, Puisne Judge £800, Establishment of General Government £4700, Native Purposes £7000.

LXV. Authority and conditions for changing Civil List. Mandatory reservation of Bills altering Governor's salary or sum for Native Purposes.]

LXVI. After and subject to the Payments to be made under the Provisions herein-before contained, all the Revenue arising from

Taxes, Duties, Rates, and Imposts levied in virtue of any Act of the General Assembly, and from the Disposal of Waste Lands of the Crown . . . shall be subject to be appropriated to such specific Purposes as by any Act of the said General Assembly shall be prescribed in that Behalf; and the Surplus of such Revenue . . . shall be divided among the several Provinces . . . in the like Proportions as the gross Proceeds of the said Revenue shall have arisen therein respectively, and shall be paid over to the respective Treasuries of such Provinces for the public Uses thereof, and shall be subject to the Appropriation of the respective Provincial Councils of such Provinces. . . .

LXVII. It shall be lawful for the said General Assembly, by any Act or Acts, from Time to Time, to establish new Electoral Districts for the Purpose of electing Members of the said House of Representatives, to alter the Boundaries of Electoral Districts for the Time being existing for such Purposes, to alter and appoint the Number of Members to be chosen for such Districts, to increase the whole Number of Members of the said House of Representatives. . . .

LXVIII. It shall be lawful for the said General Assembly, by any Act or Acts, to alter from Time to Time any Provisions of this Act and any Laws for the Time being in force concerning the Election of Members of the said House of Representatives, and the Qualification of Electors and Members; provided that every Bill for any of such Purposes shall be reserved for the Signification of Her Majesty's Pleasure thereon, and a Copy of such Bill shall be laid before both Houses of Parliament for the Space of Thirty Days at the least before Her Majesty's Pleasure thereon shall be signified.

LXIX. It shall be lawful for the said General Assembly, by any Act or Acts from Time to Time, to constitute new Provinces in *New Zealand.* . . .

LXX. It shall be lawful for Her Majesty, in and by any Letters Patent to be issued under the Great Seal of the United Kingdom, from Time to Time, to constitute and establish within any District or Districts of *New Zealand* One or more Municipal Corporation or Corporations. . . .

LXXI. And whereas it may be expedient that the Laws, Customs, and Usages of the aboriginal or native Inhabitants of *New Zealand,* so far as they are not repugnant to the general Principles of Humanity, should for the present be maintained for the Government of themselves, in all their Relations to and Dealings with each other, and that particular Districts should be set apart within which such Laws, Customs, or Usages should be so observed:

It shall be lawful for Her Majesty, by any Letters Patent to be issued under the Great Seal of the United Kingdom, from Time to Time to make Provision for the Purposes aforesaid, any Repugnancy of any such native Laws, Customs, or Usages to the Law of *England*, or to any Law, Statute, or Usage in force in *New Zealand*, or in any Part thereof, in anywise notwithstanding. . . .

LXXII. Subject to the Provisions herein contained, it shall be lawful for the said General Assembly to make Laws for regulating the Sale, Letting, Disposal, and Occupation of the Waste Lands of the Crown in *New Zealand;* and all Lands wherein the Title of Natives shall be extinguished as herein-after mentioned. . . .

LXXIII. It shall not be lawful for any Person other than Her Majesty, Her Heirs or Successors, to purchase or in anywise acquire or accept from the aboriginal Natives Land of or belonging to or used by them in common as Tribes or Communities. . . .

[LXXIV. One quarter of proceeds of land sales to discharge the principle and interest of the New Zealand Company's £268,370 15*s*. 0*d*. debt.

LXXV. Confirmation of Canterbury Association's right to dispose of land under 13 & 14 Vict. Cap. 84.

LXXVI. Canterbury Association permitted to transfer its rights.

LXXVII. Confirmation of New Zealand Company's right to administer the fund for public purposes in Nelson under 14 & 15 Vict. Cap. 86.

LXXVIII. Confirmation of the rights of the Otago Association.

LXXIX. Delegation of H.M.'s powers to Governor.]

LXXX. In the Construction of this Act the Term 'Governor' shall mean the Person for the Time being lawfully administering the Government of *New Zealand;* and for the Purposes of this Act '*New Zealand*' shall be held to include all Territories, Islands, and Countries lying between Thirty-three Degrees of South Latitude and Fifty Degrees of South Latitude, and One hundred and sixty-two Degrees of East Longitude and One hundred and seventy-three

Degrees of West Longitude, reckoning from the Meridian of *Greenwich*. ...

[LXXXI–LXXXII. Proclamation and publication of Acts.]

U.K. *Public and General Statutes*, 15 and 16
Vict., Cap. 72, 30 June 1852

THE CONSTITUTION AMENDMENT ACT OF 1857

(An Act to amend the Act for granting a Representative Constitution to the Colony of New Zealand. 20 & 21 Vict., Cap. 53. 17 August 1857.)

... 1. [Sections 67, 68, 69, and 74, and part of section 62 of recited Act repealed.]

2. It shall be lawful for the said General Assembly of New Zealand, by any Act or Acts, from time to time to alter, suspend, or repeal all or any of the provisions of the said Act, except such as are hereinafter specified ... namely. ...

The provisions contained in sections three, eighteen (save the exception therein contained), twenty-five, twenty-eight, twenty-nine, thirty-two, forty-four, forty-six, forty-seven, fifty-three, fifty-four, fifty-six, fifty-seven, fifty-eight, fifty-nine, sixty-one, sixty-four (save so much as charges the Civil List on the revenues arising from the disposal of waste lands of the Crown), sixty-five, seventy-one, seventy-three, and eighty of the said Act. ...

U.K. *Public and General Statutes*, 20 and 21
Vict., Cap. 53. 17 August 1857

29. THE DEMAND FOR RESPONSIBLE GOVERNMENT—DR. ISAAC FEATHERSTON

Speech by Dr. Featherston at a meeting in Barrett's Hotel, Wellington, 18 April 1853, acknowledging a requisition that he accept nomination for Superintendent of the Wellington Province.

... With respect, then, to the [1852] Constitutional Act,—I hesitate not to say, that it is infinitely more liberal in all its main provisions, and confers a far greater amount of substantial power, than any Constitution, yet granted to the Australian Colonies.

In getting rid of the Nominee element, both in the Provincial Councils, and in the lower House of the General Assembly; in the curtailment of the Crown's Veto; in the reduction of the Civil List, to (comparatively speaking) a very trifling amount; in the election of the Superintendents; in the power to alter and amend the Act itself; but, above all, in the acquisition of the entire management and control of the Waste Lands—you have gained great and important advantages—and achieved as those have been, in a great measure by your own exertions—by your own steady adherence to the principles of Constitutional Government, they constitute a triumph of which you may well be proud. It may in truth be said, that the Colonists of New Zealand and their friends at home, have fought and won, the battle of Constitutional Freedom, not only for themselves but also for all the Australian Colonies.

But the chief merit of the Act to my mind, undoubtedly is, that it confers, or at least is intended to confer, not merely Representative, but Responsible Government:—by the term Responsible, I mean, that system of Government under which the chief administration of affairs is entrusted to those who possess the confidence of the Representative body—that system of Government under which the Chief Executive Officers, or Heads of Departments, as we term them here, must consist of those who have both obtained seats in the Legislature and can command a majority in support of the measures, which they, as the Ministers of the day, may deem it advisable to bring forward;—I mean in short, Government by the Leaders of the Parliamentary majority. Such, as you well know, is the practice of the British Constitution; such is the system, which has within the last few years been introduced with so much success, into Canada, and I believe, the other North American Colonies, and such is the system, which you must insist upon being established in this Colony, if you are really desirous of carrying out the principles of the Constitutional Act, or of reaping the full benefits of Free Institutions. Tolerate any other system—permit the administration of your affairs to be carried on by an Irresponsible Executive—by men not enjoying the confidence of your Representatives—by men not able to obtain seats in the Legislature, and you must be prepared to encounter the evils which were experienced in Canada, under a similar system; you must be prepared to see, an effectual stoppage put upon all useful Legislation, and ultimately to find the whole machinery of Government brought to a dead lock; for as Lord Durham well expressed it, the natural state of every Government conducted upon such a principle, must be that of 'perpetual collision between the Executive and the Legislature'. . . .

For just picture to yourselves your representatives assembled in Council, without a single member of the Executive having a seat in it; and then ask yourselves the question how the ordinary business is to be transacted. Suppose, for instance, that one of your honourable members for Wellington requires certain explanations— that the honourable member for Wanganui moves for certain returns—or that the honourable member for the Hutt makes a furious onslaught upon the whole policy of the government;—what a farce, what a sham, mockery and delusion—will this Constitution be made, if the Executive be not present to give the required information, or to defend their own acts! . . .

The Wellington Independent, 20 April 1853,
8(785): 3

30. THE DEMAND FOR RESPONSIBLE GOVERNMENT— EDWARD GIBBON WAKEFIELD

In moving the resolution calling for the establishment of Ministerial responsibility, in Auckland, 2 June 1854, Edward Gibbon Wakefield lectures the House of Representatives on the 'ABC' of responsible government.

. . . To those who ask, 'What is meant by Responsible Government?' I answer, government according to the principles and usages of the British Constitution. . . . And I may therefore not improperly begin by reciting in a few words the A, B, C, of the British system of government. This will be best done by stating what is meant by responsibility in government, and then drawing a distinction between the two ways in which government is made responsible under the republican and monarchical systems. Addressing myself therefore to every honourable member individually, I would ask, What is representation for? Why are we assembled here? We have not been brought here for the purpose of making speeches to each other, or for that of discussing abstract principles of government, though such discussion may be necessary as one means towards very different ends. We are here to reflect the well-understood wishes of the people, to represent their wants, to give effect to their settled desires. . . .

... Now, there are two distinct and very different ways in which representation is made to tell upon all the operations of government. The first occurs under the republican system. The best example is that of the United States of America—. . . There, representation extends, beyond the representative bodies, to the officers of the Executive Government. All the Governors of the several States are elected, and, in many cases, the principal officers under the Governor. In the United States Government, besides the President, the highest officers, such as the Secretaries of State, are indirectly elected by the people, being appointed, though nominally by the President, still virtually by the second Chamber of representatives, the elected Senate. . . .

... To some extent, and, in passing, I cannot help saying that, in my own opinion, to a lamentable extent, the principle of direct executive responsibility by means of election was admitted into the New Zealand Constitution when the office of Provincial Superintendent was made elective. If the conduct of any Superintendent should be opposed to the wishes of the people in his province, he will be made to feel his responsibility at the next election. Believing that entire responsibility in the Provincial Governments might have been provided for without making the Superintendents elective, I regret that the American principle should have been at all intermixed, in our system of government, with the British principle as adopted in all the rest of our Constitution. Since the year 1688, the Crown of England has never, I believe, exercised its prerogative of the veto on Bills passed by both Houses of Parliament. Of course not; because the veto could only have been exercised by the advice of Ministers, who, of course, would never think of advising the disallowance of measures which they themselves had recommended, and carried through the legislative Houses. The system may be described in a few words. The Sovereign, at his own free will and pleasure, chooses a certain number of persons to give him advice with respect to every use of his high authority. They are commonly, for the sake of convenience, but not necessarily, persons holding seats in the legislative Houses. When the advice given by them is unpalatable to the people as represented in the House of Commons, the bad Advisers retire from office, to make room for others who enjoy the popular confidence. Thus the Sovereign escapes all responsibility, and—his office being in no way elective—escapes all risks of suspension or disturbance. The Advisers, the Ministers, alone are responsible for everything. When they differ from the representatives of the people, instead of a conflict between the people and the Sovereign, instead of angry passions of political strife, ending perhaps in revolution, some half-dozen gentlemen walk out of a room and another half-dozen walk in, when peace is restored, and the people throw up their hats for the Crown and the Constitution. Such is the operation of responsibility under the monarchical form of government. If we, being Englishmen, had to choose, can it be doubted that we should prefer that form to the other? . . . But now comes the question of the applicability to colonies of this plan of indirect responsibility. Not very long ago it was the fashion in England, and especially in Downing-street, to say that the British Constitution is all very well for the people at Home, who understand it, but is totally unfit for the purposes of colonial government. Instead of controverting that doctrine, I will state a fact. It is that now, in every one of the colonies of England which enjoys full representation, which has a House of Representatives without admixture of nominees, and which is ocupied entirely or chiefly by people of British race, the British Constitution, including Ministerial responsibility, is in full force. It was first established in Canada, where it worked admirably, and was then extended to Nova Scotia, New Brunswick, and even to Prince Edward Island, in the Gulf of St. Lawrence, a colony whose population scarcely exceeds in number the colonists of New Zealand. But, further, only yesterday I came to the knowledge of a yet more remarkable fact. I then read in a London newspaper . . . a notice of the speech delivered by Governor Sir Henry Barkly to the House of Assembly of Jamaica. Everybody knows that government in Jamaica was lately brought to a standstill by conflict between the representative body and the Executive. . . . In his Speech when opening the Assembly, he states that his intention is to establish Responsible Government without delay, because he is instructed to do so, and because he regards this as one of the principal means whereby the disorders of the colony may be remedied. . . . The House of Assembly of Jamaica is already, in some measure, composed of negroes, who will probably soon be a majority in that body. . . . Sir, if Her Majesty's Government think the Jamaica negroes fit for Responsible Government, surely the gentlemen who now holds the office of Governor in this colony must think that the colonists of New Zealand are not less fit. . . . Sir, we have all lately seen in print, and have heard in private discourse, that difficulties, insuperable difficulties, oppose themselves to the adoption of the policy which I have indicated; that the proposed change may be good to make, but cannot be made, that in order to the establishment of Ministerial responsibility or parliamentary government, there must be two hostile parties tearing each other to pieces. I can see no such necessity. I trust that we may remain for years without violent party animosities. . . . We may well suppose that years will probably last before there can be in this country a banded party of Outs, always striving to turn out the Ins. I believe myself that the absence of party has nothing to do with the matter. In due time, no doubt, rival parties will grow out of events. There may even soon be a Conservative party and a Movement party,—such as all free countries exhibit; or perhaps the day may not be distant when parties will be distinguished by Provincial and Federal preferences. But, instead of regretting that there are not two hostile parties, we may surely rejoice at observing the general and earnest desire of this House to make the Constitution work as well as possible, instead of throwing party obstacles in the way of that most desirable consummation. . . .

. . . Further in the background there is another set of objectors: I mean those who insist that this thing cannot be done without an Act of Parliament. When this so-called difficulty was mentioned, I called to mind what had been done in Canada, and by what authority. The Canadian Constitution under which Responsible Government was fully established is the Canada Union Act; and I will venture to state positively that it does not contain one word about Ministerial responsibility, or even an allusion, direct or indirect, to the subject. That Act was principally framed on the recommendation of Lord Durham's report, a copy of which is now in my hand; and I can assure the House that Lord Durham, when urging the necessity of adopting the system of Responsible Government, expressly declares that an Act of Parliament is not required; that the change may be accomplished by a few words in a dispatch. Nor does he say that even a dispatch is necessary. He describes it as a means, not of enabling the Governor to change his Ministers and make the new ones responsible, but of compelling him to do so if he should be unwilling, if he should be advised to be so unwise as to refuse the desire of the people. . . . I beg leave to move, as a resolution, That, amongst the objects which this House desires to see accomplished without delay, both as an essential means whereby the General Government may rightly exercise a due control over the Provincial Governments and as a no less indispensable means of obtaining for the General Government the confidence and attachment of the people, the most important is the establishment of Ministerial responsibility in the conduct of legislative and executive proceedings by the Governor. . . .

N.Z.P.D., 1st Parliament, 1854, pp. 27–32

31. BRINGING THE EXECUTIVE AND LEGISLATURE INTO HARMONY

Henry Sewell's account, 11 June 1854, of the forming of the so-called 'FitzGerald Ministry', an arrangement whereby the Officer Administering the Government added to the Executive Council three members who had the confidence of the Assembly.

. . . The Revolution is accomplished. Responsible Government is un fait accompli. FitzGerald is Prime Minister, with Weld as Colonial Secretary about to be, and myself as Solicitor General pro tem; that is, such is the present outline of arrangements agreed to by the Governor and accepted by the House; and which will in all probability be effectuated in the course of next week. This is a strange affair, is it not? Now as to how it came about. After the Governor's speech, we all took counsel under Wakefield's leadership as to what course to take. There were Meetings, public and private. . . . A few preliminary meetings of the House gave us an opportunity of skirmishing a little. . . .

Wakefield . . . gave notice that he should on Friday the 2nd move a Resolution affirming the principle of Ministerial responsibility, and further stating that, if the house adopted that Resolution, he should afterwards move an address to the Governor, founded on it. Then he moved an adjournment till Thursday, suspending all business till these matters were disposed of. I must say Wakefield is an admirable political General, bold, skilful, and above all things, knowing where to plant his weapon deepest and deadliest in his enemy's side. It was just one of those coups which he delights in. . . .

Saturday, June 10th, began our Ministerial life. A strange position to be in. FitzGerald completed his arrangements with the Governor. . . . So we three [FitzGerald, Weld, Sewell] are the

Cabinet. . . . It was a queer affair our walking into the Government Offices. They turned some clerks out of a Survey Office, and put us into it desks and all official—and we three sat down together to make a Government. A carteblanche to do what we liked and a promise of absolute confidence from the Governor. I can hardly help rubbing my eyes, and asking whether it is not all a dream. It was the March of Conquerors into the Citadel—the occupation of Paris by the Allies on a small scale. The Garrison, to wit, the old Officials, surrender at discretion, reserving only a certain peculium in the shape of retiring pensions.

Well—now comes the main question—what to do? It is all mighty fine getting into power, and there is just for a moment a gratification in it. But then comes the grave part, what to do? . . .

Sewell's Journal, 1852 to 1857: i, pp. 544–5, 555–6

32. RESPONSIBLE GOVERNMENT APPROVED

Dispatch from the Secretary of State, Sir George Grey, to Lieut.-Col. Robert Henry Wynyard, officer administering the government, 8 December 1854, indicating approval and a procedure for the adoption of responsible government.

. . . Her Majesty's Government have no objection whatever to offer to the establishment of the system known as 'responsible government', in New Zealand. They have no reason to doubt that it will prove the best adapted for developing the interests, as well as satisfying the wishes, of the community. Nor have they any desire to propose terms, or to lay down restrictions, on your assent to the measures which may be necessary for that object, except that, of which the necessity appears to be fully recognized by the General Assembly, namely, the making provision for certain Officers who have accepted their Offices on the equitable understanding of their permanence, and who may now be liable to removal. The only Officers mentioned in your dispatches as likely to fall within this category, are the Colonial Secretary and Treasurer, and the Attorney General; nor am I myself aware of any others; but I do not wish to fetter your discretion, if further consideration makes it, in your opinion, desirable to alter the list.

Should the arrangements made for this purpose be in your judgment satisfactory you are authorised to admit at once the new holders of office under the responsible system, reporting their names for confirmation in the usual manner. There will be no occasion, on this supposition, for a further reference to the home Government before the change is carried into effect. . . .

The preliminary steps for the introduction of responsible government being thus few and plain, I do not understand the opinion . . . that legislative enactment, by the General Assembly is required to bring the change into operation. In this country, the recognised plan of Parliamentary government by which Ministers are responsible to Parliament, and their continuance in Office practically depends on the votes of the two Houses, rests on no written law, but on usage only. In carrying a similar system into effect in the North American Colonies, legislation has indeed been necessary, to make a binding arrangement for the surrender by the Crown of the territorial revenues which has generally formed part of the scheme; and for the establishment of a Civil List; but not for any other purpose. In New Zealand the territorial revenue has already been ceded to the Assembly, and Her Majesty's Government have no terms to propose with reference to the Civil List already established. Unless therefore there are local laws in existence which would be repugnant to the new system, legislation seems uncalled for except for the very simple purpose of securing their pensions to retiring Officers. . . .

No. 39 received 30 March 1855. G1/39

33. RESPONSIBLE GOVERNMENT— RESERVATION OF MAORI AFFAIRS

Minute by Governor Gore Browne, 15 April 1856, stating his relationship with his responsible advisers and signed by himself, Henry Sewell, and Frederick Whitaker.

The view the Governor takes of the relation between himself and his responsible advisers is as follows:—

1st. In all matters under the control of the Assembly, the Governor should be guided by the advice of gentlemen responsible to that body, whether it is or is not in accordance with his own opinion on the subject in question.

2nd. On matters affecting the Queen's prerogative and Imperial Interests generally, the Governor will be happy to receive their advice, but when he differs from them in opinion he will (if they desire it) submit their views to the consideration of Her Majesty's Secretary of State, adhering to his own until an answer is received.

Among Imperial subjects the Governor includes all dealings with the Native tribes, more especially in the negotiation of purchases of land. He will receive and act on the advice of his responsible advisers in reference to the amount of money they may desire to have expended in any one year in the purchase of land, but beyond this he considers himself bound to act on his own responsibility.

The Governor alone is responsible to Her Majesty for the tranquillity of the Colony which would be endangered by the ordinary and inevitable change of opinion consequent on a change in his advisers.

It follows as a necessary consequence of these views, that the Chief Land Purchase Commissioner and his subordinates must take their orders from the Governor alone.

Before giving his assent to Acts passed by Provincial Councils and other matters of a legal nature, the Governor will require the annexed Certificate from the Colonial Secretary and Attorney General; and in approving appointments to vacant Offices, he will require to be assured that the gentlemen recommended are fit and eligible for their respective situations.

> Enclosed in Governor Browne to Henry Labouchere, no. 43, 30 April 1856. C.O. 209/135, pp. 420–2

34. HENRY SEWELL'S 'CENTRALIST' INTERPRETATION OF THE CONSTITUTION

On forming the first, short-lived, responsible ministry, Henry Sewell outlined his views on the respective roles of General and Provincial governments to the House of Representatives, 25 April 1856.

. . . The question now before us is, How establish instantly, and without delay, Responsible Government? . . . What is our Policy? And, first, as to the seat of Government . . . Sir, I believe that it is not possible that New Zealand should remain one united colony except by mutual concession. . . .

. . . Say that every third session shall be held at Auckland, the other two in the South, if asked at what place in the South we should now fix the alternate sitting of the Assembly, conscientiously I believe Nelson to be best. Nelson is, I believe, nearest the Australian Colonies. It is, besides, the most convenient for members attending the Assembly. . . . I turn to another question of even more difficulty than the seat of Government, . . . I refer to the relations between the General and Provincial Governments. On this point the Constitution Act was extremely vague. It created six Provincial Legislatures, with full powers of legislation upon all but thirteen excepted subjects; a General Assembly, with paramount powers of legislation; and Superintendents with no defined powers. A Constitution has been created of which, I believe, there is scarcely another example. From this vagueness and indistinctness in the respective powers and jurisdiction of these bodies great difficulties have arisen in its practical working. The difficulties inherent in it were aggravated by the policy of Sir George Grey in bringing into operation first the Provincial Councils—the inferior and subordinate bodies—before the General Assembly had been brought together. This measure has been attended with most injurious consequences. It has almost defeated the spirit and intention of the Constitution. Six independent Governments, armed with plenary authority fresh in the exercise of their newly-acquired rights, and eager to rush into the possession of them, were set in motion, without any authority to keep them in check. The consequence has been that the real aim of the Constitution has been almost destroyed. These six bodies, acting independently of all control— for the General Government was so weak as to be unable to exercise any practical control over them—have been usurping, day by day, larger powers, and, should they continue unchecked in their present career, will soon be in the position of six independent States. That was not the intention of the Constitution. To break up and divide the colony in this way is to deal treacherously with the institutions committed to our charge. How to apply a remedy is matter of great difficulty. Two remedies have been suggested: one, to strip the Provincial Governments of all but their purely municipal powers, reducing them to mere municipalities. That I will not consent to. I believe that, rightly used, and under proper checks, the large powers of the Provincial Governments may be turned to valuable account. I would not deprive them of one particle of their present power. I would but direct and control its exercise. Another remedy has been proposed, of an opposite kind. It is to establish at once the independence of the Provincial Governments, upon all but a few excepted subjects—to limit the jurisdiction of the General Assembly and the General Government to these subjects—and to establish a federal union of the provinces, after the American model. That view is advocated by my honourable friend the member for Wanganui [Fox]. . . .

. . . I am not prepared to break up the colony into six independent republics, united by a confederation, and to establish, even were it practicable, an American Constitution. Such would be the result of giving to the provinces independent powers of legislation. For my part, I believe it possible to work the Constitution, as it stands, without material change. I would neither curtail in any formal way the powers of the Provincial Councils, nor would I limit those of the General Assembly. At all events, I would not meditate such a change until the experiment has been fairly tried. Let me state my own views as to the true character of the Provincial Governments. I may describe them as consisting of one body and two souls. That they were intended as municipal bodies—using the term 'municipal' in its restricted sense—no one can doubt who has read Sir John Pakington's dispatch accompanying the Constitution Act. As municipal bodies, intended for the management of local affairs, they should be independent, and subject to the slightest possible interference on the part of the General Government. If they commit blunders within their own municipal sphere, it is their own concern, not ours. But, beyond this, they possess powers of a wider scope. The Constitution Act enables them to 'make laws for the peace, order, and good government of the province'—words ordinarily conveying to legislative bodies the fullest power—except upon thirteen subjects. The exception proves the rule. Nothing can hinder them from dealing with all matters except the specified subjects. But, then, this power of legislation is distinctly declared to be subordinate to the paramount control of the General Assembly. In this character the Provincial Governments are to be regarded as subordinate branches and in the nature of departments of the General Government. It is impossible that the Constitution Act should have meant to create independent Provincial Legislatures. The Superintendent in an elective officer. That of itself stamps the Provincial Governments with a municipal character; for British statesmen, in framing our Constitution, could not have meant to invest with independent powers of legislation a body with an elective head. Such an institution would have been fundamentally at variance with the British Constitution, which furnished, of course, the model for our own. When the Superintendent assents to provincial ordinances, he does so, not in his own name, but in that of the Governor. And the Governor may disallow them. And I specially desire you to notice that, in giving such assent, the Superintendent is bound to obey the Governor's instructions. Viewing the Provincial Governments in this light, I would apply the principle I have laid down to practice. With all provincial legislation of a purely municipal kind I would interfere as little as possible; but, when the provinces legislate on subjects of wider scope, I think that the General Government is bound to exercise its controlling power. I do not wish to stop provincial legislation even upon those wider subjects; I believe that much of it may be of a very useful character; but, in general, to make it useful, it must be made uniform throughout the colony. That which may be a valuable improvement in the law if uniform and general, may be injurious by being partial and provincial. . . .

N.Z.P.D., 2nd Parliament, 1856–8, pp. 16–18

35. 'PROVINCIALISM', 1856

Dr. Isaac Featherston and William Fox argue for a 'Provincialist' interpretation of the constitution in the debate on the Address in Reply, in the House of Representatives, 2 May 1856

Dr. Featherston . . . My honourable friend, in touching upon the relations between the General and Provincial Governments, commenced by bewailing the great evils inflicted upon this colony by Sir George Grey in calling the Provincial Councils into life before convening the General Assembly. He attributed to this proceeding the weakness of the Central Executive, and what he was pleased to term 'the usurpations' of the Provincial Governments. As, however, the Constitution Act required that the writs for both Councils should be issued within six months after the Act was proclaimed, and as it was physically impossible to convene the General Assembly for some months after their elections had taken place, it is somewhat difficult to see how Sir George Grey could, without violating the Constitution, have prevented the Provincial Councils meeting before the General Assembly.

. . . It cannot and will not be denied that, since the proclamation of the Constitution, the only Government that has existed for beneficial purposes has been that of the provinces. . . . Surely, if it was not intended that the General Assembly should meet oftener than once in every two or three years—an opinion in which my honourable friend now expresses his concurrence—the conclusion is irresistible that the authors of the Constitution intended that the colony should be governed, as it has been and as it will be, by the Provincial Governments. . . . His great object is to reduce the Provincial Councils to Municipal Councils, the Superintendents to Mayors, or the mere servants of the General Government. And how does he proceed? Admitting that the colony cannot by any possibility be governed by a central Executive, he proposes to govern it by means of the Superintendents, provided the Superintendents will consent to become the agents of the General Government and forswear their allegiance to their constituents. Unwilling to confine the General Government to its only legitimate functions— to restrict its action to those interests which are common to all parts of the colony—he is anxious that it should likewise have a controlling power over those interests which concern the provinces only—that it should have a finger in every provincial pie. . . . He ignores the great principle which breathes in every line of the Constitution Act, the great principle of localized self-government, and proposes to substitute for it a centralized administration. The Superintendent is no longer, as the chief executive officer of the province, to be responsible to the people by whom he has been elected, but is to sink into the obedient servant of the central Executive: he is to obey mandates of a distant authority necessarily ignorant of the wants and requirements of his province. Instead of carrying out a policy acceptable to and approved by his constituents, he is to adopt the views of, it may be, an incompetent and an ever-changing Ministry. . . . My honourable friend's policy is to clothe the central Executive with legislative powers—a combination of power which has been justly described to be the very definition of tyranny. The whole scheme seems to have been imported from China, a country in which centralization exists in the greatest extent, one in which a celebrated author has declared, 'the people have peace without happiness, industry without improvement, and public order without public morality.' But a slight difficulty, which has even occurred to my honourable friend, presents itself in the way of carrying out his scheme. Suppose the Superintendents refuse to obey the instructions or to accept these delegated powers. What then! The remedy provided by the Constitution Act is to dissolve the Provincial Councils. . . .

Mr. Fox said the time was now come when he felt he ought to state his views on the policy of the honourable member for the Town of Christchurch. . . . That policy was Centralism against Provincialism, and that was the issue to be tried. The real question between them was, To what power were the Provincial Governments to be subordinated? He (Mr. Fox) said, To the controlling legislative power of the General Assembly, in accordance with the Constitution Act. The honourable member for the Town of Christchurch sought to subordinate them to the control of the Executive, and, by the details of his scheme, to convert the General Executive into a legislative body for the long interval he proposed between the meetings of the Assembly. . . .

Nothing could be more dangerous than this fusion of legislative and executive functions. The true object of a central power was to regulate the external relations of a country, to adjust conflicting interests between its minor divisions, and to regulate all matters in which they had a common interest; but not, as the honourable member proposed, to intrude into provincial action. And what was the excuse for all this intermeddling? It was to secure uniformity of legislation. The idea of uniformity was the feeble offspring of the brain of the political student sitting in his closet, and not of the statesman who, by extensive travel in countries possessing institutions analogous to ours, had acquired a practical knowledge of their working. Political institutions, to succeed, must be in conformity with the realities of the case. Here there were six settlements, physically, socially, nay, even in their religious creeds, essentially different from each other: why put them all into the provincial bed of uniformity, that child's-toy of a dreamy theorist? . . .

Another evil that he foresaw in this centralized scheme was the amount of central legislation which would be required by the Assembly. That table would groan under piles of correspondence, reports, and Bills. Members would be kept for months from their homes, and the country would be disgusted with representative institutions—a result which perhaps some of the gentlemen opposite earnestly desired. . . . The great argument for Provincialism was that it had entirely succeeded. For nearly three years, till His Excellency's arrival, there had been no central Government in New Zealand: at least, it was in such feeble and incapable hands as to be utterly powerless. Yet never had the provinces made such progress. . . .

> *N.Z.P.D.*, 2nd Parliament, 1856–8, pp. 49–51,
> 55–6

36. THE 'COMPACT OF 1856'

A working compromise for settling the financial arrangements of the Colony and the Provinces introduced by the Stafford Ministry. Henry Sewell outlined the compromise to the House of Representatives on 10 June 1856 and Edward William Stafford, the Premier, defended them. They were adopted on 2 July and thus a stable Ministry could proceed.

Mr. SEWELL.—

Sir, in asking the House to consider a plan which embraces a complete and permanent settlement of all its outstanding burdens, by means of a great charge to be imposed on its revenue, involving with it the transfer of the waste lands and Land Fund to the control of the Provincial Governments, it is my duty to lay before you, in a clear and explicit form, the exact financial position of the colony— its resources, on the one hand, and, on the other, its liabilities, present and prospective. My first business is to show the state of the revenue. The two great sources of revenue are the Customs and the Land Fund. These alone are items of magnitude, and on these the Government of the colony mainly depends for its maintenance. Besides these, there are the Post Office, registration and Supreme Court fees, and other small items, not sufficiently important to deserve special consideration. The Customs revenue is necessarily in a great degree uncertain. It fluctuates from year to year according as it is acted on by various circumstances, and in particular by the accidental excitements and depressions of trade. In a young and rising colony like this its growth and development must affect its revenue in the way of gradual and progressive increase. In the long-run, we may safely calculate on such an increase. But we must deal in this matter as men of business, basing our transactions on certain and reliable data, with the same prudence which we should apply to our private affairs. In regulating these we rest, or ought to rest, on facts and certain calculations, not on loose speculations and uncertain theories. Sir I apply these rules to our present case. Comparing the past and current year I observe a falling-off in our Customs revenue. I am told that we may safely look forward to future increase. I admit that this may be fairly relied on in the long-run; but I am not so sanguine as to that immediate future which is before us, the next year or two, to which it is our duty especially to direct our attention. It is an undeniable fact that at the present time there is a great depreciation in the value of our agricultural produce, the main export, at least of this part of the colony. That results from the state of the Australian markets, which may or may not revive. We must look to our exports as our real source of wealth, and the real test of probable revenue. Our imports are a fallacious test of commercial prosperity. It is not what a country spends, but that which she produces, which constitutes her wealth. In order to a sound and healthy state of things the exports of a country ought at least to balance its imports; and—just as in private life—as we are compelled, in the long-run, to entrench our expenditure within our income, so, if our exports fall off, our imports, and with them our revenue, must diminish likewise. It may be that the present depreciation may not continue for any length of time; but, as men of business and common-sense, we must not indulge in loose and uncertain conjectures on such a subject. . . .

Mr. STAFFORD.—

. . . Folios of figures had been inflicted on the House; but it might, with no injustice, be said that these figures—which would more properly have been referred to in Committee—were as inconclusive as the assertions with which they had been accompanied. Honourable gentlemen approached the House with pockets full of figures; quires crossed and recrossed; studiously poring over these ominous characters, with grave shakings of the head and solemn whispers, as if some phenomenon of calculation, some gigantic exploit of numbers, was about to be ushered forth. The difference between the financial schemes of the late and the present Ministry was, that one was, as it had been justly described, the finance of youth and hope; while the other, fairly considering the present financial circumstances of the colony, was founded upon logical deductions, upon fixed and certain data. . . . One great principle that distinguished the present scheme was that it apportioned to each province and each individual their fair proportion of the present burdens and the expenses of the Government. It did not require a few to provide for the government of the many. It did not take, as did that of the late Ministry, the funds contributed by the man who had worked hard to acquire a freehold as a lasting means of support for himself and his family, from their legitimate use of providing for public works and immigration, whereby the waste lands of the country might be settled and improved; but it proposed, subject to the repayment of the sums by which those waste lands had been acquired, to devote the revenue arising from the sale of them to those local improvements which alone justified any price being imposed by a Government on the sale of waste lands. The scheme of the late Ministry was unjust, as, instead of providing for the necessary expenses of the Government from the Customs revenue—that was to say, from funds contributed by all in proportion to their means—it would have deprived a small and particular class in each community of the funds essential to the improvement of their properties. Was this policy, so diametrically opposed to all sound principles of political economy, the result of the American experience of the honourable member for Wanganui? Was that the plan which he proposed as an encouragement to the peopling of the wilderness; or was it likely that, under his plan, the wilderness would ever be peopled? The scheme of that honourable member, which this amendment asked them, in other words, to affirm, was so unwise and fallacious, that, when it came to be analysed, the House could come to no other conclusion than to reject it. The real question to be decided, which could not be mystified by any amount of figures, was, whether the expense of governing the whole community was to be borne by the whole people, or only by a small portion, and that portion often comprising many who, from their isolated and, it might be, distant position, received the least benefit from the Government. The present Ministry believed that the first was the only just policy, and they proposed, accordingly, to liberate the Land Fund and place the expenses of the General Government upon the Customs; and they had founded their estimates of the revenue of the ensuing year upon a safe probability. . . .

101

FINANCIAL RESOLUTIONS

The resolutions were then reported to the House, as follows:—

1. 'That it is expedient, without delay, to make provision for all ascertained outstanding liabilities, and permanently to adjust the public burdens of the colony, which adjustment ought to embrace a settlement of the New Zealand Company's debt, and the charge on the Land Fund for the purchase of Native lands.

2. That, as part of such arrangement, it is necessary to make provision by loan for sums absolutely required for Native land purchases for the ensuing financial year, and to make permanent provision for the same object.

3. That amongst the liabilities to be provided for by the colony this House recognizes the following: Balance due to the Union Bank of Australia; deposit accounts; arrears of fourths due to the New Zealand Company; balances due to provinces; outstanding liabilities on contracts for purchase of Native lands.

4. That, as a provisional arrangement for satisfying immediate liabilities, providing for the purchase of Native lands, and for general services, it is desirable to raise upon debentures a loan not exceeding £100,000, at interest not exceeding 10 per cent., payable off, at the option of the colony, in one or two years: any portion of such loan which, in excess of the amount required to complete existing contracts, shall be expended in the purchase of Native lands, to be repaid with interest out of the permanent loan of £180,000 to be provided for affecting such purchases.

5. That it is expedient, as part of a general and permanent arrangement, to redeem the New Zealand Company's charge on the Land Fund upon the terms offered by the Company and assented to by the Imperial Government—namely, that payment be made to them on the 5th April, 1857, of a sum of £200,000, towards which all moneys in their hands at that date in excess of the interest shall be applicable by way of reduction, the Imperial Government guaranteeing a loan for that object of £200,000 to be obtained in England upon the most favourable terms practicable.

6. That, as further part of such general and permanent arrangement, it is expedient to exonerate the Land Fund from its liability for the purchase of Native lands, and to provide a capital fund for carrying on such purchases; with which object it is expedient to borrow a sum of £180,000 to form such capital fund, such sum to be raised and made available as circumstances may require, in such

manner, and subject to such conditions as to the application thereof, as the Legislature may direct; and that it is expedient to make application to the Imperial Government for a guarantee for a loan for such purpose of £180,000, to be raised in England upon the most favourable terms practicable.

7. That, as further part of such general and permanent arrangement, in order to pay off the before-mentioned provisional loan and the old debentures, but exclusive of land scrip, it is expedient to make application to the Imperial Government for its guarantee for a further loan, to be raised in England upon the most favourable terms practicable.

8. That the aggregate of such loans ought not to exceed £500,000, and that such loans should be secured on the general and territorial revenue of the colony.

9. That the ground on which this House conceives itself entitled to claim the guarantee of the Imperial Government for the required loans is, that burdens have been imposed on this colony by the Imperial Parliament unjust in themselves, and greatly disproportioned to its revenue, and which, without such aid, must prove deeply injurious to its progress and prosperity.

10. That, as further part of such general and permanent arrangement, and in order to adjust equitably the public burdens, the New Zealand Company's debt be borne by the provinces of the Middle Island in equal proportions, and the charge of purchasing Native lands by the provinces respectively within which such purchases shall be made.

11. That, in accordance with a former resolution of this House, the Province of Auckland be relieved retrospectively, as well as prospectively, from the New Zealand Company's debt, and that, after payment of the sum due to the Company on the 5th April, 1857, the balance of the loan of £200,000 be made applicable to that purpose, leaving any deficiency or excess to be adjusted when the same be ascertained, the Province of Auckland on its part bearing the sum of £911. 8s. 9d. under the Lands Claimants Ordinance, New Ulster, as a debt incurred for its exclusive advantage.

12. That this House is of opinion that the administration of the waste lands of each province should be transferred to the Provincial Government of such province, and the land revenue thereof made provincial revenue, subject to the following charges: The Province of Nelson to be subject to a charge of £66, 666. 13s. 4d., to bear

interest at the rate of 4 per cent., with a sinking fund of 2 per cent.; the Province of Canterbury to be subject to a charge of £66,666. 13s. 4d., to bear interest at the like rate, with a sinking fund at the like rate; the Province of Otago to be subject to a charge of £66,666. 13s. 4d., to bear interest at the like rate, with a sinking fund at the like rate; the respective Provinces of Auckland and Wellington to be subject respectively to charges equal to the proportion of the permanent loan borrowed for the purchase of Native lands in such provinces respectively, with interest at the rate of 4 per cent. per annum, and a sinking fund of 2 per cent.; the Province of New Plymouth to be subject to a charge equal to the proportion of permanent loan borrowed for the purchase of Native lands in such province, with interest at the like rate, and with the like sinking fund, but after allowing the sum of £20,000 as a first outlay to be made in the province in the purchase of Native lands, without charge to such province.

13. That, until such outlay of £20,000 shall have been made in the Province of New Plymouth as aforesaid, the colony do guarantee, out of its general revenue, to make up any deficiency in the gross proceeds of land sales within such province, so that the sum derivable from such gross proceeds be not less than £2,200 in any one year.

14. That the loan to be obtained for fresh purchases of Native lands be distributed in the following proportions: Five-tenths to the Province of Auckland, £90,000; three-tenths to the Province of Wellington, £54,000; two-tenths to the Province of New Plymouth— without interest £20,000, with interest £16,000: total, £180,000.

15. That the scheme of arrangement and adjustment embodied in the foregoing resolutions be brought into operation on and from the 1st day of July, 1856, and the revenue of the colony distributed and appropriated on that basis on and from that day; the contributions from the Land Fund to the New Zealand Company's debt ceasing on and from that day, and the purchase of Native lands being thenceforth provided for out of the before-mentioned loans.

16. That such scheme of arrangement and adjustment be effectuated by an Act of the Imperial Parliament, to be applied for forthwith, and that an appeal be made to the Home Government for its guarantee for an aggregate loan of £500,000.

17. That, failing such Act of Parliament and guarantee, the entire scheme be open to revision by the General Assembly; and

that this House guarantees to the provinces all moneys which may be received by them under the foregoing arrangement, without liability to future account.

18. That application be made to Parliament forthwith for effecting the before-mentioned objects.'

The House divided on the question, 'That the foregoing resolutions be adopted'. . . .

N.Z.P.D., 2nd Parliament, 1856–8, pp. 138, 184, 248–9

37. 'PROVINCIALISM' AND 'CENTRALISM'

Editorial from The Lyttelton Times, *11 September 1858, which suggests that 'Provincialism' and 'Centralism' are little more than party 'nicknames', and warns Stafford's Ministry that the country prefers 'practical good to theoretical uniformity'.*

CENTRALISM and Provincialism;— these appear to be the antagonistic war-cries under which New Zealand politicians are ranging themselves against each other on almost every question of importance. It is to be feared that in each succeeding session—unless we are prepared to take a more practical view of the political necessities of the colony—these war-cries will become louder, and the division between the ablest men in New Zealand will grow wider and wider.

After all, the names 'Centralist' and 'Provincialist' do not in most cases give a truer impression than party nick-names generally convey. 'Centralism', properly so called, is repugnant to all the political instincts of Englishmen. 'Provincialism' is as repugnant to their educated sympathies. Many of those who are called or erroneously call themselves Centralists are truer friends of local self-government than many of the defenders of 'Provincialism', while some who find themselves classed under the name of Provincialists have the most profound contempt for the assumption and local tyranny that have distinguished one or two of our little centralisms.

We are at present in a very anomalous position. How we have been so placed is not now the question, but how we are to use it practically to the best advantage. We colonists hate, as Englishmen have ever hated, fine-spun well-balanced political theories; but still more hateful to the Anglo-Saxon is a logical deduction from a paper theory. This is the only sufficient reason that occurs to us for the uncertain way in which the several provinces and individual members from the provinces have looked upon different measures which affect the relations between the General and Provincial Governments. And any Government that wishes to succeed must respect the anxiety to prefer practical good to theoretical uniformity. We have no doubt but that the interests of the colony practically considered must gradually lead to the union of the whole under one Government; but this consummation will not be attained by interfering with any local Governments now established in matters in which they are the best judges and the best operators. It is not wise, either for the good of the colony or for the stability of his Ministry, that great Mr. Secretary Stafford should contemptuously pooh-pooh the Governments, one of which little king Stafford initiated in the most florid cocked-hat-and-feathers style. Nor on the other hand is it right that Her Majesty's lieges should be in fear lest the magnates of the 'Empire City' should declare war against the rest of New Zealand, or vilify every opponent till he succumbs or leaves his own province in disgust.

A judicious General Government might manage matters now very well. Our Representatives have been throughout the Session most forbearing; ministers have had every opportunity of initiating their policy; they have taken votes for two years, so that they may have an opportunity of giving it a fair trial; let us only hope that they may show judgment. They have shown ability and industry; but towards the end of the Session they got a broad hint not to presume too much upon the patience of the country. It lies with them to prove to us during the next two years that the changes made in our institutions are not injurious; and this can only be done by a wise discretion in the use of the powers entrusted to them.

The Lyttelton Times, 11 September 1858, p. 4

38. FOX'S POLICY, 1861: ARGUMENTS AGAINST THE SUSPENSION OF THE 1852 ACT

Memorandum by the Premier, William Fox, 8 October 1861, suggesting that the outbreak of war in Taranaki was an Imperial responsibility, but that suspension of the Constitution would be impracticable.

Ministers are aware that the question has been raised, and may be raised again, how far the form of Constitutional Government bestowed upon this Colony by the Imperial Parliament in 1852, is adapted to its present circumstances, and whether a suspension of the Constitution might not facilitate the adjustment of the difficulties of the present crisis.

Before entertaining any such proposition it ought to be made clear, 1st that, the existing system of government has in any way contributed to the present difficulties; and 2ndly that the suggested suspension would be likely to lead to their removal.

Ministers are decidedly and unanimously of opinion that neither position is tenable.

As to the first—The difficulties referred to have arisen solely in reference to the administration of Native affairs. Now this has, (partly by the operation of the Constitution Act, and partly by the action of the late Governor on the introduction of Responsible Government,) been practically reserved in the hands of the Governor as the Representative of the Imperial Government, and the Colonial Government in fact, has had little or nothing to do with it. The Colonial Government has done what it could, consistently with the limited powers vested in it, to advise and legislate in support of the Governor's administration of Native affairs—but substantially the whole control and action has been with him; and it may be safely asserted, that the present difficulties are in no way chargeable on any exercise by the Colonists of the Constitutional powers vested in them by Parliament.

As to the Second point, the proposed suspension of the Constitution: The principal result of this would in the opinion of Ministers be this; that while at present one department of Government, the Native Administration, is in difficulty and confusion, the whole Government of the Colony would by such a course be placed in the same predicament.—In considering this question it is necessary to bear in mind the character of the Constitution of the Colony, and the distribution of functions created by it in the hands of the General and Provincial Governments; the latter, in particular being charged with what may be termed all the Constructive work of the Colony, immigration, public works, the Survey and Sale of Land, as well as with the organization and control of the Police, and other social régime of the community. The machinery by which these functions are executed is in active operation, and nothing but the most inextricable confusion and paralysis would arise from any sudden suspension of its exercise. Even the General Government of the

107

Colony would prove incapable of taking over the functions of the Provincial Governments, and if the General Government itself as at present constituted were suspended also, the difficulties of the Colony would be indefinitely increased. . . .

C.O. 209/164, pp. 60–3

39. ENDING IMPERIAL RESPONSIBILITY FOR MAORI AFFAIRS

Dispatch from Governor Grey to the Duke of Newcastle, 30 November 1861, in which Grey begins the process whereby Gore Browne's responsibility for Maori affairs is ended and eventually passed to the General Assembly.

2. . . . whilst the Colonial Ministers are virtually responsible for all other matters of Government in this Colony, the Governor has hitherto retained the management of Native affairs in his own hands. . . .

5. At the present crisis, it is quite impossible that Her Majesty's Government could be advantageously carried on under such a system. I therefore immediately arranged to consult my Responsible Ministers in relation to Native affairs, in the same manner as upon all other subjects; and in like manner to act through them in relation to all Native matters. If any serious differences take place between us upon these subjects, I must, as in other cases, resort to other Advisers, and appeal in fact to the General Assembly.

6. Your Grace will, I have no doubt, inform me if you wish me to discontinue this arrangement, but I think it would be well to leave it permanently in operation until difficulties arise under it, which I do not see any probability of. . . .

Any attempt to set up either the Governor, or any special body between the Natives and the General Assembly, as a protective power for the Natives against the presumed hostility of that body, will, I fear, produce an ill effect upon the Native mind as making them regard the Assembly as their admitted natural enemies. Whilst it will perhaps create in the minds of the General Assembly some prejudice against the Natives, and against what may be done for them, and a carelessness for their interests, with the protection of which the Assembly would be in no way charged.

9. Another disadvantage of the system of making the Governor chiefly responsible for Native affairs, is, that it will be thought that

the wars which may arise under it have sprung, whether rightly or wrongly, from the acts of the representative of the British Government, over whose proceedings the Colonial Legislature had but very imperfect control, so that it would seem difficult to call upon that body to find the means of defraying the cost of a war, for the origin, continuance, or conduct of which it was only in an indirect manner responsible.

10. Under the system I have adopted, the Governor and Ministers act as mutual checks each upon the other. If either of them wishes to force on some proceeding, which the other party regards as unjust to the Natives, or as injurious to their reasonable interests, it is known to both that the ultimate appeal must be made to the General Assembly, and that the justness of the intentions of each party will become a matter of public discussion. It is therefore reasonable to think that each of them would carefully consider the grounds on which they were acting before incurring the risk of an appeal of this nature.

11. Certainly this plan . . . throws a greater responsibility on the General Assembly in regard to the expenditure on account of any war which their acts might bring on. But this would indirectly prove a protection for Native interests. The Assembly will now know that the justness of their acts, if disturbances spring from them, will be publicly canvassed in the British Parliament. That if misfortunes and dangers have undeservedly been brought upon Her Majesty's European subjects by the misconduct of the Natives, then the General Assembly will receive from England that generous and liberal support which she has never failed to afford to British subjects, under such circumstances, whilst on the other hand, if, which one may hope would be impossible, the Colonial Assembly had been attempting to oppress Her Majesty's Native subjects, its unrighteous conduct would meet with that public reprobation, which it would so justly deserve. . . .

No. 36. C.O. 209/165, pp. 201–9

40. AGREEMENT TO END DOUBLE GOVERNMENT: WELD'S 'PROPOSITIONS', 1864

After Sir George Grey summoned Frederick Weld to form a Ministry, the incoming Premier submitted a series of 'propositions' on 22 November 1864 and secured the Governor's written assurance of support, providing Weld could retain a majority in the General Assembly.

. . . 2. Mr. Weld is of opinion that the system of double government by Governor and Ministers, has resulted in evil to both races of Her Majesty's subjects in New Zealand;—he recognises the right of the Home Government to insist upon the maintenance of this system, so long as the Colony is receiving the aid of British troops for the suppression of internal disturbances: he is prepared to accept the alternative, and will recommend the Assembly to request the Home Government to withdraw the whole of its land force from the Colony, and to issue such instructions to the Governor as may enable him to be guided entirely by the recommendations of his constitutional Advisers, excepting only upon such matters as may directly concern Imperial interests and the prerogatives of the Crown.

3. Mr. Weld is aware that the Governor, before taking action upon a proposition which would change the whole aspect of the relations between the Mother Country and the Colony, may probably feel it his duty to ascertain the views of Her Majesty's Home Government; he would, therefore, pending their decision, recommend to the Colonial Parliament that the Colony should undertake a reasonable liability for the services of troops actively engaged in the field, at the especial recommendation of His Excellency's Ministers, and for such troops only.

4. Mr. Weld would recommend that a small standing Colonial Force be kept on foot, armed and trained with special reference to the nature of the service required.

5. It would be his duty to advise that at least one strong Military Post should be occupied about the centre of the coast line of the Ngatiruanui country, with such force as the Lieutenant-General may deem requisite; and that a road be made from Wanganui to the Northern part of the Taranaki Province.

6. The Colony having entered into arrangements with a large number of Military Settlers, Mr. Weld would propose that sufficient land, being part of the territory belonging to the insurgents and now in military occupation, should be taken to fulfil those engagements, and that the description of such confiscated lands, and proper plans thereof, should be made public without delay.

7. In its last Session the General Assembly resolved that the Seat

of Government should be removed to some place in Cook's Straits, to be determined by a Commission specially appointed for that purpose. In accordance with the recommendation of that Commission, Mr. Weld would propose that the Seat of the General Government be at once removed to Wellington.

8. Mr. Weld thinks it right to state frankly that if the Governor should feel it his duty to differ on any material point with his Constitutional Advisers, Mr. Weld would, without hesitation, place his resignation in His Excellency's hands; he therefore considers it essential that in such a case, the Assembly should at once be called, or other Advisers summoned.

A.J.H.R., 1864, A–2

41. THE ABOLITION OF THE PROVINCES, 1876

Although the 'Abolition of Provinces Act' was passed on 12 October 1875, it was not to come into effect until the day following the end of the next parliamentary session and thus after the 1875 Elections. In a final Provincialist move a Resolution was proposed on 19 September 1876 that the Act should be held in abeyance until a new Provincial Council in Otago might discuss it. In the House of Representatives Major Harry Atkinson, for the Government, argued that Provincialism had had its day. Sir George Grey feared that abolition would leave New Zealand's land to the mercy of 'professional politicians'.

Major ATKINSON.—For more than twenty years we have tried Provincialism, and . . . during that time we have never been able to apply the revenues of the colony to the wants of the people evenly throughout the land. That to my mind would alone be a sufficient reason for reconsidering our position. I say we have tried Provincialism; we have given it a fair and independent trial, and we have found that it has not supplied throughout the colony good and fair government. Some parts of the colony have been rolling in wealth, while others have been reduced almost to starvation; and so long as we have to put up with Provincialism, so long will that be the case. Although Provincialism has done much for the provinces— although it has done a great deal for Otago—I say, without fear of contradiction, that the Immigration and Public Works scheme, inaugurated and carried out by this House, has done more for Otago than Provincialism has from first to last. . . .

I am certain that this House and the people of New Zealand are determined that this shall be one united colony; and that the House, nothwithstanding the strong feeling of some honorable members, can and will provide a suitable form of local self-government, which will thoroughly satisfy the people of New Zealand.

Sir G. GREY.—I have on several previous occasions felt a sense of shame at some things I have heard stated in this House . . . but my sorrow and regret at the language used by the Premier to-night are still greater. What has been done? He has appealed to nothing but the lowest motives. 'Money, money, money,' was the one theme that ran through his speech. It was represented as being the one great thing we all desired, the one thing we strove for. He spoke as if liberty, freedom, and the right to govern ourselves were as nothing—that we cared nothing for them. I felt shame when I heard Auckland pitted against Otago, and Otago against Auckland —each province against the other, as a set of thieves, dividing the booty and quarrelling over the spoil. Was it right that the leader of the Government of New Zealand should stand up and speak in that way in this House? No, Sir. I never felt moved with greater sorrow than I did this night to think that the supposed leader of this country should thus speak to the representatives of New Zealand. . . . We desire that Provincialism should be restored to the state in which the people of Great Britain gave it to us—not in the mutilated form to which this Assembly and the friends of the honorable gentleman had reduced it. That is the very thing we ask for, and the honorable gentleman said that to meet our wishes it would be necessary to clip the wings of Provincialism. Clip the wings of Provincialism! Why, they have torn every feather out of them now. What we ask is, that the plumage of which they have deprived us for their own selfish ends shall be allowed to grow once more. . . .

. . . Now, Sir, I will tell the honorable gentleman what abolition means. It means that a small number of wealthy men should obtain possession of the public lands, and that the rest of the people throughout New Zealand should be reduced to the condition of serfs. That is what abolition means. It means that those great estates, acquired, as I believe, unlawfully, by honourable gentlemen who sit, or have sat, on those benches, or which belong to their friends, shall be unlawfully secured to them. It means that the mass of the

112

inhabitants of the people of New Zealand, deprived of the power they now have of legislating for themselves, shall be reduced to a state of poverty, of abject subjection of spirit. That is what abolition means. It means to set up one governing race and one governing class, and to lower the rest of the people beneath their feet. It means to attempt to re-establish in this country a system the existence of which in the old country is the lament of all right-thinking people. It means to set in power, not an hereditary nobility sprung from the feudal system, but a class of people who, by an adroit use of the land laws or an adroit use of political power, have accumulated and will accumulate lands and wealth, who will deprive their fellow-citizens of what rightfully belongs to them, and will sink the rest of the people of New Zealand in poverty and want. It means to introduce people of a foreign race, who have no knowledge of the British Constitution, who cannot speak our language, who know nothing of the rights they ought to possess, for the purpose of settling them upon their estates. It means to make the free British subjects in this colony contribute largely, often from their small means, to bring these people out, and then to compel them to compete in the labour market with people of a lower status than themselves, to go to the wall and lose their status in society. . . .

. . . The honorable gentleman stated in his place that some provinces were wealthly and some were in a state of beggary, and they could not manage to expend the revenues of New Zealand in such a way as to benefit all alike on account of the existence of the provinces. I say in making a statement of that kind he either knows nothing of the law of the land, or he wilfully and knowingly made representations which must have led the people of New Zealand astray. The sole reason these difficulties have arisen is that this Assembly departed from the law of Parliament, and thus brought about the difficulties itself. If this Assembly had confined itself to reasonable expenditure, and then, having deducted that reasonable expenditure from the revenues as a whole, had allotted to each province its share of the remainder in the fair proportion of population in each province, none of these financial difficulties would have arisen: none of the log-rolling of which we hear so much would have taken place. It is the assumption by this Legislature of the power, in violation of the Constitution, to expend the whole of the revenue, and to give really nothing back to the provinces, which had led supplicants and mendicants from all parts of New Zealand to resort to this place, from which funds can be obtained. When they have squandered the millions they have raised, when they have expended everything the provinces gave them, and forestalled the future to an extent unknown in any other country in the world, and squandered all that also, is it a wonder that they should have brought about them, as I said before, supplicants and mendicants from all parts of New Zealand? They have at once altered the character of the people of New Zealand, and inflicted serious injury on the country. . . . I cannot believe the people of New Zealand are yet so dead to every virtue that Britons should possess that they will tamely yield up privileges and rights which the British Parliament has bestowed upon them, or that they will sink to that degradation which must necessarily follow from allowing the management of their revenues and their lands to fall into the hands of a few professional politicians; or, further, that they will sink to that baseness which necessarily must follow from the abrogation on their part of all the duties and toils of public and political life. . . .

N.Z.P.D., 1876, vol. 22, pp. 376–7, 378–9

3

RACIAL POLICIES AND ADJUSTMENTS

---

42. THE TREATY OF WAITANGI, 1840

Official English text of the treaty, signed at Waitangi, in the Bay of Islands, on 6 February 1840, by Captain Hobson and about fifty Maori chiefs. Over 500 signatures or marks were eventually included. A translation from the Maori text, back into English, follows.

HER MAJESTY VICTORIA, Queen of the United Kingdom of Great Britain and Ireland, regarding with Her royal favour the Native Chiefs and Tribes in New Zealand, and anxious to protect their just rights and property, and to secure to them the enjoyment of peace and good order, has deemed it necessary, in consequence of the great number of Her Majesty's subjects who have already settled in New Zealand, and the rapid extension of emigration both from Europe and Australia which is still in progress, to constitute and appoint a functionary properly authorized to treat with the Aborigines of New Zealand for the recognition of Her Majesty's sovereign authority over the whole or any part of those Islands. Her Majesty, therefore, being desirous to establish a settled form of Civil Government with a view to avert the evil consequences which must result from the absence of the necessary laws and institutions, alike to the Native population and to Her subjects, has been graciously pleased to empower and authorize me, William Hobson, a Captain in Her Majesty's Royal Navy, Consul and Lieutenant-Governor of such parts of New Zealand as may be or hereafter shall be ceded to Her Majesty, to invite the confederate and independent Chiefs of New Zealand to concur in the following articles and conditions:—

Article the First

The Chiefs of the Confederation of the United Tribes of New Zealand, and the separate and independent Chiefs who have not

115

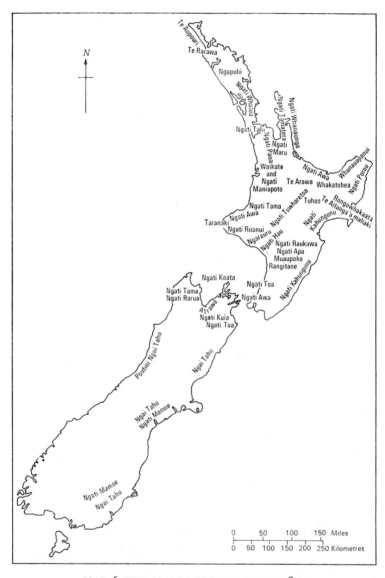

Te Aopouri
Te Rarawa
Ngapuhi
Ngati Whatua
Ngati Tahi
Ngati Maru
Ngati Paoa
Waikato and Ngati Maniapoto
Ngati Tamatera
Ngati Whanaunga
Ngati Awa
Te Arawa
Whakatohea
Whanauapanui
Ngati Porou
Ngati Tama
Ngati Tuwharetoa
Tuhoe
Rongowhakaata
Te Aitanga a mahaki
Taranaki
Ngati Awa
Ngarauru
Ngati Hau
Ngati Kahungunu
Ngati Ruanui
Ngati Raukawa
Ngati Apa
Muaupoko
Rangitane
Ngati Koata
Ngati Toa
Ngati Tama
Ngati Rarua
Ngati Awa
Ngati Kahungunu
Atiawa
Ngati Kuia
Ngati Toa
Pouttini Ngai Tahu
Ngai Tahu
Ngai Tahu
Ngati Mamoe
Ngati Mamoe
Ngai Tahu

N

| 0 | 50 | 100 | 150 | Miles |

| 0 | 50 | 100 | 150 | 200 | 250 | Kilometres |

MAP 6. THE MAORI TRIBES ABOUT 1840

116

become members of the Confederation, cede to Her Majesty the Queen of England, absolutely, and without reservation, all the rights and powers of sovereignty which the said Confederation or individual Chiefs respectively exercise or possess, or may be supposed to exercise or to possess, over their respective territories as the sole Sovereigns thereof.

Article the Second

Her Majesty the Queen of England confirms and guarantees to the Chiefs and Tribes of New Zealand, and to the respective families and individuals thereof, the full, exclusive, and undisturbed possession of their lands and estates, forests, fisheries, and other properties which they may collectively or individually possess, so long as it is their wish and desire to retain the same in their possession; but the Chiefs of the United Tribes and the individual Chiefs yield to Her Majesty the exclusive right of pre-emption over such lands as the proprietors thereof may be disposed to alienate, at such prices as may be agreed upon between the respective proprietors and persons appointed by Her Majesty to treat with them in that behalf.

Article the Third

In consideration thereof, Her Majesty the Queen of England extends to the Natives of New Zealand Her royal protection, and imparts to them all the rights and privileges of British subjects.

W. HOBSON,
Lieutenant-Governor.

Now, therefore, we, the Chiefs of the Confederation of the United Tribes of New Zealand, being assembled in congress at Victoria, in Waitangi, and we, the separate and independent Chiefs of New Zealand, claiming authority over the tribes and territories which are specified after our respective names, having been made fully to understand the provisions of the foregoing Treaty, accept and enter into the same in the full spirit and meaning thereof; in witness of which we have attached our signatures or marks at the places and the dates respectively specified.

Done at Waitangi, this sixth day of February, in the year of our Lord one thousand eight hundred and forty. . . .

Translated from the original Maori by Mr. T. E. YOUNG, Native Department.

VICTORIA, Queen of England, in her kind thoughtfulness to the chiefs and hapus of New Zealand, and her desire to preserve to them their chieftainship and their land, and that peace may always be kept with them and quietness, she has thought it is a right thing that a chief should be sent here as a negotiator† with the Maoris of New Zealand—that the Maoris of New Zealand may consent to the government‡ of the Queen over all parts of this land and the Islands, because there are many people of her tribe who have settled on this land and are coming hither.

Now the Queen is desirous to establish the Government, that evil may not come to the Maoris and the Europeans who are living without law.

Now the Queen has been pleased to send me William Hobson, a Captain in the Royal Navy, to be Governor for all the places of New Zealand which may be given up now or hereafter to the Queen; and he gives forth to the Chiefs of the Assembly§ of the hapus of New Zealand, and other Chiefs, the laws spoken here.

The First

The Chiefs of the Assembly, and all the Chiefs also who have not joined in that Assembly, give up entirely to the Queen of England for ever all the government‡ of their lands.

The Second

The Queen of England arranges and agrees to give to the Chiefs, the Hapus, and all the People of New Zealand, the full chieftainship‖ of their lands, their settlements, and all their property. But the Chiefs of the Assembly, and all the other Chiefs, give to the Queen the purchase of those pieces of land which the proprietors of the land may wish, for such payment as may be agreed upon by them and the purchaser who is now appointed by the Queen to be her purchaser.

The Third

This is an arrangement for the consent to the government of the Queen. The Queen of England will protect all the Maoris of New Zealand. All the rights will be given to them the same as her doings to the people of England.

WILLIAM HOBSON,
Consul and Lieutenant-Governor.

---

† He kaiwhakarite. ‡ Kawanatanga. § Whakaminenga. ‖ Tino Rangatiratanga.

Now, we, the Chiefs of the Assembly of the Hapus of New Zealand, now assemble at Waitangi. We, also, the Chiefs of New Zealand, see the meaning of these words: they are taken and consented to altogether by us. Therefore are affixed our names and our marks. . . .

Journal and Appendix of the Legislative Council of New Zealand, 1869, pp. 69–71

43. CAPTAIN GEORGE GREY'S INSTRUCTIONS AS LIEUTENANT-GOVERNOR, 1845

Dispatch from the Secretary of State, Lord Stanley, dated 13 June 1845, giving Grey general instructions as to his duties as Lieutenant-Governor. In view of Hone Heke's resistance he is instructed to enforce order, and to uphold the promises of the Treaty of Waitangi insofar as this was consistent with the welfare of the settlers.

. . . I enclose a Commission under the Royal Sign Manual appointing you Lieutenant-Governor of the Colony. . . . You are aware that the Colonization of New Zealand was not the spontaneous Act of the Queen's Government, but was forced on them as the only means of averting the evils with which unauthorized Settlements of Her Majesty's Subjects there appeared to threaten the inhabitants, whether European or aboriginal. Among the motives dissuading the establishment of British dominion within those islands, not the least considerable was the extreme difficulty which would evidently attend on the protection which in that case, every class of the people would be entitled to demand. . . .

. . . My predecessors in Office declined to engage for the employment in New Zealand of a garrison to be composed of the regular army. It appeared . . . better that the experiment should first be tried, of enrolling the Colonists in Militia Corps. . . . Of course we were . . . well aware of the objections to which such a measure was open. . . . To arm the British Colonists might excite, among their aboriginal neighbours, jealousies of a dangerous nature, or that the European Settlers might be reluctant to undertake a service of so much toil and cost. . . . I am still without proof of the impracticability of the plan of enrolling a Militia. . . .

But in the meantime, an exigency has arisen, which I fear may

119

not brook any delay and measures have . . . been taken for detaching to New Zealand a sufficient Military force. . . .

Among the circumstances which have forced on Her Majesty's Government this measure, the chief is that of the unfriendly relations which appear to have arisen between the Colonists and the Aborigines. . . .

From the commencement of the Colonization of New Zealand to the present time, it has been the anxious and unremitting desire of Her Majesty's Government to avoid if possible any actual conflict with the Native Tribes. . . . I repudiate with the utmost possible earnestness the doctrine maintained by some, that the treaties which we have entered into with these people are to be considered as a mere blind to amuse and deceive ignorant savages. In the name of the Queen I utterly deny that any Treaty entered into and ratified by her Majesty's Command was, or could have been made in a spirit thus disingenuous or for a purpose thus unworthy. You will honourably and scrupulously fulfil the conditions of the Treaty of Waitangi.

Further as representing the person and authority of your Sovereign, you will omit no measure within the reach of prudent legislation, or of a wise administration of the law for securing to the Aborigines the personal freedom and safety to which they are entitled, and the most unrestricted access to all the means of religious knowledge and of civilization provided for them by the pious zeal which has established, and which principally maintains an Episcopal See and Christian Missionaries for their instruction.

It will also be your duty to take care that in the government of this class of Her Majesty's subjects every possible respect be shewn, both in the structure of the Law and in the administration of it, for the opinions, the feelings, and the prejudices by which they may be possessed, and from which they cannot be rudely or abruptly divorced. I of course refer to opinions, feelings and prejudices not in themselves opposed to the fundamental laws of morality, nor inconsistent with the peace and welfare of the Colonists of European descent.

Subject to these general rules, you will of course require from these people an implicit subjection to the Law, and you will of necessity enforce that submission by the use of all the powers, civil and Military, at your command. . . .

No. 1, G1/13

44. MAORI AFFAIRS UNDER RESPONSIBLE GOVERNMENT

Dispatch from Governor Gore Browne to the Secretary of State, Sir George Grey, 12 March 1856, indicating that he favoured the reservation of Maori affairs to the Royal Prerogative.

. . . Within the last few days it has come to my knowledge that different opinions are entertained as to the meaning of the 73rd clause of the Constitution Act, and as the subject appears to me to be one of great importance, and one which must affect the relation between the Governor and his responsible advisers, I beg to submit it for your consideration.

2. The view I have taken of the relation which ought to exist between myself and my responsible advisers (when they take office) is, that as these gentlemen are responsible to the Assembly, I should be guided by their advice in all matters under the control of that body, even when I differ from them in opinion. On matters affecting the Queen's prerogative and Imperial interests generally, I should receive their advice, but when I differ from them in opinion, I should, if they desire it, submit their views for your consideration, but adhere to my own until your answer is received.

3. Among Imperial subjects I include all dealings with the Native tribes, more especially in the negotiation of purchases of land. My responsible advisers would probably fix the amount to be expended in any one year in the purchase of land, but at that point their interference should cease.

4. The Governor alone is responsible to Her Majesty's Government for the tranquility of the Colony which would be endangered even by the ordinary and inevitable change of opinion consequent on a change of my advisers. It is also necessary to observe that though I might be judiciously advised by gentlemen who have lived among the Natives and have had experience of their habits and feelings, I should also be liable to advice from gentlemen of great influence who have never resided among them, and from others whose known opinions would, if acted on, plunge the country into war or inextricable difficulties.

5. If my views are correct, it is evident that the Chief Land Commissioner and his subordinates must take their orders from me alone. My late dispatches will have satisfied you that in all dealings with the Natives the utmost caution and the most careful

management is necessary, and if the power of interference with them is confided to gentlemen liable to the pressure of public opinion, and whose tenure of office is dependent on the confidence of a public Assembly, it will be impossible to foresee the result. . . .

No. 25. C.O. 209/135, pp. 256–8

45. MODEL FARMS AND VILLAGES FOR MAORIS

Minute dated 13 October 1856 by Francis Dart Fenton, who as Native Secretary from March to August 1856 had noted the effects of competition with settlers on Maoris and advocated a policy of developing model farms and villages by example, which would eventually remove opposition to land sales.

. . . The Maories have been constantly told, and at one time partially believed, that it was the wish of the Europeans to raise them to their own level, and that the object of Government was, by well-concerted measures, gradually to amalgamate the two races into one. This belief is still held, though in a very different sense, and the interpretation now placed upon these assertions is one deeply humiliating to their pride as a people, and discouraging to each man as an individual. . . . But among the tribes generally, the amalgamation of the races is now construed to mean the local union of the Maories with the Europeans, founded on the supremacy of the one, and the reduction of the other to the class of hewers of wood and drawers of water. . . .

. . . I now respectfully record my opinion that the alarm and dissatisfaction which I have previously referred to, and the resolution consequent thereon, cannot be effectually obviated, until the causes which give rise to this state of feeling are carefully removed. . . . When the uneducated Maori is placed side by side with the intelligent and highly cultivated member of an elaborate civilisation, he is at once subjected to an amount of competition which first astonishes and ultimately disheartens him. In the great contest for livelihood, for which every member of a civilized community is educated, and to which his energies are entirely devoted, the bewildered Maori clearly distinguishes nothing, beyond an all-absorbing eagerness to acquire property, and suspects the professions which are made to him, that the success and advancement of his own race is an object that interests every European. Unable to endure the social attrition to which he is subjected, he abandons the contest, or pursues it in a listless and indolent manner that can never result in any great measure of success. It is therefore the duty of the governing body, either to relieve him from the liabilities to which he is subject, as one of a civilised community, or by rendering him assistance which the educated member does not require, place him in a position in which the general conditions of success may be equalised. . . . Though at present the Maori cultivator is possessed of three or four small patches of land, generally removed at considerable distances from each other, amongst which his time is divided, yet the obstacle presented by this custom will not be difficult of removal. Having an object before him, with the means of attaining it, he will readily concentrate his exertions on the one spot from which the prospect of speedy and ample recompense appears most certain. Thus will be achieved a *fixity of residence*. And the success of the small body of new farmers will quickly raise up imitators, many of whom will settle in the immediate vicinity of the exemplar farm, and thus will gradually be secured the *thickening of the population*. . . .

I propose, then, that a subdivision of a tribe should be carefully selected, combining as many external conditions necessary to success, as can be found united, and that the Government should furnish them with an agricultural instructor, and with sufficient funds, to enable them to establish a farm on the European system. And, I suggest, for the commencement of this practical attempt at civilization, Ngatikaiotaota, a subdivision of the tribe Ngatitipa. . . .

They will enclose in a permanent fence one hundred acres or more of the best land, and, working under the instructions of the resident agriculturalist, they will divide it into the portions requisite for production of the proper proportions of grass, wheat, potatoes, &c., and as the breadth of the grass land gradually increases, they will enclose fresh land for the growth of the cereals and other crops intended for sale. Collected at one extremity of the farm, they will place their houses, built as at present with *raupo* in the Maori fashion, for, until their wealth is increased, and their social habits improved, they will have no desire to inhabit wooden houses. The inclination for better habitations and greater comforts will spontaneously arise as they gradually feel themselves more at ease, as to the first necessities of subsistence.

Though eminently a people of agricultural tastes, the Maories, in their own system of cultivation, are careless and improvident to a degree that is astonishing to any person who is acquainted with their covetous disposition. The moment a succession of crops has lessened the productive powers of land, it is abandoned, and immediately becomes covered with a prolific crop of docks and other noxious weeds, which spread their seeds into the adjoining plantations. By proper instruction in the utility of grass, this great evil will be stopped, and the country will be gradually covered with an enduring sward.

The amount of produce raised by each individual will probably be increased twenty-fold by the adoption of the proposed system, and with their economical habits of living, the profits derived from the sale of the surplus produce will be very considerable. I think it is not extravagant to expect that in the fourth year they will be in a condition to repay the whole, or the greater part, of the money advanced to them by the Government. . . .

The obnoxious custom of abandoning partially-exhausted land, to be taken possession of by weeds, will be stopped, and the Maories, possessing abundant means of feeding stock, will become breeders of cattle and growers of wool.

Communities, established as proposed, will fill the void existing, and will fitly receive the adult Maori who leaves the school, a comparatively civilised being. The female school-Maori, marrying one of a community, will find that she is capable of carrying with her the habits of order, and many of the ideas of comfort to which she has been for years accustomed. At present, she rapidly sinks to the level of the surrounding rudeness or, unable to endure the miserable change, seeks to ameliorate her position by connection with a European, or adds another to the degraded class who minister to the appetites of our town populations.

The Maories will recognise the truth of our professions of interest in their welfare when they see the practical results of our propositions, and will regard the British authority with affection and respect, and gradually abandon the deep-rooted feeling of a distinct nationality. . . .

A.J.H.R., 1860, F–3, pp. 133–8

46. THE ELECTION OF A MAORI KING, 1858

Translations from the text of an account of the meetings held at Ngaruawahia, 2 June 1858, and at Rangiaowhia, a few days later, by Wiremu Tamihana, Te Waharoa. The account was probably sent by him to a missionary and appeared in the Southern Cross *on the 3rd and 6th August 1858. Editorial comment and an interpretation of the verse is by Professor Keith Sinclair, Auckland University, who discovered the account and republished this text.*

. . . We assembled ourselves together on the occasion of Potatau's [Te Wherowhero] coming hither to Ngaruawahia, and we thought that we should now take him [i.e., elect him as King] as he came to us, but the meeting was not willing that Potatau should be taken,—they did not consent to his being elected as king. . . .

. . . We accordingly wrote letters to the leading chiefs to say that on Wednesday at 8 o'clock on the 2nd of June, the proceedings would commence, and the flag of New Zealand would be hoisted. The people who reside at the place [Waikato] were up while it was yet dark at four o'clock in the morning, and food having been prepared and all parties in readiness, the flag was hoisted at 8 o'clock and the guard of honour moved forward. It consisted of the following tribes:—Ngatihaua, Ngatikoroki, Ngatiruru, Ngatimahuta, and Ngatimaniapoto. When the guard had reached the tent of Potatau, it stood, and presented arms. The women also in a body moved forward and arranged themselves on the other side. No person sat down,—all stood motionless, and not one word was uttered, nor could even the rustling of any one's garment be heard. I then stepped forward holding in my hand the Old Testament, the Psalms, and the New Testament of our Lord. Potatau was in his tent, which I entered and said, 'Peace be to this house, and to him who is within it'. I then sat down by his [Potatau's] side and presented to him the Old Testament open at the 20th chapter of Exodus from 1st verse to the 17th—the Commandments. I presented the Psalms also pointing the xxiii-5-6; also the New Testament, pointing out Matthew xi-28, John xiv-15, John x-11.

'Now,' said I, 'let me ask you which of these two titles do you prefer, that of *Chieftain* or that of *King*?'

He replied, 'I prefer the title of *King*.'

I then said, 'Who is to be your protector?'

'Jehovah,' was the reply.

'Yes,' said I, 'the only—is there no other?'

'Jesus Christ,' was the answer.

'Even so,' said I, and I read to him the words of David, 'The Lord is my shepherd,' and the words of Christ 'I am the good Shepherd' &c.

I then said, 'Let us pray to God in order that he may bless us and succeed our present movement.'

After we had prayed together, I said to him, 'You had better come outside in order that your people may see you.' He came forth therefore, and all the men, women, and children saw him, and they all uncovered their heads, and did obeisance to him.

I then addressed the flag which had been hoisted, saying unto it, 'Potatau has consented to become King.'

Paora Te Ahuru immediately proceeded to an eminence, and addressing the mark that was put up [i.e., the flag] called in a loud voice, 'Are you willing that this man should be your King?'

All cried out 'Yes,'—both great and small, women and children.

Paora said secondly, 'Are you willing that this King should put down that which is evil, and stay the hand of him who persists in doing wrong?'

'Yes' was the reply of them all.

After this, those who composed the meeting took part in the proceedings. The first two who came forward were Te Awarahi [Te Katipa] and Ihaka [of Pukaki]. The part they took in the proceedings was most imposing; those who bore arms followed the chiefs,—when they came near, Te Awarahi said,—

'O Potatau, you will be a father to us, will you not?'

'Yes,' was Potatau's reply, which was greeted by great cheering; and a salute was fired the noise of which, together with the cheering, was like the roaring of the sea on the ocean shore.

When the firing was over, the people sat down, and I addressed the meeting, I said,—

'Hearken, O my fathers and my friends. This is the basis (I here held up in my hand the scriptures). We have not regarded the word of God, which saith, "Come unto me all ye that are weary and heavy laden, and I will give you rest;"—we have not obeyed the call. The Apostle says, "Mortify your members which are on the earth;" but we hearken not, therefore it is deemed proper that the chiefs should be of one mind, and select a person who shall be entrusted with these treasures for the earth [that is, the protection of our property, the management of our lands, etc.]. We have seen that the wars arise from disputations about land, wherefore we seek out him, that he may be a depository for our lands. He will restrain the father who is badly disposed towards his son, and the elder brother who would take advantage of the younger brother. He will manifest his displeasure in regard to that which is evil; he will do away with the works of confusion or disorder, and he will be a covering for the lands of New Zealand which still remain in our possession.'

It was half-past nine, we broke up therefore to get refreshments, and thus ended the meeting for this day.

We arranged that another meeting should take place at 8 o'clock the following morning. Accordingly at 8 o'clock we met again, when the lands were given up to king Potatau.

Paora said,—'this is the basis upon which we act,—the knowledge which is manifested by the night and by the day [that is, the laws of nature]. It is written in the Psalms, "Day unto day uttereth speech, and night unto night showeth knowledge." Now we remain ignorant whilst the day and the night show forth their knowledge. The waves of the sea also obey their law, they roll on to the great ocean whose offspring they are. So in like manner are our own islands looking to God; even this island and that island are feeling after God. [i.e., the islands of the sea, not including New Zealand]. But this island [i.e., New Zealand] is without reflection. What God is He who had discovered evil [amongst us?] Christ says, "Go ye forth unto all nations and preach the Gospel to every creature." Paul the Apostle says, "Be it known therefore unto you, that the salvation of God is sent unto the gentiles and they will hear it." '

This was the conclusion of Paora's address.

On the following day there was a subscription by the people for the King. . . .

On the 8th of the month of June, the tribes went from Waikato to Rangiaowhia. The numbers were:—

Ngatihaua	267
Ngatikoroki	30
Waikato	240
Ngatimaniapoto	200
Ngatihau	60
Ngatituwharetoa	100
Ngatihinetu } Ngatiapakura }	140

When these tribes assembled, the king came outside the railing, and they met the king and his guard, 240 men. The king and his people tarried at the entrance of the gate, and Te Ngatihaua, numbering 297, went forward to make their obeisance to the king. Next in order came the people of the place, and then the tribes of Taupo, Ahuriri, Whanganui, Kawhia and Mokau. They all stood in the entrance of the gate, so that they might meet King Potatau.

There was also present a youth named Keremete, brother of Wi Karamoa, holding in hand a paper, which he read. This is the first portion,—'Welcome hither, O king Potatau. Establish thou the nationality of New Zealand!' The remaining sentences I do not know. After this address was read, the people walked backward and fired a salute, even three vollies, and the sound thereof was as the roar of thunder. After this they did obeisance, and arranged themselves in procession. First came the people resident in that locality, bearing aloft the flag of New Zealand; then followed the king with his own people; then followed the other tribes; and lastly the women. Those who went before the king were the inhabitants of the settlement and the visitors (that is, the Ahuriri and Whanganui people). On arriving at the camp they halted, and ranged themselves on each side of the court yard in rows three deep. Then stood up Te Tapihana, a teacher of the Ngatihikairo, and said, 'Name the king, O Io, O Io!' [Io is a Maori deity dwelling in the heavens, and represented as being all powerful, wise and good.] He meant, 'Name the king, O William, O William.' [William Thompson Tarapipipi, one of Potatau's chief supporters.] After this they did obeisance to to the king, and the 23rd hymn was given out by the same monitor—

'From Egypt lately come,
Where death and darkness reign,
We see a new, a better home,
Where we our rest shall gain:
Halleluia,
We are on our way to god, &c.'

After this Te Heuheu spoke, but his speech was not of consequence. The tribes now dispersed to their encampments, and met on the 9th, when the chiefs spoke. Policemen were appointed to keep order; the Superintendent of Police was Aihipene Kaihau. When all was arranged, Kiwa, the brother of Hoani Papita stood up and said, —'Welcome, O son, welcome, welcome, to your people. Hold the authority of your ancestors and your fathers. You shall be king.'

128

Wiremu Te Akerautangi stood up and said,—
'Welcome O King;—welcome to Waikato.
> "The shame I feel is great
> For thou hast made a hapless exit.
> And now thou art as fish caught from the sea
> And placed upon the stalls to dry:
> Are we to feed upon the things that come
> From lands far distant?
> O son, thou gavest this to me
> And caused these lips to be polluted
> Which once were sacred. Lo, I'll lop it off.
> Lest it should lead me to adopt its measures." '

[The Poet feels shame that the sun of the Maori nation should have gone down. The present social condition of his countrymen is compared to fish once healthful swimming at ease in its native water, but now ruthlessly cast upon the stalls no longer to be admired, but simply looked upon as an article of food. He asks whether the New Zealanders should be satisfied with the systems of foreign people which they have been called upon to adopt. He then censures the natives who were so credulous as to take for granted that the foreigner sought only the benefit of the New Zealanders by coming to this land and introducing other customs that came into collision with their own sacred usages; and concludes with a determination to maintain the national independence of the Maoris.]

Kingi Waikawau said,—

'Welcome, O son, welcome.
> "The pangs I feel are of a two-fold nature.
> Some are without and as the wind beyond my grasp.
> O King welcome, and be thou enthroned." '

Toma Te Ipuinanga spoke and chaunted a song complimentary to the King.

Te Awarahi [Te Katipa] now stood up; he said,—

'Oh my elder brethren and my children, you have given us [a hearty] welcome.
> "O this deafening noise and dread confusion
> How am I pained for thee O wife
> Gone from me to another!" '

[*O wife gone from me*, &c.—i.e. the lands sold to the Government. He bitterly regrets that his *wife*—i.e., Maori lands—should have been sold, and now that he is anxious to raise the Maori standard, and organize a Maori system, impediments will arise from the fact that many valuable native lands are in the possession of a power they are not prepared to either respect or obey. The above speech is a reply to those which preceded it.]

Then rose up Te Mutumutu, grand son of Turoa, the Chief of Whanganui. He said,—

'Return hither, O my relative, and steer the canoe
        [i.e., guide the people].
Mat which Hotunui and Hoturangi
Reclined upon, thy face was broken,
Thy face was beaten, and yet thy face
Was worn as ornaments around the neck.
Thy face too was concealed, yet it was grand,
And beautiful the while.
Hither bring my treasures—
The treasures that I got me from the northern
        countries,
And from the eastern lands, that I may
Cover now that face.
Lo, the mat is spread,—how great a treasure!
Give the King to beautify the features of each man
And rid the land of evil.'

[Hitunuku and Hoturangi deified men. If we understand the thing rightly, mats were made and offerings presented to these deities, and when the priests prayed and muttered their incantations, the gods came and reclined upon the new mats spread for them. Of course the mats were highly venerated, and although broken, or beaten by accident, or trampled upon and partially destroyed by enemies in war, the fragments were collected and worn as relics. Although thus debased they were considered *grand* &c. So in like manner, Te Wherowhero, or Potatau, though denuded of his native dignity by residing in the heart of a European settlement, still the tribes looked upon him with a feeling of veneration. His return to his kindred and people is embodied in the figure 'Lo the mat is spread.' Lest there should be any doubt, however, on the minds of the audience, in reference to the metaphorical language used, the poet concludes in plain terms, 'Give the King' &c.]

Tuhikitia stood up and said,—'Welcome O Te Mutumutu; welcome O wi Pakau; welcome O Te Moananui; welcome O Te Heuheu; welcome O Te Poihipi; welcome O Pakake; welcome O Te Wetini Pahukohatu; welcome O Takerei Hikuroa; welcome O Waikawau and Wiremu Te Ake.

> "O sacred glory! how I love to dwell on thee,
> Streaming forth along the narrow way,
> Come hither daughter, let us go together
> To Isaiah, he will make us Teachers;
> And he'll gather us together
> That we may seize upon the Word of God,
> And lean upon the Saviour."

'Welcome; let us be one;—let us cling to God and the King,'
Hori Te Waru stood up, and said,—

'Let us be one,—one with God and the King.'
Te Heuheu rose up and said,—

'O Hoani, be energetic; O Hori, be energetic; O Tamihana, be energetic; O Te Wetini be energetic for the King, and drive away wickedness and disorder.'

Then rose up Kapara Ngatoki; he said,—

'Let those who have been named be brave, and adhere to the King.'

Then Wiremu Pakau [a Southern Chief] stood up and said,—

'Ye have called, and bid me welcome. Lo I have journeyed hither to Waikato.

> "It is being flung that way
> Where the clump of forest trees are growing.
> Even at Tongaporutu, herewith shall cease
> The sorrow for my land." '

[*Being flung that way,*—i.e., he is drawn to Waikato the people of which are compared to forest trees growing luxuriantly, he hopes by joining the king confederation to secure the well being of his countrymen, and mitigate the sorrow he feels on account of their present degraded state.]

On this day a collection was made for the printing press. . . .

(Signed) WILLIAM.

(*Southern Cross*, 6 August, 1858.)

Appendix to J. E. Gorst, *The Maori King*, 1959 edn., edited by K. Sinclair, Hamilton & Auckland, Paul's Book Arcade, pp. 265–74

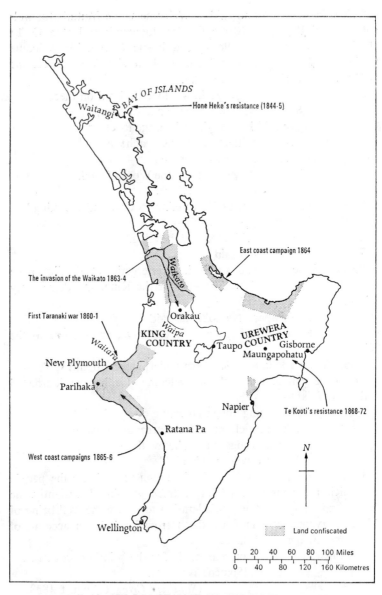

BAY OF ISLANDS

Waitangi ———— Hone Heke's resistance (1844-5)

East coast campaign 1864

The invasion of the Waikato 1863-4

Waikato

First Taranaki war 1860-1

Orakau

Waipa

KING COUNTRY

UREWERA COUNTRY

Taupo

Gisborne

Waitara

Maungapohatu

New Plymouth

Parihaka

Napier

Te Kooti's resistance 1868-72

Ratana Pa

West coast campaigns 1865-6

N

Wellington

Land confiscated

| 0 | 20 | 40 | 60 | 80 | 100 Miles |

| 0 | 40 | 80 | 120 | 160 Kilometres |

MAP 7. MAORI RESISTANCE IN THE NORTH ISLAND

132

47. THE KING MOVEMENT

Passages from Chapter Four, 'The Revolt', of John Eldon Gorst's classic account of the King Movement, in which he suggests that it was a national movement caused by growing anxiety over the loss of land, a realization that the settler population was becoming dominant and by humiliations arising from the settler attitude of white superiority.

... The cause of what is called 'the king-movement' has been much disputed among New Zealand politicians. The fact is, that there has been no single cause.

... as the number of Europeans increased, ... relations were altered; a sale involved parting with the dominion of the soil; towns sprang up, inhabited by strange and powerful white men, who neither knew nor cared for the original proprietors. If the native visited the spot where he was once lord and master, he found himself insignificant and despised in the midst of a civilization in which he did not share. The hopes of social advancement which the natives had formed when they first consented to share their country with the stranger, were disappointed. They did not fail to contrast the rapid alienation of their land with the slow improvement of their condition, and they feared that at this rate their lands would be gone before they had attained the desired equality with their white neighbours. Every function of Government seemed paralysed in comparison with the Land Purchasing Department. They were willing to sell their land for civilization and equality, but at no other price. . . .

They were still more painfully conscious of their social than of their political inferiority. To view men whose skin differs in colour from our own as 'damned niggers,' is a weakness of our Anglo-Saxon character, which proves our civilization and Christianity far from perfect. It destroys all chance of our gaining the affections of our native subjects in any part of the world; for uncivilized men will forgive any amount or kind or wrong sooner than a single personal insult. The Maories are exceedingly sensitive of any appearance of personal slight. . . . Men habitually told that they emit a disagreeable smell, are not likely to feel a very strong affection towards the race that smells them. I know that the petty rudeness of Europeans is so disagreeable to many chiefs in Waikato, that they dislike going into Auckland, or any of the English villages, and are very shy of visiting at English houses. Their own behaviour to strangers affords a striking contrast, not very creditable to our-selves; a chief of the highest rank will unsaddle the horse of his guest with his own hands, and either pitch his tent or give him the best house in the village to sleep in. . . .

At the close of this catalogue of Maori grievances, I must, to avoid misconstruction, state that I am quite aware there were wrongs on both sides, and that the European race has had just grounds of offence against the Maori. My reason for not enlarging upon these here is, that the cause of the King movement, with which we have now to do, was the sense of wrong felt by the natives for what their side had suffered; of the wrongs they had done, they were, like mankind in general, unconscious. At the time the King was set up, the hostile feeling was not nearly strong enough to create a desire for war, but there was quite enough to make the mass eager for separa-tion and independence, and to this the easy and rapid success of the King party is to be attributed. . . .

J. E. Gorst, *The Maori King*, 1959 edn., pp. 40, 44, 50–2

48. THE WAITARA PURCHASE

Governor Gore Browne's announcement that he would accept individual land sales; Te Teira's offer of land and Wiremu Kingi's prohibition of the sale, New Plymouth, 8 March 1859.

On Tuesday a meeting of the Moturoa, Town, Waiwakaiho, Puketapu, and Waitara Natives was held in a paddock adjoining the residence of the Land Purchase Commissioner. It was less numerously attended than many former ones, the muster of the Waitara natives being particularly small. Shortly after 11 o'clock His Excellency the Governor, accompanied by his Private Secre-tary and the Chief Land Purchase Commissioner, arrived on the ground and was welcomed by the assembled natives the whole rising up to receive him, with the exception of William King and some few of his followers.

The principal chiefs then paid their respects to the Governor.

Tahana, a Native Assessor, opened the proceedings by acknow-ledging the benefits conferred on the Natives by the introduction of Christianity and European customs and expressed the desire of himself and his tribe to have British law established amongst them.

Mr McLean on behalf of his Excellency spoke as follows:—

The Governor wished them to understand that the Queen regards equally all her subjects; that all her Governors have had and would have the same instructions, viz.:—to do their utmost to promote the welfare of her subjects without distinction of race. The missionaries had imparted to them the blessings of Christianity and translated the Bible for their use. It was not in the power of man to confer any other gift which would bear comparison with that of the Bible; but, out of regard for the natives, his Excellency had caused an abstract of English law to be translated into Maori. He had no wish to enforce this law; on the contrary, it would only be put in force in those districts where the people are wise enough to desire it, and prepared to carry it into effect themselves. Some tribes in the North had already desired to have English law; and a Magistrate had been appointed to instruct them how to put it into practice. They were now engaged in doing so, with every prospect of becoming a peaceful and prosperous people, and uniting themselves with the Pakeha. This tribe is the Ngapuhi. The Governor had but two subjects on which he desired to speak, particularly, to the tribes living near Taranaki, and they were— First, in reference to criminal offences; second, in reference to land. He wished these subjects to be considered separately, and as having no sort of reference to each other. The tribes in the vicinity of Taranaki have greater advantages than most others, as they are much intermixed with the Pakeha, and ought to profit by their intercourse with them. If they chose to live peaceably and culti- vate their lands they would grow rich and multiply, instead of which they were constantly at war with each other, and their numbers were decreasing. Their disputes were almost always about matters of little or no importance, or about land which was not worth quarrelling for. Had the Governor been in New Zealand when Katatore slew Rawiri he would have had him arrested and brought before the Judge, and, if the Judge had sentenced him to be hanged, he would have caused him to be hanged; that he had not thought proper to arrest Ihaia, because though the murders to which he was a party were horrible and disgraceful, yet they admitted of some extenuation, inasmuch as they were committed in retribution for the murder of Rawiri. All this, however, now belongs to the past; but, for the future, he had determined that every man (whether he be Maori or Pakeha) who may commit any violence or outrage within the European boundaries shall be arrested and taken before the Judge, and the sentence of the Judge, whatever it may be, shall be carried into effect. He was determined that the peace of the settlers should no longer be disturbed by evil doers, and that those Maories who are not content to live in peace among the Pakehas had better go elsewhere. In reference to the second subject, the Governor thought the Maories would be wise to sell the land they cannot use themselves, as it would make what they could use more valuable than the whole; but that he never would consent to buy land without an undisputed title. He would not permit any one to interfere in the sale of land unless he owned part of it; and, on the other hand, he would buy no man's land without his consent.

Tahana again addressed his tribe approving of that portion of his Excellency's speech declaring that if murder were again committed that the murderer should be arrested and tried by British law. He then supposed a case of a native policeman or assessor (himself) shot whilst arresting a murderer, and inquired who would avenge him. He stated that if he were assured of the support of his Excellency, as he knew his Excellency would receive the support of the Queen, he could hereafter single handed arrest offenders.

Te Teira, a Waitara Native, then stated that he was anxious to sell land belonging to him, that he had heard with satisfaction the declaration of the Governor referring to individual claims, and the assurance of protection that would be afforded by his Excellency. He minutely defined the boundaries of his claim, repeated that he was anxious to sell, and that he was the owner of the land he offered for sale. He then repeatedly asked if the Governor would buy this land. Mr McLean on behalf of his Excellency replied that he would. Te Teira then placed a parawai (bordered mat), at the Governor's feet, which his Excellency accepted. This cere- mony, according to Native custom, virtually places Teira's land at Waitara in the hands of the Governor.

Hemi Kuku then followed and stated his desire to dispose of land at Onairo, but in consequence of violent opposition his offer was not then entertained.

Piripi, a relative of Ihaia's, then offered his land at Waitara; his right to sell was denied by Te Teira, Te Waka (a town native,) and several of the Waitara natives, who asserted that his land was forfeited as payment for the murder of Katatore by his relatives.

Paora then informed the Governor that Te Teira could not sell the land he had offered without the consent of Weteriki and himself, as they had a joint interest in a portion of it.

Te Teira replied to him, and was immediately followed by William King, who, before addressing the Governor, said to his people 'I will only say a few words and then we will depart,' to which they assented. He then said 'Listen, Governer. Notwithstanding Teira's offer I will not permit the sale of Waitara to the Pakeha. Waitara is in my hands, I will not give it up; *ekore, ekore, ekore*,' (i.e., I will not, I will not, I will not). 'I have spoken!' and turning to his tribe added 'Arise, let us go'—whereupon he and his followers abruptly withdrew.

Kipa, a Waiwakaiho native, then expressed the satisfaction that the Governor's speech afforded him and proposed that henceforward British law should not prevail beyond the Waitaha.

Matiu, a Hua native, wished to address His Excellency on the King movement, but was informed that another opportunity would be afforded him.

The meeting then separated.

[Editorial comment] . . . His Excellency the Governor's acceptance of Teira and Retimana's offer of land at Waitara may be considered as the first step towards the re-occupation of that district, and opens out a new era for Taranaki. Yet important as the offer is, especially when considered in relation to the expressed determination of the Governor to purchase the claims of individual natives as opportunity offers, it is to its consequences rather than to any immediate results that we have to look. It may be some time, a considerable time perhaps, before the great benefits to be derived from the offer will be realized, but it is highly gratifying to know that the system we have so long advocated, (and which completely succeeded in the purchase of the Bell district,) is at length formally recognised and assented to. It is true that the natives named have only assigned their individual interests to His Excellency, but in so doing they have shaken off the ban that has so long enthralled them, and set an excellent example which will not be lost upon the natives. The practice hitherto adopted of requiring the assent of all the natives before accepting offers of land from any of them has tended directly to the non purchase of land—placed the seller at the mercy of the non seller—discouraged him in his efforts, and in more than one instance has added him to the list of dissentients.

At the meeting of Natives on Tuesday the Governor most distinctly stated that he was prepared to buy individual claims to land, but that he would not consider the purchase of a district complete until every claimant had given his consent to the sale and been fairly compensated. The declaration will have the effect of pacifying the natives on their most fertile subject of quarrel since the reliance they feel in the integrity of the government will leave the most turbulent and unruly amongst them no pretext for the adoption of violent steps in defence of their rights.

The Taranaki Herald, 12 March 1859

49. THE WAITARA DISPUTE, 1860

Letter from Revd. Octavius Hadfield, Archdeacon of Kapiti, to the Secretary of State, the Duke of Newcastle, 29 May 1860, upholding Wiremu Kingi's position in the Waitara dispute.

. . . It is fortunate that the merits of the question lie within very narrow limits. The right of natives to their lands is not now a subject of dispute. The Governor says, 'The Queen has said that all the natives shall be free to sell their lands to her, or to keep them, as they may think best.' The question at issue is simply this—Is a native chief to be forcibly ejected from his land, because an individual member of his tribe tells a subordinate land agent that it is his, and not the chief's, and that agent believes him? The Governor says—Yes; the chiefs say—No. We have resigned our sovereignty to Her Majesty the Queen; and in return for that, Her Majesty has guaranteed to us the protection of the law. We claim to have disputed titles to land, which it is desired to purchase, decided in some competent court on evidence given upon oath, for we have never consented, and we will never submit, to have the titles to the land on which we live, and on which we cultivate the food for our subsistence, decided by a mere subordinate land agent, interested in acquiring land, and resting his decision on the bare assertion of a man of no note or rank in the tribe. This is really the question at issue between the Governor and William King. Were Teira's title as good as I am quite certain it is bad, and had William King no valid title whatever, still the real question raised by this act of the Governor's is what I have now stated it to be. Are chiefs to be debarred from all right to defend their titles in a competent court of law? Is the *ipse dixit* of an interested subordinate land agent to deprive a chief of his land, and justify the Governor in having recourse to arms? If so, of what conceivable use or meaning is the guarantee in reference to their land contained in the Treaty of Waitangi? . . .

Before I endeavour to refute the Governor's statements as to the respective titles of the claimants, it will be necessary to seek the origin of the dispute. Before his death, William King's father obtained a promise from his son that he would not sell Waitara. This took place in the presence of the leading men of the tribe. This alone would shew what native law or custom on the subject has been, otherwise the promise would not have satisfied the old chief. But I mention this to account for the apparent obstinacy of William King in reference to the small district of Waitara, which he and his tribe have possessed for ages, and which has rendered a remarkably mild and inoffensive chief generally unpopular. Not long since a girl, who was affianced to Teira's brother, preferred William King's son and married him. It is well known here that Teira immediately meditated revenge for this slight put upon his brother. He was well aware of William King's promise to his father. He knew the district land commissioner wished to obtain land. He made an offer of the land, hoping to do, what he has succeeded in,—make use of the Governor to avenge the insult he had received. It even appears that Teira was not satisfied in receiving the payment for the land he sold, which is all that a vendor usually expects, but actually obtained a promise from Colonel Browne that he would push the matter to extremities. The document above referred to, says, . . . 'The Governor has given his word to Teira, and he will not go back from it. The land has been bought and must be surveyed. The Queen's soldiers will protect the surveyors.' This admission in an official document widely circulated among the natives has been very severely animadverted on by the chiefs as derogatory to the Governor, who they consider has allowed himself to be made a tool of by a low-bred man in gratifying his feelings of revenge against his chief. . . .

I now proceed to consider the grounds publicly set forth by the Governor in defence of his extraordinary act at Taranaki, in forcibly ejecting William King and his tribe from a block of land situated on the south side of the river Waitara, consisting of about

139

six hundred acres, on the bare assertion of a district land commissioner, that it belonged to another person, who had sold it to the Government. It is stated that the land belonged to Teira and a few other persons, who were the real owners, and who have sold it to the Government;—that Teira's title to the land was 'carefully investigated and found to be good;'—that William King and those who acted with him had no title to it;—that 'William King never pretended to deny Teira's right of property, but insisted on his own right to put a veto on all sales at Waitara.' I deny the truth of all the statements. . . .

I have already cited the Governor's own admission that William King positively told him that 'Waitara was in his hands,' and that he would not part with it. I am unable to conceive in what manner the old chief could more distinctly deny his opponent's title. It is true Mr. Parris, the district commissioner says, that in answer to his question—'Does the land belong to Teira and his party?' He replied—'Yes; the land is theirs, but I will not let them sell it.' I am credibly informed that the chief did not intend to convey the meaning here attributed to him; that what he said was, that Teira and his party were part owners of the land, but that did not justify them in selling the whole. I can easily conceive how such a mistake would arise, as it is quite in accordance with the idiom of the *Maori* language to begin an objection by 'Yes,' *i.e.* you are right to a certain extent, but, &c. And that was exactly the chief's meaning: Teira has a right to a small part; but he wishes to avail himself of that to establish a claim to the whole block of land now under discussion, and that I will not allow him to do. Here the irregularity of the whole proceeding appears; for had such a question been put in a court of law, and the alleged answer been returned, William King's counsel would have taken care that no inference prejudicial to his interests should be drawn from it. But to return to the chief's plain assertion to the Governor that Waitara was his, and that he and the other principal owners declined to sell it; and the claim implied in this. How does the Governor deal with it? How does he escape from the difficulty implied in his own admission that he will not purchase land the title of which is disputed? He merely pretends that William King 'insists on his own right of putting a veto on all sales at Waitara.' . . .

Octavius Hadfield, *One of England's Little Wars*, London, 1860, pp. 5–6, 7, 10–11, 13–14

50. CONTROL OF MAORI AFFAIRS BY THE GOVERNOR CONDEMNED, 1861

Minute by the Premier, William Fox, 8 October 1861, addressed to the incoming governor Sir George Grey, and criticizing the reservation of Maori affairs by his predecessor.

... The result is, that while on all other subjects the Responsible Ministers are the sole advisers of the Governor, and exercise the entire executive functions of the Government, on Native Affairs, the Governor has, in addition to his Ministers, another Adviser, his Native Secretary, who is not a responsible Minister nor under the control of responsible Ministers, but who exercises, (subject only to instructions from the Governor himself) all the Executive functions of Government in relation to Native affairs.

In 1856 the two departments were amalgamated by the union of the two offices of Native Secretary and Chief Land Purchase Commissioner, in the person of Mr. McLean. A prominent result of this union of the political function of the Government with its Commercial function as Land purchaser, has been the creation in the Native mind of a suspicion that all the acts of the Government originate in a desire to get possession of their land. They have learned to look upon the Government as a gigantic land broker, and every attempt made by it either to improve their social condition or to control them by the necessary restrictions of law, is supposed to have for its ultimate object the acquisition of territory. This feeling, to a great extent lies at the foundation of the unsatisfactory relations at present existing between the Natives and the Government.

The House of Representatives, on two separate occasions in the last two Sessions, unanimously condemned the fusion of the two departments. . . .

Ministers are bound to state that they regard the existence of the Native Secretary's Department, free as it is from all control on the part of the Responsible Ministry, as a very serious evil. While its existence paralyzes all independent and vigorous action on the part of the Ministry, it is itself inefficient and powerless. Receiving no sympathy, and little support, at the hands of the Assembly or the Responsible Ministry, it neither originates nor can it carry out any persistent or large policy, & it is only capable of obstructing,

by mere vis inertiæ the attempt of the Colonial Government to
bring its energies to bear on Native interests. . . .

C.O. 209/164, pp. 41–51

51. THE POLICY OF THE FOX GOVERNMENT, 1861: CONCILIATION IN THE WAIKATO; FIRMNESS IN TARANAKI

*Minute by the Premier, William Fox, 8 October 1861, advising the
incoming Governor, Sir George Grey, on Maori policy.*

. . . Only a small part of the Natives have been in overt insurrection;
except the Ngatiruanuis and Taranakis no whole tribe has been
committed. Such of the Waikatos as took part in the Taranaki war
did so on their own individual responsibility and not as the result
of any tribal action. Admitting that these individuals and the
Ngatiruanui and Taranaki tribes have placed themselves in a
position to justify severe treatment, why should the larger part of
the Waikatos and all the other tribes who have taken no part in the
insurrection be included in the same sentence? . . .

. . . The Governor might instal himself at Auckland without
making any direct overture to the insurgents. It is pretty certain that
before long he would be visited by many of the most influential
Chiefs belonging to or connected with the Waikatos, indeed, with
all the other Tribes. Friendly communication with them in a spirit
of firmness and conciliation, accompanied by acts of personal kindness would result in their return to their Tribes in a temper which
would probably go far to promote a pacific solution of difficulties. . . .

. . . The Ngatiruanui and Taranaki Natives remain in a state of
passive insurrectionary sullenness,—refuse submission to the Terms
proposed—retain possession of large quantities of the Settlers'
Stock carried off during the war, have stopped the Mail though
carried by Natives, and threaten death to all Europeans who venture beyond certain lines;—so that, no one dare travel beyond a few
miles from the Town of New Plymouth on the one side, or Wanganui
on the other. The Tataraimaka block, purchased from the Natives,
and which has been parcelled out into thriving farms, for the most
part under cultivation, may now be said to be practically in the

142

possession of the Insurgents. The Homesteads of the Settlers, their fences and cultivations, have been destroyed:—and no Settler will incur the risk of going on his own land. In fact, the Natives boast that they hold the land by right of conquest.

This state of things cannot in the opinion of Ministers be suffered to continue. . . .

. . . If there must be a War, it is better far that it should be at Taranaki, than elsewhere. For whatever mischief could be inflicted on British Settlements by a state of War has been done there. The penalties of War have been already paid. Besides this, the case of the Ngatiruanui and Taranaki Natives is the one which presents the fewest grounds of sympathy with other Natives. They engaged in the quarrel without provocation, and were guilty of gross outrages. Their present attitude is one of such open hostility, as in the eyes of well affected Natives themselves would not merely justify, but demand on our part active measures against them, and retribution for the wrongs done. . . .

. . . There appears to Ministers no inconsistency in dealing with the main body of the Natives, the Waikatos in particular, with a gentle and even friendly hand—and endeavouring by all legitimate means to recall and attach them to us; and at the same time assuming a stern and decisive attitude towards the Ngatiruanuis and Taranakis with a view to compel from them material guarantees for their future good behaviour.

One other topic requires to be brought under Sir George Grey's consideration: viz: the recent Gold Discoveries as affecting Native Policy.

The fact of paying Gold Fields existing in New Zealand is now placed beyond a doubt. The auriferous district extends through the Northern and Middle Island from Cape Colville downwards. Already there are signs of a large influx of population, directed at present to the Otago Gold Fields, but which will in all probability spread to the Northern Island particularly in the direction of Coromandel. What may be apprehended is lest gold seekers should force themselves into Native Districts against the will of the Native owners, the result of which would probably be a Collision between the races leading to fresh political complications.

It will in the opinion of Ministers be the duty of Government to guard against the risk, by all means in their power. . . .

C.O. 209/164, pp. 16–39

52. THE RUNANGA SCHEME

Governor Grey's scheme for dividing the North Island into twenty districts, within which Maori assemblies would be developed in co-operation with the Government, as outlined in a Minute of October 1861.

. . . Inasmuch as, up to this time, large portions of the Northern Island of New Zealand have never been provided with any machinery by which law and order could be maintained, the good and well-disposed be protected, and the violent restrained, it is now intended to create the following machinery to give effect to the laws which have, from time to time, been made for the security and welfare of Her Majesty's subjects, both European and Native.

Division of Native portions of Northern Island

1. The Native portions of the Northern Island to be divided into, say, twenty Districts, each under a Civil Commissioner, with a Clerk and Interpreter, and a Medical man as district surgeon attached to his District.

Hundreds and Officers of Hundreds

1. Each District to be divided into about six Hundreds, from the Runangas of each of which will be selected two persons to represent such Hundred in the Runanga of the District, and to act as Assessors or Native Magistrates.

2. The Governor will generally select Native Officers from the candidates whose names may be submitted to him by the Runangas of the Hundreds.

3. In selecting Native Officers the preference will be given to those candidates who have a knowledge of the English language.

4. The two Native Magistrates to receive, the one a salary of £50 per annum, the other a salary of £40 per annum.

5. A Warden or Chief Police Officer will be appointed to each Hundred, with a salary of £30 per annum.

6. Five Constables will be appointed to each Hundred, with a salary of £10 per annum each and a uniform for each year.

Constitution of District Runangas

1. The District Runanga will consist of the Civil Commissioner, and say twelve members.

2. The Civil Commissioner will preside at all meetings of the Runanga, and will have an original vote and a casting vote.

144

Powers of District Runangas

1. The District Runanga shall have the power of drawing up, from time to time, bye-laws, for the purpose of putting in force within their District regulations respecting all matters regarding which the Governor is by 'The Native Districts Regulation Act, 1858,' empowered to make and put in force regulations within Native Districts: . . .

[cattle trespass, public pounds, boundary fences, cattle branding, cattle disease, weed control, prescribing and enforcing rights and liabilities among tribes, bush fires, cleansing of buildings, health, drunkenness, suppression of injurious customs, reporting on Native Schools, gaols, hospitals, district roads, disputes over boundaries.]

Native Clergymen and Schoolmasters

In order that assistance may be afforded to the Civil Commissioners and the Runanga in establishing Schools in their District, and promoting the spread of piety and order, salaries of £50 per annum each will be provided for three Native Clergymen and Schoolmasters in each District, subject to such conditions and regulations as may be agreed on between the Government and the head of the religious body to which such ministers may belong.

Resident Magistrates, Native Assessors' Courts

1. The Civil Commissioners, Resident Magistrates, and Native Assessors, shall periodically hold Courts within their several Districts, at such convenient times and places as may, from time to time, be appointed by the Governor for that purpose. . . .

Locations of Europeans, in Native Districts

1. In order to promote the welfare of the two races inhabiting this country, and to lead to a community of interests, and the frequent interchange of friendly offices between them, as well as with the view of fostering the development of the resources of the interior, the Civil Commissioner and Runanga of each District will be authorised to report the size of the farms which farmers would require in that District for the purpose of carrying on their calling, whether agricultural or pastoral, reference being had to the situation and soil of each District.

2. So soon as the boundaries and ownership of any lands in any District have been ascertained and defined, in accordance with the regulations of the Runanga, and have been registered in the Civil Commissioner's office and approved by the Government, the Native

owners will be permitted to dispose of any such lands, not exceeding the extent of one farm, by direct sale to any purchaser who may be approved of by the Government on the recommendation of the Runanga, on such conditions as may be agreed on between the seller and purchaser. . . .

A.J.H.R., 1862, E–2, pp. 10–12

53. GREY'S VISIT TO THE WAIKATO, 1861

Speeches at Kohanga, 12 December 1861 and at Taupiri, 16 December, when Sir George Grey indicated his attitude to the King Movement and outlined his runanga scheme.

Kohanga, 12th December.

Waata Kukutai (Ngatitipa): Welcome, Governor. Welcome to Waikato. Welcome to the house which is injured, to the path which is overgrown, to the fence which is broken down. Welcome to the scattered sheep. The sheep have no shepherd, and so they are scattered abroad. It was I who fetched you from the forests of Taane. Welcome to your old resting-places. The roads are filled up. . . .

His Excellency: . . . I am come here as a stranger, and so I seek to know what it is which is desired by you. Do you want to know if I am come here in peace? Yes. I have come in love and regard for you all, and I wish to find out what I can do for you.

Herewini: Friend the Governor, listen to me. There are three things that I think of: love, peace, and Christianity. There are also three other things which I think of: the king, the flag, and the roads.

His Excellency: I am a stranger here, and should like it to be made clear what all these things mean. What is the king, according to your thoughts?

Herewini: This is the interpretation of it. There are three things which I consider: the king, the flag, and the road; this is my explanation.

His Excellency: Well, what is it that you mean by the king?

Herewini: He is a king belonging to us, to us of this Island of New Zealand, belonging to (or over) us the inhabitants of New Zealand.

His Excellency: Is he a king for the Europeans?

Herewini: If you, O Governor, are willing to accept my king, it will be well.

His Excellency: Is he then only a king for those who wish to have him?

Herewini would not answer at first; then he said: He is for us, the men of New Zealand.

His Excellency: What about those who do not wish to have him?

Herewini: All the men of New Zealand wish to have him.

His Excellency, repeating the last question, said: What about those who refuse him?

Herewini: I do not know that there are any; there are none who have fled beyond the bounds of New Zealand.

His Excellency: But I know there *are* many. What about those? Do you intend to force them to have him as a king?

Herewini: Ha! There are none unwilling; all are consenting.

His Excellency: Have the Ngapuhis consented?

Herewini: All, all belong to New Zealand.

His Excellency: Have the Ngatitipa consented?

Herewini: Yes, all belong to New Zealand; and Waikato belongs to New Zealand.

His Excellency: What power is the king to have? What is he to do?

Herewini: His work. You know that wars have been the constant practice in this Island of New Zealand. The Scriptures having come to me, I search, and in the Scriptures I find: Hence I build up this enclosure as the means of stanching my blood; thus I have considered in the years that have passed.

His Excellency: Have you thought of no other plan for stopping war and bloodshed, in which all the country could join?

Herewini: The destroyers of this evil are Christianity and love: these are its destroyers. Speak, O Governor, about evil and good; I thought that love should be joined to love, and hence I spoke about the three things.

December 16th, 1861.

Waata Kukutai: O Waikato and the Governor, listen to me. This is my opening speech to you now, that the two *tikangas* may be seen. My thoughts during the two last years have been respecting the soiling (troubling) of this land, and I thought how good could arise for it. The splinters of Waikato flew to Taranaki, and evil

147

came: the splinters of the Pakeha flew at Taranaki, and evil came. As for this, Waikato has now come here with the Governor, and it is good for us all to talk this day. I merely now call out to you: Welcome, welcome. There is good in the two plans (meaning the King movement and the Governor's proposals): how can that good be made to grow? You have raised before the Governor the road and the King, and the Governor does not tread them down. Now how must good spring up or evil grow? This is my invitation for you all to speak.

His Excellency spoke after Waata Kukutai, and said: Salutations to you all! I have returned to this country to see my old friends, and to be the Governor of the two races, the Europeans and the Maories. You must not think I am only come as a friend of the Europeans, to punish the Maories for anything they have done. I am come as the friend of both, and as an impartial person, to see what can be done. I have been sent with a very large force at my disposal, to put an end to war and discord, and to establish law and order; and if the force now here is not sufficient, I can have as much more as I like. . . .

Having now said these things, I will talk to you with reference to the points of difference between you and the Government, and tell you my news.

The first point is the property stolen from the Europeans. You will remember that this has been demanded to be given up, if you do not wish to be attacked. In my position as Governor, I do not care whether this is given back or not; but I will tell you what I think. You know, if in a tribe one steals from another, that the whole tribe rises and punishes the thief. Now I say that the Maories and the Europeans are one tribe; and to say that I will attack the tribe that has the plunder, is to say that it is of a different tribe to ourselves, which I will not admit; and, therefore, whenever a man is caught with any of the stolen property, he will, even it be 20 years hence, be taken before the Judge, and if found to be a thief, he will be punished. . . .

So when I see Taranaki has been plundered, I know the Europeans can never feel reconciled to the Maories unless some restitution is made; and I would persuade them to make it.

The next thing is about the Roads. You seem to think that roads through the country would do no good. I think they would improve the value of the lands through which they pass; and if you think

I want to spend money in making roads through the land of people who don't want them, thereby enriching them at the expense of others, you must think me a fool. In the country of the Europeans, they have to pay the greater part of the cost of the roads before the Government helps them. In the same way I should be very unwilling to make roads through Native land, even if the owners came and asked me to do so, unless they paid part of the money. . . .

Now the third thing—the King—I will talk about. You heard Waata Kukutai say, I assented to the king and the flag. I must explain what I mean. If a tribe, or two or three, or more, call their Chief a king and stick up a flag, I think it nonsense, and don't mind it. I think it a foolish thing to do, and that it may lead to bad consequences; but I shall not quarrel with them until the bad consequences come. You must recollect that this king affair is mixed up with many things that ought not to be. . . .

I will now speak to you on one other point—the land.

I understand that there is a jealousy that I shall buy land from a few people, and take it by force from others; you may depend on it I shall not do this. Until all that are concerned are consulted, no land will be taken. I will not send people about the country teasing and troubling you about the sale of your lands. I should be a bad man if I did so,—particularly in the Waikato—as whenever I have asked you for land you have given it to me. . . .

Now, I will tell you what I propose to do for the future. I do not mean to say, that in as far as institutions for the maintenance of law and order have not been established in the country among you, your interests have not been overlooked. You must have seen that the Europeans have been allowed to make rules and laws for themselves, and those who made them have been paid for doing so; while the Maories have been left unprovided for, and those that did make laws were ill paid. I do not feel that I am without blame in the matter myself. When I was the Governor here formerly, I ought to have seen farther ahead, and what civilization would lead to and require. I propose therefore now, that wherever people live in considerable numbers, the island should be divided into Districts, and Runangas appointed to make laws for them, and to determine if roads are to be made, and what share of the expenses the people of the district will have to pay. They will also determine the ownership and boundaries of land, and if it may be sold, and by whom—and whether spirits may be sold, and under what regulations. In fact they will have to make laws on all subjects concerning their own interests, and when these are sent to me and I have consented to them, they will be binding alike both on Maori and European.

Native Magistrates will also be appointed, and people under them, to administer the laws: and all these people that are employed will have salaries, and be paid regularly on the 1st of each month like Europeans. You will thus see by what I have said, that the way I intend to put down *evil* is by putting up *good,* not by employing force.

One thing I have omitted to tell you. In each district a medical man will be stationed, and salaries will be provided for the Native Clergymen or Schoolmasters, and for each 'hapu' that wishes to put aside land for the support of a clergyman I will endeavour to get a minister. One of the great evils has been, that there has been no opening for the young men, Chiefs and others, who have been highly educated. Now I make all these openings, clergymen, magistrates, doctors, &c., and a young Chief may become one of these, and not have to go to work (manual labor) on his land like a common man, but live like a gentleman.

Now don't you say I am not come here to conquer and kill you; I have come to conquer and kill you too—*with good*. Now I have done, and if any of you want to ask questions about what I have said, I am here to answer. . . .

Tipene (Ngatimahuta): What I shall speak about is the king, the flag, and the plunder. You formerly were the Governor of this island; and as for us, we were with you. Now the things you gave us at that period were Magistrates. After your departure, we considered that we should raise up a king for ourselves, to stop blood shedding and repress the evils of the land, and put an end to wars. For two years this *korero* has been maintained. While the magistrates which you speak about were still residing, men were selling land throughout the island. We thought, New Zealand will be gone. We saw the land which had gone covered with cattle, and horses, and sheep, and the men employed fencing the land against cattle, &c. We then said let the land be withheld. We (Waikato) began it, and others joined. We saw that the elder brother was quarrelling with the younger; and so one man was appointed to suppress fighting, and stop the blood.

Land was bought at Taranaki: we heard it was bought improperly, and presently disturbance arose about it. We held two runangas to consider it, in the course of which we heard that Taranaki was destroyed. Afterwards came news about the Ngatiruanui, and here we were perplexed. We had not heard that the Pakeha was fighting at Taranaki until the soldiers had gone aboard the ships: then we heard. Now this offence was from the Pakeha: hence we said, we are strangers to one another. This is our thought; we are divided, you on one side, and we on the other.

Three things we worked at after you left us; the gospel, the king, and the flag. We did not know it was wrong till after it was set up; then, for the first time, we knew it was considered wrong. I now say, work gently. Enough about that. This is another thing, about the roads. Formerly you commanded them, and they have been withheld by us. The roads are not simply for fetching food from a man's farm; throughout the island, it is this which creates fear. At Taranaki, the road being there, your guns reached the pa. This is our fear, lest that strange cart (gun carriage), the cart of terror, should travel on it. But for this fear, roads would have been allowed long ago. Enough of that.

Now, it was we (Waikato) who established the king. I have not heard that the roads are stopped up; the great road of the Waikato river is not stopped, the road of the Waipa river is not stopped, the Pakehas and the Maories are travelling upon them; the road of the Union Jack alone is closed. The words of Potatau, and yours, are still held: we adhere to the advice of Potatau 'do not do anything, do not fight, do not be angry with the Pakeha, but be kind to him.' Waikato adheres to these words. Our runangas are similar to your own, some are good and some are bad. At the present time, the only thing we will look at is goodness, that it may be joined and made fast. If we rise up against you, what would be the result? If you rise up against us, what would be the result? Formerly we, the Natives, were separate tribes: but now if I go to the other end of the island, it is still I (we are now one people). Let the error, if any, be sought out of our conversation during this day.

Tipene: . . . I will ask a question: Are you opposed to my king?

His Excellency: I do not care about him. But I think it is a thing which will lead to trouble. If you ask my opinion as a friend, I should say, Stop it. It will be stopped by such means as I have adopted, and it will die out. But I advise you to stop it. I fear it will lead to quarrels and so forth.

Tipene: Behold! if you say that it (the king) is a road which will

151

lead to future difficulty, the error is our own: that is right. You have heard the reason why he (the king) was set up; if evil arise, it will fall upon ourselves (for we shall be the cause of it.) But if it (the king movement) is brought to nought by your plans, well and good. You say what is the king to you? We say it is a thing of importance to us. And the reason why we say so is this, that we have seen the good of it: the quarrels of the Maories amongst themselves have for the last two years diminished. Therefore I say, if evil arise from it in future, we shall have caused it (brought it on ourselves.) Listen. Formerly both races were living together, our plans were the same and the work of this island remained unbroken. We worked together and talked together at that period, about the evils of the land; until the separation took place which we have been speaking about. Then, for the first time, I saw it was well. And now, by means of it many evils that have arisen have been put down (without war); and, therefore, I say it (the king) is an important thing to us. Now, I ask you, 'Are you altogether opposed to my king?' If you consent to my question, we shall then work quietly, because we are not the chief cause of the king: whereas with you is the final decision as to your own system. So I ask you 'Are you altogether opposed to our king?' that you may say whether you are so or not.

His Excellency: If you ask me as a friend, I tell you I think it a very bad thing.

Tipene: I say it has not arisen from us (Waikato), but from the whole island: but my question still remains unanswered. I ask, in order that the word of condemnation or otherwise may be spoken out. Will you condemn it in anger with war? Rather let him (the king) stand: if you let him alone he will fall of himself.

His Excellency: I think that each Chief in his own tribe, should, with his Runanga, come under the Governor; then they could all work with me.

Tipene: Leave that, we will convey it to the people. We are not going to pluck out the various tribes, *i.e.*, for their adherence; if a man comes to join us, we will not tell him to stop away. This will be our plan of scooping (gaining adherents); if a tribe come to us, we shall say, the system is with us (Waikato). This will be right, for they will have come of themselves. . . . At the present time, whilst both races are at peace, perhaps we shall be divided, or perhaps we shall be united. Let goodness, peace and love be joined together: that may be done now, and I say therefore, proceed gently (cautiously) in working out the plans you (the Governor) have spoken about. The only thing that remains dark (unsettled) is the king: your own plan is to unite us all. . . .

A.J.H.R., 1862, E–8, pp. 3–10

54. THE POLICY OF THE WHITAKER GOVERNMENT—CONFISCATION

Memorandum by the Premier, Frederick Whitaker, 4 January 1864, for Governor Grey, explaining the law which made provision for the confiscation of Maori land as a punishment for resistance.

'THE NEW ZEALAND SETTLEMENTS ACT, 1863'

. . . The complete defeat of the rebels would have but little effect in permanently securing the peace of the Colony, unless some ulterior measures are adopted for that object. In former wars in New Zealand, the natives have been permitted to leave off fighting when they though fit; to keep all the plunder they had obtained; and they have not been subjected to any kind of punishment for disturbing the peace of the country, killing Her Majesty's subjects, and destroying their property. If native wars are to be prevented for the future, some more effective mode of dealing with those who create them must be adopted. The question then is, in what way, for the future, can the peace of the Colony be maintained, and the peaceable inhabitants of both races best secured against the aggression of lawless men?

For the most part, the natives of New Zealand possess but little personal property, and therefore suffer but little from losing temporary possession of their settlements. What they have most dreaded in their own wars has been slavery and the permanent loss of their landed possessions. There is no doubt that the native lands afford the most effectual means of securing the object the Government has in view. They may be made, by affording a striking example, the means of deterring other tribes for the future from engaging in rebellion, and at the same time of securing the rebellious districts against future outbreaks.

The object of the Settlements Act is to give effect to these views. Already 3,000 men have taken military service under conditions, copies of which are included in the papers herewith, and it is intended to increase that number to 20,000. The provisions of the Act are framed with the intention of enabling the Government to fulfil the promises made to those who have already been enlisted in the service, and to meet future engagements of a similar kind.

The mode by which effect is proposed to be given to the intentions of the Government is by authorising the Governor in Council to proclaim districts, of which the native inhabitants have been engaged in the rebellion, to come within provisions of the Act, and then to authorise the taking of land within such districts for the establishment of settlements.

It will be observed that the provisions of the Act may be made to include lands belonging to persons who have not justly forfeited their rights by rebellion. In order to carry out the scheme, this is absolutely necessary. The principal difficulty which would arise from the want of such a power would be in those cases in which portions of a tribe have joined in the rebellion, leaving a few behind them, in some instances, with the avowed object of preserving the tribal land from forfeiture. The New Zealand native tenure of land is for the most part, in fact with little or perhaps no exception, tribal; and if the principle were admitted that the loyalty or neutrality of a few individuals would preserve the lands of the tribe, the Act would for the most part be a dead letter, and that in districts in which it is most required, and in which its operation would be perfectly just.

Care has been taken on the one hand that satisfactory provision is made for granting compensation to those who may be entitled to it, and on the other hand those are excluded who have fairly forfeited all claim to consideration. It is a recognised principle that, when the public interests require it, the property of individuals, on fair compensation, may be taken as available for the purposes of the State. A great public object, essential to the peace and security of the country, is to be gained in this instance, fully justifying the practical application of the principle. Again, it is undoubted natural justice that those who violate the fundamental principles of the Government under which they live, justly forfeit their right to the advantages which they derive from that Government. The rebellious natives have placed themselves in that position, and fairly subjected themselves to the penalty due to their offences. . . .

A.J.H.R., 1864, A–1, pp. 3–4

154

55. THE MAORI LAND LAWS OF 1862 AND 1865

The preamble of the 1862 Act recites the provisions of the Treaty of Waitangi relating to land, and the Act goes on to provide for the recognition of individual title to Maori land and to waive the Crown's pre-emptive right, thus permitting individual sales. In 1865 the new system was consolidated and provision made for the Native Land Court. A system of Maori land-dealing was brought into being which caused Maoris to part with millions of their ancestral acres over the next twenty-five years.

(a) *The Native Lands Act, 1862.*

An Act to provide for the ascertainment of the Ownership of Native Lands and for granting Certificates of Title thereto and for regulating the disposal of Native Lands and for other purposes. . . .

WHEREAS by the Treaty of Waitangi entered into by and between Her Majesty and the Chiefs of New Zealand it was among other things declared that Her Majesty confirmed and guaranteed to the Chiefs and Tribes of New Zealand and the respective families and individuals thereof the full exclusive and undisturbed possession of their lands and estates which they collectively or individually held so long as it should be their desire to retain the same. And it was further declared that the Chiefs yielded to Her Majesty the exclusive right of pre-emption over such lands as the proprietors thereof might be disposed to alienate AND WHEREAS it would greatly promote the peaceful settlement of the Colony and the advancement and civilization of the Natives if their rights to land were ascertained defined and declared and if the ownership of such lands when so ascertained defined and declared were assimilated as nearly as possible to the ownership of land according to British law AND WHEREAS with a view to the foregoing objects Her Majesty may be pleased to waive in favor of the Natives so much of the said Treaty of Waitangi as reserves to Her Majesty the right of preemption of their lands and to establish Courts and to make other provision for ascertaining and defining the rights of the Natives to their lands and for otherwise giving effect to the provisions of this Act And it is expedient that the General

Assembly of New Zealand should facilitate the said objects by enacting such provisions as are hereinafter contained. . . .

New Zealand Statutes, 1862, 26 Vict., no. 42, pp. 195–6

(b) *The Native Lands Act, 1865.*

AN ACT to Amend and Consolidate the Laws relating to Lands in the Colony in which the Maori Proprietary Customs still exist and to provide for the ascertainment of the Titles to such Lands and for Regulating the Descent thereof and for other purposes.

[*30th October* 1865.]

BE IT ENACTED . . .

I. CONSTITUTION OF COURT UNDER THIS ACT

V. The Native Land Court of New Zealand (hereinafter called the Court) shall be a Court of Record for the investigation of the titles of persons to Native Land for the determination of the succession of Natives to Native Lands and to hereditaments of which the Native owner shall have died intestate and for the other purposes hereinafter set forth. . . .

XII. Every Judge of the Court acting with at least two Assessors shall have the same jurisdiction and may exercise the same powers as the Court in all judicial matters whatever under this Act Provided always that there shall be no decision or judgment on any question judicially before the Court unless the Judge presiding and two Assessors concur therein. . . .

II. JURIES

XVI. In any matter brought before the Court under this Act for judicial investigation it shall be in the discretion of the Court on its own motion or on the request of any party interested made at any time before the commencement of the hearing to order that the matter shall be tried by a jury and the matter shall if necessary be adjourned until a jury can be formed. . . .

III. JURISDICTION AND DUTIES OF THE COURT

(1) *Investigation of Titles*

XXI. Any Native may give notice in writing to the Court that he claims to be interested in a piece of Native Land specifying it by its name or otherwise describing it and stating the name of the tribe or the names of the persons whom he admits to be interested therein with him and that he desires that his claim should be investigated by the Court in order that a title from the Crown may be issued to him for such piece of land.

XXII. Upon the receipt of such application notice thereof may be given by the Court and circulated in such manner as shall give due publicity thereto and in the same or in a subsequent notice shall be notified the day and the place when and where the Court will sit for the investigation of the said claim.

XXIII. At such sitting of the Court the Court shall ascertain by such evidence as it shall think fit the right title estate or interest of the applicant and of all other claimants to or in the land respecting which notice shall have been given as aforesaid and the Court shall order a certificate of title to be made and issued which certificate shall specify the names of the persons or of the tribe who according to Native custom own or are interested in the land describing the nature of such estate or interest and describing the land comprised in such certificate or the Court may in its discretion refuse to order a certificate to issue to the claimant or any other person Provided always that no certificate shall be ordered to more than ten persons Provided further that if the piece of land adjudicated upon shall not exceed five thousand acres such certificate may not be made in favor of a tribe by name. . . .

XXIV. It shall be lawful for the Court to order the making and issue of two or more certificates respecting any piece of land comprised in one claim if they shall find on investigation that there is more than one owner or set of owners thereof who desire that their respective estates or interests therein shall be divided or that the land shall be apportioned.

XXV. Subject as hereinafter mentioned the Court shall not proceed to a decision upon any such claim or make any order for a certificate of title unless there shall be produced before the Court during the investigation a survey of the lands the subject of the claim made by a surveyor duly licensed by the Governor on such a scale and in all respects so prepared as shall be provided in the rules aforesaid and unless it shall be proved to the Court that the boundaries of such land have been distinctly marked on the ground. . . .

XXXVII. The Court shall refer every such application to the Governor and if it shall appear to the Governor in Council that it would be fit and proper that such boundary line should be so defined and that no political difficulty is likely to arise by reason of entertaining the question it shall be lawful for the Court to give notice of the application aforesaid to the other tribe (if only one shall have joined in such application) and in the same or in a subsequent notice may state the day and place when and where the matter will be inquired into and the Court may take further judicial proceedings for the investigation of the matter aforesaid and may make a provisional or conditional order thereupon and may afterwards make a final order defining such boundary line after the same shall have been surveyed as hereinafter provided in such manner as to the Court shall seem just.

XXXVIII. Subject as hereinafter provided no such final order shall be made until the boundary line shall have been surveyed and mapped by a surveyor licensed as aforesaid at the expense of the applicant or at the joint expense of the tribes (as may be decided by the Court) and the same shall have been well and effectually marked off on the ground.

XXXIX. Such order shall be deemed to be conclusive as to the boundary and dividing limits of the lands therein referred to in all future proceedings of the Court respecting the same or adjoining lands. . . .

New Zealand Statutes, 1865, 29 Vict. no. 71, pp. 264–8

56. TE WHITI, THE PROPHET OF PARIHAKA

An account of the village of Parihaka, Taranaki, and the aims and methods of Te Whiti, including the passive resistance offered to government forces when they occupied the village.

. . . Te Whiti does not pretend to exercise jurisdiction over any lands excepting those situated and owned by his tribe, the Ngatiawa, in the vicinity of Parihaka. . . . He is more-over a most intelligent, and far-seeing man. By past experience he has known how the Maori has been debauched and impoverished by having parted with his lands. . . . He and his then become a burden on his relatives and friends, who may themselves barely possess sufficient for their own sustenance. . . . The Maori has never been taught to work; consequently he looks upon labour as a degradation. He says only the 'tutua' (or low-class) Europeans work; the 'Rangatiras' sit around and are waited on. . . .

Knowing the evils that have and are decimating his race, Te Whiti has thought out, and is carrying out, his scheme for saving the remnant of his tribe, the Ngatiawa. His principle is to discourage all sales of lands and drawing of rents by his people, but instead of encouraging them to follow in the good and beneficent works of pakeha. No man understands these benefits . . . more than Te Whiti. This can be demonstrated by anyone visiting his settlement of Parihaka. Ten years ago it was a collection of the usual insanitary Maori whares. What do we see here to-day? A model village, which would be a credit to any European community. A good macadamised road, culverted, fenced, and smooth as a bicycle track, leads one to the village, where one observes well laid out streets and wooden residences built in the best European style. . . . Largely and tastefully furnished dining rooms are there, which can seat 100 to 250 settlers. These tables are laden with good, wholesome food, roasts of beef, mutton, pork, several kinds of vegetables, ending with plum and other kinds of pudding, jam tarts, etc. Tea, coffee, or cocoa is always to be had; but intoxicants of every description are strictly tabooed by Te Whiti and his people. The tables are provided with every requisite, right down to the serviette, and one is looked after by young Maori waiters, who would be a credit to any European hotel. All visitors are welcome, whether European or Maori, and they will fare as well as in the best European hotels. The larger houses are fitted up with hot and cold baths. . . . Altogether, the accommodation is not surpassed on the coast.

The village has its bake, slaughter and butcher houses, blacksmith shops, etc., the different houses getting their water supply from a very fine reservoir. This reservoir is supplied by clear mountain streams flowing from Mount Egmont, the water being beautifully clear and icy cold. It has concrete sides and bottom. The water is then pumped by means of a hydraulic ram for a distance of about half a mile on to the top of a large hill overlooking the village. On this hill it is received into a large concrete cistern, from thence the water is carried by main and pipes to the houses. The pressure is very strong, many of the houses having five or six services led to the different parts. The overflow or waste water from the reservoir is shortly to be utilised for driving the machinery for lighting Parihaka by electricity, and for flushing the street drains . . . all these buildings and works have been carried out by the natives themselves, under the able superintendence of Taare Waitara, Te Whiti's son-in-law. . . .

Te Whiti in the first place secured the services of European tradesmen to instruct his leading men in the different avocations. The Maoris proved apt pupils, and quickly picked up all the European could teach them; then they in turn taught their own people; consequently they are tradesmen of all descriptions, and very good ones too. Te Whiti will not tolerate a drone in his village. . . . Te Whiti himself is scarcely ever idle; he takes a hand at everything, showing his people a practical example. The gongs at the different eating houses are sounded three times a day, and the natives are provided with a fare that most Europeans would envy. Active young fellows, who thoroughly understand their duties, wait at table, and everything as before mentioned is carried out in thorough European fashion—the men, women and children sitting down to the tables and observing the decorum of well-bred Europeans. . . .

At daybreak the whole village is astir, each busying about his different duties until the gong sounds for breakfast about seven, dinner is at twelve and tea at five. At midnight numbers gather into the large meeting halls, where the young people amuse themselves with the poi dance and other innocent recreations. As Te Whiti does not believe in the principle of all work and no play, the men meet together to discuss local, political and other matters, and to chat away generally while smoking their evening pipes. Te Whiti does not allow any intoxicants or any intoxicated person in his village; on the evil of drink he is very decided; and no immorality or wrong-doing of any kind is tolerated. . . . On the 18th of March each year he observes what he calls his 'Ratapu', or sacred day.

On these occasions only Te Whiti, so to speak, address his people politically. They gather in from the surrounding settlements to listen to him. He is a fluent and brilliant orator, and sometimes talks right on for hours, never repeating himself. Every word is the utterance of a sage. True it is, many of his words are metaphorical, and his people have occasionally to think over his sayings for many days before able to grasp their real meaning; some they have never been able to solve. . . . A Maori chief, to be thoroughly respected and feared by his people, must appear to be somewhat inspired and to lead a good and consistent life. No one sees faults and shortcomings in others quicker than the Maori.

Te Whiti's speech and actions have on occasions appeared to be those of a madman, such as instructing his people to plough up land in the occupation of the Europeans. There was method in this. All these lands which were interfered with belonged to him and his tribe; this was his manner of entering his protest; thus demonstrating that he and his claimed these lands. . . . Te Whiti considered that, if the European was left in peaceful occupation, these lands would in time pass away from him and his, and titles for them would be issued to those who had no claims whatever. Thus he offers his passive resistance to the leasing of these lands. He has always counselled his people to use no force, and show every forbearance. He is aware that directly the law is broken he and his people must be arrested and imprisoned, thus drawing attention to their grievances and also preventing outside natives from claiming their lands. We know that he and his have several times been imprisoned and deported to the southernmost parts of the colony. This did not in any way cool their ardour.

Even the celebrated expedition of force under Mr. Bryce did not cause him to flinch. He treated the whole thing as a huge farce, sending out the little children to dance a welcome to the European warriors as they approached the pah. On the investment of the place by the thousand or more constabulary and volunteers, cannon was placed on the hill commanding Te Whiti's house, in front of which he assembled all his people, counselling them to offer no resistance, saying: "Even if the soldiers fire on us and kill our women and children, better to do thus on the lands of our fore-fathers than be hounded off as vagrants". How well he exercised his influence, and kept his young, hot bloods in check, is a matter of history. He has also for years back told his followers to have no fear, but that their lands will be returned to them. . . . They are still there, and they have not been induced to sign them away so far. The rents lie still intact with the Public Trustee. So much the better. In the meantime he will teach the Maori to work and be self-reliant. When he has learnt this, he will value and put his moneys to good use.

What is the condition to-day of the Maori who has sold his lands? . . . The remnants on the whole are a poor and miserable lot. Well would it have been for them if a man or two of Te Whiti's stamp had lived amongst them and shown them how to work out their own salvation. . . .

By 'Rawiri Matangi', *The New Zealand Times,*
29 March 1899, p. 2

57. THE MAORI PARLIAMENT MOVEMENT

Part of an interview in Auckland, 1893, with Hone Heke, Member of the House of Representatives for the Northern Maori seat, in which he tells of Maori grievances about land and the movement for a Maori Parliament.

'. . . Ever since 1842 the land troubles have been recurring between Europeans and natives, and no change, as far as beneficial legislation is concerned, has occurred since the advent of the native members.'

'There were troubles in respect to titles to land, were there not?'

'Yes; ever since the first Native Land act, in 1862, the trouble with respect to native titles has existed. This act was introduced for the purpose of investigating titles to native owned lands in New Zealand, and also to repeal the Crown's right of pre-emption, which was embodied in Clause 2 of the treaty of Waitangi. In our native land tenure there was no individual title to land; it was held in common. In former days the chief of each tribe was the recognized person who held sole *mana* (authority in a wide sense) over the people, and over the land held by the people. After the introduction of legislation and European ways, in respect to putting everything down on paper, a tendency arose to alter the former true Maori honesty of settlements. In olden days the chief made the agreement, which was held sacred. If that was broken, the usual result was compensation or bloodshed. But under the new state of affairs, natives who were neither chiefs nor owners of the soil gave signatures to deeds of land to the Crown as well as private individuals.'

'Since then you have had legislation? With what result?'

'Disastrous results to the native races, who are dissatisfied, and who now take a deep and absorbing interest in the land question—a personal interest. Education has spread and the Maoris are great students of the politics of the country. They fully understand also that they can only look for redress through constitutional methods.' . . .

'What is it that the native race wishes for now as regards the land question?' . . .

'Ever since 1865 the native mind continually referred back to the treaty of Waitangi, contending that several provisions of acts passed since then were contrary to the treaty that their rights have been ignored and the confiscation of their lands is a direct violation of its clauses. After the Waikato war the lands of the Waikato people were confiscated as payment of a war indemnity, and this extended also to land in the Taranaki district. The land was taken away and sold.'

'Now for later times. The Parihaka affair was a land trouble, was it not?'

'Yes, and I may tell you that the action of the government in respect to the Parihaka trouble against Te Whiti was of a very provoking character. Te Whiti took a very reasonable stand, and submitted to all the hardships imposed upon himself and his people by the then government. There was a smoldering feeling of resentment left in the native breast. . . .

'The white population have been clamoring for the native lands to be thrown open for settlement. I suppose the Maoris are feeling very nervous about it?'

'The Maoris quite agree that the Europeans ought to be able to obtain lands, and to have the whole matter settled under favorable conditions. The impression some people seem to have, that the Maori race desire to remain in a state of seclusion and to exclude Europeans from gaining a foothold, is entirely erroneous. We would welcome settlement but for the unfair terms imposed upon us by acts of Parliaments. . . .'

'And what are the aims of the movement now organizing?'

'Our first aim is to ask the New Zealand Parliament to grant to the natives a separate constitution, the main reason being that in former years and up to the present day every government has been passing experimental legislation with regard to the administration of native lands. This the natives find has been most detrimental to their interests, and therefore they consider that the time has now arrived when Parliament ought to allow them the right of making laws for the administration of their own properties. They base their right, first upon the treaty of Waitangi, and then upon the Constitution act of 1852. In the former case the Crown guarantees to the natives the full and exclusive right to their own lands.

163

In the latter case they are given the right to establish legal government among themselves. They contend that the provisions of the treaty have been violated, and in the latter case they have not had the opportunity or the privilege of obtaining the right set forth in Clause 71. The movement was first originated by the northern natives, and also a similar movement was made by the Waikato natives and on lands about there. . . . They are shown that the time has come to try and organize themselves into one body—in other words, to federate. By doing that they may be able to make themselves felt in the New Zealand Parliament in respect of their grievances and desires.'

'And how does the movement stand now?'

'The scheme of federation has been accepted by more than half of the natives of New Zealand now, and the organization is going on steadily toward success. The result of this abandoning of jealousies has been an actual federation amongst the native tribes and chiefs. Hereditary enemies have met, and casting aside the memories of former days of bloodshed, have made compact to stand by each other for the common good. . . .

L. Becke and J. D. Fitzgerald, 'The Maori. Politics and Social Life of the Native New Zealander', *Review of Reviews*, 1895, pp. 440–4

58. BILL FOR A MAORI PARLIAMENT, 1894

The 'Native Rights Bill' presented to the General Assembly by Hone Heke (M.H.R. for Northern Maori) in 1894.

AN ACT to empower the Aboriginal Natives of New Zealand to enact Laws for the Government of themselves and their Lands and other Property.

WHEREAS the legislation heretofore in force relating to Native lands and the powers of Native Lands Courts, and relative to property and rights of the aboriginal inhabitants of New Zealand, have been found to be and are inadequate and unjust, whereby the progress of a great part of the colony has been retarded, and the said aboriginal natives have been subject to great wrongs and grievances for which they have now no remedy: And whereas, by reason of the matters aforesaid, the said aboriginal natives have suffered much loss in lands and moneys and otherwise: And whereas it is to the benefit of both the European and aboriginal inhabitants of New Zealand that the said aboriginal natives and their lands and other property should be governed by laws enacted by themselves:

BE IT THEREFORE ENACTED by the General Assembly of New Zealand in Parliament assembled, and by the authority of the same, as follows:—

1. The Short Title of this Act is 'The Native Rights Act, 1894.'

2. A Constitution shall be granted to all the persons of the Maori race, and to all persons born of either father or mother of the Maori race who are or shall be resident in New Zealand, providing for the enactment of laws by a Parliament elected by such persons.

3. Such laws shall relate to and exclusively deal with the personal rights and with the lands and all other property of the aboriginal native inhabitants of New Zealand.

> *Bills Thrown Out,* 1894, Government Printer,
> Wellington

59. KING TAWHIAO'S CONSTITUTION, 1894

A translation published in a Wellington newspaper of the constitution for the 'Kingdom of Aoetearoa' adopted by the Kauhanganui. First published in Te Paki o Matariki, *the gazette of 'The Independent Royal Power of Aotearoa', Maungakawa, 12 April 1894.*

. . . notice to the 'Hapus and Tribes of New Zealand, from the tail to the head of Maui's fish, crossing the sea of Raukawa (Cook's Straits) to Te Waipounamu, that the following laws have been adopted by the Maori Kauhanganui (Convention), and assented to by King Potatau Tawhiao under his Royal seal and sign manual.'

1. That he has been pleased to appoint Taua Taingakawa Te Waharoa (son of the King-maker William Thompson) to be Premier of the Maori kingdom of Aotearoa.

2. That the Kauhanga (Convention) of manukura (nobles) and matariki (commoners) shall assemble on the 2nd of May in each year.

3. That the Convention shall then assemble before the Prime Minister and submit their deliberations (laws) to King Tawhiao on his throne.

4. Special provision will be made for those chiefs who may hereafter join the King movements that they shall be equal with the Europeans.

5. On 2nd May in each year returns will be published . . . of the amount raised by the Poll Tax of 2s. per head, and careful statements given showing the just and equitable expenditure of the same. . . .

6. Every Act of the Assembly must be confirmed by King Tawhiao by affixing the seal of the kingdom.

7. The leasing of land under the King's authority is assented to.

Sub-section (1) provides that land may be leased for a term not exceeding 22 years including kore-kore or 'lean' years; (2) each year is divided in three 'quarters' of four months, and rents all payable at end of each quarter, unless arranged differently between the contracting parties; (3) Any breach of agreement shall be followed by instant eviction and determination of the lease; (4) All metals—gold, silver, iron, copper, coal, road metal, clay for bricks or pottery—to belong to the State; (5) Leases only give the lessee power to graze stock and cultivate; (6) Arrangements may be made by which all metals, &c., can be acquired by the lessee; (7) The King reserves power to make public roads through such leased land, also for purpose of working any of the aforesaid metals; (8) Nothing growing on the land, such as timber and flax, shall be affected by the preceding sub-sections.

Clause 8.—Part 1 defines various classes of land, such as land which has not been affected by European laws. Claimants must apply to the Premier of the Kingdom for ascertainment of individual or tribal rights. Part 2—Native lands which have been dealt with by the European Native Land Court, being lands inherited by the Maoris from their ancestors, can be dealt with under the laws of the Kingdom. Part 3—For judgements and rehearings for lands dealt with by European laws special provision by regulations will be made.

Sub-section 1.—Lists of Maori owners' names to be given, &c., inclusive of halfcastes. It shall not be lawful for any halfcaste or halfcastes to set aside Maori rights or customs, nor to assume supreme control of the land; (2) halfcastes are defined as consisting 'only of those persons who are peaceful and law-abiding, who will not bring trouble and ruin upon their mother race;' (3) the Maori Government to have full power to enquire into and adjust any dispute or trouble of whatever kind. The European Government may take part in any such enquiry should it so desire, and it makes written application to, and obtains permission from, the Maori Premier.

Part 4.—Single individuals will not be permitted to force on surveys. Permission must be obtained from the Prime Minister after the whole of the reputed owners or tribe have expressed their covenance.

Part 5.—Defines Crown lands . . . lands which have been Crown granted, but since placed by the Maori owners under the King's protection. Maoris or Europeans having claims thereto must apply to the Premier in order to prevent confusion.

Sub-sections 1 to 4 provide for dealing with such lands in a 'spirit of truth and justice.' Where lands the lawful property of others have been wrongfully Crown-granted, such grants will be annulled. Then follow a number of amendments relating to the leasing of Crown-granted lands which have not been dealt with by Europeans.

Part 6.—Deals with gifts of lands, and with land placed by the owners under King Tawhiao's sovereignty.

Part 7.—Lands given to the missionaries for school endowments. Where the trusts have not been fulfilled, the area shall be assumed to be no more than five acres in each case, residue to revert to original owner.

Part 8.—Disputed lands not to be dealt with till all troubles connected therewith have been decided by the Maori tribunals.

9. Public lands to be dealt with under clauses 1 and 6.

10. Provides for the appointment of magistrates within the Maori kingdom, to uphold the laws, keep the peace, settle all disputes as to persons, live stock, property, offences, &c.

Laws as to marriage, under the ancient customs and manners of the Maori race.—

(1) If the parents, brothers, and the hapu generally, consent to the marriage of a girl with the man of her choice, the union shall be binding in law, without further ceremony. (2) If one or more of the parents or relations object to a marriage, then full enquiry shall be made to endeavour to remove reason of objection; but the wish of the majority must be final. (3) Under these laws it shall not be lawful for a Maori woman to marry a pakeha. Should the woman still cling to her European spouse, she may be given her own way, but she will henceforth be deemed 'a child of the night,' and an

167

outcast from the native race; such being ancient Maori custom. (4) No licenses shall be granted to individuals to perform the marriage ceremony.

Part 2.—Settlement of Europeans on the land.—It shall not be lawful for the owners of such land to locate Europeans upon any land whatever unless sanction is first obtained. Any natives so offending will be punished in the event of trouble and loss coming upon the European.

11. Makes regulations for printing the Paki o Matariki.

12. For the appointment of a capable person as editor, Government printer, &c.

13. The Government of the Maori kingdom have assented to the establishment of licensed stores in Maori districts under King Tawhiao's authority, but the sale of ardent spirits is strictly prohibited.

The names of ten chiefs are gazetted as Justices of the Peace in certain districts, 'all being good men and true.'

A number of chiefs notify that they have banded together to prevent the sale of spirits, and agree to fine every person breaking this agreement £5.

Issued by order of the Prime Minister of the Maori Kingdom.

(Sd.) T. T. RAWHITI.

The Evening Post, Wellington, 30 May 1894

60. THE MAORI COUNCILS ACT, 1900

'An Act to confer a Limited Measure of Local Self-government upon Her Majesty's Subjects of the Maori Race in the Colony', 18 October 1900.

WHEREAS reiterated applications have been made by the Maori inhabitants of those parts of the colony where the Maoris are more or less domiciled and settled, forming what is known as Maori centres and surroundings, for the establishment within those districts of some simple machinery of local self-government. . . .

BE IT THEREFORE ENACTED . . .

3. The Governor may proclaim any district a Maori district. . . .

6. For every Maori district established under this Act there shall be a Council consisting of the official member and of not less than six or more than twelve members to be elected from among

the Maoris of such-and-such a district as hereinafter provided; and the number of members shall be fixed by the Governor on the establishment of the district; and it shall be lawful for the Governor, by Proclamation, to subdivide any such district into convenient sections, and to appoint and declare the number of such members to be elected for each such section. . . .

8. In every Maori district established under this Act the Stipendiary Magistrate at the chief town within such district, or such other person as the Governor may from time to time appoint, shall be *ex officio* a member of such Council. . . .

15. It shall be the duty of the Council to formulate, and from time to time report to the Governor upon, a general plan that would be acceptable to the Maoris of the district, and be best adapted for the purposes following; that is to say,—

(1.) For ascertaining, providing, and prescribing for the observance and enforcement of the rights, duties, and liabilities, amongst themselves, of tribes, communities, or individuals of the Maori race, in relation to all social and domestic matters.

(2.) For the suppression of injurious Maori customs, and for the substitution of remedies and punishments for injuries in cases in which compensation is now sought by means of such customs.

(3.) For the promotion of education and instruction, both ordinary and technical, and the conduct and management of Native schools.

(4.) And generally for the promotion of the health and welfare and moral well-being of the Maori inhabitants of the district. . . .

And it shall be the duty of the Council to collect and tabulate facts and statistics in relation to, and to report to the Governor upon, the following matters:—

(1.) The general health of the Maori inhabitants of the district, the causes of death as far as it is possible to ascertain them;

(2.) The movement of the population, the extent of consanguineous connections or marriages and their effect, and the extent of the absorption of the Native race by inter-marriage with Europeans;

(3.) The number of persons engaged in industrial pursuits and the nature of such pursuits, the extent of land cultivated or under pasture, and the number and nature of stock depasturing thereon;

(4.) And other matters that the Council may deem necessary in order that the Governor may know from time to time the condition of the Native race, the fluctuations of population, the causes of decrease of population if there is a decrease, any influences that may be at work to ameliorate the condition of the race, and the progress that may be made towards the adoption of healthier habits and pursuits.

16. It shall be lawful for the Council of any Maori district constituted under this Act to make, and from time to time vary or revoke, by-laws respecting all or any of the matters following, that is to say,—

[Health. Cleansing of houses. Common nuisances, Drunkenness. Tohungas. Meeting-houses. Dogs. Branding of cattle, &c. Eel-weirs. Oyster-beds, &c. Burial-grounds. Recreation-grounds. Hawkers. Smoking. Gambling. Water-supplies. Sanitation. Diseases of animals.] . . .

17. The Council shall have power to appoint from among the Maoris of any Maori kainga, village, or pa a Committee of not less than three or more than five, who shall be called the Village Committee (Komiti Marae), and who shall, subject to the control of the Council, order the abatement or removal of any nuisance, or the destruction of rubbish likely to prove detrimental to the Maori inhabitants of any Maori town, village, or pa; who shall enforce the proper sanitation of all whares or other buildings. . . .

29. A general Conference of delegates from the Councils may be held annually. . . .

> *New Zealand Statutes*, 1900, 64 Vict., no. 48, pp. 252–60

61. THE MAORI LANDS ADMINISTRATION ACT, 1900

'An Act to provide for the Administration of Maori Lands', 20 October 1900. The district Maori Land Councils were to have a non-Maori majority.

WHEREAS the chiefs and other leading Maoris of New Zealand, by petition to Her Majesty and to the Parliament of New Zealand, urged that the residue (about five million acres) of the Maori land now remaining in possession of the Maori owners should be reserved for their use and benefit in such wise as to protect them from the risk of being left landless: And whereas it is expedient, in the interests both of the Maoris and Europeans of the colony, that provision should be made for the better settlement and utilisation of large areas of Maori land at present lying unoccupied and unproductive, and for the encouragement and protection of the Maoris in efforts of industry and self-help: And whereas it is necessary also to make provision for the prevention, by the better administration of Maori lands, of useless and expensive dissensions and litigation, in manner hereinafter set forth:

BE IT THEREFORE ENACTED . . .

PART I

PRELIMINARY

3. In this Act, if not inconsistent with the context,— . . .

'Maori land' means any land or estate or interest in land in New Zealand held, or which may hereinafter be held, by any Maori under any class of title, and includes papatupu land, but does not include,—

(*a*.) Land which, although owned by a Native, has been acquired in fee-simple by purchase from the Crown or a European: nor

(*b*.) Land which is subject to or administered under the provisions of any of the following Acts, that is to say,—

'The Taiaroa Land Act, 1883,'

'The Westland and Nelson Native Reserves Act, 1887,'

'The West Coast Settlement Reserves Act, 1892,'

'The Native Townships Act, 1895,'

'The Urewera District Native Reserves Act, 1896,' and

'The Kapiti Island Public Reserves Act, 1897';

nor

(*c*.) Native land in the Middle Island or Stewart Island, or any other lands controlled by any other special Act: . . .

'Papatupu land' means any land claimed or owned by Maoris the title to which has not yet been investigated and determined: . . .

'Papakainga' means an inalienable reserve set aside for the occupation and support of any person of the Maori race. . . .

171

PART II

DISTRICTS AND COUNCILS

As to Districts

5. For the purposes of this Act there shall be within the North Island of New Zealand not less than six Maori land districts. . . .

As to Councils

6. For each Maori land district there shall be a Maori Land Council, . . . and shall consist of not more than seven and not less than five members, to wit,—

(1.) A President, to be appointed by the Governor. . . .

(2.) Not less than two nor more than three other persons to be appointed by the Governor, one of whom shall be a Maori.

(3.) Not less than two nor more than three Maoris to be elected by the Maoris of the district out of their number.

(4.) No elected Maori shall be a member of more than one Council. . . .

PART III

POWERS OF COUNCIL AND ADMINISTRATION OF MAORI LANDS WITHIN EACH DISTRICT

9. The Council shall, in respect of all Maori lands within its district, have and exercise all the powers now possessed by the Native Land Court as to ascertainment of ownership, partition, succession, the definition of relative interests, and the appointment of trustees for Native owners under disability:

Provided that the Council shall not proceed to exercise its powers in any matter under this section unless and until directed so to do by the Chief Judge of the Native Land Court. . . .

As to Papatupu Block Committees

16. Maoris claiming to be the owners of any specified block of papatupu land within a district may, in the prescribed manner, elect a committee, to be called 'the Papatupu Committee of the Block'; and with respect to such committee the following provisions shall apply:—

(1.) The committee shall consist of such number of persons, being not less than five nor more than nine, as is prescribed.

(2.) In no case shall a member of the Council be a member of the committee.

(3.) The term of office of each member of the committee shall

172

be three years, but retiring members shall be eligible for re-election; and every election shall be held at such time and place as the Council appoints.

(4.) Subject to regulations under this Act, the committee may direct its own procedure.

17. The committee, having due regard to Maori customs and usages, shall make full investigation into the ownership of the block, and, as the result of such investigation, shall cause a sketch-plan of the block to be prepared by an authorised surveyor setting forth the situation and boundaries of the block, adopting hapu boundaries as far as practicable. . . .

As to Papakaingas

21. With respect to all Maori lands within the district of the Council the following special provisions shall apply:—

(1.) The Council shall with all convenient speed proceed to ascertain and determine what land each Maori man, woman, or child has suitable for his, her, or its occupation and support, and to determine how much thereof and what portion is necessary to be a papakainga for each such Maori for his or her maintenance and support and to grow food upon, and shall issue a papakainga certificate declaring that such land is a papakainga for such Maori, and notice of such allocation shall be given by the Council to such Maori preparatory to the issue of a certificate therefor.

(2.) Such land shall be absolutely inalienable. . . .

As to Alienation

22. Immediately upon the coming into operation of this Act, Maori land shall not be alienated by way of lease either to the Crown or to any other person except with the consent of the Council first obtained, and in accordance with the provisions of this Act. In the case of alienation by way of sale where the land belongs to more than two owners, the consent of the Governor in Council to such sale shall be first had and obtained; in the case of alienation by way of sale where the land belongs to not more than two owners, the passing of this Act shall in no way affect the same unless the land is transferred to the Council.

23. No Maori shall alienate any Maori land, either to the Crown or to any other person, unless and until he has had issued to him a papakainga certificate as hereinbefore provided, or he is able

to produce the notice of the Council that lands have been allocated to him preparatory to the issue of a papakainga certificate therefor, as provided in section twenty-one hereof.

24. For the purposes of this Act the Governor may, on the recommendation of the Council, remove and revoke any and all restrictions existing against the alienation of Maori land, whether contained in any Crown grant certificate or other instrument of title, or in any Act heretofore passed; and thereafter, but subject in every case to the provisions of this Act, the Maori owners of the land against the alienation whereof the restrictions have been so removed and revoked shall have the same rights and privileges to alienate the land as a European possesses in respect of his land:

Provided that nothing in this Act contained shall be construed to authorise the alienation of papakaingas. . . .

29. With respect to any Maori land which is duly transferred as aforesaid to the Council the following provisions shall apply:—

(1.) The Council shall have full power and authority, at the request in writing of a majority of owners, to reserve and render inalienable such portion of such land as may be required for their occupation and support, and also to reserve any land as burial-grounds, eel-pas or eel-weirs, fishing-grounds, or as reserves for the protection of native birds, or the conservation of timber and fuel for the future use of the Maori owners.

(2.) As regards the balance of such land, but subject to the provisions of the instrument creating such trust, the Council shall have full power and authority to lease the same by public tender upon such terms and conditions as may to it seem fit. . . .

New Zealand Statutes, 1900, 64 Vict., no. 55, pp. 469–83

62. INTEGRATION BY THE MIDDLE OF THE TWENTIETH CENTURY?

Dr. Maui Pomare, then a district health officer under the Maori Councils Act (1900), comments on improving health conditions in Maori villages and predicts that there will be a fusion of the races into 'a new race entirely' in fifty years.

. . . 'On the West Coast of this island, the natives have made splendid progress. They have abandoned the whares, and are living in cottages which would compare well with those in the cities. They have a water supply laid on, and their slaughter-house is an up-to-date building which would be an object lesson to many European communities, the abbatoir being floored with concrete, and having a plentiful water supply. In the South Island and in the Wairarapa district they have reached a high level, and considerable improvement is visible in Hawke's Bay.' . . .

'Among the Ngapuhis great improvement is manifest. Three sanitary inspectors are employed there, and they have done a vast amount of good. Progress has not been so rapid among the Waikatos, and in the King Country where there are no sanitary inspectors, but opportunities will probably be made shortly. The Kingite influence has retarded progress there. The Urewera natives are gradually improving their domestic conditions, but the prophet Rua is keeping them back.

'. . . they still believ in him; he is established on the borders of the Urewera country, inland from Whakatane, where he presides over a kind of court. At his instructions the natives are keeping their children away from the schools, and is thus further interfering with the progress of the tribes. . . . Where two superior races meet they are bound to fuse; but where the line of demarcation is wide, as between negroes and whites, then they will never fuse. In the South Island 80 per cent of the natives have European blood in their veins, this within fifty years. In another fifty years there will be a new race entirely. . . .'

Auckland Star, 14 February, 1907, p. 5

63. THE PROPHET RUA TAPUNUI HEPETIPA

Account of a visit to Rua's settlement at Maungapohatu in the Urewera Counry in 1908. The reporter records Rua's intention of improving the conditions of the Maoris.

. . . Rua impressed me as a very charming personage, and the reverse of the overbearing despot one expected to meet. He affects European clothes, and is scrupulously clean. The profusion of hair completely removes any resemblance to the Maori, as he is commonly known; in fact, the greater number of his followers have rather the appearance of Mexican-Indians. Others remind one forcibly of the fuzzy-headed Fijian, while those who allow their hair to fall down in ringlets after the manner of their leader have a great likeness to the characters depicted in Scriptural illustrations, which is perhaps not surprising, considering that they take these old Israelites for a pattern. As far as I could learn only Rua affects a plurality of wives.

. . . Rua's strong point is his religion, which seems to be a mixture of the Old Testament and the New, and cannot, perhaps, be better described than as a slightly modernised form of Hauhauism. He poses as the Messiah come to save the world again, and takes pride in drawing attention to what he thinks is his remarkable resemblance to the Saviour, proudly pointing to several coloured oleographs that adorn the walls of his room, in support of his contention. . . . He emphasises the fact that he is not preaching 'Maoriland for the Maoris,' but is really Europeanising Maori customs and ways. He strongly objects to being called a tohunga or prophet, claiming to be above them in his desire for the better-ment of his race. He insists that the pakeha is more than foolish (though admitting that he is actuated by good motives) in trying to lift the Maori to his level with a few short years of schooling, whereas, it has taken the white man many centuries to reach his present standard of enlightenment. Questioned as to his reasons for withdrawing the children of his followers from the schools specially erected for their benefit, he said that after leaving these places most of the children soon forgot what had been taught them educationally, but never forgot the vices that frequently come in its train. In his settlement (which he likened at present to a child in short clothes), the children had no bad example of smoking and drinking before them, and when his village was properly established they would be taught the use of tools and farming. . . . Speaking of the old Maori style of living, he said he disliked those who lived in filth. In his settlement he was trying to induce all who came into his fold to adopt European ways as much as possible. . . .

. . . The village, built upon the lands of Rua's parents 8000 acres of which he claims to be entitled to, consists, roughly speaking, of 50 dwellings of the split-paling variety, though the great man's residence of 16 rooms and portions of his tabernacle (of which more anon) are built of good pit-sawn timber. There are several streets (?), a store, butchery, and a council office, in connection with which a bank has been opened. A number of smaller huts and tents are scattered about the hillside, which will be done away with so soon as the present occupants erect more pretentious structures. The land has been denuded of its heavy rimu forest, cleared, and the whole place laid out in less than eight months, which speaks well for the energy of the Maori when he has an object in view. . . . the great man insists that his followers must be cleanly in person and dwelling, that food shall be served on raised benches in buildings set apart for the purpose, and that platter of a kind and cutlery shall be in daily use. The old Maori style is done away with, and meals are served three times a day after the manner of the pakeha. . . .

Near the centre of the village, occupying a prominent position, Rua's house, a single storey, two-gabled structure, roofed with rubberoid, has been placed. A verandah stands at either end, and the whole building, including doors and window-sashes, has been cut out of the virgin bush, and put together by native labour and brains. At the present time calico is used as a substitute for window-panes, but the necessary glass is already on hand. The front verandah boasts of a peculiar decorative finish, having, I was told, some kind of Biblical significance. Service is held twice daily, at seven a.m. and three p.m., before this dwelling, which is known as 'Hiruharama hou' (the new Jerusalem), Rua being conspicuous by his absence, though at times he appears later on and harangues his people. The service, consisting mostly of chanting in Maori, and the reading of a short chapter from the Old Testament, is conducted by one of the elders. . . . The most striking feature of the settlement is the tabernacle, or house of parliament, a peculiar spherical-shaped structure surmounted by a smaller rounded conical-roofed storey, in which the business of the place is debated. From two entrances placed on opposite sides of the building, railed stairways lead up to an elevated rostrum, which occupies the middle of the lower room. In the centre of this platform, a rotunda-shaped cupboard, with a circular table and nest of lockers running round its outside, has been built. Two witness-boxes, one half-moon in shape and the other square, standing at the head of the stairways, in close proximity to the platform, give the place a sort of Police Court appearance. Light is admitted by the removal of ingeniously-arranged wooden shutters, completely encircling the building. Several tiers of high-backed circular benches, filling the intervening space between the rostrum and wall, complete the inside fittings of the lower compartment. The only internal connection between this room and the upper one is a funnel-shaped orifice directly above the platform, but admittance is gained to this storey (which, minus rostrum and benches, is a smaller fac-simile of the one just described) by means of an outside stairway, on one side of which a belfry is in course of construction. In here, but out of sight of those below, Rua sits alone and listens to the discussions of his elders, and when occasion demands passes judgment. A strange decorative border of clubs and diamonds painted in two colours alternately, runs round the outside, while a fiery comet, and what may be described as a pair of inverted monograms, add to the general grotesque appearance of this extraordinary structure. Probably the most remarkable thing in connection with this unique edifice, which is a model of native skill and ingenuity, is that the builders had no idea of what sort of building they were called upon to erect, simply taking their instructions from day to day from Rua, who superintended the erection personally, and who is responsible for the design. . . .

The New Zealand Herald, 20 April 1908, p. 7

64. THE RATANA MOVEMENT

About the time of the influenza epidemic, 1918, Tahupotiki Wiremu Ratana, a farmer in the Wanganui area, had visions and soon began a mission of healing which attracted mass support among Maoris. Both the King Movement and the churches were divided over Ratana and in 1925 the Ratana Church was registered. In 1928 Ratana turned to political action and called for four 'Quarters' to win the Maori seats. Eruera Tirikatene, the first successful Ratana candidate made his maiden speech in the House of 29 September 1932.

(a) *From the Creed of the Ratana Church.*

1. I believe in Jehovah—Father, Son and Holy Ghost—the Creator of all things that do exist, and the Author of all life, Who in Infinite Wisdom and Love presides over all His creation. . . .

7. I believe, as Jesus Christ has taught us, that Jehovah is our Heavenly Father, and all men are brethren; that all our labours should be, not for personal gain, but in co-operation with each other as co-workers with Jehovah for the benefit

of mankind and the honour of God. That all men should be honest workers and in love and justice and knowledge each bear his share of the burden of life thus serving Jehovah and his fellow men. . . .

10. I believe that Tahupotiki Wiremu Ratana is a mouthpiece of Jehovah, spreading abroad new light as the above truths concerning the salvation of the spirit and the vitalising of the body.

> English copy of creed deposited with the Registrar General, 21 July 1925. Appendix 2, J. McLeod Henderson, *Ratana. The Origins and the Story of the Movement*, Wellington, Polynesian Society, 1963, pp. 118–19

(b) *From Eruera Tirikatene's maiden speech in Parliament, 29 September 1932.*

. . . I have been returned to this honourable House as an independent member, to see that the interests of the Maori people are restored. I represent the Ratana party, which is practically a household name throughout the Dominion and across the seas. My policy is to stand for the rights and privileges of the whole Maori race, as embodied in the Treaty of Waitangi, standing foursquare. . . .

N.Z.P.D., 1932, vol. 233, p. 120

4

POLITICAL DEVELOPMENTS, 1870s TO 1919

65. A CALL FOR LIBERAL AND CONSERVATIVE PARTIES, 1876

Robert Stout, Member for Dunedin East, denounces 'Oligarchy', Localism, and Ministerial domination, in a speech to the House of Representatives on 18 August 1876, when he called for 'Liberal' and 'Conservative' parties.

. . . Sir, I look upon the course adopted with reference to this Counties Bill as one of the curses of the want of party in this House. I admit that the existence of parties is attended with a great number of evils; but I ask, if you have no party, what would happen in any representative body? A representative body would be landed in chaos. What does it mean? It means that there should be no such thing as proper legislation in this House, but Ministers will be able to do what they please, because, if there is no organized Opposition, what happens? Ministers are masters of the situation. . . . I can understand in New Zealand two kinds of parties. I can understand what may be termed a Central party, or a Country party, and a Provincial party. That is a fair battle-ground, and let them fight it out, each trying to win, because I conceive that any member and all members must have ideas upon this constitutional question. I can conceive, Sir, what may be a Conservative party and a Democratic party. . . . But if you are going to obliterate all these party distinctions, as you are actually doing, and have done since 1870, what will be the result? It would tend to create national life, to have created a broad line of demarcation between two parties in this House. If we had Conservative and Liberal parties, or even a Provincial party, as opposed to a Centralist party, this Parliament would have done far more to promote national life than by passing a Counties Bill. . . . those honorable members who talk of national life have never yet risen up to the conception of that which creates a nation. It is not by merely cutting up a lot of districts, and allowing them to quarrel over roads and bridges. . . . Parliament has ceased to be a Parliament in anything but name, and has become a huge Board of Works, in which every member scrambles to get all he can for his own district. That is the way in which this Parliament has been drifting; and do honorable members believe that by passing the Counties Bill, and by creating a property class in this colony, and by giving over to them all the administration of this colony, excepting the administration of railways, the telegraph, postal service, and a few marine matters, which will be left to the people of New Zealand, everything else being vested in the property class, who are to be the rulers of New Zealand—do honorable members believe this is the way to raise a great nation? How do nations grow? One has only to look to history to see that no nation has ever grown to be great that has been an oligarchy. That nation will only grow to greatness that gives, in the true spirit of national life, to every man equal rights with his neighbour, and tells him to look upon that country as his home. . . .

N.Z.P.D., 1876, vol. 21, pp. 481–2

66. A RADICAL PROGRAMME, 1877

Speech by Sir George Grey during the taxation debate, 17 August 1877, in which he advocates changing the basis of taxation from Customs Duties to Land and Income Taxes in order to 'raise up a race of freemen in New Zealand'.

Sir G. GREY said,—I move as an amendment, to be added to the resolution, That the system of taxation should immediately be altered with the view to impose taxes upon income and property, and relieve the people of the colony from some onerous Customs duties now paid. . . . It is monstrous that the labouring population of New Zealand—the industrious portion of the population—should have to pay the far larger part of the interest upon those enormous sums that have been spent in giving value to the property of the wealthy. . . .

Why should not those people who have despoiled the Native race of immense tracts of land be compelled to pay a tax for what they hold? . . . With an income-tax which would not be levied on incomes below a certain amount, and a property-tax which would touch the large landed estates, we should have a system of taxation that would fall fairly on all alike. . . . Then let that taxation increase in proportion to the extent of the property. Let it increase fairly and justly, and you will soon have an income from that source alone; and you will save the country from that gigantic evil of an aristocracy with enormous tracts of land, unfairly acquired in many instances, which is growing up in it—an aristocracy which every effort is being made to build up here by the aristocracy at Home. . . .

. . . whilst the income-tax should perhaps not touch incomes below a certain amount, I thought that portion of the property-tax which touched land should be imposed upon even small landed properties, so that every individual, in so far as practicable, not only in indirect taxation, but also in direct taxation, should contribute to the revenue of the country, which, in some respects, I regarded as a common guarantee fund by contributions to which during a great part of his lifetime and the period of health and strength each man in New Zealand might establish a claim to relief from the State if he fell into sickness, destitution, or helpless infirmity in old age. I contended that to make him contribute to the taxation of this country in every possible respect was to educate him as a free man, to train him in habits of self-respect, and to make him know that, if he was compelled to claim assistance from the public, he claimed a right—which I believe would not be often claimed, for provision for many cases would be made by societies or clubs, such as benefit societies or similarly-managed institutions, which would, in ordinary cases, provide for sickness. . . . That is the plan which I propose, and I do not know that I really can add anything to this outline. I think it presents this advantage: that it will raise up a race of freemen in New Zealand who will take a great interest in the country, from a feeling that representation in this House is equal. . . .

N.Z.P.D., 1877, vol. 24, pp. 499–502, 505–7

67. A LIBERAL PARTY

Speeches by Sir George Grey, the Premier, and John Ballance, during a debate on a 'no confidence' motion in the House of Representatives, 29 October 1877.

Sir G. GREY . . .

The House is ranging itself into two great parties. . . . Honorable gentlemen who think with me have been taunted with what are called their radical principals. Sir, we care nothing for such taunts. We are determined to establish a policy for the people—a policy for the country at large. We have resolved that in New Zealand there shall be a party of progress, as well as a party of conservative notions. What is conservatism? We know what it is in Great Britain. There it is a time-honored institution, the growth indeed of centuries, meant to uphold and to conserve principles and traditions which are potent elements in a great monarchical country. What is conservatism to honorable gentlemen opposite? To them, Sir, it means a conservatism of place and power—of privileges which they have usurped against the interests of their fellow-subjects in this colony. To them it is the maintenance of the undue right of acquiring place, and land, and wealth. Let them strive for all this. Let them strive to keep their fellow-countrymen out of a due share of influence and of the direction of public affairs in this House. We, Sir, will strive to allow the people to have a fair share of the direction of public affairs. For years those honorable gentlemen have withheld advantages from their fellow-countrymen—have shut them out of a due share of influence and of the direction of public affairs in this House. . . . We will try to change all that, Sir. We will strive to do our best to initiate a policy by which equal laws may exist in this country for all; laws under which every family may hope to obtain its home and its land, and under which the best of the land of the country shall not be given unfairly, often in vast tracts, to the friends of the Government. A new era is dawning, new times are coming, and new men will soon be found in this House. New principles will prevail, and I believe that in New Zealand will be established that great principle that all men have equal rights in the property and in the lands of the colony—that the Crown lands are the property of all, and not of a party of squatters. . . .

Mr. BALLANCE.— . . .

I will conclude by expressing the opinion that the way to create and consolidate a Liberal party in this country is to defeat the present Government. That the elements of a Liberal party exist on this side of the House I have no doubt whatever. Your 'unity of the colony' and your 'seat of Government' questions are not really at issue. They are dead issues which you are attempting to galvanize into life. The great question of the day is the question of Liberalism *versus* Conservatism—of advance and progress in all matters of

public policy *versus* monopoly and antagonism to progress. We have these two parties, and there is no doubt whatever about the question. . . .

N.Z.P.D., 1877, vol. 26, pp. 489, 542

68. A LAND TAX OF A HALFPENNY IN THE POUND ON LAND EXCEEDING £500 IN VALUE, 1878

Speech by John Ballance, Colonial Treasurer in the Grey Government, to the House Committee of Ways and Means, on the Financial Statement for the year, 6 August 1878.

. . . The policy of opening up for settlement the lands of the colony by means of railways, roads, and other works, executed out of loans contracted in the foreign market, has entailed upon the colony a heavy responsibility in the form of interest, which has reached on the total debt a sum of about a million and a quarter annually. On the other hand, one of the most marked effects of that policy has been to enhance the value of all property—especially land— which derives a permanent benefit from the extension of the railway system and other means of communication. The increase in the value of land is due to the additions which the population has received by means of assisted immigration in a degree scarcely inferior to that caused by public works, and, as the same cause will continue in existence, a similar result may confidently be expected. The exemption of this accumulating wealth—land—from contributing to the general revenue of the colony has been condemned by the House as unjust to those who have been paying on the perishable necessaries of life the principal portion of the taxation. We propose, therefore, to extend the taxable basis, with the double object of establishing more firmly the finance and credit of the colony, and of fairly adjusting the fiscal burdens according to the capacity of the different classes to bear them.

And here I may take the opportunity of disclaiming and repudiating the charge which is sometimes made, that the Government have in contemplation a class tax. The very contrary is the fact. We hold that the system which we propose to correct has worked unfairly in the past, that it has favoured the escape from taxation of the greater portion of the wealth of the colony, and has implanted a strong sense of injustice in the minds of the wages class. . . .

. . . We believe that no form of wealth is more legitimately called upon to contribute a portion of the public revenue of the colony than the value of land *minus* improvements, which, for brevity, I shall call the unimproved value, as no other commodity increases so rapidly in value from the increase of population and the natural progress of a country. By exempting improvements we award a premium to industry, and discourage a system of speculation which thrives only upon the labour of others. . . . The principle, then, we propose is, to tax the actual value to sell, *minus* improvements, embracing both town and country, with a re-valuation every third year. . . . Every holder will be entitled to claim an exemption to the extent of £500 on the total value of all his holdings, and no one will be called upon to pay the tax the value of whose property is not more than that sum. The leaseholder, except where the lease is held from the Crown, will have the right to deduct from his rent at the time of payment the amount of the tax. The minimum unimproved value of land will be fixed at a pound an acre. . . .

. . . We propose that property under this head shall contribute a halfpenny in the pound, which on £50,000,000 will yield to the revenue a sum of £104,166, or in round numbers say £100,000. The net gain to the revenue will, however, not reach this amount by £10,000, the estimated cost of valuations and collection. The Government believe their proposals on this subject will be received as characterized by fairness and moderation, as founded on a principle just in itself, and so applied as to inflict the least hardship on any class of the community. . . .

N.Z.P.D., 1878, vol. 28, pp. 88, 90–1

69. THE LACK OF PARTY DIVISIONS IN THE HOUSE OF REPRESENTATIVES, 1882

A few months after resigning from the Premiership in April 1882, John Hall comments on the 'unreality of political divisions in New Zealand'.

It is true we have been sitting on opposite sides of the House, but there has not been much opposition between us in matters of principle. Our case I think illustrates the unreality of political divisions in New Zealand, if they are supposed to represent real differences of principle. Where, since the settlement of the provincial question, is the real difference in political principle between 3/4ths of our public men? Stout & Hutchison differ in toto from you and me—and Grey differs from everybody, himself included; and beyond this, & a few others, the differences are mainly personal & accidental—and men sitting on opposite sides often are more nearly in agreement, than are members of the same party, or even of the same cabinet—I don't see how this can be cured, or even whether it is desirable to cure. Much the same state of things seems growing up at home. It secures moderate compromises. In our own case, sorry as I was to see you the other side of the mace, I was consoled by the belief that to your experience and moderation we owe it, that many crude, rash and dangerous proposals were modified— . . . It has been very slow & unsatisfactory, owing chiefly to the evenly balanced state of parties— The opposition also is split into two divisions, apparently quite irreconcilable, altho' their differences are ostensibly only personal. . . .

> John Hall to William Gisborne, 10 August 1882, Hall Letter Books, vol. ii, pp. 173–4. General Assembly Library, Wellington

70. PROPOSAL FOR A NATIONAL INSURANCE SCHEME, 1882

Speech by Major Harry Atkinson in the House of Representatives, 10 July 1882, proposing a resolution that provision should be made against sickness and pauperism by compulsory national insurance.

. . . We see malign influences and agencies at work in all old countries which seem to be producing more and more destitution as the nation advances in material prosperity. In other words, as the aggregate of wealth increases so does the unevenness of its distribution. . . . the truth must be apparent to all that the line is being made sharper and sharper between the enormously rich and the wretchedly poor. These agencies, whatever they are, are ascribed by various classes of thought to different causes. Those who think with Malthus set them down to over-population in all old and densely-peopled countries. Those who think with George ascribe our woes to the monopoly of land—that is, the private ownership of land—which enables the landlord by means of rent to obtain far more than his fair share of the profits arising from the soil; while others, like Musgrave, believe that it is the middle-man—the merchant, the distributor—who, through the economic laws which govern our system of unlimited competition, succeeds in obtaining the lion's share at the expense of the landowners, the labourers, and the producing capitalists. But, be the causes what they may, the authorities are all but universally agreed that they exist and are in full operation, and are illustrated in every country which has passed a certain stage of its growth. After very carefully watching this matter it seems to me that these agencies are gradually extending their baneful influence over this colony, and that the state of things which I have described is present here, and increasing in intensity. The ratio of expenditure upon hospitals and charitable aid and benevolent institutions is gradually increasing in proportion to our population, and, as far as we can see, the ratio will steadily increase, and unless we take some special course—unless we can devise some means to remedy the evil that is coming upon us —we must be prepared to see a large number of persons supported by private charity, or public charity, or both. Then, Sir, must follow inevitably, as it seems to me, a poor-law, and I venture to think that no greater curse would come upon any country—upon this country, not to generalize—than the English poor-law in all its intensity. . . . We have then to consider in what way we can provide against destitution without demoralizing the people. I think it must be evident to all that private thrift is quite useless in this matter, because it must take considerable time to insure any result, and is absolutely powerless to provide against premature sickness or death. The only effectual remedy against pauperism seems to me to be not private thrift or saving, but co-operative thrift or insurance, and that to be thoroughly successful, I venture to think I can show before I sit down, it must be national and compulsory. . . .

. . . Now, I would ask, what are we doing as a nation to prevent the spread of pauperism? I think the answer of every honorable member must be, 'Practically nothing.' We grant charitable aid, we have benevolent institutions and hospitals, but they are merely temporary palliatives. They do not touch the root of the evil, and, while undoubtedly they relieve much misery, they also tend to produce much evil. The only efforts that are being made upon sound principles are those of the friendly societies, and I say all honor to those twenty thousand men, good and true, who are doing their utmost to suppress poverty and destitution. . . . But, from the very nature of their organization, they are powerless to deal with the question of national poverty. That can only be dealt with by the nation itself. . . . I think, by the process of elimination, we may come to the conclusion that national and compulsory insurance is the only mode of meeting the difficulty; and, if honorable members have followed me so far, they will, I hope, admit that a strong case has been made out for the necessity of some action in this matter. And now I come to the practicability of the scheme: and first I would like to say a few words with regard to the minimum fixed. . . . I do not think the State has a right to ask its subjects to provide a minimum which would be more than sufficient to cover the necessities that we propose to provide for; but the amount I have fixed has been arrived at by inquiry as to the least amount which the most economical benevolent societies find to be sufficient to keep the people they are called upon to provide for. . . . We propose as a minimum that every man and woman, being single and between the ages of eighteen and sixty-five, shall receive, when ill, 15s. a week; that married men shall receive 22s. 6d., and married women 7s. 6d. between the same ages. This is a mere arbitrary division between married people. Husband and wife will be each entitled to 15s.; but it seemed desirable, as the man is usually the bread-winner of the family, and if he is sick the arrangements of the family are thrown out to a much greater extent than by the sickness of the wife, to give the man the larger amount, and the smaller amount to the woman. . . . The proposal is that every young man and young woman should pay into a fund £41. 1s. 4d. between the ages of sixteen and twenty-three, or £41. 17s. 1d. between eighteen and twenty-three. If they began their payments at sixteen, they would have to pay at the rate of 2s. 3d. per week; if they began their payments at eighteen, they would have to pay at the rate of 3s. 3d. per week. The total payment that could be made, if they paid the amount down, would be £36. 3s. 9d. at the age of sixteen, or £38. 7s. at the age of eighteen. Now, this amount of £41. 1s. 4d. at the age of sixteen, or £41. 17s. 1d. at the age of eighteen, paid at the rate I have mentioned, would provide sick-pay up to sixty-five years, and an annuity of 10s. a week after that age until death; but there is no provision in that for orphans, and each man and each woman would have to continue a payment of about 2s. per week each, or about £5 a year, for another five years; and that would give what I have stated as an orphan benefit of 15s. for each woman and one child up to 30s. a week, according to the size of the family. Thus the total payment from each man and each woman would be between £66 and £67 to obtain the whole of the benefits named, spread over a period of from ten to twelve years, thus showing that an average payment of about 2*s.* a week for twelve years would be all that was necessary to make the required provision. . . . Then, assuming that the necessary provision can be made, we want to consider the machinery by which we can secure the premiums. There is no doubt that it would be necessary to divide the colony into districts, coterminous with the districts of the local bodies; the local bodies would be charged with the duties of registration within their own boundaries. . . . Each person coming of age would receive a pass-book showing the amount to be paid by him, with a column showing the amounts as paid in by him, and every employer would be bound to pay in at the nearest Post Office Savings-Bank the weekly or monthly instalment which might be due by any of his employés; the right being reserved to him to stop the amount due from wages earned. . . . Every one who has made one payment will be entitled to the full benefit, and no one who has made any payment can ever lose his right in respect of that payment. There will be no forfeiture—the premiums cover all that. . . .

. . . I am told that we are going outside the proper functions of Government. Well, I would be very glad if any honorable gentleman who thinks so would tell me what the proper functions of Government are. I entirely disagree with writers of the Herbert Spencer class who would confine the functions of Government simply to police duties. I would ask, what is the meaning of civilization but combination; and what is the meaning of a State but that we all band together to do certain things and to promote certain ends that we desire? In this country the Government has already done many things which fifty years ago the greatest Radical would probably have declared quite beyond the functions of Government. We have State railways, State telegraph, State post office saving-banks, and last, though not least, State education, all of which in their turn have been declared entirely beyond the proper functions of Government, and ruinous to the independence of the people who adopt them. But I will point out this fact: that nothing can be done nowadays without combination, and that the practical wisdom of a nation is shown not in talking about what are and what are not the proper functions of Government, but in deciding whether a particular object which it is desired to promote can with the greatest advantage be undertaken by the Government or by private enterprise. And so, when . . . I beg one and all to give this matter their very serious consideration. It is a subject of the greatest importance to this country. It is a subject we must deal with if we are not going to see the same terrible effects of poverty and misery that exist in the Old Country. Now is the time, when we are comparatively rich—when we can put by—when we can start the population in a course which will, as it were, protect them from themselves, and make proper provision for themselves when old or sick. I see that one of the papers describes me as desirous of turning New Zealand into one great benefit society; and that is advanced as a matter of reproach. All I can say is, I should be delighted if I could have a hand in doing it; for I am convinced that if, from one end of the country to the other, every man belonged to a benefit society the nation would be more independent and prosperous than it is possible for us under our present arrangements to conceive of. Sir, I hope it will yet be said of this Parliament, the first elected under universal suffrage, that it was prepared to face this difficulty and to deal with it, if not upon the lines I have submitted, at all events upon some other better lines that any honorable member may propose, so that the difficulty may be faced and dealt with, and the fear of having repeated in New Zealand the amount of misery and wretchedness that prevails in the Old Country disposed of once and for ever. . . .

N.Z.P.D., 1882, vol. 42, pp. 183–90

71. BRITAIN—MORTGAGEE AS WELL AS SUZERAIN

Sir William F. D. Jervois, the Governor, comments on the indebtedness of the Australasian colonies to the United Kingdom, in a dispatch to the Secretary of State, Lord Knutsford, 16 May 1888.

. . . The condition of these Colonies is highly artificial. This is chiefly due to the discovery of precious metals and to unlimited credit. Their growth has not been gradual and healthy, but forced and unnatural. . . . Australasia with an aggregate population of $3\frac{1}{2}$ millions has an aggregate public debt of £150,000,000. The aggregate private debt may be estimated at as much again. It is fair therefore, and probably not above the mark, to set down the total liabilities of those Colonies at 300 millions sterling; nearly all of which is owing to England. The Colonies are in fact absolutely mortgaged to the mother-country. That their resources are equal —indeed superior—to the value of the money advanced upon them, I have no doubt whatever; but the Australasians have deliberately anticipated the profits of several years, and devoted them, in many cases to unremunerative objects. Therefore it is that I think these Colonies must at no distant date encounter serious financial difficulties. This fate is already overtaking New Zealand, and cannot, I think be escaped by the rest; and, if we are to judge from New Zealand, the task of bringing down a whole community from an artificial to a natural standard of living will be one of extreme difficulty.

. . . British statesmen may perhaps look forward to the day when the Australasian Colonies will form independent States, and hope that it may not be far distant. Separation would be a simple method of settling all difficulties, were England merely a suzerain and not also a mortgagee —But when we consider the enormous sums owed by Australasian Governments and Australasian people to British capitalists, I apprehend that Great Britain cannot relax her hold upon these Colonies, and that she must feel bound to watch over the safety of her own interests in Australasia. . . .

> Jervois to Knutsford, Confidential, 16 May 1888, C.O. 209/248

72. REEVES'S ARTICLES ON SOCIALISM AND COMMUNISM, 1890

From articles by William Pember Reeves, the editor, in The Lyttleton Times *during April 1890. Writing under a pseudonym, Reeves surveyed the Utopian schemes from Plato onwards, and outlined communistic societies such as Sparta, the early Christians and Essenes, the Incas, the mission communes of Paraquay, Russian village communes, American communistic experiments, before considering the differences between communism and socialism. He concluded that New Zealand had already gone a long way towards 'unconscious socialism'.*

. . . The words 'Communistic' and 'Socialistic' are in everybody's mouth. They are the most hackneyed commonplaces of political warfare. If we dislike any new proposal we call it Socialistic, much in the same loose way as our political fathers called novelties 'unconstitutional'. . . .

What is the difference between Communism and Socialism? One is often asked the question, ...

Socialism is something more definite than charity, sympathy, vague yearnings after better things, and divine discontent with the present. Socialism is not one and the same with Liberalism or Radicalism, though Socialists can often join hands with parliamentary reformers. On the other hand, Socialism does not insist upon the abolition of private property, a community of goods, or a community of living. In these it stops short of the Utopia of the Communist.

The logical Communist must withdraw from society, to make a fresh society of his own. His societies must try to be as far as possible self-dependent, so many little worlds within the world. Look at the attempts made to form Communes. ...

The Socialist says, 'Stay where you are, go on with your daily labour, but keep your eye on the ideal, upon attaining which we are all agreed.' Communism demands from each admitted member the complete surrender of all private property at the outset. Communism denies the right of the individual to possess property. Socialism does not do that. Its aim is to nationalise land and capital. It considers that the State should control the sources of production and manage the processes of industry. All production should be the State's work, and all labourers should be the State's workmen. ...

[German] State-Socialism professes to be ready to remedy the evils of the poor by legislation and State interference while strenuously supporting existing political institutions. ...

The State-Socialist is the cousin of the Tory Democrat. He will give the masses just as little as will content them. The Social Democrat, on the contrary will wring from the 'classes' as much as he can possibly get by persuasion or political war. The results of State-Socialism have been Protection, compulsory national insurance, the State ownership of railways and the Berlin Labour Conference. All these are Socialistic interferences with private industry. ...

... In England the thing hardly began to be more than vaguely talked about before 1882. Even now the avowed Socialists are few—I mean the Socialists who aim at the nationalization of land and capital, who know what they want and mean to get it. These open and avowed Socialists, who are ready to go all, or pretty nearly all, the way with Marx, are as yet but a little band. Their creed is the creed of the German Socialists. Their work in England is mainly missionary work. They are trying to educate England up to 'Das Kapital'.

But at the back of this scanty band of emissaries and proselytisers is the great mass of what is called Unconscious Socialism. This is made up of the opinions of the millions of respectable persons who either do not know what the doctrines of Socialism are, or profess to repudiate them. But these millions are all ready to do bit by bit what the Socialists want. They either do not see or do not admit that they are drifting into Socialism; but they go on. They sanction interference after interference by the State with industry. They begin timidly and cautiously to lay special burdens on wealth. . . .

To come to New Zealand. When Sir Harry Atkinson introduced into the House of Representatives his National Assurance Bill he probably would have resented, in his most emphatic manner, any suggestion that his Socialistic new departure could be in the direction of blotting out the private capitalist and employer of labour. When Mr Rolleston dwells upon the beauties of Perpetual Leasing he does not commit himself to absolute hostility to private ownership of land. When the Canterbury Chamber of Commerce clamours for the resumption of State-aided immigration, its members are so far from being conscious Socialists that they would probably be extremely wroth at having it hinted that they are advocating what is most assuredly a purely Socialistic undertaking. Scores of our politicians wax more or less eloquent on the virtues of our State system of education—free and secular, if not compulsory. Nine out of ten of them are innocent of a notion that State Education is one of the best known planks in Socialism's platform. There is hardly a public man in New Zealand who is not in favour of carrying some Socialistic reform, or maintaining some already established Socialistic institution. . . .

. . . The State, nowadays, confronts the individual from the moment at which it registers his birth to the day on which it takes care he is buried in a cemetery duly set aside by Government for the interment of the dead. . . .

In this part of the British Empire the State is the largest land-owner, the chief rent-collector, and the owner of the largest industrial 'going concern'—the railways. It not only manages the Post

Office, the lighthouses, the telephones, and the telegraphs, but has established a powerful Life Insurance Company. Its Public Trustee takes care of private estates. Its Land Transfer Office has taken away a whole branch of business from the lawyers. The State not only provides for the sick and the aged helpless, but finds work for the unemployed and teaches, free of charge, every child in the Colony whose parents will accept State teaching. It has subsidised colleges, high schools, and libraries. Above all, it has interfered with the labour market by State immigration, by factory and mines inspection, and by regulating with some care the labour of women and children. Municipalities, in addition to lighting and maintaining the streets and doing sanitary work, sometimes establish gasworks and provide their ratepayers with water. In the country it is the State which in one form or another makes roads, bridges, and water-races, and pays for them. All these acts are Socialistic. All are so much State interference with private enterprise. All are so many steps onward in the march towards making industry one national thing. All show that we live in an age of unconscious Socialism. . . .

Socialism is many-sided; it appeals all round. To the philanthropist it holds up the ideal of a comfortable and happy world. To the Christian it comes as the embodiment of Gospel teaching —a vision of hope and faith white handed. To the small or over-weighted capitalist it promises relief from the relentless ferocity of competition. To the fighting Democrat it talks of the downfall of capitalist tyranny and class insolence. . . . To the old and worn it speaks of rest and kindness: to the young and ambitious of equality, the open career, and the thousand thoroughfares to fame and greatness. Socialism has over Individualism the same advantage which Christianity had over classic Paganism. It is a gospel of hope. It pours into the ear of the slave of Industry such bright words of counsel and comfort as the Christian preacher whispered in secret to the Roman slave. It speaks of a bettered world and a happier state, where even if all tears shall not be wiped away, at any rate greed and rapacity, wearing anxiety and carking care, strife and covetousness, envy, hatred, and malice shall not or need not be. The Socialist holds the strong vantage-ground of the man with a remedy for great and confessed evils. No one denies that the world is a bad world; that society, as it now is, is a clumsy, cruel unrighteous system. The Socialist offers to change all this:

the Individualists, when appealed to for a cure, can only cry, 'I know not; am I my brother's keeper?'. . . .

> 'Pharos', *Some Historical Articles of Commun-ism and Socialism. Their Dreams, Their Experiments, Their Aims, Their Influence,* Lyttelton Times Office, Christchurch, 1890, pp. 1–2, 38, 43–5, 49

73. THE SWEATING COMMISSION, 1890

Extracts from the 'Report of Royal Commission into Certain Relations Between the Employers of Certain Kinds of Labour and Persons Employed Therein', 5 May 1890. The Commission was appointed in January 1890 to examine conditions of employment in shops, wholesale and retail trading, places of manufacturing, and in hotels and licensed houses.

. . . we have been obliged to content ourselves with voluntary witnesses, having reason to believe that a compulsory summons would in many cases lead to the dismissal of the witness: . . .

8. The evidence as a whole goes to show that in whatever branch of industry a union has been formed the condition of the operatives has improved, wages do not sink below a living minimum, and the hours of work are not excessive. . . .

11. Any new or amended Factory Act should include amongst others the following provisions:—

All factories, workrooms, and places where work for hire is executed, irrespective of the number of workers employed, shall be registered, and the Inspector shall satisfy himself as to the sanitary and other arrangements necessary for the health and morals of the workers; and without his sanction no factory shall be registered.

12. A certain number of cubic feet, as determined by expert evidence, shall be allowed for each worker.

13. The Government shall provide the Inspectors of Factories under the Acts with a form of table to be forwarded with their annual reports, showing the number of adults and young persons employed in each factory or workshop, distinguishing the sexes, the number of cubic feet of space for each person, as also the sanitary arrangements in connection with all establishments under their supervision.

14. Penalties shall be imposed in cases of workrooms being kept open for working purposes during meal-hours.

15. No boy or girl shall be allowed to work in any factory under the age of fourteen years. . . .

17. The Inspector shall have the right to enter any factory at any reasonable hour. Any obstruction to him shall be punishable by fine. . . .

26. This Commission expresses its entire sympathy with the movement to secure early closing; but, having in view the diversity of opinion on the part of its promoters, is unable to recommend any direct method by which this desirable object is to be attained.

27. We recommend that steps should be taken to establish at an early date Boards of Conciliation and Arbitration based on an equitable representation of labour and capital. . . .

A.J.H.R., 1890, H–5, pp. iii–vi

74. THE SWEATING COMMISSION, 1890

Evidence on the benefits of trade union activities from Harriet Morrison, Vice-President of the Tailoresses' Union, John Andrew Millar, Secretary of the Seamen's Union and the Tailoresses' Union, and Ellen Wilson, a Dunedin shirt-finisher. Dr. William Lamb, a Dunedin practitioner, speaks of the damage to health caused by poor working conditions.

MISS HARRIET MORRISON examined.

I am Vice-president of the Tailoresses' Union. . . .

. . . Working ordinary hours in the factory, the girls earn 2*s.* 6*d.* per day, take the average all through. When they take work home, perhaps they could make an extra shilling. Including both day and night work, they could earn 3*s.* 4*d.*, not including Saturday. This was previous to the establishment of the Union. It has stopped entirely the taking of work home. Since the formation of the Union I have made it my business to inquire strictly, and keep a very strict watch. I have others to watch too, for me, with the exception of one or two instances which have been done away with since. . . .

JOHN ANDREW MILLAR examined

I am a master mariner, and am Secretary of the Seamen's Union and of the Tailoresses' Union . . .

. . . The introduction of labour-saving machinery is constantly throwing numbers out of employment, and the only way to meet that in future will be to reduce the hours of labour. The more machinery is brought in the less work is there for men to do. . . .

I am decidedly in favour of Courts of Arbitration. No one desires to see a strike. Strikes are not to the interests of employed or employers. It is not the loss of money only, but a strike engenders bitter feelings that take years to abate.

. . . My idea is that the greater the combination of trades-unions the less chance there is of strikes on either side, because of the great responsibility on both sides. Both sides would hesitate more about causing a strike of a body of, say, fifteen thousand men than they would if only five hundred were concerned. . . .

So far as New Zealand is concerned, it is only within twelve months that trades-unionism has made a start at all. There were three or four unions, but they had gradually died out; but things have lately taken a start. Since the big London dock-strike has opened men's eyes to the necessity of trying to protect themselves there has been a regular epidemic of trades-unions throughout the colony. . . .

ELLEN WILSON examined.

I am a shirt finisher. . . .

. . . There is very little to complain of now. Sixteen months since it was hardly possible to earn a living. The best week I had then, working hard, was 10s. 6d.; that was working from 9 in the morning till 11 at night, with no hours off for meals. I got about ten minutes for dinner, and when I got home at night I used to take a short time to do a little extra cooking; but I could scarcely take time to get my meals. I can now make 12s. to 13s. a week; and a good finisher would make 18s. a week inside the eight hours per day. I can make 12s. per week now, working eight hours per day, whereas before it took me fourteen hours to make 1s. 10½d.

. . . The Union has been a great boon to us. I would not for anything it was dissolved, because it has done away with taking work home at night. . . .

Dr. WILLIAM LAMB examined.

909. I am a duly-qualified medical practitioner, and have been in practice in Dunedin for about eight years. I am one of the medical officers to the Oddfellows, Foresters, and Druids at the present time, and in my practice I am brought much in contact with the labouring-classes.

910. I do think there must be something far astray that induces in so many girls here the condition called anæmia—that is, poverty of blood. I have found factory girls very prone to that.

911. When I find them like that I tell them at once to leave their work and to take at least six weeks or so out in the country, and to get into the fresh air. My opinion is that the breathing of vitiated air in close, confined places deteriorates their health, and the blood gets poor. The thing is easily understood: the air they breathe is deprived of oxygen that ought to be in it, and its place is taken by carbonic-acid gas. In some cases this anæmic condition leads to consumption.

912. I have had one case of a young woman serving in a shop suffering from varicose veins, due to standing too long.

913. Another class of artisans who are very pale and pasty are the boot-makers. They are subject to the same conditions as other factory workers where there are a number of operatives in one room, and no doubt in boot factories there is a great deal of effluvia from the leather, and in other factories from woollen materials. The remedy for that—that is, the anæmic condition—would be proper ventilation. . . .

919. Want of proper closet-accommodation would have a tendency to create constipation; and, as regards urination, it would not be the best thing for the bladder. In connection with every establishment there should be such accommodation. . . .

A.J.H.R., 1890, H–5, pp. 4–5, 10–13, 23, 33

75. THE MARITIME STRIKE, 1890

New Zealand's only regular Labour paper of the day sets out the issues involved in the strike and counsels moderation and a spirit of conciliation, 1 September 1890.

The position with regard to the shipping dispute, grave as it is in itself, is rendered still more serious by the attitude of these members of the general public who systematically consider everything is wrong which affects their purses. They are out of pocket because of a strike—*ergo*, the strikers must be in the wrong. They totally overlook the fact that the strikers impose at least five times as much hardship upon themselves as upon others, and no body of men would do that were they not impelled by strong principle to a course they felt was the only right one. Still, the hard fact remains that such a strike as the present one is little less than disastrous for the colony as a whole; and every moderate person, no matter how staunch a Unionist he may be, must regret that the workers of New Zealand have been dragged into the dispute. From an independent standpoint it is even worse that Unionists expect to reap in personal advantage from the struggle. If ever a bitter fight was fought for the sake of pure principle, it is that now waging in New Zealand. The Australian marine officers demanded certain concessions. These were granted, provided the officers withdrew from their affiliation with labour bodies. They refused, and the Australian labour bodies had in honour no option but to support them in the struggle. These, in their turn, have helped us in the past, and must be helped by us in their necessity. Upon the advisability of officers affiliating with the sailors and other labour bodies we offer no opinion. There is much to be said on both sides, and a decision at present is impossible, the employers having *demanded* the withdrawal of the officers as the only alternative to working at what they admitted, by granting conditional increases, were inadequate rates of pay. This is an explicit denial of the right of employés to combine, an infringement of the most fundamental principle of Unionism, and at all costs the workers must cling to that right as the one door which offers a means of escape from the inequities of the present social system. We would counsel both parties to the struggle to note the urgent necessity for moderation and the encouragement of a spirit of conciliation. If the shipowners can see their way clear to conceding any points at all, we would strongly urge the Labour party to accept any reasonable compromise that does not actually affect the right of Labour to combine.

The Evening Herald, Dunedin, 1 September 1890

76. THE 1890 GENERAL ELECTION—
THE GOVERNMENT'S CASE

Address to the Egmont electorate, published in November 1890, from Sir Harry Atkinson, the Premier, who was ill at the time.

Our Future Course

. . . Let us have no political or financial fireworks, no great or heroic policy, no great schemes to dazzle or to lead us astray.

What we want and what we must insist on is a strict but not parsimonious economy, combined with cheerfulness, and a firm belief in the unbounded resources of our colony. . . .

Finance

. . . You will see that we have succeeded in getting our finance under control, but the most rigid economy and careful administration are still necessary before we can hold own own and pronounce our work of establishing a satisfactory finance fully accomplished. . . .

Further borrowing

. . . Can we do the necessary work of extending colonisation with the aid of ordinary revenue only? I regret to say that, in the opinion of the Government, this is not possible without such a large increase of taxation as no Government would propose and no Parliament would sanction: and yet this work must be done. If the settlement of our unoccupied lands is to be pushed forward— and this the Government think of the greatest importance—it cannot be efficiently done without continuing to expend an amount at least equal to that which has been for some years past devoted to this purpose. . . .

The Strike

. . . There are two lessons which I hope it has clearly taught us. The first warns us of the danger and unwisdom of our local unions being so connected with outside associations as to make it possible for them to be coerced into lines of action which they themselves may strongly deprecate. We have seen our whole trade and commerce seriously embarrassed by a quarrel in another colony upon a question in which the local unions were only remotely interested. . . . The second lesson which this strike has, I hope, taught us is that it is the duty of every one of us to do his utmost to devise some ready means, which shall be acceptable alike to capital and labour, to settle disputes which may in future arise between them, without resort to the most cruel expedient, the boycott and the strike. There is no doubt that unionism has been of great advantage to the working classes, and consequently to the community at large, for there can be no country really prosperous where its prosperity does not extend to its workers. It is impossible, however, that any section should be allowed to dictate to its parent community, and no community can permit unions to assume functions which of right . . .

can only be properly exercised by Parliament. Individual liberty must be preserved, and at the same time the right of the people to organise in such societies as they think will benefit themselves must be protected. . . . The solution must be the outcome of deliberation and mutual agreement between labour and capital, and must be mainly, I think, in the direction of legalising the decisions of such tribunals as may be set up by the parties themselves for the purpose of determining the disputes. . . .

The New Zealand Herald, 6 November 1890, p. 6

77. THE 1890 ELECTION: THE OPPOSITION CASE

Speech by John Ballance at Wanganui, 23 September 1890.

. . . As to the great question between labour and capital, he thought there was not the slightest reason why these matters should not be discussed and spoken of in public. There was no need for concealment. Let the question be faced and probed to the bottom, so that means might be found of adjusting the difficulty which at present exists. . . . He looked upon strikes as disastrous. This strike was disastrous to the community, and it was peculiarly unfortunate from the fact that it arose not in this colony but in another. But the unions held by the unions, and there was a great deal to be said for it that, in order to maintain unionism, these must affiliate with different unions in different colonies. That was why the unionists of New Zealand had responded to the call of their brethren in Sydney. He would not pretend to say which side was right, but he did say it was the duty of every politician in the colony to bring about a reconciliation between these two parties, recognising the patent fact that labour and capital were indispensable to each other. . . .

Whatever might come of that business, his own impression was that the one great remedy for all strikes and disputes of this kind was to have a tribunal that would command the confidence of both parties to settle disputes between labour and capital. . . .

. . . We must not lose our population in the way we have been losing it. During last year we lost 9000, while last month 1035 left our shores, and the immigration was only 803. He held most strenuously that population was the life blood of the colony, and if we lost our population it meant poverty, and the causing of a state of depression from which the country could never recover. Although we might be increasing our exports to a very large extent, and at the same time the population was not increasing, the colony would certainly get into a worse condition. They had a right to demand that the continued exodus of the population should be brought to an end. The great question was how to bring it to an end. . . . One cause of the exodus of population was wholesale dummyism that was going on in the public lands. It had been proved by evidence given before the Committee during the session that dummyism of a very peculiar character existed to an alarming extent. Bogus applications were being sent in at the instance of speculators for sections and the result was that lands were passing into the hands of speculators. The result was unfortunate. People who required land for settlement purposes, failing to get it, became disgusted, and left the country. Another thing was that large landowners were buying out deferred-payment settlers, who had improved their lands to a certain extent, and these settlers went with their money to other shores. The estates of large landowners were thus considerably extended. That was one of the causes of the exodus of population, and another cause was the large number of absentees who held land in the colony. The number of absent landholders was 43, and the area owned by them was 1,029,399 acres, valued at £1,635,280. . . .

. . . With regard to the monopoly of lands in the colony there were 84,547 freeholders in the colony, and the value of the land held by them was £84,208,000 and of these there were 2353 who owned land valued at £43,395,000, or more than half the whole value of the land. Then, again, there were 528 holders of over 5000 acres each, who owned seven million acres, while the whole of the lands disposed of in the colony was not more than 14 or 15 millions. They would find nothing to be compared to that in the mother country. The remedy was twofold, and they ought to face it and see that legislation in that direction was carried out. It was practical, simple, specific, and that was a graduated land tax. . . .

. . . With regard to the future, there should be initiated a vigorous policy of land settlement. Every man who had the opportunity should be given the right to go upon the land, surveys should be pushed on, roads made, and dummyism, speculation, or monopoly should be stopped at once. Such a policy would contribute greatly to the restoration of prosperity, or to removal of the depression which had so long existed. The remainder of the public estate should be only disposed of on perpetual lease. . . . After alluding to his leadership of the Opposition, he said there was a great battle now going on all over the colony between the champions of the people and the champions of privilege. The latter class would not fight fair, and would not run straight. They would run with the hare and hunt with the hounds; and he warned the people that it was their duty to return men who would work for the interests of the colony as a whole rather than for a class. . . .

The New Zealand Herald, 24 September 1890, p. 5

78. THE SIGNIFICANCE OF 1890

Editorial from The Lyttelton Times, *6 December 1890, suggesting that the adversities faced by Liberals during that year caused the 'masses' to unite against the 'classes' and ensure the victory of Liberal principles.*

The battle has been fought, and won. Notwithstanding the fact that the Conservative Government have had the prestige and influence attaching to the occupancy of the Treasury Benches in their favour; notwithstanding that they manipulated and delayed the elections in the hope that they and their capitalist friends would be able to con- solidate and strengthen their supposed power over the majority of the voters of the Colony—the people have proved true to Liberal principles, and have by a substantial majority declared against Sir Harry Atkinson and his policy and party. Reviewing the history of the last few months, there can be no doubt that the Liberal party passed through a crisis. The labour troubles, and the strikes which arose out of them, were, to those who regarded them super- ficially, rocks and breakers which threatened the Liberal bark. But those who looked beneath the surface must have felt that the adversities such as these were the very things required to unite the masses of New Zealand as against the classes. The heart of the people was true to Liberal principles. The adversities passed through were eminently calculated to develop and intensify the determination that henceforth—and for ever—the legislation of the country should proceed in the direction of Bentham's great maxim —'the greatest good of the greatest number'. Thus do adversities lead to benefits, and every step forward in the race of human progress is helped by difficulties, and sometimes secured by apparent defeats. So has it proved in this case. Beaten in one direction, the Unions and the people have conquered in the other—and at the arbitrament of the ballot-box the people of New Zealand have declared in favour of Liberal principles, Liberal measures and the Liberal party.

The Lyttelton Times, 6 December 1890, p. 4

79. VOTES FOR WOMEN

Sir John Hall, the chief parliamentary advocate of the female suffrage in the early 1890s, privately expresses his expectation of the conservative effect of the female vote.

. . . About Female Suffrage we must agree to differ—Your experience in the towns under the influence of strikes, may be an argument against women's suffrage, but in the country districts, and even throughout the Colony generally, it will increase the influence of the *settler* and *family*-man, as against the loafing single men who had so great a voice in the last elections. But for them all the country seats would have come to our side. I cannot believe that those who have anything to lose, will fail to bring to the poll, the female voters belonging to them. And generally among womankind the drunkard and the profligate will not have much chance, which will be a great gain for us. . . .

Hall to G. G. Stead, 30 June 1891. Hall Letter Books, vol. xii, p. 120

80. BALLANCE'S LAND TAXATION PROPOSALS, 1891

The Timaru Herald *turns against the Ballance Ministry on its land tax proposals, regarding a graduated tax as simply an abomination, 11 August 1891.*

The whole scheme bristles with points of objection, and even the Colonial Treasurer himself has been compelled to admit the validity of some of them. The graduated tax is simply an abomination. It is dishonest. Its principle is not fair taxation but confiscation, and its effects will prove disastrous. It is intended to burst up large estates. If it accomplishes that object what becomes of the revenue, which all agree must be raised from some source or other? If it fails as a bursting up agent, it remains a huge fraud, because it takes from the taxpayer more than his fair contribution as a member of the community. It punishes him for being the possessor of property which he has bought and paid for under the laws of the country . . . The revenue will very likely not be realised, and the mischief done indirectly will be great, and will adversely affect the revenue in other directions. We firmly believe that the uncertainty has already had that effect, but when the graduated tax becomes an accomplished fact a serious blow will have been struck at the wages fund, and the principal sufferers will be the working classes. Improvements will to a great extent be stopped. The wealthy owners will not feel the change to the same extent as the labourers. The former will still have their living and their luxuries, but how about the men travelling round the country and looking for work, and finding it more scarce than ever as a consequence of the new Liberal policy? Honestly, we are afraid the outlook is bad, and we confess that we cannot see how help is to come from any other quarter—how can there be a reasonable expectation of such improved markets and expanding trade as might enable New Zealand to view with indifference the losses occasioned through the experiments of her political and financial doctors. We have not the smallest faith in Mr Ballance as a financier. He failed most egregiously in the past, and his experience does not appear to have taught him to be cautious. . . .

The Timaru Herald, Tuesday, 11 August 1891, p. 2

81. LAND FOR SETTLEMENTS BILL, 1894

The Hon. John McKenzie, Minister for Lands, introducing the 1894 Land for Settlements Bill in the House of Representatives, 20 July 1894.

. . . Every year that passes by, the area of Crown lands of the colony, which we have had in the past to deal with, so as to supply the number of people who come to the country and want to get land to settle upon, is diminishing, while the number of people who are anxious to obtain homes for themselves is every year increasing. . . . Here we are in this colony, with a population less than three-quarters of a million of people, and we already find a scarcity of land for people to settle upon. We could in this country, with comfort and ease, settle at the very least five millions of people; so that if we have arrived at such a stage in our early history that so many people could be settled in the country, and yet we already find a scarcity of land to settle them upon, it is evident that we have, to a certain extent, abused our trust in the past. . . .

. . . we have still a certain area of Crown lands, and also lands that we are obtaining from the Natives in the North Island, where we can supply the demand for settlement, to a certain extent, for some time to come; but there are other parts of the colony where this is not the case, where the Crown lands have already been disposed of, and it is impossible for us to settle any large number of people without getting land from those who have taken it up in large areas in the past. This refers notably to North Otago, Canterbury, Marlborough, and Hawke's Bay. It is notable, I say, that in these districts large estates prevail to a greater extent than in any other portion of the colony. So far as Canterbury itself is concerned, I may say that the whole of the Crown lands suitable for small settlement are disposed of, and there is no chance there for the progress of settlement unless we are prepared to obtain land in this way for the purpose. I might ask this honourable House, what would have happened in Canterbury this last year had it not been for the acquisition by the Government of the Cheviot Estate? Through the fact that we had the Cheviot Estate to dispose of last year, we were able to meet the demand for settlement in that portion of the colony to a certain extent, . . . In many cases these large estates that are in existence in the colony are so hampered that it would be impossible for the people who own them—or who are the nominal owners—to deal in any way with them, owing to the fact that they are in the hands of companies and monetary institutions. . . . We know as a fact that a large number of these large estates have been created in the past by very questionable means indeed, in many cases. We have had gridironing and dummyism to a considerable extent in Canterbury. . . .

. . . And then we have had—what shall I call it, in the Hawke's Bay District?—I should say 'Native-land jobbery' would be a very good name to call it. And through these processes we have had large estates created in various parts of the colony, which at the present time force us to take the course we are now taking. . . . Honourable gentlemen opposite may say that I have had an Act on the statute-book which would enable me to purchase fifty thousand pounds' worth of land per annum, and that I have not exercised the rights I have under that Act to within £10,000 of the amount which I could have dealt with. . . . There are numbers of people who are not prepared to sell their property to the Crown at a fair value. . . . So that you have here a clear reason why the Crown should come to the House and ask for compulsory clauses in the Land for Settlements Act. If anything could be more clear, then I am sure I do not know where to find it. In asking the House to pass this Bill, I think I can safely claim that the colony at the last election pronounced in favour of the Land for Settlements Bill. . . .

. . . Now I will come to the Act itself, and explain its various provisions to honourable members. It first provides for getting land for settlement by purchase voluntarily from people who are prepared to sell it, and, in the event of the Board of Commissioners reporting that land is required in certain portions of the colony for various purposes, that land can be taken compulsorily if it cannot be purchased privately and at a voluntary bargain. . . . Now, I say we should meet the demands of all classes of settlers who come to the colony, and the demands of those who are now here, and we should induce people with capital to come here and settle: it is only by doing that, in the same way as at Cheviot, where we have been able to induce a number of people with capital to come and settle, and employ some of the smaller people who have not the same means at their disposal—it is only, I say, by that means that we can make these settlements prosperous; so that curtailing the area to fifty or a hundred acres is not advisable, in my opinion. . . .

N.Z.P.D., 1894, vol. 83, pp. 631–8

82. ADVANCES TO SETTLERS, 1894

Joseph G. Ward introducing the second reading of the Government Advances to Settlers Bill in the House of Representatives, 14 September 1894.

. . . The object of this Bill is to enable people in this colony to obtain money at lower rates of interest than have hitherto prevailed.

. . . In many cases, those who have mortgages already know that when they have become due they have had considerable difficulty in renewing them. I could, if I desired to take up the time of the House this evening, give numbers of cases which have come to the knowledge of the Government of people who with good securities have endeavoured to get renewals of their mortgages during the past three or four years, and have been unable to get them renewed except on terms very much more unfavourable than existed formerly. . . .

. . . Now, Sir, I propose to refer to the manner in which it is intended to make advances under this Bill. The lowest amount is to be £50, and the highest amount £5,000. I think there can be very little difference of opinion as to the propriety of having a low minimum to enable the class of small settlers intending to go upon the land, as well as to enable the existing small settlers, to avail themselves of the advantages which the Bill is intended to confer. . . . In connection with the proposals to advance on lease-hold there is an ever-growing change, which has been going on in the colony for some time past, in connection with the land-system of the colony. It is almost useless to ask a man to take up land upon a perpetual lease, or an eternal lease, or any lease under the Land Act, or to expect a poor man at any rate to do so, in order to make a home for himself, unless he has the wherewithal to do it. . . .

. . . I may say there have been, in connection with this cheap-money scheme, many representations made to the Government by men who are anxious that the Government should undertake this function. It is very painful to have to state to the House that many settlers, and intending settlers, have made the strongest representations to the Government in order to induce them to provide a scheme such as that now submitted to the House. I can assure the House that it is a necessity. . . . I only wish to say, in conclusion, that my honest and firm conviction in connection with this matter is that it is calculated to do more good to this colony than any other proposal that has been brought down for many years. There are at the present time in the colony a considerable number of persons now paying excessive rates of interest, who, if they had an opportunity of getting money at low rates of interest, as provided in this Bill, could apply it well, and put their shoulders to the wheel and makes homes for themselves. . . .

N.Z.P.D., 1894, vol. 85, pp. 685–92

83. THE INDUSTRIAL CONCILIATION AND ARBITRATION ACT, 1894

'An Act to encourage the Formation of Industrial Unions and Associations, and to facilitate the Settlement of Industrial Disputes by Conciliation and Arbitration.' [31st August, 1894.]

BE IT ENACTED ...

PART I

REGISTRATION OF INDUSTRIAL UNIONS AND ASSOCIATIONS

(1.) *Industrial Unions*

3. A society consisting of any number of persons not being less than seven, residing within the colony, lawfully associated for the purpose of protecting or furthering the interests of employers or workmen in or in connection with any industry in the colony, . . . may be registered as an industrial union pursuant to this Act. . . .

10. The effect of registration shall be to render the industrial union, . . . subject to the jurisdiction by this Act given to a Board and the Court respectively, and liable to all the provisions of this Act, and all such persons shall be bound by the rules of the industrial union during the continuance of the membership. . . .

(2.) *Industrial Associations*

12. Any council or other body, however designated, representing any number of industrial unions established within the colony may be registered as an industrial association pursuant to this Act. . . .

PART II

INDUSTRIAL AGREEMENTS

17. The parties to industrial agreements may be (1) trade unions, (2) industrial unions, (3) industrial associations, (4) employers; . . .

21. Every industrial agreement duly made and executed shall be binding on the parties thereto and on every person who at any time during the term of such agreement is a member of any industrial union, trade union, or association. . . . and every such employer shall be entitled to the benefit thereof, and be deemed to be a party thereto.

22. (1.) If any industrial union, trade union, association, or person bound by any industrial agreement shall in any particular commit or suffer a breach thereof, such union, association, or person shall for every such breach be guilty of an offence against this Act, . . .

PART III

CONCILIATION AND ARBITRATION

(1.) *Preliminary*

24. (1.) The Governor may from time to time divide New Zealand, or any portion thereof, into such districts as he shall think fit, to be called 'industrial districts,' . . . .

27. Any Board and the Court, and, being authorised in writing by the Board or Court, any member of such Board or Court respectively, or any officer of such Board or Court, without any other warrant than this Act, at any time between sunrise and sunset,—

(1.) May enter upon any manufactory, building, workshop, factory, mine, mine-workings, ship or vessel, shed, place, or premises of any kind. . . .

(2.) May inspect and view any work, material, machinery, appliances, article, matter, or thing whatsoever being in such manufactory, building, workshop, factory, mine, mine-workings, ship or vessel, shed, place, or premises. . . .

(3.) May interrogate any person or persons who may be in or upon any such manufactory. . . .

(2.) *Boards of Conciliation*

30. In and for every industrial district there shall be established a Board of Conciliation. . . .

32. . . .

(1.) Every Board shall consist of such equal number of persons as the Governor may determine, being not more than six nor less than four persons, who shall be chosen by the industrial unions of employers and of workmen in the industrial district respectively, such unions voting separately and electing an equal number of such members.

(2.) The Chairman of such Board shall be in addition to the number of members before mentioned, and be elected. . . .

42. Any industrial dispute may be referred for settlement to a Board either by or pursuant to an industrial agreement, or in the manner hereinafter provided: —

(1.) Any party to such dispute may, in the prescribed manner, lodge an application with the Clerk requesting that such dispute be referred for settlement to a Board.

(2.) The parties to such dispute may comprise—

(*a.*) An individual employer, or several employers, and an industrial union, trade union, or association of workmen; . . .

(5.) Every party appearing by a representative or representatives shall be bound by his or their acts. . . .

(7.) No counsel or solicitor shall be allowed to appear or be heard before a Board, . . . unless . . . all the parties shall expressly consent thereto. . . .

44. In the course of any . . . inquiry and investigation the Board shall make all such suggestions and do all such things as shall appear to them as right and proper to be made or done for securing a fair and amicable settlement of the industrial dispute between the parties, and may adjourn the proceedings for any period the Board thinks reasonable, to allow the parties to agree upon some terms of settlement; and, if no such settlement shall be arrived at, shall decide the question according to the merits and substantial justice of the case, and make their report or recommendation. . . .

46. If the Board shall report that they have been unable to bring about any settlement of any dispute referred to them satisfactory to the parties thereto, the Clerk on the receipt of such report shall transmit a copy (certified by him) of such report to each party to the industrial dispute, whereupon any such party may, in the manner prescribed, require the Clerk to refer the said dispute to the Court. . . .

(3.) *The Court of Arbitration*

47. There shall be one Court of Arbitration for the whole colony for the settlement of industrial disputes. . . .

48. (1.) The Court shall consist of three members to be appointed by the Governor, one to be so appointed on the recommendation of the councils or a majority of the councils of the industrial associations of workmen in the colony, and one to be so appointed on the recommendation of the councils or a majority of the councils of the industrial associations of employers of the colony. . . .

No recommendation shall be made as to the third member, who shall be a Judge of the Supreme Court, and shall be appointed from time to time by the Governor, and shall be President of the Court. . . .

54. Within five days after any dispute has been submitted by the Clerk to the Court the President shall fix a suitable time and place for the Court to meet to hear and determine the dispute, and shall give at least forty-eight hours' written notice to the other members of the Court of such time and place. . . .

68. The award of the Court shall be made within one month after the Court shall have begun to sit for the hearing of any reference. . . .

(4.) *Enforcement of Awards*

74. Every award of the Court shall specify each industrial union, trade union, association, person, or persons on which or on whom it is intended that it shall be binding, and the period, not exceeding two years from the making thereof, during which its provisions may be enforced; and during the period within which the provisions of such award may be enforced such award shall be binding. . . .

New Zealand Statutes, 1894, 58 Vict., no. 14, pp. 23–41

84. THE OLD-AGE PENSIONS ACT, 1898

'An Act to provide for Old-age Pensions', 1 November 1898.

WHEREAS it is equitable that deserving persons who during the prime of life have helped to bear the public burdens of the colony by the payment of taxes, and to open up its resources by their labour and skill, should receive from the colony a pension in their old age:

BE IT THEREFORE ENACTED . . . .

PENSIONS

7. Subject to the provisions of this Act, every person of the full age of sixty-five years or upwards shall, whilst in the colony, be entitled to a pension as hereinafter specified. . . .

9. The amount of the pension shall be eighteen pounds per year, diminished by,—

(1.) One pound for every complete pound of income above thirty-four pounds; and also by

(2.) One pound for every complete fifteen pounds of the net capital value of all accumulated property, computed and assessed as next hereinafter provided.

10. The net capital value of accumulated property shall be computed and assessed in the prescribed manner, and for that purpose the following provisions shall apply: —

(1.) All real and personal property owned by any person shall, to the extent of his beneficial estate or interest therein, be deemed to be his accumulated property.

(2.) From the capital value of such accumulated property there shall be deducted all charges or encumbrances lawfully existing on such property, and also the sum of fifty pounds; and the residue then remaining shall be deemed to be the net capital value of all his accumulated property. . . .

PENSION-CLAIMS

15. (1.) Every person claiming to be entitled to a pension under this Act shall, in the prescribed manner and form, deliver a claim therefor (elsewhere throughout this Act called a 'pension-claim') to the Deputy Registrar of the district wherein the claimant resides, or to the nearest Postmaster, who shall forthwith forward the same to the Deputy Registrar.

(2.) The pension-claim shall affirm all the requirements and negative all the disqualifications under this Act.

(3.) Every claimant shall, by statutory declaration, affirm that the contents of his pension-claim are true and correct in every material point.

(4.) Such declaration may be made before any Justice of the Peace, solicitor, Deputy Registrar, or Postmaster, and shall not be liable to stamp duty.

16. The Deputy Registrar shall file the claim, and record it in the prescribed manner in a book, to be called 'The District Old-age Pension-claim Register,' which shall be open to inspection on payment of a fee of one shilling.

17. All pension-claims shall be numbered consecutively in the order in which they are entered in the register, so that no two pension-claims in the same register bear the same number.

18. (1.) The Deputy Registrar shall, in the prescribed manner, transmit the claim to a Stipendiary Magistrate exercising jurisdiction in the district, who shall in open Court fully investigate the pension-claim for the purpose of ascertaining whether the claimant is entitled to the pension, and, if so, for what amount in respect of the first year.

(2.) The Clerk of the Magistrate's Court shall ascertain on what date the claim may be investigated, and shall notify the claimant of a date on which he may attend to support his claim, and the Stipendiary Magistrate shall on the day so appointed, or on the first convenient day thereafter, proceed to investigate the same:

Provided that where the Stipendiary Magistrate is satisfied that

213

the documentary evidence in support of the claim is sufficient to establish it, and also that by reason of physical disability or other sufficient cause the attendance of the applicant should be dispensed with, he shall not require the personal attendance of the applicant, who shall be notified accordingly. . . .

New Zealand Statutes, 1898, 62 Vict., no. 14, pp. 48–51.

85. SEDDON AFTER EIGHT YEARS IN POWER, 1901

Critical editorial comment on Seddon's eight years of office which left him 'supreme' in the 'most advanced' democracy in the world.

To-day the Premier finds himself with a record of eight years of continuous power as the first Minister of the most democratic community in the English-speaking world. It is a unique position, and one that his most ardent admirers twenty-one years ago . . . could hardly have dreamed that he would ever attain much less hold so long and yet be in the full zenith of his power. It is as remarkable a career as is the seeming lack of equipment of the man who has made it. With many of the methods by which this power and distinction have been achieved we can express, as time and again we have expressed, nothing but condemnation, but it would be idle to blink the fact that for eight years he has ruled New Zealand by the expressed will of its people. The leader of the most advanced and probably the most intelligent Democracy of the age he has in turn ignored the forms and precedents of constitutional usage, denied the plain rights of the Legislature, and trampled on Parliamentary practice, and yet today he is supreme. Under his sway the Democracy has been in some ways corrupted and degraded, and yet he remains its ruler.

What then are the compensating services to the people that have impelled the country to maintain him in power? It is a question that may well be asked and answered on this the eighth anniversary of his supremacy. The answer is not far to seek. . . .

. . . With an intrepid faith in the gullibility of the people he has had the vision to perceive and the power to gratify the most ardent wishes of those whose voices alone could maintain him in power. Whether it was for love of the people or greed of power, or something of each that impelled him, no man can say; but from whatever cause, the Premier stands today triumphant in the policy he has pursued. And in the broad lines of the policy we read the secret of his success, notably the Land for Settlements, Conciliation and Arbitration, Advances to Settlers, Old-Age Pensions, and various labour enactments. It is true that Messrs John McKenzie, W. P. Reeves, and J. G. Ward were respectively the authors of the three first mentioned measures, but the Premier has Old-Age Pensions to his personal credit, besides being the head of the Government that has placed all these measures on the Statute Book. It is true that he has had some able lieutenants, but his most adverse critics will admit that the continuous success of the 'Liberal' Party in the State has been primarily due to the consumate generalship of its leader. . . .

The Evening Post, Wellington, 1 May 1901, p. 4

86. THE LIBERALS AND THE FARMERS' UNION, 1901

Unfavourable editorial comment on the 'weakest spot' in the policy of the Seddon Government, 12 November 1901, including a denunciation of the policy of playing off farmers against the 'workers'.

. . . Ever since the late Sir John McKenzie retired from the Ministry the farming interests have been seriously neglected. . . . The Premier has never evinced any great knowledge of the farmers' needs or any great sympathy with their aspirations. He has talked vaguely of things his administration would do for them, . . . During the past two years it has become more and more apparent that, so far as country matters are concerned Sir John McKenzie was the strong man of the Ministry. The recent indifference of the Government, which, as Mr Glass [Chief Organiser of the Farmers' Union] points out, has miserably failed in the fulfilment of its promises, is steadily alienating a class that had for some years been a strong support to the 'Liberal' Party. Unless there be a distinct change of policy in this respect, and the Departments of Land and Agriculture become once more live and energetic branches of the Administration, the Ministry may suffer a rude awakening at the next general election. . . . Although we cannot accept all the planks of its platform, we do not fail to recognise the good work being done by the Farmers' Union. It is supplying the producers of the country, the pastoralists and the agriculturalists who form the backbone of the population and the chief source of New Zealand's prosperity, with a powerful organisation, by means of which they can express their wants. . . . In future the Government of the colony, whatever its party denomination, will have to deal with organised producers as well as with organised 'workers'. . . .

Past experience induces a belief that the Farmers' Union, as soon as it becomes sufficiently numerous and can command enough votes, will receive the Premier's sincerest consideration. He will then—and the time seems to be fast approaching—probably try to absorb it into his Party, as for a time he absorbed the organised labour of the colony. Signs of transition were not wanting last session, but Mr Seddon, like a practical political Don Juan, thinks it best to get rid of the old love in a friendly way before he devotes himself to the new. In order to keep the new interested in him and attached to his person he is lavish of promises, but he does not fulfil them lest he should prematurely offend the old, who might become troublesome and even dangerous if ignominiously cast off. Hence it is that no amendment has been made in the Workers' Compensation Act and that other country measures have had to go by the board while preference was given to Bills of other kinds. Were it not that Mr Seddon is a past master in the art of counting up votes, his present attitude would seem to be fraught with grave danger to his own and his Party's political prospects. The playing-off of farmers against unionists and unionists against farmers with the obvious intention of ultimately heading the stronger faction might be expected to lead to a schism in the Liberal Party. It might not be safe to conclude that both factions were so short-sighted as not to understand the game even when it is being played by such a skilful professional player. However, there is the nine years' record of the Premier's sensitiveness as a political barometer, and that disposes his friends and opponents alike to suspect that he may still find himself upon the winning side when there is a fresh cut for partners. . . .

The Evening Post, Wellington, 12 November 1901, p. 4

87. FREEHOLD TENURE

William Ferguson Massey, Leader of the Opposition, welcomes the retreat of the Ward Ministry from its 'Leasehold policies' in a

*speech to the House of Representatives, 16 November 1909, during
the debate on the Budget.*

. . . I should like before going on to take the opportunity of con-
gratulating the members of the Government, from the Right Hon.
the Prime Minister downwards, on becoming converts to the doctrine of the freehold tenure. . . . According to . . . the first policy
measure of the present Administration—it was intended that the
Crown lands should be disposed of on the renewable-leasing system only, without any possibility of the freehold existing. Now the
Minister comes along with his policy proposals, which are quite
a reversal. . . . let me say here that we are glad to see the honourable
gentlemen on the penitent-stool, and there is joy in the freehold
camp over every leasehold sinner that repenteth. . . . I think that on
an occasion like this the members of the freehold party—the men
who have stood by freehold when it was not nearly so popular in the
House or in the country as it is at the present time—have good
reason to shake hands with themselves. We can remember when
an attack—the most serious and deadly attack ever made on the
freehold tenure—was made by those men who are now anxious to
call themselves its friends; but we know perfectly well that if the
leaseholders were in a majority, those gentlemen would be just
as anxious to support the leasehold then as they are to support
the freehold to-day, and on that account I, for one, do not trust
them. But, Sir, there is still much to be done. I feel certain that
though we are now on a right track, and the Government is giving
way, still it will be some time before we are able to gain everything
we want. For our part we have never deviated from the straight
course in the past, and we do not intend to deviate in the slightest
from the straight course in the future. The goal we are aiming at
is simply this: to place as many men as we possibly can on the
land, under the best possible conditions and under the best tenure
the law can provide; and if we can accomplish that, we shall do
a good thing for the settlers themselves and for the country. . . . so
far as the lease in perpetuity is concerned I admit that the proposal
is most important. In the case of the lease in perpetuity the proposal
is, in the first instance at any rate, that the settler shall be able to
buy the land at the original value, plus half the increase between
the original value and the present value. There is also the alternative
to the effect that if a tenant pays one-tenth of the increase on the
unimproved value for thirty-three years for a term of 165 years the

217

land is to become freehold. That is the most utter nonsense. You cannot make a land law to last 165 years. . . .

. . . I believe the prosperity of the country depends on successful settlement; but if we are to have successful settlement, the conditions must be favourable from every point of view. The conditions must be favourable from the point of view of the land and of the settler. . . . As a practical man I have been astounded at times at the extraordinary opinions we have heard in this House, and sometimes outside of it, in regard to land-settlement. We have heard it said—and it is a common saying now—that it is necessary to have the leasehold in order to provide land for the people who want it. Now, what difference does it make to the man who is not on the land whether those who are on it occupy it on leasehold or freehold tenure? The fact of the tenure does not give one additional inch of land. It is the most utter claptrap, and yet we hear it repeated over and over again in the House. And then we hear members who toil not, neither do they spin, talking about the profits of dairy-farming and the beauties of sheep-farming. The honourable gentlemen who express those opinions are probably better occupied in milking the State cow or shearing the innocent elector. . . . When a man has done his duty to his country, when he has been a good settler, when he has gone out and carved out a home for himself he is reviled and vilified; and it is no wonder if under such circumstances they lose confidence in the country to which they belong, and begin to look with wistful eye on other countries where the land-nationalisers cease from troubling and the settler is at rest. This sort of thing has been and is inducing men with rising families to go to other countries, instead of keeping their families and their capital in this country to which they rightly belong. I say this: that when a man is benefiting his country by raising products—in the first instance directly for his own benefit, and indirectly for the benefit of the country—that man should be encouraged rather than harassed and discouraged as we have been inclined to harass and discourage him by our legislation in recent years. It is our duty to find land for all those who require it, and to settle them on unoccupied land if it is possible. When a farmer has a field which is lying waste and unoccupied, what does he do? The first thing he does is to make arrangements for bringing that field into cultivation. He does not devote his time and energy to the paddocks that are productive, but he never rests till he has made productive the

218

land that was lying idle. That is what we ought to do with this country. New Zealand is our farm, so to speak. . . .

88. LEASEHOLD DEFENDED

Thomas E. Taylor, Member for Christchurch North, in his speech on 16 November 1909 during the debate on the Budget, presents the 'Leasehold' Liberals' case against the Ward Ministry's proposal to allow state tenants to purchase the freehold of their sections on certain conditions.

. . . Now, I ask, what right has the State to give the lessee some portion of the unimproved value? If it is wrong to take all the increased value that we have already a title to under these leases— if that be the case, then it is wrong to take any part from the lessee, either now or at the end of thirty-three years. . . . Now, we ought to be honest. We either ought to give the freehold right out, or we ought to maintain the right of the State in all these leases, and in the increased values that will accrue as times goes on. I do not believe in tricky provisions such as these undoubtedly are, because they are not fair to the lessee and they are not fair to the people. It is clear that these tricky clauses are not designed in the interests of the lessee, because I frankly do not think that the lessee will be able to get the freehold title under some of them. If this surmise is correct, the Ministry is still blamable for its attempt to deceive lessees and people. . . . I consider that these clauses in the Budget are utterly disgraceful. I am not blind to the fact that on the Liberal side of this House there are a number of freeholders, but the truth is clear that for the last eight or nine years the Radical sentiment of this country has been gradually betrayed. . . . I am confident that if the issue were put before the people of the country to-day, whether they desired the whole of the remaining Crown lands for all time to be dealt with under the leasehold system, six at least out of every ten men and women throughout the Dominion would vote for the preservation of the remnant of the national estate. It may be said that if you take a referendum vote you still have sent back to this House a majority of freeholders. When the Liberal party was in its youth in the early 'nineties,' it was able to capture country constituency after country constituency. But to-day it has lost its nerve. . . .

89. THE FIRST LABOUR PARTY

The first New Zealand Labour Party adopted its constitution at the Trades and Labour Council's conference, Auckland, July 1910, and the 'Platform and Objective' were adopted at a conference in the Trades Hall, Christchurch, 19 April 1911.

Introduction to the People

This Party is formed as an expression of the great Labour Movement which is to-day finding voice in every country of the world. . . . Our Party takes the name of 'Labour' for its distinctive title not as seeking to represent and uphold a section of our people alone. . . . To all producers within the Dominion, whether their labour be of the brain, the hand, or the eye, the Party holds out the hand of fellowship and good-will. Let all come together in the one great Party to secure the political and economic reforms required by the mass of the people; that the day may soon dawn upon our fair land when in all matters of government, both local and general, humanity shall take precedence of mere wealth, and the well-being of the masses be considered before the enrichment of the few. . . .

OBJECTIVE

. . . To enact comprehensive measures, and establish such conditions as will foster and ensure equality of opportunity; also the moral, material, and educational advancement, and the general comfort and well-being of the whole people, based upon the gradual public ownership of all the Means of Production, Distribution, and Exchange.

PLATFORM

Immediate Nationalisation of Monopolies

(A) Establishment of State ferry service, and State colliers.

(B) Establishment of competitive State factories.

Land Reform

(A) Establishment of State ferry service, and State colliers.

(B) Leasehold tenure, with right of renewal and periodical revaluation every 21 years.

(C) Tenant's absolute right to improvements.

(D) Limitation of area, based on value, to ensure an equitable distribution of our lands.

(E) Resumption of native and other lands for closer settlement on renewable lease.

(F) Increment Tax on all land sales to secure to the State all socially created values.

(G) The retention and direct operation by the State of sufficient land to meet the demands of the National Food Supply.

(H) Increased Graduated Land Tax. . . .

Currency Reform

(A) Establishment of a State Bank with sole right of Note issue.

(B) Cessation of public borrowing, except for redemption of loans and completion of works already authorised by Parliament. . . .

Electoral Reform

(A) Abolition of Legislative Council.

(B) Proportional representation on single transferable vote.

(C) Initiative and Referendum.

(D) Parliamentary Franchise to apply to the election of all local bodies.

(E) Full political rights to all State employees.

Industrial Reform

(A) Right to Work Bill.

(B) Insurance against unemployment.

(C) Extension of State Labour Agencies, and abolition of private registry offices.

(D) A maximum eight-hour day, a six-day week, with a gradual reduction to a forty-hour week.

(E) Statutory preference of employment to unionists.

(F) Equal pay for equal work for male and female workers.

(G) Amended Workers' Accommodation Act.

(H) Amended Workers' Compensation Act.

(I) Amended Conciliation and Arbitration Act.

(J) The Prohibition of labour under contract.

(K) Legislative Minimum Wage.

Taxation Reform

(A) A Graduated Income Tax based on scientific principles, with a super-tax on unearned incomes.

(B) A Graduated Absentee Tax.

(C) That power be given to Municipalities to specially tax all socially-created land values within their boundaries. . . .

Education Reform

(A) That a system of free, secular, State education be maintained, with compulsory attendance up to the age of fifteen years; and that the necessary books and stationery be printed by the Government and supplied free by the Department of Education. . . .

Social Reform

(A) Pensions for widows and orphans, and State assistance in maternity.

(B) The right of the people to decide all questions submitted to them on a bare majority vote.

International Arbitration

That this Party endorses the policy of arbitration, and the establishment of treaties of peace towards the settlement of international disputes between civilised nations. . . .

'New Zealand Labour Party', 1912, *Society Rules*, Pamphlet

90. PLANKS IN THE REFORM PARTY PLATFORM, 1911

Summary of the Reform Party's policy, with a stress on land reform in the interests of the small farmer.

FINANCE

(1) REFORM of the financial system of the Dominion, by instituting a thorough investigation into the Dominion's finances with a view to keeping borrowing within reasonable bounds, and of preventing wasteful expenditure.

(2) REFORM of the fiscal system of the Dominion, by reducing taxation wherever possible, in order to lessen the cost of living.

LAND

(3) REFORM of the Land system of the Dominion.
  (*a*) By giving all facilities possible to men of small capital to get on the land by means of the leasehold, as a stepping-stone to the freehold if they so desire it.
  (*b*) By giving the option of the freehold to leasees of Crown lands on L.I.P.* at the original value, plus the difference between the rental on O.R.P.* and L.I.P.

> *L.I.P.—L[ease] I[n] P[erpetuity]
> O.R.P.—O[ccupation with] R[ight of] P[urchase]

(c) By giving the option of freehold to leasees of settlement land on L.I.P. at the original value.

(d) By providing for limitation of area to effectually prevent aggregation.

(e) By providing for the payment of the purchase money in instalments, if so desired by the leasee.

(f) By providing that the money derived from the sale of the freehold be utilised for the acquisition of further land for settlement.

NATIVE LANDS

(4) REFORM of the Native Land legislation:

(a) By a determined and sustained effort to settle the native land question.

(b) By the rapid individualism of Native land wherever possible.

(c) By affording to the Native race the common privilege of disposing under proper safeguards of such portions of their land as are not required for their personal use.

(d) By making provision against the creation of large holdings.

(e) By promoting legislation having for its ultimate aim the placing of the Natives in the same position as the Europeans, with the same privileges and responsibilities.

LEGISLATIVE COUNCIL

(5) REFORM of the Legislative Council by replacing the present nominative Council by one elected on the same franchise as the House of Representatives, on the proportional system of voting in larger electorates.

CIVIL SERVICE

(6) REFORM of the Civil Service.

(a) By improving the conditions governing the employment of Civil Servants.

(b) By eliminating political influence and patronage.

(c) By providing that all appointments and promotion shall be made and regulated by a Board responsible directly to Parliament, and absolutely free from Ministerial control.

(*d*) By granting to the Civil Servants the right of appeal to a competent tribunal from a decision of the Board.

LOCAL GOVERNMENT

(7) REFORM of local government in the rural districts of the Dominion, by giving extended powers and assured finance, thus making it unnecessary for them to depend, to the same extent as at present, on the wasteful and unsatisfactory system of Parliamentary grants for public works.

(8) REFORM of the municipal legislation of the Dominion, by promoting a town-planning scheme to meet the future requirements of the towns of the Dominion.

INDUSTRIAL AND SOCIAL LEGISLATION

(9) REFORM of the Old Age Pensions Act, by making the qualifying age for the pension for women sixty years, instead of sixty-five.

(10) REFORM of the industrial system of the Dominion by promoting legislation in favour of compulsory insurance against sickness and unemployment.

(11) REFORM of the economic system of the Dominion, in the direction of promoting industrial peace, and restoring public confidence, in order to encourage local industries.

The Dominion, 2 December 1911, p. 17

91. THE REFORM GOVERNMENT'S CLAIM OF BEING 'LIBERAL' IN THE 'TRUE SENSE' 1912

After twenty-one years of Liberal rule, William Ferguson Massey took office as leader of a Reform Ministry on 7 July 1912. The Dominion *argues that the principles of the party are 'progressively Liberal', that while Ward and Mackenzie had strayed from the Liberalism of Ballance, Reform would take up matters considered too radical by Ballance. The real struggle was now between 'Liberalism' and 'Socialism' and that in this Reform provided the 'true' Liberals.*

. . . More than half the Parliamentary voters of New Zealand are those who have never known any Government save the SEDDON, WARD, and MACKENZIE Governments. The majority of the electorate, therefore, have always thought of the two main parties as simply 'the Government' and 'the Opposition'. The WARD and MACKENZIE Governments have been in most essentials entirely opposed to the Liberal principles of BALLANCE, but they insisted on calling themselves the guardians of Liberalism. The Reform party to-day is quite different from the party in Opposition in the 'eighties and the early 'nineties: it has preserved little more of that party's character than its devotion to principle and honesty. To-day it is, as its name declares, primarily a party bent upon purging the nation of the evils engendered by a long and unbroken period of bossism, but its general political principles are progressively Liberal. BALLANCE indeed, might have shrunk from, as being too advanced, many of the democratic beliefs of the Reform party.

There has thus been a confusion of names. Some of the Wardist newspapers called MR MASSEY and his friends Tories, and it is a testimony to the great power of plain fact that nobody was deceived by this absurd attempt to misrepresent the Reformers. We doubt whether there is a Tory in the Empire outside Britain, . . . Of course it was ignorance that inspired this curious fashion of referring to the supporters of the Reform movement. The better-informed of the Wardist papers shrank from venturing any greater misrepresentation than the use of the term 'Conservatives' when speaking of the Reformers. The actual line of division, however, as everyone knows who has troubled to think about it, is between Liberalism in the true sense and Radicalism shading into Socialism. This line chances, too, to divide honesty and sound principles and fidelity to principle from shadiness, bossism, misgovernment, and opportunism. . . .

The necessity for readjusting its mental attitude will force upon the public a revaluation of party labels. When he brings down the Liberal and democratic policy that his speeches and the speeches of his supporters have led the country to expect the new PRIME MINISTER can afford to let the heterogeneous and incoherent Opposition call him by any name it chooses. The nation will be less concerned with the label than with the goods. In one respect, namely, in respect of finance, the nation does want the Reform Government to show itself a party of reaction—of reaction towards the honesty and prudence of BALLANCE. For our own part, knowing that in politics there is a good deal in a name, and that names and phrases can be very potent things, we are glad that the change in our politics will force people to think—and in the case of a great many people, to think for the first time—of the fundamental principles underlying party names. For the present, the main duty of the Government must be the establishment of the reforms to which it is pledged. It was the nation's fervent and uncompromising demand for reform that put MR MASSEY in power. . . .

The Dominion, 10 July 1912, p. 4

92. MILITANT TRADE UNIONISM

Preamble to The Federation of Labour's constitution adopted at the 1912 conference—inspired by the constitution of the 'Industrial Workers of the World' of the United States. It came into force on 1 January 1913.

The working-class and the employing class have nothing in common. There can be no peace so long as hunger and want are found among millions of working-people and the few, who make up the employing class, have all the good things of life.

Between these two classes a struggle must go on until the workers of the world organise as a class, take possession of the earth and the machinery of production, and abolish the wage system.

We find that the centreing of the management of industries into fewer and fewer hands makes the trade unions unable to cope with the ever-growing power of the employing class. The trade unions foster a state of affairs which allows one set of workers to be pitted against another set of workers in the same industry, thereby helping defeat one another in wage wars.

These conditions can be changed and the interest of the working-class upheld only by an organisation formed in such a way that all its members in any one industry, or in all industries, if necessary, cease work whenever a strike or lock-out is on in any department thereof, thus making an injury to one an injury to all.

Instead of the conservative motto: 'A fair day's wages for a fair day's work,' our watchword is: 'Abolition of the wage-system.'

It is the historic mission of the working-class to do away with capitalism. The army of production must be organised, not only for the everyday struggle with capitalists, but also to carry on production when capitalism has been overthrown. By organising industrially we are forming the structure of the new society within the shell of the old. . . .

'New Zealand Federation of Labour. New Constitution and Rules', *The Worker*, Print Wellington, 1912, p. 1

93. INDUSTRIAL UNIONISM

A Federation of Labour view of the significance of the Waihi Gold-miners' Strike 1911–12.

Constituted as it is, it would have been too much to expect that the Massey Government could have approached the situation from any viewpoint other than that of the material interests of the class the Government reflects. There are no men in our bourgeois Government, or for that matter in our bourgeois Parliament, intellectually big enough to rise superior to class considerations—to decline to figure as the scouts and tools of the moneyed few in a 'land of Labor'. . . .

. . . The miners had not struck for fun. As a matter of fact, action had to be taken at Waihi or the Miners' Union be gravely imperilled and straight unionism dealt a heavy blow. Unionism has never yet been able to tolerate the establishment of a scab union without itself becoming the servant of the scab union, and thereby a menace to the organised working-class. . . .

. . . For everybody to see, sectionalism, with its agreements expiring at different dates, forbids united industrial action—and if we are to have united action, then we must have the form of organisation which permits of united action. This being so, how could there be united action at Waihi if a section of the workers was allowed to become Arbitrationist, while the remaining workers favored other methods? . . .

. . . The outburst of outrage and lawlessness at Waihi was undeniably planned by the mine-owners, with the Government for aiders and abettors, the police for organisers, plices, and the law courts for instruments of oppression. Recognising this, we may not blind our eyes to the burden or responsibility that rests on those craft unions proclaiming for arbitration and taking sides with the enemies of Labor. . . .

. . . It is true a thousand times over that there are red stains of blood on the hands of the men of the Massey Government; that there are black stains of guilt on their souls; that there is a mantle of conspiracy and corruption and crime over their administration. . . . But it was not Massey that brought about the defeat at Waihi. It was Labor that defeated Labor. Class-unconsciousness, reflected in craft unions whose sectionalism refused to recognise that an injury to the working-men of Waihi could possibly be an injury to the working-men elsewhere, was the fundamental weakness of our national industrialism. But the awakening comes apace. Our dead comrade is destined to speak louder from the silence of the grave than ever he might have spoken in life, and the lesson to be read from the eternal gloom of that great tragedy is for the working-class a message of industrial life, proclaiming the need for and pointing the way to revolutionary working-class organisation, and hastening the consolidation of the working-class forces into one big revolutionary union on the industrial field in a way that will abolish Arbitration Courts and make scab 'unions' impossible, and one big revolutionary party on the political field with the overthrow of the Class State for its objective and the replacing of political class rule with industrial administration by the workers themselves. . . .

. . . We do not forget that Waihi was but a skirmish of the advance guard in the great class war. . . . Waihi has furnished an indelible contribution to the history of world struggles for freedom; and out of its tragedy has sprung the magnificent promise of working-class solidarity—as demonstrated at the Unity Congress (held since the substance of this book has been in type)—and even now the workers are preparing to unite industrially and politically for the overthrow of their historic class enemies. . . .

> H. E. Holland, 'Ballot Box', and R. S. Ross, *The Tragic Story of the Waihi Strike*, Wellington, 1913, pp. 47, 81, 171–2, 191–3

94. THE SOCIAL DEMOCRATIC PARTY'S PLATFORM, 1913

After the defeat of the unions in the Waihi strike of 1912 a 'Unity Congress' was held in Wellington, 1–10 July 1913. The congress represented about 50,000 workers, and W. T. Mills proposed a 'united Labour movement' in New Zealand with two organizations —one industrial, the other political. Before adopting the Platform, the Social Democratic Party proclaimed a series of principles, beginning: 'The Social Democratic Party stands for the common ownership of all the collectively used agencies of wealth production for use.'

The Fighting Platform

1. Proportional representation, the initiative, the referendum, and the recall.

2. The abolition of the country quota; full civil rights to all public employees; the removal of the Parliamentary disabilities of women.

3. A Right to Work Bill, with minimum wage and maximum hours of six per day, a weekly day of rest, and a Saturday half-holiday.

4. Reorganisation and extension of the powers of the Labor Department to include scientific investigation of matters pertaining to the wages of labor and the cost of living, and to publish all findings thereon.

5. The right of unions to register or not to register without the loss of legal standing; Dominion awards, with power to regulate a minimum on a sliding scale in ratio with the rise in the price of commodities; and protection against the creation of bogus competing organisations of labor.

6. Increased taxation of unimproved land values both in town and country, and a graduated income tax, and a corresponding reduction in tariffs on goods not produced in New Zealand, and in railway freights and fares.

7. No further alienation of Crown lands, and the establishment of homes and of improved farms as going concerns to be within the reach of all workers.

8. The direct representation of the workers on any governing boards in all departments of the Public Service and of local government authorities.

9. Free and secular education from kindergarten to the University, with compulsory attendance in all primary grades. All books and stationery shall be supplied by the State free of cost.

10. To establish State-owned shipping, to extend and promote State fire, life, sick and accident insurance, and to establish a State Bank with the sole right of note issue, and when the time is opportune to take over insurance and banking as sole monopolies of the State.

11. Old-age pensions after 15 years' residence for all men at 60, and for all women at 50; the endowment of motherhood, including maternity care and infant life protection; free hospital care for married and unmarried, and medical aid in the direction of maintaining the national health, rather than simply in the treatment of disease; and pensions for all widows, orphans, the blind, and the incurably helpless.

12. The repeal of the present inadequate Defence Act, and the creation of a citizen army on a volunteer basis, democratically organised with standard wages while on duty, which shall not be used under any circumstances in time of industrial disputes, together with practical measures for the promotion of peace.

'Report of the Proceedings of the Unity Congress held in Wellington, July 1st to 10th, 1913, *The Worker*, Wellington, 1913, pp. 78–9

95. THE 1913 WATERSIDE STRIKE— HARRY HOLLAND IMPRISONED FOR SEDITION

Harry Holland's speech from the dock, and the Chief Justice Sir Robert Stout's remarks in delivering sentence, in the Supreme Court, Wellington, 29 April 1914.

[Holland read from the *Maoriland Worker* report of his speech at Newtown Park, 2 November 1913.]

Mr. Holland . . . said in effect that Wellington had seen what was unique in Australasia. It had been declared that a Gatling gun was in readiness on the wharf, and . . . in the daily papers Col. Heard had made it clear that if the soldiers were called out, and if the civil authorities (meaning the Massey Goverment) deemed it necessary that the crowd should be fired upon, even though there should be women and children in the crowd, the soldiers would not hesitate to fire, although they would not like doing it. He (Holland) said he feared that if one woman or one child were shot down by the Government's order, the fact would light the

RED HELL OF REVOLUTION

in this country, and he deprecated the threat in that direction. They read day by day of farm-owners preparing to come to Wellington fully armed. They read of 2000—he was going to say men, but did not want to be guilty of libel—Waikato heroes who were prepared to come fully armed provided Mr. Massey would guarantee them protection. . . . It had been suggested that the naval men would be required to operate against the strikers, and if there were naval men from the Psyche present he wanted to urge that if they should be ordered to fire upon any body of men, women and children of the working class, they should remember where their class interests lay, and point their guns accordingly. They should refuse to shoot down either the men, women or children of the working class at the behest of the useless exploiters. . . .

It seemed to me that the Government in power had lost all control of its own passions, and that in its

BITTER HATRED OF THE WORKERS

it would even order the bluejackets and soldiers to fire on the people. I admit that fires of indignation leaped in my veins because of the threat. . . .

. . . my own knowledge of what is fundamentally right and wrong, and my own sense of duty to my fellow-men, would not permit me to do other than urge the soldiers

NOT TO SHOOT

I feel that I should be recreant to my own conscience were I to do otherwise—and the question then arises as to what extent a man must pay the penalty to class rule for the crime of possessing a conscience which impels him in such matters to the observance of of what Thoreau calls the 'duty of civil disobedience.' . . .

THE SENTENCE

The Chief Justice (Sir Robert Stout) in summing up said: . . . You have FAILED TO APPRECIATE PEACE AND ORDER. You are an enemy to the people, and you have ceased to have the brotherhood of man before you. Because a man is a capitalist is no reason why he should be attacked. Anyone knows what happened during the strike: some men, waterside workers or others, chose to assault others, and these men were not hitting them nor obstructing them in any way. . . .

. . . The brotherhood of man does not mean a brotherhood of waterside workers only, but a brotherhood that includes all classes of the community, rich as well as poor. If you think that brotherhood is to be amongst one class only, you do not appreciate what brotherhood means. Violence and disorder have come in every case not from the rich classes, but from the working classes. In the recent strike, what right had any man to stop any other man from working if he so wished? A man has the undisputed right to labour, not only the right but the duty to labour—the foundation of social life. Men were struck and assaulted simply because they were working, and that is not the way to promote brotherhood. . . . let me give a word of advice: No good can come out of violence. As you yourself said, 'Violence breeds violence.' You are not to imagine

that this community is going to permit violence towards the established authorities. That would promote civil war. . . .

. . . If you preach peace and order to your mates you may in the
end succeed in improving their status. But neither you nor anyone
else will succeed by preaching civil war. I sentence you to TWELVE
MONTHS' IMPRISONMENT, to count from February 2, and I make
it without hard labour. . . .

. . . I am sorry to inflict hardship upon your family by sentencing
you, but unfortunately you did not stop to consider that point
when you committed the crime. People never do consider the suffering they inflict upon others when they do wrong. As to your plea
that no sentence should be imposed, you must understand that if
the Court acquitted you it would go forth to the world that the
community permitted violence. If you would lead your fellows
you ought to try and show them that there must be a kindly feeling
between all classes, the workers and the employers alike, and the
only progress that can come is by promoting that kindly feeling. . . .

> *Twelve Months for Sedition*, pamphlet pub-
> lished by *The Maoriland Worker*, Wellington,
> 1914

96. THE SOCIALIST OBJECTIVE OF THE
LABOUR MOVEMENT

*Harry Holland's maiden speech in the House of Representatives,
30 October 1918, in which he proclaimed Labour's socialist objective and indicted the National Government's War Administration.*

. . . We come into this House as representatives of the working-
men in certain electorates of the Dominion, and we come to state
not our views alone, but the views of the men and women who have
sent us here. We do not come merely to attempt to make a change
of individuals on the Government benches. We of the Labour party
come to endeavour to effect a change of classes at the fountain of
power. We come proclaiming boldly and fearlessly the Socialist
objective of the labour movement throughout New Zealand; and we
make no secret of the fact that we seek to rebuild society on a
basis in which work and not wealth will be the measure of a man's
worth. What is wrong with the men on the Government benches
to-day is not that they are worse than other men—they are bad

enough, the Lord knows—but that they represent powerful class interests, which class interests are always in conflict with the interests of the community, with the interests of the men and women who render social service. We do not seek to make a class war. You cannot make that which is already in existence. We recognize that the antagonisms which divide society to-day into classes are economically foundationed, and we are going, if we can, to change those economic foundations, to end the class war by ending the causes of class warfare. . . .

. . . We come first and foremost to take our place as the party that is in the end destined to occupy the Government benches in this chamber. We come to function as the legitimate Opposition to the National Government, and to indict the Government on both its legislation and its administration. The . . . fight in the future is between Toryism on the one hand and the Labour party on the other hand. The Liberal party can never again regain the position which it held in days gone by, for this reason if for no other: that it to-day stands for a repudiation of the things that mattered in the policy of Ballance and Seddon. . . .

. . . We of the Labour party indict the National Government on its war legislation. In the first place, it passed a conscription law which it did not dare to permit the people to vote upon, which it would not to-day dare to put before the people. . . . As a result of conscription and the War Regulations you have between two hundred and three hundred of the very best men that New Zealand possesses lying in prisons cells to-day. You have thousands of men fugitives in their own country, many of them in the bush, gazetted as deserters, and who are being hunted down in the hills and tracked in the towns. The land is filled with sorrow as a result of the militarizing of New Zealand. . . .

N.Z.P.D., 1918, vol. 183, pp. 92–9

5

COLONY INTO NATION, 1870 TO 1948

---

97. COLONIAL RESPONSIBILITY FOR INTERNAL SECURITY

Dispatch from the Secretary of State, Earl Granville to Governor Sir George Bowen, 7 October 1869, in which he argues that it is wrong in principle for the British Government to be responsible for internal security in a Colony whose policies it might disapprove of. He sees the withdrawal of the last British troops as in the best interests of the Colony.

All experience, and not least the experience of New Zealand itself, has shown the fatal consequences of carrying on War under a divided authority. It can but lead to continual differences, imperfect co-operation, interrupted enterprizes and the other evils which are alleged to have characterized the Maori War. . . .

. . . If the active employment of British Troops in a Colony in which Responsible Government has been established under ordinary circumstances is fraught with difficulties, it is still more objectionable when the presence of these Troops is calculated to encourage the Colonial Government in a policy which the Home Government have always regarded as pregnant with danger.

The present distress of the Colony arises mainly from two circumstances, the discontent of the Natives consequent on the confiscation of their land, and the neglect of successive Governments to place on foot a force sufficiently formidable to overawe that discontent.

That the discontent of the Natives does mainly arise from the confiscation of their lands is manifest. The neighbourhood of Tauranga and other confiscated Districts on the East Coast is that in which Te Kooti maintains himself. In Taranaki your own officer states that 'the larger and more generally operative incitement to rebellion is the hope of recovering land and status,' while the restoration of the large extent of land confiscated in the Waikato is unequivocally put forward by the Advisers of the so-called Maori King as the condition of pacification.

These being the sources of the danger to which the Colony is exposed from the Natives it is pressed upon Her Majesty's Government that the task of reducing the Natives is beyond the strength of the Colony; and this is conclusively shown both by the experience of the last war, in which as you have frequently observed, the Colonial Forces has the assistance of nearly ten thousand Regular Troops, and by the present state of the North Island, where a few hundred Insurgents suffice to impose a ruinous insecurity on large numbers of Settlers, and a ruinous expenditure on the Colony.

Meanwhile I perceive that the average strength of the Colonial Forces on foot during the year preceding the commencement of these disturbances, hardly exceeded 700 men, having in the month of March been allowed to fall to 496, and although it has been of late greatly increased and improved yet that your present Ministry on its accession to office contemplated its speedy reduction.

Large concessions therefore are unavoidable to appease a pervading discontent with which the Colony is otherwise unable to cope, and still larger concessions will be required unless a force is kept on foot capable of commanding the respect of the Natives when the Queen's Troops are withdrawn.

But the abandonment of land, the recognition of Maori authority and the maintenance of an expensive Force, however indispensable some or all of these may be, are distasteful remedies, which will not be resorted to while the Colony continues to expect assistance from this country. And a decision to supply the Colony even with the prestige of British Troops, objectionable as I have shown it to be on grounds of practical principle, would in my view, be also immediately injurious to the settlers themselves as tending to delay their adoption of those prudent counsels on which, as I think, the restoration of the Northern Island depends.

It is in no spirit of controversy that I make these remarks. I should not gratuitously have criticized the proceedings of the Colonial Government, who are entitled to the entire management of their own affairs. But this Country is asked for assistance; it is asked for assistance to sustain a policy which it does not direct, and which it is not able to foresee. Upon such a state of facts many questions arise; and among them it becomes material to enquire whether that assistance is for the real advantage of those who seek it. Judging from the best materials at my command I am satisfied that it is not so, and that it is not the part of a true friend of the Colonists by continuing a delusive shadow of support, to divert their attention from that course in which their real safety lies—the course of deliberately measuring their own resources and, at whatever immediate sacrifice, adjusting their policy to them.

No. 115 received 13 Dec. 1869, G1/71

98. A POLICY OF SEPARATION DISAVOWED

Dispatch from the Earl of Granville (Secretary of State for the Colonies) to Governor Sir George Bowen, 25 March 1870.

. . . Her Majesty's Government absolutely disavow any wish on their part to abandon New Zealand, or to bring about the separation between this Country and the Colony. The refusal to retain the Troops in New Zealand did not proceed from any indifference to the true welfare of the Colony, but from a conviction that on the one hand the employment of British Troops in a Colony possessed of responsible Government was objectionable in principle except in the case of Foreign War, and under conditions arising out of such a War; and on the other hand it is not for the true interest of the Colony itself that New Zealand should be made an exception from that rule, which, with due consideration for circumstances, is in course of application to other Colonies. . . .

No. 35 received 2 June 1870, G1/72

99. DEFENCE AGAINST EXTERNAL AGGRESSION

Memorandum by the Premier, William Fox, 30 December 1870, (for transmission by the Governor to the Secretary of State for the Colonies).

Ministers respectfully desire to represent, through His Excellency, to the Imperial Government the position of the Colony of New Zealand in the event of Great Britain being unhappily involved in war with any Foreign Nation, and the claim which the Colony has for adequate protection against external aggression.

The Imperial Government have adopted and acted on the policy of repudiating all concern in civil war in the Colony, and have removed from it the Military Force which not only served as a moral support to Her Majesty's loyal subjects of both races, but which also constituted a material protection in the case of foreign war.

Meanwhile, the action of the Imperial Government,—action in which the Colony has no share, and over which it can exercise no control—may suddenly plunge the Colony into foreign hostility, expose to serious damage its ports and its trade, and stimulate internal Native rebellion into renewed activity.

Under these circumstances, the Colony has irresistable right to claim that the Imperial Government should take such steps as will secure it against the serious consequences, external and internal, of foreign war in the origination of which it has no voice and of which it will be compulsorily the passive victim.

The present state of Europe makes this question one of vital import to the Colony, and Ministers feel it their duty to ask to be informed distinctly what measures of protection the Imperial Government will adopt, in case of war between England and any other nation.

There appear to be two courses open,—either that the Imperial Government should supply adequate defence, which does not now exist, or sanction an arrangement with foreign powers that in the event of war the Colony should be treated as neutral.

In making this representation, Ministers desire to reiterate the expression of the loyalty of the Colony to the Crown, and of their anxiety that it should always be preserved as an integral portion of the Empire. The same anxiety for the integrity of the Empire which actuated them in their recent appeal to the Imperial Government when the question at issue was confined to civil war, now actuates them in their present appeal, when that question is extended to a wider range and assumes a greater significance. The Colonists of New Zealand will cheerfully bear their due share, as loyal subjects to Her Majesty, in the maintenance of her Crown and dignity, and in the preservation of her Empire. . . .

C.O. 209/221, pp. 15–18

100. THE QUESTION OF NEUTRALITY

Reply from the Earl of Kimberley, Secretary of State for Colonies, to Governor Sir George Bowen, 15 March 1871.

. . . the Memorandum raises the further question whether the Colony could be treated as neutral in a War in which Great Britain was engaged.

On this I would remark that if a British Colony is to remain neutral when England is a Belligerent, the following among other questions would require to be considered. Could the other Belligerent be expected to recognize that neutrality?

Would the people of England be content to remain under the obligation of resenting injuries offered to that Colony in time of peace?

In what manner and in what terms is it proposed upon this hypothesis to define the connexion between the home Country and the Colony, to which I am glad to notice that your Ministers reiterate their attachment?

No. 30 received 4 May 1871, G1/74

101. NAVAL PROTECTION

Memorandum by the Premier, William Fox, 26 June 1871 (for transmission by the Governor to the Secretary of State for the Colonies).

His Lordship has in his remarks apparently misconceived the intention of their Memorandum. Its object was not to recommend that in the event of War the Colony should be treated as neutral, but humbly to represent, in the immediate interests of the Colony either that the Imperial Government should, in such case adequately defend it, or secure its neutrality,—and thus more strongly to urge on them the duty of defence by showing the alternative into which they would otherwise be logically forced,—an . . . alternative altogether impracticable, consistently with the Sovereignty of the Crown. . . .

In simply stating the grounds on which they are endeavouring to arrive at some definite understanding with the Imperial Government as to the protection which will be afforded to the Colony, Ministers have no desire to revive past controversy, or to raise unnecessary discussion, but they do so from a settled conviction that uncertainty on this point, or reliance, as at present, on the drift of accidents will, sooner or later, inevitably lead to results ruinous to the Colony, and fatal to the integrity of the Empire. . . .

In consequence of the course of Imperial Policy towards it, the resources of New Zealand are at this time necessarily absorbed in giving effect to large measures for its internal security;—and therefore the imminent probability, last year, of a war between England and Russia was viewed with great alarm, in the absence of all Military and any adequate Naval Imperial protection—and in the apparent unlikelihood, as far as could be seen, of any such protection being forthcoming. It is now known that, in contemplation of war, a Russian Corvette was in the Australian Waters and would have been able, if war had been declared, to have inflicted incalculable damage on British commerce and property before any steps could have been taken for her capture.

It was under these circumstances that a respectful representation was made to the Imperial Government urging them, unless they wished altogether to abandon this Colony, to take some steps for increasing its Naval protection, and supplying it with other means of defence, and to lay down specifically some principles and conditions on which these Colonies could systematically and harmoniously cooperate with the Mother Country in their external defence.

[Minute on the memorandum by the Earl of Kimberley.]

. . . I think we might answer by stating that it is impossible to give any further assurances as to the manner in which the British fleet would be employed in the case of foreign war than those already given. So much must depend on the nature and circumstances of the conflict which cannot be precisely foreseen, that the particular manner in which H.M.'s ships would be employed, cannot be laid down. . . . It is obvious that it would be impossible that H.M.'s ships should always be at hand on the far extended coasts of the Australasian colonies, and that it would greatly conduce to the safety of New Zealand and the general strength of the Empire if N.Z. were to take advantage of the Naval Defence Act and gradually establish an armed Colonial Navy. Such a navy would be of great service to N.Z. in her internal affairs, and when supported by H.M.'s ships in time of war would secure the colonial coasts and trade from insult; . . .

C.O. 209/222, p. 61–4

102. REDUCED POLITICAL POSITION OF THE GOVERNOR UNDER RESPONSIBLE GOVERNMENT

Governor Sir Arthur Hamilton Gordon's descriptions of his position in private letters to Lord Selborne, 1881.

... The official duties of a Governor of New Zealand or any similar Colony are few, and excepting once or twice in five or six years when he may be called on to decide whether he will dissolve a Parliament or dismiss a ministry, they are altogether formal and mechanical. They make no demand whatever on his thoughts—and but little on his time—not occupying perhaps more than two or three hours *a week*. . . . The fact that the Governor has 'absolutely nothing whatever to do in the way of business' which one of my predecessors Lord Normanby in writing to me mentions as constituting one of the main attractions of the place is to me just the reverse. . . . How completely perfunctory a 'Governor's' action is you in England altogether fail to realize. It is quite a mistake to compare his official position with that of the Queen at home. Things move fast in this part of the world. We are no longer in the earlier days of 'responsible' Government when the Governor though powerless still exercised a sort of traditional influence. There is as much difference between the position of a Constitutional Governor in 1860 and 1880 as between the Queen now and George III an hundred years ago. I presume that whatever the theory may be the practical authority of a constitutional Sovereign is that of which the Legislature tacitly permits the exercise and which usage sanctions. . . . Here the jealousy of the legislature, and the arrogance of successive ministries have deprived the Governor not only of all influence in public affairs but to a great extent even the means of obtaining any knowledge of them. . . . [2 January 1881]

. . . Sir Hercules Robinson devoted himself entirely to racing, which gave him ample employment. Lord Normanby shot a great deal, and played cards at the club every afternoon, when he did not shoot. Sir James Ferguson (sic.) (who was unable to endure it much more than a year) had a yacht, in which he spent most of his time. I do not yacht, or play cards, or shoot, or race; so I have none of their resources. . . . [20 May 1881]

. . . Once a week—on Tuesdays,—there is what is called an Executive Council;—that is to say, the Premier, and one other member of the Cabinet, (two are required for a quorum), meet me in the Council Room. The Clerk gabbles over the *Caption* of a lot of papers. The Premier says 'I advise Your Excellency to approve these recommendations', and hands me a pen. The Clerk puts the schedule before me, and I write on it 'appd. A.H.G.'. The whole of the proceedings do not occupy more than ten minutes or a quarter of an hour.—After the Council, the Premier frequently, (but not always), comes to my room, for five minutes, and asks me, (in a way which always irresistibly reminds me of the *Lieutenant of the Tower* asking a state prisoner whether he can in any way oblige him), whether there is anything I want done in the house, or garden; whether anything requires amendment there; or whether I wish to use the Government boat? During the whole five months he has never once spoken to me on public affairs, and any attempt on my part to speak to him would be, at once, peremptorily checked. The other ministers I never see, (except at a dinner), and have no communication with them except through the Premier.

Two or three times a week, batches of papers are sent up for my signature, with a memorandum of advice. . . . Sometimes the signatures, especially of grants, are very numerous. I have had as many as 600 in a day, and as many more a day or two after. But beyond the signing of my name, I have nothing to do, and this is looked on as so mere a formality that the papers are seldom sent for signature until some days after the sanction that signature is supposed to convey has been acted on, and the steps taken by 'the Government' announced in the papers. Mr. Hall (the Premier) and I are on the best possible terms . . . but he makes no secret of his conviction that he, or any other minister, would be considered by the public to betray his trust if he discussed *any* matter with the Governor, and tells me that it is now an understood thing that no *reasons* are ever given to the Governor for ministerial 'advice'. The Governor is perfectly at liberty to refuse it, if he can find another Ministry, but unless he does so, he must accept it *because* it is their advice, and, when the ministers have made up their minds, discussion with the Governor is unnecessary, and 'might lead to false impressions.' As, however, advice is only needed when a *signature* is required, the most important acts of the Government, which require *no* signature, are not submitted to the Governor at all. I know no more of them beforehand than you do in Portland Place; and I learn them, when done, as the rest of the world does, from the morning newspaper. . . . [23 April 1881]

. . . (1) Twenty years ago, though one was not present at Cabinet meetings, the business done was,—as it is (or at least used to be) in England,—reported to the Governor by the Prime Minister. Now, not the smallest hint of Cabinet proceedings is allowed to reach the Governor.

(2) One was allowed free intercourse with all the ministers. All communications now pass through the Premier exclusively.

(3) Though the ultimate decision, of course, rested with Ministers, all questions were freely discussed with the Governor. His opinion was listened to, and sometimes taken. Now, unless his signature is required, no matter is mentioned to him, and then only in the shape of 'advice', which must be taken.

(4) No step requiring the Governor's approval was taken until it had formally been submitted to him. Now, the general rule is to act first, and advise approval, as a matter of course, afterwards.

(5) The Governor was the *sole* medium of communication between the local and home governments. Now, all the larger Colonies have an 'Agent General' in London, who communicates direct with the C.O., and none of whose correspondence with the local Government is ever seen by, or mentioned to, the Governor.

(6) The Governor's dispatches were simply an affair between himself and the Home Govt. They were of course liable to be published, and he might, if he chose, communicate them to his ministers, but the claim of the local ministers as a matter of right, to see them was refused, time after time, by the Secretary of State. Now, they not only see all, but affect practically to dictate those written from hence.

(7) The Governor exercised a *personal* command over the Militia and Volunteers, as Commander in Chief. It was subject, of course, to the general control of the Government, but was real, and afforded some employment. Now, the control of the armed force is so completely in the 'Defence Minister', that not even the Governor's formal approval is required for any matter relating to it and had the Government accepted, instead of rejecting, Mr. Bryce's warlike policy, the force would have been ordered to Parihaka without any sort of communication with me previously, and war commenced without my knowledge.

And all these are very important 'developments' of the responsible government system. . . . [20 May 1881]

> From the Stanmore Papers, quoted by D. K. Fieldhouse, 'Autochthonous Elements in the Evolution of Dominion Status: The Case of New Zealand', *Journal of Commonwealth Political Studies,* 1962 1(2): 89–92

103. THE CROWN AND MINISTERIAL ADVICE IN CONSTITUTIONAL MATTERS, 1881

After the occupation of Parihaka and the apprehension of Te Whiti in November 1881 the Premier, John Hall, sought a Dissolution of Parliament and although the Governor, Sir Arthur Gordon, attempted to attach conditions he had to give way when the government threatened to resign. When Hall then asked that the meeting of the new General Assembly be prorogued for nearly two months, Gordon again tried to interfere. Hall insisted that his 'Advice' be accepted and the Secretary of State, Lord Kimberley, firmly upheld the doctrine of ministerial responsibility.

[Memorandum from Gordon for Ministers, 16 December 1881.]

The Governor has been advised to prorogue the meeting of the General Assembly from the 22nd December to the 13th February.

His Excellency has without hesitation assented to this advice, but at the same time he thinks it his duty to state some reasons which lead him to consider that the principles of Constitutional Government require the assembly of the new Parliament at the earliest possible moment consistent with public convenience.

It is the duty of the Governor to act upon the advice of Ministers possessing the confidence of Parliament; and to enable him to do so, it is necessary that he should have reasonable ground to believe that such confidence exists.

On the election of a new Parliament this can be shewn only in one or other of two ways; either by public declarations of support given by a majority of the members returned to the House of Representatives; or by a Vote of the House itself, after it has been called together.

In the present instance, declarations of support to the existing Administration have not been made by an absolute majority of the House of Representatives. That its confidence is possessed by

Ministers cannot therefore be said to be proved until the commencement of the next session of Parliament.

His Excellency consequently believes that—wholly apart from the consideration of any question of policy—constitutional principle requires that the meeting of the Legislature should not be delayed, as he understands is contemplated, for a period of six months from the date of the dissolution of the late Parliament.

Again; since the close of the last session the Government has taken measures of great importance involving the risk of open hostilities between different sections of Her Majesty's subjects in this Colony; and it would appear to be only consistent with constitutional usage, and certainly in accordance with the principles of Parliamentary Government that the judgement of the newly elected Parliament upon these transactions should be pronounced as speedily as possible.

Thirdly; it appears to His Excellency that an Act of Indemnity may be required to sanction some of the steps taken by direction of Ministers in carrying out the measures above referred to. Should this be so, it is almost needless to observe that no time should be lost in seeking such indemnity, whether it be regarded simply as a matter of Constitutional propriety, or in view of the possible institution of legal proceedings with regard to any act for which legislative indemnity may be required.

For these reasons His Excellency conceives an early session of the Parliament lately elected to be desirable.

[Minute by John Bramston, Assistant Under-Secretary in the Colonial Office, 28 February 1882.]

I think Sir Arthur's lecture to his Ministers rather uncalled for; he might have been at any rate less oracular as to their misfeasances if he meant them to pay any attention to him.

[Minute by Leonard Courtenay, the Parliamentary Under-Secretary, March 1882.]

I think Sir Arthur is right constitutionally.

[Minute by Lord Kimberley, 2 March 1882.]

I am not prepared to say that Sir A. Gordon was right. If he is persuaded, as he says, his Ministers have most probably the confidence of the newly elected Parliament, he has it not in his power to require them to call Parliament together on pain of dismissal. Where then is the use of his lecture? It is for his Ministers to judge what advice they will give him on this and other points.

C.O. 209/241, p. 8–12

104. NEW ZEALAND'S DEFENCE AND ROYAL NAVY SUPREMACY

From an address 'The Defence of New Zealand' by the Governor, Sir William Jervois, to the New Zealand Institute on 4 October 1884, in which he placed New Zealand's defences in the setting of the defence of the British Empire.

. . . The defence of New Zealand should be regarded from an Imperial and an Australasian, as well as from a local point of view.

The first line of defence of this, as of every other part of the British Empire, is on the lines of maritime communication. If the steamers and sailing-vessels that carry our exports and imports to and fro along the ocean highways were liable to be captured or destroyed by hostile ships, our commerce would be stopped. The result to the colonies would be disastrous. To Great Britain, it would be starvation. . . .

Bases for the naval defence of the empire are maintained and fortified by Great Britain, not only . . . in the United Kingdom, but also at numerous places throughout the world, in positions advantageous for coaling, victualling, and refitting the vessels of war charged with the defence of our commerce. . . .

. . . You will also understand that it is of paramount importance that these stations be rendered thoroughly secure. They cannot fulfill the conditions required of them if their anchorages, and the depots and repairing establishments they contain, are not protected against hostile occupation, capture, or destruction, during the absence of the squadron they are intended to support. It is, I know, often said that the defence of these stations should be dependent upon our fleet, but this view will not bear examination. The depots are provided to enable our vessels of war to command the sea, and those vessels cannot possess the freedom of action which is necessary for the performance of their duties if they are either tied down to particular places, or are obliged to manoeuvre with a view to the protection of those places. The Admiral on station requires his ships for the defence of our commerce at sea, and he cannot detach them for the purpose of guarding particular ports. . . .

Now, considering the question from an Australasian point of view, the security against attack of certain ports in Australasia is an essential part of the maritime defence of this portion of the empire, and it will be seen that there are some, which are of common interest to all these colonies. For instance . . . all ships approaching Australia by the Cape or Red Sea routes must pass comparatively near to King George's Sound. If, therefore, this harbour were held by an enemy, his war-ships acting therefrom might cut off our steamers and merchant-vessels. . . . Again . . . the Derwent, on which is the Town of Hobart, occupies a central position, whence attacks might be directed against Australia and New Zealand. . . . Again, New Zealand is, as it were, an advanced shield to the south-eastern part of Australia. . . .

The defence of these harbours is therefore not only important to the places themselves and the colony to which they belong, but has a considerable bearing upon the defence of Australasia generally. There is, perhaps, no harbour in Australasia more suitable as a centre of naval defence than Auckland.

It will then be readily understood that it is most desirable that all the Australian Colonies should unite to carry out defences in which all are interested, making an arrangement by which each would bear its fair share of the expense. . . . Unity of organization, and especially measures required for general naval protection which are common to the whole of these colonies, can only be carried out under federal arrangement. So far as defence is concerned, New Zealand is probably more interested than any other Australasian Colony in the question of federation. . . . In the absence, however, of any such organisation, each colony must do what is necessary for its own defence, taking care at the same time that, as far as possible, its separate action shall harmonize with any future joint concert with its neighbours which may arise. . . .

With respect to the nature of attack to which these colonies are liable in the event of Great Britain being at war with a foreign naval Power, I have often pointed out . . . that there is no probability of an expedition on any extensive scale being dispatched against Australia. In the improbable event of Great Britain ceasing to hold command of the seas, such an expedition might perhaps be undertaken with a view of subjugating the colonies and finally annexing them. The very existence of the British Empire, however, depends upon her naval supremacy, and the question must obviously be considered on the assumption that that supremacy is, as it undoubtedly will be, maintained.

In the event of Great Britain being engaged in hostilities with any great maritime Power, the enemy would retain the most powerful portion of his fleet in European water, or in the Atlantic, for the protection of his country, or for operations in the immediate neighbourhood of hostilities. If he sent his fleet, or any considerable portion of it, on an expedition against the Australasian Colonies, a sufficient part of our Home Fleet would in turn be set free to intercept it; and our squadrons in the Pacific, on the China, the Australasian, and Indian stations, might, if necessary, be concentrated to oppose it.

But, whilst the bulk of the enemy's naval forces would be occupied in the immediate scene of action in Europe or America, he might no doubt dispatch one or more cruisers, and possibly an ironclad, to operate against our maritime commerce, or make a descent upon Australasian ports, which, if undefended or insufficiently protected, would offer tempting objects of attack. Eluding our cruisers, and appearing suddenly on the coast of New Zealand or Australia, the enemy might capture the merchant-vessels in the harbours, or— under threat of bombardment, or after actual firing into one of the towns—demand and obtain payment of money. Or the object might be attained by an enemy landing a small force in the vicinity of a town, if steps were not taken to meet such a contingency. . . .

Of all parts of Australasia, New Zealand, owing to her extensive seaboard and numerous harbours, is most in need of local naval protection. The principle on which the defence of the colony must be based is, that whilst the general protection of its commerce and seaboard is provided for by naval means, the chief cities and ports should be rendered secure in themselves by land batteries, submarine mines and other local defences. By fortifying these places, the chief centres of wealth are absolutely protected, whilst each becomes a focus of refuge or action for the general naval defence.

The main general plan should therefore be to fortify Auckland Harbour, Port Nicholson, Port Lyttelton, Port Chalmers, and the Bluff Harbour; thus setting free the Imperial cruisers and any local naval force we may possess, and thereby greatly strengthening our power of general maritime defence. In fact, the fortification of these five ports is part and parcel of the Naval defence of the colony.

It is obviously impossible, however, to fortify all the harbours of New Zealand. . . . The protection of all these . . . must be provided for by local naval forces acting as auxiliaries to Her Majesty's cruisers, and combined as far as practicable with other means of defence. At or near most of the places . . . field forces of riflemen and field guns would also be available for their protection. . . . In the distant future New Zealand may become—I venture to foretell she will become—a considerable Naval Power; but meanwhile she must be content with what her present resources will enable her to accomplish. The most practicable suggestion that I can now make with regard to provision by the colony of vessels of war is to make arrangements for utilizing certain vessels of the Union Steamship Company as auxiliary cruisers for local defence. . . . 'But how much will all this cost?' . . . The whole thing could be done for a capital sum of £400,000. Of course, there would also be some annual expenditure. . . .

New Zealand . . . at present expends scarcely anything for the purpose of resisting foreign aggression. . . .

. . . I *do* . . . venture to suggest that she should not rest content in her present unprotected state. It is not only impolitic, but rash, for her to remain in a passive, defenceless state, unprepared to resist aggression, trusting to the forbearance of any Power possessing the means of attack. . . .

. . . New Zealand is happily united to the greatest maritime Power the world has ever seen, which, by her fleets and squadrons acting from her naval stations, protects the commerce of the empire. The old 'Mother-country', as she is sometimes called, cannot, however, do everything. Australasia must do her part. . . .

> W. F. D. Jervois, *The Defence of New Zealand*,
> New Zealand Institute, Wellington, 1884, pp.
> 3–21

105. AN IMPERIAL FEDERATION

Memorandum submitted to the Governor by Sir Julius Vogel, Colonial Treasurer, 24 February 1885.

. . . By Federation of the Empire Sir Julius Vogel understands to mean the promulgation of such a Constitution as will indissolubly knit all Great Britain's vast territories into one dominion, without power to any part to retire from the Federation. . . . It is certain that when the population of Australasia and Canada combined equals the population of Great Britain, and probably long before that time, neither Canada nor Australasia will be content to remain without a voice in the Government of the British Empire, so far as relates to external subjects, or indeed to all subjects upon which the issues of peace and war depend. It is manifestly impossible that they will feel otherwise, educated as they will have been in a deep veneration for representative institutions. How can it be imagined that many millions of self-governing, wealthy, and powerful people will consent, without exercising substantial control, to the horrors of war being thrust upon them. . . .

. . . If, then, what to the writer seems the mathematical certainty is recognized, that the colonies will within a few years insist upon having a voice in the affairs upon which peace, war, and treaties depend, it becomes a question, Should they attain to this voice gradually or by a violent wrench, when endurance is stretched to its extreme limit? . . .

If it be conceded that Federation is the sole alternative to the breaking-up of the Empire within a comparatively short period, and that it means that the several parts of the British dominions must have a share in the Government of the whole, it becomes necessary to consider how that share can be given. Obviously the share must be proportional to the importance of the portions represented. . . . As to absolute cost, it is probable that any contribution the colonies would have to make on any reasonable basis to the cost of the forces and defence of the Empire would fall far short of what they are now spending in more or less isolated efforts in the way of defence. . . .

There remains an alternative, which is free from many, though not all, of the objections touched upon, and which is by far the most promising course, inasmuch as it may be brought to a conclusion at any time if not found satisfactory, whilst, if it should prove acceptable, it is capable of being worked out to the ultimate end desired. That plan is to give the colonies the right to elect a certain number of members to the House of Commons. . . .

. . . The proposed representation might be made experimental, to extend, for example, over the duration of three Parliaments. The number of representatives given to the whole of the constitutional colonies need only be small, say twenty in all. Much may be said as to the advantages of this proposal. It is free from the principal objection to other plans that they involve the recognition of a new official position. A colonial representative would be neither more nor less than a member of Parliament. His influence in the House, or with members, or with the Government would depend upon the force of his character, the strength of his abilities, and the nicety of his tact and judgment. . . .

A.J.H.R., 1885, A–I, pp. 28–31

106. FIRST OFFICIAL OFFER OF TROOPS FOR SERVICE OVERSEAS, 1885

The Governor Sir William Jervois reports a Cabinet decision on 4 June 1885 to offer 1,000 men for Imperial service.

. . . My Ministers, on the 4th May, as soon as they considered that the defences of this Colony were in a state to justify them in taking such a step, requested me to telegraph to Your Lordship that they proposed to ask Parliament to sanction the expense of sending one thousand well trained men, one fourth to be Maoris, for active service in Afghanistan, or any other part of the globe where Her Majesty's Government might require them. . . .

Jervois to Derby, 20 June 1885. C.O. 209/245

107. TRADE NEGOTIATIONS WITH FOREIGN POWERS, 1887

In a memorandum for the 1887 Colonial Conference, Francis Dillon Bell, the New Zealand Agent General in London, requests that the governments of New Zealand and the Australian colonies should be given the same rights of access to foreign governments as Canada and that all colonies might be allowed to negotiate commercial treaties under the general aegis of H.M. Ambassadors in the relevant countries.

I beg permission to bring before the Conference the expediency of extending to the Governments of Australasia the same privilege which has been repeatedly granted to Canada, of entering into negotiations with foreign countries, under the sanction of the Foreign Office and in concert with Her Majesty's Ambassadors or Ministers at other courts, in matters of trade and commerce.

Without referring to transactions of an earlier date, I may mention that in 1878–9 the Government of the Dominion desired to negotiate with the French Government for a relaxation of the duties on Canadian products, and Sir Alexander Galt, G.C.M.G., who had already been charged with a mission of a similar character to the Spanish Government on behalf of Canada, was formally accredited by the Marquis of Salisbury to Viscount Lyons, Her Majesty's Ambassador at Paris, in order that the Ambassador might place him in communication with the proper authorities in that capital for the purpose. . . .

Lord Salisbury . . . decided that while the formal negotiations between the Governments of England and France were to be conducted by Lord Lyons, the settlement of the details was to be made by Sir Alexander Galt. . . .

I ought to add that some time ago, upon a postal question, I was accredited in the same way to Lord Lyons by Lord Granville, and placed in direct communication with M. Cochery, who at that time controlled the French postal and telegraphic services.

The immediate cause of my asking permission to bring the question before the Conference is that very recently communications of a private nature have been passing with the French Customs authorities, on a matter of much commercial interest to New Zealand. A trade in our frozen meats has sprung up at Paris, and it is capable of large extension; but the heavy duty of 10 fr. 50 c. per 100 kilos, lately increased under fresh protective legislation to 12 fr., has hitherto been greatly in the way of a profitable trade. An opportunity, nevertheless, exists now for reconsidering these duties, with a view to reciprocal trade advantages; and I have been asked to go over to Paris and discuss the particular points requiring arrangement. I propose accordingly to ask permission of Her Majesty's Government to communicate with Lord Lyons, and through his Lordship with the French authorities, for this object.

But in the meantime, as there are many commercial questions in which reciprocal trade concessions might be secured with advantage to British interests generally, and to Australasian interests in particular, by friendly negotiations between the Australasian colonies and other countries, it seems desirable for the Conference to consider the general question whether the privilege should not be extended to all Colonial Governments alike, of being allowed to negotiate commercial treaties with foreign powers, under the sanction and supervision of Her Majesty's Ambassadors at foreign courts. The Foreign Office would reserve to itself, of course, the right of judging in each case as to the expediency of the proposed arrangements, and as to their bearing on the commercial interests of this country;

but generally it will no doubt be admitted that the removal of difficulties affecting Colonial trade which arise out of foreign tariffs, must tend to the advantage of the trade and commerce of the Empire. . . .

Memo. by Sir F. Dillon Bell, 27 April 1887, Proceedings of the Colonial Conference, 1887, vol. ii, Great Britain, *Parliamentary Papers,* 1887, C-5091-I, pp. 135–6

108. THE AUSTRALASIAN NAVAL AGREEMENT, 1887

Portions of the Australasian Naval Defence Act, 1887, which authorized payments of about £20,000 per year as New Zealand's contribution to a reinforced Royal Navy Squadron.

'An Act to provide for the Payment by the Colony of New Zealand of a Proportional Part of the Cost of the Establishment and Maintenance of an Additional Naval Force to be employed for the Protection of the Floating Trade in Australasian Waters.'

[23rd December, 1887.]

. . . 3. In each of the ten years during which the said agreement shall be in force, there shall be issued and paid to Her Majesty, out of the Consolidated Fund, for the purposes of the said agreement, a sum bearing the same proportion to the total amount payable under Article VII. of the said agreement as the population of New Zealand bears to the total population of the Australasian Colonies whose Governments are parties to the said agreement. . . .

SCHEDULE
AGREEMENT AS TO ADDITIONAL FORCE TO BE EMPLOYED FOR THE PROTECTION OF THE FLOATING TRADE IN AUSTRALASIAN WATERS

Article I
There shall be established a force of sea-going ships of war, hereinafter referred to as 'these vessels,' to be provided, equipped, manned, and maintained at the joint cost of Imperial and Colonial funds.

Article II
The vessels shall be placed in every respect on the same status as Her Majesty's ships of war, whether in commission or not. . . .

Article IV

These vessels shall be under the sole control and orders of the Naval Commander-in-Chief for the time being appointed to command Her Majesty's ships and vessels on the Australian Station.

These vessels shall be retained within the limits of the Australian Station, as defined in the Standing Orders of the Naval Commander-in-Chief, and in times of peace or war shall be employed within such limits in the same way as are Her Majesty's ships of war, or employed beyond those limits only with the consent of the Colonial Governments.

Article V

Notwithstanding the establishment of this joint naval force, no reduction is to take place in the normal strength of Her Majesty's naval force employed on the Australian Station, exclusive of surveying vessels.

Article VI

These vessels shall consist of five fast cruisers and two torpedo gunboats, as represented by the 'Archer' (improved type) and 'Rattlesnake' classes in Her Majesty's navy. Of the above, three cruisers and one gunboat to be kept always in commission, the remainder being held in reserve, in Australasian ports, ready for commission whenever occasion arises.

Article VII

1. The first cost of these vessels shall be paid out of Imperial funds, and the vessels fully equipped, manned, and sent to Australia.

2. The colonies shall pay the Imperial Government interest at 5 per cent. on the first and prime cost of these vessels, such payment not to exceed the annual sum of £35,000.

3. The colonies shall, in addition, bear the actual charges for maintaining from year to year the three fast cruisers and one torpedo gunboat, which are to be kept in commission in time of peace, and also of the three other vessels, which are to remain in reserve, including the liability on account of retired pay to officers, pensions to men, and the charge for relief of crews; provided always that the claim made by the Imperial Government under this head does not exceed the annual payment of £91,000.

4. In time of emergency or actual war the cost of commissioning and maintaining the three vessels kept in reserve during peace shall be borne by the Imperial Government.

Article VIII

In the event of any of these vessels being lost they shall be replaced at the cost of the Imperial Government. . . .

Article XI

Nothing in this agreement shall affect the purely local naval defence forces which have been or may be established in the several colonies for harbour and coast defence. Such local forces in each colony to be paid for entirely by that colony, and to be solely under its control.

Article XII

In time of peace two ships, either of the normal Imperial squadron, or of these vessels, shall be stationed in New Zealand waters as their head-quarters. Should, however, such emergency arise as may, in the opinion of the Naval Commander-in-Chief, render it necessary to remove either or both of such ships, he shall inform the Governor of the reasons for such temporary removal.

SCHEDULE

LIMITS OF AUSTRALIAN STATION

The Australian Station is bounded—

N.—On the north from the meridian of 95° east by the parallel of the 10th degree of south latitude to 130° east longitude; thence northward on that meridian to the parallel of 2° north latitude; thence on that parallel to the meridian of 136° east longitude; and thence north to 12° north latitude and along that parallel to 160° west longitude.

W.—On the west by the meridian of 95° east longitude.

S.—On the south by the Antarctic circle.

E.—On the east by the meridian of 160° of west longitude.

New Zealand Statutes, 1887, 51 Vict., no. 39, pp. 129–31

109. NEW ZEALAND SUPPORT FOR THE ROYAL NAVY, 1891–1908

In a speech to the House of Representatives on 8 December 1909 concerning New Zealand's offer of a 'Dreadnought' for the Royal Navy, the Prime Minister, Sir Joseph Ward, outlined the history of New Zealand's payments under the Australasian Naval Agreements.

... I would like here also to state what the position is in connection with the contribution this country was giving under the agreement that existed for the support of the Australian Squadron. The amount that we were paying at first varied. The first payment was made in 1891-2 under 'The Australian Naval Defence Act, 1887,' which fixed the annual contributions on a population basis for ten years. The first payment by this country was for £20,712, and the amount varied from £20,304 to £21,523 per annum, and the last payment under that agreement was made on the 11th November, 1903. 'The Australian and New Zealand Defence Act, 1903,' next provided for a further ten-years agreement at £40,000 per annum, and the first payment was made in 1904-5, as from the 12th November, 1903, and £40,000 per annum was paid up to the 12th November, 1908. Then this country passed 'The Naval Subsidy Act, 1908,' which authorised the payment of £100,000 per annum in half-yearly payments, due on the 12th May and the 12th November, 1909, and the authority was given for these payments to be made in the ordinary way. I have alluded to this to show the position that exists at the moment and that existed at the time this country offered to present a Dreadnought to the British Government. . . .

N.Z.P.D., 1909, vol. 148, p. 809

110. THE CROWN ACTS ON THE ADVICE OF MINISTERS IN COLONIAL MATTERS

After its defeat in the 1890 Election, the Atkinson Ministry advised the appointment of six additional members of the Legislative Council in order to strengthen the 'conservative' composition of the Upper House. In 1891 the new Ballance Ministry advised the appointment of twelve Liberals to the Council but Lord Onslow, the Governor, refused on the ground of 'swamping'. The matter was still unresolved in June 1892 when Lord Glasgow became Governor, but although he tried to maintain Onslow's refusal he was firmly instructed by the Colonial Office to accept his Ministers' advice.

[Minute by John Bramston, Assistant Under-Secretary, 16 September, 1892]

I fear we cannot support Lord Glasgow: but the whole case shows the difficulty of attempting to interfere in local matters from Downing Street. The Colonial Ministry must have the responsibility of making such appointments, and if the Colony agrees with them no opposition by the Governor can prevail, if the advice is opposed to the general opinion of the Colony they will be called to account in Parliament. . . .

[Dispatch to the Earl of Glasgow from the Secretary of State, Lord Ripon, 26 September, 1892.]

. . . 4. In the House of thirty-five members, I gather that your Government could only rely on the consistent support of five. I do not assume that the remaining thirty members could all be considered to be opposed to the policy of your Ministers; but it seems to me that your Government is entitled to hold that it is not adequately represented, either for speaking or voting purposes, in the Upper Chamber, and that, if the twelve members were added as they desire, they would only have seventeen consistent supporters in a House of forty-seven. . . .

5. I cannot, therefore, conclude that the proposed appointments constitute one of those cases to which the term 'swamping' has been applied, in which the proposed addition of members at the instance of the Government for the time being has been so great, in proportion to the balance of parties in the Upper Chamber, as to overthrow that balance altogether.

6. Your Lordship was willing to appoint nine new members, and your Government desired that twelve should be appointed. It can hardly be considered that the difference between these limits is so great or important as to require a Governor to assume the very serious responsibility of declining to act on the advice of his Ministers, and possibly of having in consequence to find other Advisers. Moreover, it must be remembered that these appointments, under the colonial law of 1891, will be for seven years only, and not for life as in the case of some other colonies possessing a nominated Upper House.

7. I have thus far dealt with the merits of the particular case on which my advice has been sought. But I think it right to add that a question of this kind, though in itself of purely local importance, presents also a constitutional aspect, which should be considered on broad principles of general application. When questions of a constitutional character are involved, it is especially, I conceive, the right of the Governor fully to discuss with his Ministers the desirability of any particular course that may be pressed upon him for his adoption. He should frankly state the objections, if any,

which may occur to him; but if, after full discussion, Ministers determine to press upon him the advice which they have already tendered, the Governor should, as a general rule, and when Imperial interests are not affected, accept that advice, bearing in mind that the responsibility rests with the Ministers, who are answerable to the Legislature, and, in the last resort, to the country.

8. A governor would, however, be justified in taking another course if he should be satisfied that the policy recommended to him is not only in his view erroneous in itself, but such as he has solid grounds for believing, from his local knowledge, would not be endorsed by the Legislature or by the Constituencies.

9. In so extreme a case as this, he must be prepared to accept the grave responsibility of seeking other Advisers; and I need hardly add, very strong reasons would be necessary to justify so exceptional a course on the part of the Governor.

C.O. 209/252, pp. 113, 203–7

111. THE CROWN ACTS ON THE ADVICE OF MINISTERS—THE 1892 LETTERS PATENT

Royal Instructions to the Governor of New Zealand passed under the Royal Sign Manual and Signet, 26 March 1892. Revoking previous instructions, the new instrument provides for Ministerial Advice and codifies the types of Bills the Governor must Reserve under Section 57 of the 1852 Constitution Act. When the Instructions were revised on 18 November 1907 sections V and VII were retained, but the list in VI was revoked.

. . . Quorum

IV. The Executive Council shall not proceed to the dispatch of business unless two members at the least (exclusive of the Governor or of the member presiding) be present and assisting throughout the whole of the business at which any such business shall be dispatched.

Governor to take advice of Executive Council

V. In the execution of the powers and authorities vested in him, the Governor shall be guided by the advice of the Executive Council; but, if in any case he shall see sufficient cause to dissent from the opinion of the said Council, he may act in the exercise of his said powers and authorities in opposition to the opinion of the Council, reporting the matter to Us without delay, with the reasons for his so acting.

In any such case it shall be competent to any member of the said Council to require that there be recorded upon the minutes of the Council the grounds of any advice or opinion that he may give upon the question.

Description of Bills not to be assented to

VI. The Governor shall not, except in the cases hereunder mentioned, assent in our name to any Bill of any of the following classes:—

1. Any Bill for the divorce of persons joined together in holy matrimony:

2. Any Bill whereby any grant of land or money, or other donation or gratuity, may be made to himself:

3. Any Bill affecting the currency of the colony:

4. Any Bill imposing differential duties (other than as allowed by The Australian Colonies' Duties Act, 1973):

5. Any Bill the provisions of which shall appear inconsistent with obligations imposed upon Us by treaty:

6. Any Bill interfering with the discipline or control of our forces in the colony by land or sea:

7. Any Bill of an extraordinary nature and importance, whereby our prerogative, or the rights and property of our subjects not residing in the colony, or the trade and shipping of the United Kingdom and its dependencies, may be prejudiced:

8. Any Bill containing provisions to which our assent has once been refused, or which have been disallowed by Us,—

Powers in urgent cases

unless he shall have previously obtained our instructions upon such Bill through one of our Principal Secretaries of State, or unless such Bill shall contain a clause suspending the operation of such Bill until the signification in the colony of our pleasure thereupon, or unless the Governor shall have satisfied himself that an urgent necessity exists requiring that such Bill be brought into immediate operation, in which case he is authorised to assent in our name to such Bill, unless the same shall be repugnant to the law of England, or inconsistent with any obligations imposed upon Us by treaty. But he is to transmit to Us by the earliest opportunity the Bill so assented to, together with his reasons for assenting thereto.

Regulation of power of pardon

VII. The Governor shall not pardon or reprieve any offender

without first receiving in capital cases the advice of the Executive Council, and in other cases the advice of one, at least, of his Ministers; and in any case in which such pardon or reprieve might directly affect the interests of our Empire, or of any country or place beyond the jurisdiction of the Government of the colony, the Governor shall, before deciding as to either pardon or reprieve, take those interests specially into his own personal consideration in conjunction with such advice as aforesaid. . . .

> Published in Wellington, 12 July 1892. *The New Zealand Gazette*, 1892, no. 57, p. 1026

112. THE COLONIAL CONFERENCE, 1897

When the colonial Premiers met under Joseph Chamberlain's chairmanship at the time of the Diamond Jubilee of Queen Victoria in 1897, Seddon and the Premier of Tasmania were the only Premiers who were willing to support more formal ties of unity between Britain and the self-governing colonies.

POLITICAL RELATIONS

On the question of the political relations between the mother country and the self-governing Colonies, the resolutions adopted were as follows : —

1. The Prime Ministers here assembled are of opinion that the present political relations between the United Kingdom and the self-governing Colonies are generally satisfactory under the existing condition of things.

   Mr. Seddon and Sir E. N. C. Braddon dissented.

2. They are also of opinion that it is desirable, whenever and wherever practicable, to group together under a federal union those colonies which are geographically united.

   Carried unanimously

3. Meanwhile, the Premiers are of opinion that it would be desirable to hold periodical conferences of representatives of the Colonies and Great Britain for the discussion of matters of common interest.

   Carried unanimously.

Mr. Seddon and Sir E. N. C. Braddon dissented from the first resolution because they were of opinion that the time had already come when an effort should be made to render more formal the political ties between the United Kingdom and the Colonies. The majority of the Premiers were not yet prepared to adopt this position, but there was a strong feeling amongst some of them that with the rapid growth of population in the Colonies, the present relations could not continue indefinitely, and that some means would have to be devised for giving the Colonies a voice in the control and direction of those questions of Imperial interest in which they are concerned equally with the mother country.

It was recognised at the same time that such a share in the direction of Imperial policy would involve a proportionate contribution in aid of Imperial expenditure, for which at present, at any rate, the Colonies generally are not prepared.

Proceedings of the Colonial Conference, Great Britain, *Parliamentary Papers*, 1897, C-8596, pp. 14–15

113. THE SOUTH AFRICAN WAR CONTINGENT, 1899

Debate in the House of Representatives, 28 September 1899, on a proposal to send a Volunteer Contingent of Mounted Rifles to fight against the Transvaal.

Mr. SEDDON (Premier).—

. . . The question will naturally be asked, Why should New Zealand take the course which I am now proposing? The answer is simple. We belong to and are an integral part of a great Empire. The flag that floats over us and protects us was expected to protect our kindred and countrymen who are in the Transvaal. There are in the Transvaal New-Zealanders, Australians, English, Irish, and Scotch; and others from British dependencies: they are of our own race and our kindred. As one coming from the goldfields, I know what tempted many from our shores to the Transvaal. I know what transpired years ago when they left the Mother-country, other countries of the globe, and other colonies, and came to New Zealand; but when they came here they had their freedom. They had their civil rights granted to them, and there is nothing so dear— almost next to life itself—as civil rights to the British race. Our kindred to the number of 150,000 in the Transvaal have been deprived of these civil rights and civil freedom. Now, in considering carefully the situation in the Transvaal, and what has led to it, we must acquit the Imperial authorities of any desire on their part to make unreasonable, unjust, or unfair demands. I say the demands made upon the Transvaal Government are moderate and righteous. . . .

. . . Another reason why we should take action is that we are a portion of the dominant family of the world—we are of the English-speaking race. Our kindred are scattered in different parts of the globe, and wherever they are, no matter how far distant apart, there is a feeling of affection—there is that crimson tie, that bond of unity, existing which time does not affect, and as years roll by it grows firmer, stronger, and in the end will become indispensable. It was said in years gone by that the moment the colonies became sufficiently strong they would seek to sever the tie between themselves and the Mother-country. There were those misguided statesmen who said the only way to bind the colonies to the Mother-country was by using a firm hand and denying them self-government; but there were others, again, who said, 'Give the greatest freedom; trust to better nature and the natural tie, and that trust will not be misplaced.' To-day we have that faith justified. We have undoubted proof that with a free Constitution, with the right of self-government, mutual confidence has been established, and with the greater freedom has grown a patriotism hardly possible to conceive, and as the years have rolled on, the tie between the Mother-land and her colonies has grown so strong, so firm, that to-day we have a sight which, whilst gratifying to us, mystifies and almost paralyses the other nations of the globe. This pleasing feature, this drawing closer together, gladdens the hearts of our kindred at Home, and tends to their prosperity and well-being, and it is especially pleasing also to those in this colony. When adversity comes there is sincere sympathy, and there is a feeling on our part in the colonies to as far as we can mitigate and help to remove and minimise that adversity. . . .

. . . Take it on sordid grounds if you like, and we know how much to us is the Empire. We know that the Mother-country has given us our birthright of freedom. We know, of course, what she is doing for us each and every day of our existence. The British flag is our protection; without belonging to the Empire where would New Zealand be? What would be the natural result? We should be under some other nation, perhaps treated as are the Outlanders in the Transvaal. Should we enjoy the rights and privileges which are dear to Englishmen, and which we at present possess? The answer is, No. I therefore say it is to our interest to remain as we are. It is our bounden duty to support the Empire, and to assist in every way the Imperial authorities whenever occasion demands. . . . In prosperity we share, in adversity likewise, and will not shirk our share of the responsibility. Let us, in the hour of trouble and anxiety, show to the world we are a free and enlightened people, and in rendering this assistance all we seek, all we ask for, is freedom and civil rights for our oppressed kindred in the Transvaal, and in that spirit and on these grounds I ask the House to unanimously pass this resolution. . . .

Captain RUSSELL (Hawke's Bay).—Mr. Speaker, I feel it a great privilege to be allowed the honour of seconding a resolution so momentous as that proposed by the Right Hon. the Premier. It is not for me, Sir, as an Englishman, to inquire deeply into the origin of the quarrel in the Transvaal. We know, of course, what has been published in the newspapers, but the cause of quarrel has little concern for me. Feeling that the Government of the Mother-land has displayed every patience that it was possible to use, believing, as I do sincerely, that the sense of justice of the Mother-country would never precipitate a war which it was honourable to avoid, I stand as a citizen of the Empire to say that I feel it to be my duty to support the proposal made by the Right Hon. the Premier to send volunteers to prove that, however remote New Zealand may be from the Old Country, its inhabitants are loyal at heart to the Imperial idea. . . .

Mr. TAYLOR (Christchurch City).—Mr. Speaker. It seems to me, Sir, that we can find time for discussing the question of federating for warfare although we cannot find time this session for discussing the question of the Australian Commonwealth, the issues of which aim at peace and progress. It is no use our blinding ourselves to the fact that the threatened war in the Transvaal is a territorial war. The humanitarian element does not enter into the calculation from start to finish. Great Britain is demanding in the Transvaal electoral rights for her people that she denies to Englishmen in England. . . .

. . . The Imperial sentiment is a sentiment that as frequently leads men into wrong actions as into right actions—quite as frequently—and I am conscious of this fact: We are asked to spend money upon a purely sentimental mission. England has not asked for our assistance. We know perfectly well that the Empire is not endangered at all by the war in the Transvaal—it has not been suggested either here or in the Old Land; and I am opposed to the military spirit that seizes on the people at a moment like this. England has got at her door a pauper population of over a million souls, and she is prepared to flaunt her flag and talk sentiment whilst for generation after generation she leaves a large percentage of her population in the most abject poverty. In this land we have ample problems to engage our attention until the time comes when the Empire is really threatened; and that will be quite soon enough to send our men or spend our money on a mission of the kind that is now proposed. I say again this is purely a territorial war, and if the people of the colony were to be consulted, when they had calmly considered it, I feel quite satisfied their deliberate judgment would be against participating in a trouble of this kind under existing conditions. If England were threatened by a European Power the conditions would be altogether altered; but this foe is not worthy of her steel, let alone the steel of the Empire. . . .

Mr. PERE (Eastern Maori).—I am a supporter of the resolution which is before the House. Even, Sir, though it may be said that the cause of this trouble is wrongful, still I shall support the resolution. England has on many occasions, Sir, done what is wrong. I cannot make any objections to the remarks that fell from the member for Christchurch City (Mr. Taylor), because I think England has been the means of worrying the Boers in the first place, and now that they have turned round in anger she wants to fight them. How do we treat the Chinaman in our own colony? We impose a poll-tax of £100 upon these men before they can land in this country. The Boers are only adopting a similar action as a precautionary measure against the influx of Englishmen who have been pouring into their territory for the purpose of enriching themselves with the gold which is obtainable there. But, Sir, my reason for supporting the resolution is this: that even though England acts in this way towards every nation it is not for us to judge her. But there are many peoples who have suffered at the hands of England, and who now smart under the injuries which they consider they have received. Therefore I say it behoves us to go to the assistance of England lest England be worsted at their hands, and after England we follow. That, Sir, is my only reason for supporting the resolution. All people feel their own troubles, as I have said, and what we have got to guard against is lest England's foot should slip, and we should follow immediately after. If the European population of this country is not willing that the proposed contingent should be sent, I say, 'Hand the matter over to me, and let me take a contingent of five hundred Maoris there, and I will go to the assistance of my protector.' That is all I have to say. . . .

(Mr. Seddon) . . . It has been said by the historian Macaulay that it would be a New-Zealander who, on a broken arch of London Bridge would recount the ruin of London and the downfall of the Empire. I am sorry for Macaulay; he little knew the New-Zealander. The history of the future will show that the New-Zealander will not recount the downfall of the Empire, but will fight to maintain it; and that he will on that London Bridge recount the fact that New Zealand to-day took action and a leading step which will,—if followed by the other colonies and dependencies,—effectually prevent the downfall of the Empire.

I say our strength lies in being an integral part of the mighty British Empire, and that we should help to maintain its unity intact. And the day is not far distant when, if we take responsibilities and share the burdens and expense of maintaining the Empire, we shall have representatives from this colony and the other colonies taking a direct part in the government of a federated Empire. I assert we shall, before many years have elapsed, be represented in the council of the nation at Home—the New-Zealander will be advising in council, not croaking on London Bridge. By proving ourselves worthy we shall be entrusted with increased responsibility. We must show that we are equal to the occasion. On this opportunity there should be no division of opinion, no hesitation or shirking of duty. Let it go to the Imperial Parliament, let it go to the world, that we passed this resolution to send help to the Transvaal without a division. We are the first colonial Parliament that has been called upon to do so. Ministers in the other colonies have made offers, but this is the first colony in which the representatives of the people in Parliament assembled have been called upon to give a vote upon this question. Let that vote be practically unanimous, and I trust there may, if possible, be no division taken.

The House divided.

AYES, 54 . . .
NOES, 5.

N.Z.P.D., 1899, vol. 110, pp. 75–96

114. THE BOXER UPRISING—
A NEW ZEALAND CONTINGENT FOR PEKING?

Editorial criticising the proposal of the Premier, Richard Seddon, in a speech on 28 June 1900, that the Colony should contribute to the Great Power force for the relief of the legations in Peking.

THE POSING PREMIER

Yesterday, addressing a meeting of citizens at a semi-public function, the Premier made a suggestion that caps the highest altitude of inflated Jingoism yet reached by any public man in this hemisphere. Not satisfied, apparently, with the great sacrifices made by this country for the cause of the Empire, Mr. Seddon would have us take a hand in settlement of the Chinese question. . . .

'We have served the Empire in South Africa,' the Premier seems to say, 'let us now show in China that we are a coming world power!' This rhodomontade would be ridiculous did it not have its serious side. The little we have done to serve the Mother Country was a voluntary tribute of affection as of duty, but in the doing of it we have incurred grave responsibilities, and none greater or more urgent than immediate organisation of a home-keeping citizen army for self-defence. But apparently the patriotism of the Premier does not begin at home; he must pose before the Empire as one ready to rush to her aid at any time and to any point of the globe on the smallest provocation. . . . And all because the Premier's vanity cannot resist appeal to the Imperial gallery. . . . The mere suggestion of such an act of aggression is a menace to the future of the country, and it should be at once repudiated by the voice of Parliament.

The Evening Post, 29 June 1900, p. 5

115. UNION WITH THE COMMONWEALTH
OF AUSTRALIA: THE CASE AGAINST, 1901

The Federation Commission report, 13 May 1901, gives reasons why New Zealand should not enter a union with the newly formed Australian Federation.

Your Commissioners . . . found that the question had been but little considered by the people of New Zealand. The Commonwealth Constitution Act had not even been read by many of those who attended before your Commissioners, and its provisions, generally speaking, were imperfectly understood by many of those

who professed to have considered the subject of federation somewhat attentively. . . .

I. LEGISLATIVE INDEPENDENCE

. . . The conclusion is inevitable that the legislative independence
of any colony as existing prior to Federation must be seriously
impaired when such colony becomes a State of the Commonwealth . . . whereas, without federating, New Zealand would be
able to legislate upon any subject allowed by her Constitution, upon
similar lines to any law existing in the Commonwealth. . . .

II. PUBLIC FINANCE

. . . After a careful review of [expert] evidence your Commissioners are of opinion that, in consequence of the smaller
amount that would probably be yielded to New Zealand from
Customs and excise duties under a Federal tariff than she now
obtains, together with her contributions to the expenses of the
Federal Government and new services, estimated at £110,000
annually, the revenue of the colony would be diminished by at
least £450,000. . . .

. . . Your Commissioners are of opinion that the public finances of
New Zealand would be seriously prejudiced in the event of this
colony becoming a State of the Commonwealth of Australia, and that
her State Government would be hampered and embarrassed in
respect of finance, and in the prosecution of any policy for developing her resources.

III. DEFENCE

. . . Having carefully considered the opinions of [Australian mili-
tary] officers, the Commissioners agree that, so long as Great Britain
holds command of the sea, New Zealand is quite able to undertake
her own land defence. In the event of Great Britain losing command
of the sea, Australia and New Zealand could not rely upon being
able to render material assistance to each other in defence against
a foreign Power. Your Commissioners are further of opinion that as
a separate colony New Zealand would render to Australia all
possible assistance in war-time; and similar assistance would be
given by Australia to New Zealand. . . .

V. ADMINISTRATION OF JUSTICE

. . . Your Commissioners are of opinion that whatever differences
there may be between the law of Australia and New Zealand can be
satisfactorily adjusted even if the latter remain a separate colony. . . .

VI. IMPERIAL RELATIONS

It has been alleged as a reason for joining the Australian Commonwealth that federation would consolidate British interests, and thus tend to promote the unity of the Empire. But it is possible that, in the future, Imperial unity may be better promoted by the existence of two British Powers in these seas rather than one. . . .

. . . Neither Australia nor New Zealand would be likely in future years under any circumstances to break away from the Empire without inquiry as to the attitude of the other; time would be gained, and a catastrophe probably averted.

VII. FEDERAL DEPARTMENTAL ADMINISTRATION

Your Commissioners are of opinion that the stretch of some twelve hundred miles of sea between Australia and New Zealand is a weighty argument against New Zealand joining the Commonwealth, and they believe that, should New Zealand federate, great inconvenience must at all times be experienced in the administration of the several departments controlled by the Federal Government. . . .

VIII. AGRICULTURAL, COMMERCIAL, AND INDUSTRIAL INTERESTS

Those who are favourable to federation urge the great importance of inter-State free-trade, which, it is alleged, would benefit New Zealand. It is therefore necessary to consider carefully the statistics of the trade and commerce of New Zealand, the potentialities as regards production of the several States of the Commonwealth, and the effect which federation might have upon the trade between New Zealand and Australia . . . excluding gold, the exports of New Zealand produce to the Commonwealth in 1899 amounted to only 8·4 per cent. of the total exports, and that the imports of produce of the Commonwealth to New Zealand amounted to only 5·8 per cent. of the total imports. . . .

Agriculture . . .

All the expert witnesses examined by your Commission in Australia agreed that, even under free-trade, New Zealand could not look to the States of the Commonwealth for a large permanent market for agricultural and pastoral products. But in seasons of drought a valuable market will, no doubt, always be found there. . . .

Manufactures . . .

Should . . . free-trade be established, your Commissioners do not consider that New Zealand would find any considerable new markets for her manufactures in Australia, as that country could supply her own requirements. . . .

IX. THE SOCIAL CONDITION OF THE WORKING-CLASSES

. . . The inclusion of New Zealand in the Commonwealth would . . . entail free competition with States where no attempt is now made to regulate the rates of wages or the excessive employment of boy-labour. According to the almost unanimous opinion of the employers and artisans engaged in manufacturing industries in New Zealand examined by your Commissioners, such competition would render the maintenance of the New Zealand code of labour-laws extremely difficult, and might result in reduced wages, longer hours, and a considerable displacement of labour. . . .

GENERAL REMARKS . . .

One of . . . several important matters is the provision of the Commonwealth Bill (section 127) that in reckoning the number of people of the Commonwealth, or of a State or other part of the Commonwealth, aboriginal natives shall not be counted. The result would be that New Zealand, if a State of the Commonwealth, would have one member in the House of Representatives less than she would be entitled to if the Maoris were counted in the number of the people of the State. Your Commissioners . . . endeavoured to ascertain what advantages were claimed by those advocating New Zealand joining the Commonwealth. The principal arguments advanced in New Zealand were the benefits alleged to be derivable from intercolonial free-trade, and from the broader education of the inhabitants of this colony by association with the larger community of Australia. Your Commissioners have already dealt with the question of intercolonial free-trade, and they confess that they are unable to understand how the broader education of the inhabitants of this colony is to be brought about by such association. . . .

CONCLUSION

Your Commissioners, after giving the fullest consideration to the evidence before them, and with their knowledge of the soil, climate, and productiveness of New Zealand, of the adaptability of the lands of the colony for close settlement, of her vast natural resources, her immense wealth in forest, in mine, and natural scenery, of the energy of her people, of the abundant rainfall and vast water-power she possesses, of her insularity and geographical position; remembering, too, that New Zealand as a colony can herself supply all that can be required to support and maintain within her boundaries a population which might at no distant date be worthily styled a nation, have unanimously arrived at the conclusion that merely for the doubtful prospect of further trade with the Commonwealth of Australia, or for any advantage which might reasonably be expected to be derived by this colony from becoming a State in such Commonwealth, New Zealand should not sacrifice her independence as a separate colony, but that she should maintain it under the political Constitution she at present enjoys. . . .

A.J.H.R., 1901, A-4, pp. x–xxiv

116. COLONY OF NEW ZEALAND TO BE STYLED 'DOMINION OF NEW ZEALAND', 1907

At the Colonial Conference in 1907 it was agreed that the self-governing colonies should be distinguished by the style 'Dominions'. After the return of Sir Joseph Ward, the Prime Minister, instruments were published in Wellington and London to mark the change.

BY resolutions passed by the House of Representatives on the 12th July, 1907, and by the Legislative Council on the 16th July, 1907, addresses were forwarded to His Majesty the King respectfully requesting that the necessary steps might be taken to change the designation of New Zealand from the Colony of New Zealand to the Dominion of New Zealand; and it is hereby notified that His Majesty the King, by Order in Council dated 9th September, 1907, and by Proclamation issued 10th September, 1907, has been graciously pleased to change the style and designation of the Colony of New Zealand to 'The Dominion of New Zealand'; such change to take effect on and from Thursday, the 26th day of September, 1907.

JOSEPH GEORGE WARD,

Prime Minister.

Supplement to *The New Zealand Gazette*, 12 September 1907

THE following Proclamation by His Majesty the King, which appeared in the *London Gazette*, is published for general information. . . .

EDWARD R. & I.

WHEREAS We have, on the petition of the members of the Legislative Council and House of Representatives of Our Colony of New

Zealand, determined that the title of the Dominion of New Zealand shall be substituted for that of the Colony of New Zealand as the designation of the said colony: We have therefore, by and with the advice of Our Privy Council, thought fit to issue this Our Royal Proclamation, and We do ordain, declare, and command that on and after the twenty-sixth day of September, one thousand nine hundred and seven, the said Colony of New Zealand and the territory belonging thereto shall be called and known by the title of the Dominion of New Zealand, and We hereby give Our commands to all Public Departments accordingly.

Given at our Court, at Buckingham Palace. . . .[9 September 1907]

The New Zealand Gazette Extraordinary, 26 September 1907

New Zealand Gazette, 1907, no. 81, p. 2837 and no. 84, p. 2901

117. THE NAVAL DEFENCE BILL, 1908

The Prime Minister, Sir Joseph Ward, and the Leader of the Opposition, William F. Massey, support the proposal to contribute a million pounds over ten years to the Australasian Squadron of the Royal Navy, and Mr. James Allen, the Member for Bruce, pleads the cause of 'national' defence, in the House of Representatives, 30 September 1908.

The Right Hon. Sir J. G. WARD (Prime Minister), in moving the second reading of this Bill, said, . . . This Bill proposes to provide £100,000 a year for ten years towards the maintenance of the Imperial navy, without any conditions of any sort or kind. . . . None of us can estimate the value of the British navy to the Old Land and its dependencies. We are, as British subjects, proud of it in every sense of the term, and we offer this contribution, small though it be when compared with the enormous sum that is annually spent by the British Government on behalf of the British taxpayer, as evidence of our gratitude and attachment to the Old Country—a feeling which is deep-rooted amongst all classes in this Dominion. . . .

Mr. MASSEY (Leader of the Opposition).—It is refreshing at times to have a Bill placed before Parliament upon which there is very little difference of opinion . . . if we are to have an efficient Australasian Squadron, we must be prepared to make a reasonable contribution therefor.

Mr. J. ALLEN—Sir, in connection with this expenditure of

£1,000,000—for that is what it amounts to—in the ten years that we shall continue to pay it, I want members to consider for a moment if we are doing all that is necessary when we simply say to our mother, 'Here is £100,000 per annum for ten years; you look after us.' Are we everlastingly to go crying to our mother for everything that we desire? Are we never to be grown up? Are we always to be children depending upon our mother for sustenance and support? I say that the time has arrived in this young country when we ought to go in for a national system of defence in the highest sense of the term—when every man who is capable of bearing arms should be ready, if necessary—though I hope the necessity will never arise— to do his share in the defence of his country. . . .

. . . I am not advocating conscription. I am advocating national training, the time given to it being approximately what a thoroughly good Volunteer gives now. The right honourable gentleman himself was so trained once, and why should he not advocate that everybody else should be asked to do it, and that idlers should not be allowed to look on and laugh? It will do them good, and they will become efficient in the defence of their women and children afterwards. . . .

The Right Hon. Sir J. G. WARD.—I have no hesitation in saying that if in regard to the future protection of the world-wide British interests, whether in the Old Country or in the self-governing dependencies—New Zealand among that number—if we want to have the surest, and soundest, and the strongest protection, the ships of war, wherever they are, should be under a system of absolute control by the British Admiralty, who can put their finger upon the button at any time in peace or war and direct these ships to the point from which the strongest and most effective protection to British interests can be given. It is for this reason that we recognise that with the enormous interests at stake the British authorities should not in any way be bound or fettered by an agreement for the purpose of keeping ships in any particular position, either round our coasts or in our harbours, for our protection.

. . . The interests of Great Britain are so enormous, quite apart from its internal interests, that she requires no other actuating motive to look after the interests of New Zealand than the great and binding tie of the interests of common race in whatever part of the world these British interests exist. . . .

N.Z.P.D., 1908, vol. 145, pp. 691–2, 694, 708–9

118. NEW ZEALAND AND THE ROYAL NAVY— THE 'DREADNOUGHT' OFFER, 1909

After announcing in March 1909 that New Zealand would pay for and present a 'Dreadnought' to the Royal Navy, Sir Joseph Ward, the Prime Minister, told the House of Representatives on 14 June 1909 that he was going to attend a special Imperial Defence Conference in London. He defends the strategic reasoning behind New Zealand's support to the Royal Navy rather than the building up of a 'local' navy.

. . . You could not have any local navy that would be of any use to you in combination with Australia, as in time of trouble Australia would need the full use of their own local navy. I say that the future destiny of this country is as distinct from that of Australia as is daylight from dark. And I believe that our insular position will entail the responsibility on this country as the years roll on, just as much as it has done on England and Japan, of having our own navy; but we are not in a position to undertake such a responsibility now, and we cannot look at it, and any man who is in his senses knows that is so. Supposing we were to go in for a system of submarines in four or five ports, with a view to building up a local navy, what would it mean financially? And is one cruiser of any use to us?

. . . I propose to go to [the Imperial Defence] Conference and to urge, among other things—in what actual form it is impossible for me to convey to any honourable member—our absolute sincerity that a Dreadnought, or two if necessary, on behalf of New Zealand, should be constructed to be placed under the sole control of the British Admiralty either in peace or in war. And I shall do that because I believe that is the strongest and the best course for this country to take; and unless I can be shown that that is a wrong course, I am not prepared to alter my opinion in that particular. I am prepared to go to that Conference with the full knowledge, as far as I have been able to ascertain it, that the desire of the people of this country is to take their full and fair share in connection with the support of the British navy, looking at it, as our people do, as not only the first line of defence of the Old Country, but as something which is essential to our very existence and to our membership as a portion of the British Empire. . . . I believe that the Conference will mark a turning-point which will affect our destiny for all time.

It has been recognised by responsible statesmen on both sides that there has been going on for the last few years in one powerful country a movement, silently in some respects and in other respects openly, which inevitably leads to the conclusion that that country intends within a few years to try conclusions with the Old Land; and if that time arrives, we in this country must realise that the fate, and in that fate the future, of the British Empire is involved. It will not depend upon whether we have our internal defences as completely effective as we desire, regarding which I am as much concerned as any other man in this country. The fate and future of this country is not going to depend on eighty thousand men, or even one hundred thousand, or even two hundred thousand fully trained men; it is not going to depend upon who may land in New Zealand: it is going to depend upon the victory of the British navy in some places thousands of miles from the shores of New Zealand. Our international defence is a factor that we should not neglect; but first in importance, first in effectiveness, and first in power, strength, and magnitude, is the British navy, which insures not alone the preservation of the British Empire, but the interests of the world and the preservation of peace. . . .

N.Z.P.D., 1909, vol. 146, pp. 197–9

119. THE DEFENCE OF THE EMPIRE IN THE GREAT WAR

Sir Francis H. D. Bell, Leader of the Legislative Council, speaks of New Zealand's obligation to maintain a Division in Europe, 12 July 1917.

. . . If our promise is no longer to be the measure of our obligation, then let some other men dishonour our word and the promise that we have made. But I do not believe, Sir, we have become craven. I will not believe it till the country has so declared. This country, Sir, was the first to enter upon German soil. It is true that we occupied Samoa without resistance, but that was a mere accident of the absence of the great fleet that Germany was prepared to defend it with. We were the first country—the first dominion of the Empire —to enter upon German soil. We have that to our credit. Shall we be the first to quit, and have that to our lasting dishonour and disgrace? . . .

. . . How can the entry of America into this quarrel make any difference to the obligation of New Zealand? If any part of the Empire was in danger more than another, New Zealand was that part. It is our New Zealand soil we are defending, and the enemy is at the gates of one New Zealand avenue which stretches to the other side of the seas. How can the entry of America into the battle make any difference to our duty? Is it to be said of Englishmen at last as some said in the days of old, 'We will fight with Hessians, but not with our own men and our own sons'? Are we to sit behind a rampart of Americans or of any nation? Americans are our brothers, of the same speech and of the same blood, but they are of another nation. They have different aims, different objects, different hopes, and other aspirations. What test can it be of the question whether we are doing all that we can, and making as much sacrifice as possible, that there are others who are prepared to join England and her Allies in the fight? It will make the end speedier; but shall the end come without us because the Americans are there? . . . One honourable gentleman said that New Zealand had done more than others of the dominions. Of course, in the numbers we have sent, except in proportion to our population, we are hopelessly behind the great Expeditionary Force of Canada, and even of Australia. But this is true: we said we would send a full division. We did send a full division, and we said we would reinforce that full division so that it would always go into action full in strength and full in equipment, and to this day we have fulfilled our promise. . . . I do not believe there is the smallest cause for the contention that this country will be brought to ruin by the further depletion of its manhood. It may be that it will be brought to privation. It certainly may, and I think should, be brought to privation of many of the comforts, conveniences, and luxuries that we have to-day. And if that privation comes I at least shall not be one of those who will complain of it. I do believe that privation will come—I am not dreading it—but more than that I do not believe, nor do I believe that the people of New Zealand are unable, are helpless, to organize as England has organized. . . . I trust still that every man and every woman will remember that this was no selfish war of England's; that our fear in New Zealand at first was that she would not enter into it, not that she would; that she entered into the war with the full accord of the people of New Zealand. We all heard that accord echoed in the cheer that broke out from the audience when the announcement was made from the steps of the Parliament Buildings in 1914. No selfish aim of England; no selfish hope of New Zealand: a defence of the cause of justice. . . .

N.Z.P.D. (1917), vol. 178, pp. 332–4

120. THE 'WHITE NEW ZEALAND' POLICY, 1920

Excerpts from the Immigration Restriction Amendment Act, 1920, which, while avoiding overt racial clauses, gave the responsible minister wide and flexible powers to exclude intending immigrants. In 1881 Chinese immigrants had been restricted by a law permitting the entry of only one Chinese per ten tons of ship's tonnage and imposing a poll tax of £10 per immigrant. By 1896 this had been raised to one per 200 tons and a poll tax of £100. A Bill to extend the system to all Asians was Reserved and, after discussions at the 1897 Colonial Conference, applicants were required to fill a form in a European language by an Act of 1899. After 1907 Chinese had to read 100 words in English to the satisfaction of Customs officials.

PART I
REQUIREMENT OF PERMITS TO ENTER NEW ZEALAND BY PERSONS NOT OF BRITISH BIRTH AND PARENTAGE . . .

. . . **5.** (1.) In addition to the restrictions imposed upon immigration into New Zealand . . . it is hereby enacted that no person other than a person of British birth and parentage shall (except as by this Act is specially provided) enter into New Zealand unless he is in possession of a permit to enter in the form and to the effect provided by regulations under this Act.

(2.) A person shall not be deemed to be of British birth and parentage by reason that he or his parents or either of them is a naturalized British subject, or by reason that he is an aboriginal Native or the descendant of an aboriginal Native of any dominion other than the Dominion of New Zealand or of any colony or other possession or of any protectorate of His Majesty.

6. (1.) The Governor-General may, by Order in Council, from time to time declare that the provisions of this Part of this Act shall not apply to nations or peoples specified in such Order in Council. . . .

8. (1.) Any person to whom this Part of this Act applies who arrives in New Zealand without a permit but proves to the satisfaction of the Minister of Customs that he desires to enter New Zealand as a visitor only for purposes of business, pleasure, or health, and that he intends to leave New Zealand within six months after his arrival, may be granted a temporary permit in the prescribed form by an officer of Customs. A permit under this section may be granted for a period of six months or for such shorter period in any case as the Minister may, in his discretion, determine. . . .

(4.) If a person to whom such temporary permit is granted desires to remain in New Zealand beyond the period for which the permit was granted, he may make application to the Minister of Customs, who may, in his discretion, either grant an extension or extensions from time to time of the temporary permit, or grant to such person a permit in the form prescribed with respect to persons intending to settle permanently in New Zealand. . . .

9. (1.) Application for a permit to enter New Zealand must be made in the prescribed form and signed by the applicant, and be addressed to the Minister of Customs, and be sent by post from the country of origin of the applicant or from the country where the applicant has resided for a period of at least one year prior to the date of the application. . . .

(3.) The Minister of Customs, upon receipt of such application, shall consider the same, and may, in his discretion, grant or refuse to the applicant a permit to enter New Zealand. . . .

New Zealand Statutes, 1920, no. 23, 11 Geo. V., pp. 78–83

121. DOMINION STATUS—THE BALFOUR DEFINITION, 1926

Report of the Committee on Inter-Imperial relations, Imperial Conference, 1926.

The Committee are of opinion that nothing would be gained by attempting to lay down a Constitution for the British Empire. Its widely scattered parts have very different characteristics, very different histories, and are at very different stages of evolution; while, considered as a whole, it defies classification and bears no real resemblance to any other political organization which now exists or has ever yet been tried.

There is, however, one most important element in it which, from a strictly constitutional point of view, has now, as regards all vital matters, reached its full development—we refer to the group of self-governing communities composed of Great Britain and the Dominions. Their position and mutual relation may be readily defined. *They are autonomous Communities within the British Empire, equal in status, in no way subordinate one to another in any aspect of their domestic or external affairs, though united by a common allegiance to the Crown, and freely associated as members of the British Commonwealth of Nations.*

A foreigner endeavouring to understand the true character of the British Empire by the aid of this formula alone would be tempted to think that it was devised rather to make mutual interference impossible than to make mutual co-operation easy.

Such a criticism, however, completely ignores the historic situation. The rapid evolution of the Oversea Dominions during the last fifty years has involved many complicated adjustments of old political machinery to changing conditions. The tendency towards equality of status was both right and inevitable. Geographical and other conditions made this impossible of attainment by the way of federation. The only alternative was by the way of autonomy; and along this road it has been steadily sought. Every self-governing member of the Empire is now the master of its destiny. In fact, if not always in form, it is subject to no compulsion whatever.

But no account, however accurate, of the negative relations in which Great Britain and the Dominions stand to each other can do more than express a portion of the truth. The British Empire is not founded upon negations. It depends essentially, if not formally, on positive ideals. Free institutions are its lifeblood. Free co-operation is its instrument. Peace, security, and progress are among its objects. Aspects of all these great themes have been discussed at the present Conference; excellent results have been thereby obtained. And, though every Dominion is now, and must always remain, the sole judge of the nature and extent of its co-operation, no common cause will, in our opinion, be thereby imperilled.

Equally of status, so far as Britain and the Dominions are concerned, is thus the root principle governing our Inter-Imperial Relations. But the principles of equality and similarity, appropriate to *status*, do not universally extend to function. Here we require something more than immutable dogmas. For example, to deal with questions of diplomacy and questions of defence, we require also flexible machinery—machinery which can, from time to time, be adapted to the changing circumstances of the world. This subject also has occupied our attention. The rest of this Report will show how we have endeavoured not only to state political theory, but to apply it to our common needs.

> Great Britain, *Parliamentary Papers*, 1926, vol. 11, pp. 558–9

122. SUPPORT FOR THE SINGAPORE NAVAL BASE, 1927

In 1921 the British Government decided to build a major naval dockyard at Singapore to service the Royal Navy's Main Fleet for operations in the East if they became necessary. Massey offered a New Zealand contribution of £100,000 in 1923 and on 23 April 1927 the Prime Minister, Gordon Coates, announced a further contribution of one million pounds spread over seven to eight years. The matter was debated in the House of Representatives on 21 September 1927.

The Right Hon. Mr. COATES (Prime Minister).—Sir, I move, *That this House approves of the proposals of the Government regarding the Singapore Naval Base*, . . .

The question we have to consider is whether New Zealand is really carrying her share of the burden of Empire naval defence—whether she is providing a reasonable quota. If we come to the conclusion that she is not, then it becomes a matter of deciding how she shall do so. The Government's proposal has already been set out, and it is that our further assistance should be, first, towards the cost of construction of the base at Singapore, and, second, when the Singapore base is completed, towards the cost of the maintenance of cruisers—or, to be more exact, towards the cost of maintenance of cruisers in New Zealand waters. There will be cruisers of a heavier type than the present ships, and B class cruisers will replace D class cruisers. Certain new equipment will be necessary for this purpose; and the cost of that equipment, apart from maintenance charges, combined with our annual payment towards the Singapore base, will, in the meantime, involve a cost of about 2s. per head of our population, thus increasing our annual contribution for naval defence from 8s. to 10s.

Mr. H. E. HOLLAND.—Have the other dominions come to any decision?

The Right Hon. Mr. COATES.—In answer to the leader of the Opposition, may I say that, as far as I know, New Zealand is the only Dominion that has indicated in any way what she is now prepared to do in connection with naval defence.

Mr. J. A. LEE.—Government by Downing Street.

The Right Hon. Mr. COATES.—No, it is not government by Downing Street. I give that a flat contradiction. New Zealand is quite able, I think, to come to an independent conclusion and a connected and reasoned decision in regard to the question of naval defence. There are many reasons why Singapore is an ideal spot for the purpose, and I may refer to one or two of them. . . . It is near to oil; it is a centre for oil supplies; it is in the right place with respect to our interests in the East. I speak of Empire interests now. It is a point on which the Imperial airway authorities have concentrated: it will be on the line of route when airways become an accomplished fact and we are linked up in the Imperial airway system. In addition, Singapore is thousands of miles away from any other base. It is well away from any possible enemy base. Originally, I think, the base was estimated to cost between £11,000,000 and £12,000,000. Since then there has been a readjustment of the estimates, and the estimated cost is now approximately £9,000,000. The expenditure is to cover a period of about eight years. . . .

. . . and if I might express a wish—and it would be my dearest wish—it would be that we might be able to say that Parliament was unanimous, irrespective of party, in agreeing to this contribution towards what we consider to be a vital part of Empire defence. If that were possible, then I think a great step forward would be taken, and it would give a great sense of satisfaction to thousands of people in this Dominion. . . .

Mr. H. E. HOLLAND (Leader of the Opposition).—Sir, I think the main question that the House ought to keep in mind is what effect such a proposal as the Singapore base is likely to have on the peace of the world. With the supreme tragedy of the world war fresh in the memories of the different nations, every country ought to be concerned to build in a way that will make for peace rather than for warfare. . . . What the British Labour Government under Mr. Ramsay MacDonald consistently laid down was that the Singapore base would be a serious mistake. The Labour movement of Britain is pledged against the Singapore base, just as the Labour movement of every other country connected with the British

Empire is pledged against it. There is not one country forming part of the British Empire whose Labour movement does not oppose this proposal. The Labour movement opposes it because Labour sees in the proposal an incentive to future warfare; and, as much as any other section of the community, we desire that there shall be peace throughout the world. . . .

. . . We are in this peculiar position: that New Zealand alone of the dominions is making contribution. Two Crown colonies and one protectorate are making large contributions; but, as I have pointed out, the people of these places have not been consulted—the contributions have been made by officials not controlled by the people. The Prime Minister has said in one of his statements that while other nations retain their armaments it is essential that we should do the same. The militarists of every other country are making exactly the same pronouncements. I recognize that the British Empire cannot disarm wholesale while other nations refrain from disarming; but we all know that if different countries set out to compete in an armaments race—if they each incur a huge expenditure on armaments—then each of them is providing an incentive, an invitation, a challenge to all other countries to do the same. The attitude taken up by Mr. MacDonald was undoubtedly the correct attitude. It was supremely a peace gesture; but this proposal before us tonight is essentially a war gesture. I will admit right away that the establishment of a naval base at Singapore would not be a violation of the letter of the Washington Conference, but it would be as near to it as would be possible without actually going over the line. It would certainly be a violation of the spirit that brought that Conference into existence. The idea of the Conference was to reduce armaments, undoubtedly with a view to ultimate disarmament. . . .

. . . Great scientists and men of long military experience have pointed out that in the wars of the future there will be no such thing as the immunity of non-combatants. When poison-gas is used as a general method of warfare it will be directed against the civilian population as well as the military forces. And these things should teach us that the salvation of the world lies, not in entering competitively into a race for armaments, but rather in the nations endeavouring to come together and establish international relationships and agreements which will outlaw both war and the warmaker. In the days of the future, if the great nations of the earth are wise, they will proclaim war an international crime and the warmaker an international criminal.

Mr. WILFORD.—When they have altered human nature.

Mr. H. E. HOLLAND.—The honourable gentleman says, 'When they have altered human nature.' Warfare is not the reflection of what is human in nature. The honourable gentleman should know that what war represents is the reversion of man to the primitive. It is the effective application of the ethics of the jungle: it resurrects the animal and gives us 'Nature red in tooth and claw.' Human nature reflects all that is highest in our race, and as we rise to humanity's higher levels we shall move further away from the influences of the spirit of warfare. If what the honourable gentleman says is true, what becomes of Christianity, what becomes of the gospel of love, what becomes of the brotherhood of man? . . .

N.Z.P.D., 1927, vol. 214, pp. 254–64

123. THE 1937 IMPERIAL CONFERENCE

Michael Joseph Savage, the Prime Minister, reads a statement criticising British foreign policy, 21 May 1937.

. . . I clearly recognize that a country such as New Zealand can expect to play only a small part in world affairs. I realise that the United Kingdom is much more intimately affected and menaced by the world situation than New Zealand, and that the United Kingdom, with its age-long experience in such matters and with its widespread and expert sources of information is in a better position to weigh the circumstances than we, at the other end of the world, can ever hope to be. It is for this reason of course that previous Imperial Conferences have laid it down that, while the Members of the British Commonwealth are equal in status, the United Kingdom must play a greater part than the others in the actual administration of a Commonwealth foreign policy. And that leads me to my first point, which is that if the Commonwealth is to have a foreign policy, as distinct from a United Kingdom policy, some means must be afforded—some better means than at present exist —of evolving and adhering to such a policy. . . .

. . . I wish to make one point as clearly and as positively as I can, namely, that the principles we may adopt as a Commonwealth foreign policy must be founded on a moral basis that is universally acceptable. I suggest that even the admitted necessity of self defence is not now enough—we must have a wider and more inspiring appeal. Only one such policy, I submit, is available to us—one that all right-thinking people can support with their hearts and their consciences—and that is the collective peace system of the League of Nations. . . .

The days have passed when the autonomous Members of the British Commonwealth can fairly be expected, either in fact or in principle, to accept, without question, any line of policy laid down by the United Kingdom, particularly when the principles of that policy are exceedingly difficult to discover. . . .

New Zealand's views on collective security and the League of Nations are, I think, well known, and with a few final observations I have fulfilled my purpose in addressing you. One is that the evils from which the world is at the present time suffering are, in our opinion, due almost entirely to a faulty peace; that the nations which are now most threatening in their attitude have had un-doubted and legitimate grievances, and that a proper atmosphere for the international co-operation that we all so heartily desire can, we think, never be achieved until an attempt has been made to consider and to rectify, in so far as they can be rectified, the injustices of the past.

My second observation is this, that in the present circumstances, where the democracies, devoted to peace, appear to be retreating step by step before the advancing dictatorships, the New Zealand Government can in no case be a party to any Commonwealth policy which, in the struggle we fear may come between fascism and democracy, would tend to align the Commonwealth with the former.

Thirdly, I would say that the road to a sound foreign policy and universal peace can never be built except upon foundations which will do economic justice to the peoples of the nations of the earth —beginning in our own case with the people of the British Commonwealth.

For generations past the statesmen of the various nations have ignored the fact that war was almost entirely the result of economic causes, the chief of which was the inability of the people to purchase to the same extent as they had produced, an omission which in-evitably brought them into conflict with other nations over foreign markets and which, from every point of view, was disastrous to the people involved.

We are therefore of opinion that this Conference should give a lead in the preparation of the way to peace by examining methods that would bring about an expansion of trade within the Commonwealth and with other nations, and by issuing through the League of Nations invitations to all nations willing to take part in a world conference the objective of which would be to agree upon means of raising and making more secure the standards of living of all the people. . . .

> *Imperial Conference, 1937*, E(P.D.) (37), 3rd
> Meeting, 21 May 1937, pp. 13 and 17

124. WAR WITH GERMANY, 1939

Telegram to the Secretary of State for Dominion Affairs 4 September 1939, associating H.M. Government in New Zealand with the British declaration, and the Gazette Extraordinary published later that day.

His Majesty's Government in New Zealand desire immediately to associate themselves with His Majesty's Government in the United Kingdom in honouring their pledged word. They entirely concur with the action taken, which they regard as inevitably forced upon the British Commonwealth if the cause of justice, freedom, and democracy is to endure in this world. The existence of a state of war with Germany has accordingly been proclaimed in New Zealand, and His Majesty's Government in New Zealand would be grateful if His Majesty's Government in the United Kingdom would take any steps that may be necessary to indicate to the German Government that His Majesty's Government in New Zealand associate themselves in this manner with the action taken by His Majesty's Government in the United Kingdom. The New Zealand Government wish to offer to the British Government the fullest assurance of all possible support.

> *Documents Relating to New Zealand's Participation in the Second World War*, 1939–45,
> vol. i, Department of Internal Affairs, Wellington, 1941, pp. 6–7

HIS Excellency the Governor-General has it in command from His Majesty the King to declare that a state of war exists between His Majesty and the Government of the German Reich, and that such state of war has existed from 9.30 p.m., New Zealand standard time, on the third day of September, 1939.

The New Zealand Gazette, vol. iii, 1939, no. 82, p. 2321

125. LEGAL ARGUMENTS FOR ADOPTING THE STATUTE OF WESTMINSTER, 1944

An announcement in the Speech from the Throne in February 1944 that Parliament would be asked to pass legislation to adopt the Statute of Westminster, more than a dozen years after its enactment, prompted some discussion in New Zealand. Professor R. O. McGechan, in a lecture to Victoria University, gave the legal reasons.

. . . The political status of New Zealand was determined in 1926. The legal forms do not yet fit that status. Adoption of the Statute is merely a matter of bringing legal form into line with political status; and you can measure the need to adopt the Statute by the degree of inconvenience caused by the gap between the status and legal capacity. I do not hesitate then to treat the question as a lawyer. . . .

Status at international law can be gauged by reference to recognised powers to send and receive diplomatic agents, to make treaties and to declare war. . . . All the dominions have a diplomatic representative or diplomatic representatives accredited to foreign powers. New Zealand has a minister in Washington, has just appointed another to Moscow. . . . Our treaty-making power has evolved slowly over the last ninety-eight years. Commercial treaty-making power preceded capacity to enter into political treaties. . . . Treaties are negotiated by plenipotentiaries who are for that purpose invested with full powers by the king. . . .

I should mention one limitation to the treaty-making capacity of members of the Commonwealth. They cannot make treaties *inter se*—among themselves. Nor will a treaty made by two or more of them with foreign powers bind them *inter se*—a rule of construction of treaties known technically as the *inter se* rule. . . .

. . . The Canberra pact is not a treaty: it is called an Agreement, though for, I take it, mere convenience it has been included in the *New Zealand Treaty Series*. I may add that in the same way members of the Commonwealth do not exchange ambassadors or ministers with one another. Their agents are High Commissioners. Ambassadors or ministers would spell that international relationship which has been carefully avoided. . . .

Independent declaration of war or neutrality is the latest and most decisive manifestation of international status. . . .

These powers—to send and receive diplomatic agents, to make international treaties, to declare war or to remain neutral—add up to complete legal capacity at international law *vis-à-vis* foreign states. Realise too that this capacity does not flow from the Statute of Westminster at all. . . .

Neither the enactment nor the adoption of the Statute then involves any alteration whatsoever in our status: the only effect of adopton will be to put our legislative house in order. That this is a very necessary operation we shall see. One sometimes hears wild assertions that adoption of the Statute by New Zealand in 1944 means 'cutting the painter'. Now if ever we cut the painter it was in 1926 when we agreed that we were autonomous. . . .

What then are the legislative difficulties that the adoption of the Statute wil resolve? The Balfour formula speaks of autonomy and equality of status. But the imperial parliament is a sovereign legislative body, and the New Zealand parliament a non-sovereign one. . . . The New Zealand parliament has not the capacity to make any law, and there are some laws which it cannot unmake. Under constitutional law indeed the General Assembly's legislative incompetence is threefold: (1) It cannot legislate extra-territorially (2) It cannot pass laws repugnant to imperial statutes expressly or by necessary implication made by the imperial parliament applicable to New Zealand (3) It is bound by certain specific limitations under the Constitution Act and some other acts. . . .

Let us now glance at some of the wartime legislation of New Zealand to see how the extra-territorial shoe pinches.

The Shipping Control Emergency Regulations 1939, Reg. 6, provide that 'if the master of any ship under convoy wilfully disobeys any lawful signal, instruction or command of the commander of the convoy, or without leave deserts the convoy, then . . . he commits an offence against these regulations'. The regulations are restricted in their operation to British ships whether registered in a port of New Zealand or elsewhere. . . .

Let me take one other illustration of repugnancy. You may remember, first, that some of our troops were sentenced to imprisonment in Fiji for breaches of Fijian law. We preferred to see the sentences carried out in New Zealand. It should have been possible to come to terms with the Fijian authorities to this effect. But an imperial act of 1869—the Colonial Prisoners Removal Act— enabled two colonies to agree only 'with the sanction of an order by His Majesty in Council', and provided that this might be obtained only on address of both houses of each colonial parliament. Had we sought to provide for an unimportant matter like this by legislation giving one of our ministers power to make the necessary arrangements with other colonies, our legislation would have been repugnant to the 1869 act. So we must needs go on suffering this legal rigmarole, wasting the time of our legislature and of the imperial authorities, and achieving publicity much better avoided.

These examples of extra-territoriality and repugnancy present a picture of legislative muddle and confusion. Since it has been agreed that New Zealand and the United Kingdom are equal in status, the legislative incapacity of New Zealand has been illogically, even perversely, persisted in. . . .

. . . Extra-territoriality and repugnancy are anachronisms; they have in this war shown themselves too dangerous to continue. Even in peace they spell delay, uncertainty, waste of the time of our own and of imperial authorities, clumsiness and inefficiency. . . .

> R. O. McGechan, 'Status and Legislative Inability', in *New Zealand and the Statute of Westminster*, **Wellington**, 1944, pp. 65, 67, 68–71, 73, 77, 78, 85, 96–7

126. THE ADOPTION OF THE STATUTE OF WESTMINSTER

Debate in the House of Representatives on the Second Reading of the Statute of Westminster Adoption Bill, 7 and 11 November 1947.

The Right Hon. Mr. FRASER (Prime Minister, . . . The nationhood of our country is accepted in common with that of every other

British dominion, and we expect, as our natural right and function, to be represented independently and to express opinions, as far as a Government can construe the opinions of a country on international matters, overseas and at world Conferences. It is beyond argument that that is a right of our country. That being so, we have to examine how our laws enable that to be done. Are some of our existing laws opposed to the legal development of that principle? The answer is yes, that the Constitution Amendment Act of 1857 as it stands, and the Colonial Laws Validity Act of 1865 both do that. We can get an amendment to the Constitution Act to-day without adopting the Statute of Westminster. We can apply to the British Government and request the British Parliament to amend our Constitution Act to enable us to have greater scope in legislation, that is as far as our own legislation is concerned. Say, for instance, there is a desire to alter or abolish another place. We simply cannot do it at present without the permission of the British Parliament. . . . I certainly affirm that it ought to be in the power of the New Zealand Parliament, without consulting the United Kingdom at all. . . . In certain matters, although we do not realize it, and do not feel it, and would be sorry to admit it, the New Zealand Parliament still exists as subordinate in some way to the British Parliament by the very fact of the legislation. Of course, in my opinion, that ought not to be. If the full spirit of the Balfour Declaration is translated into legal terms, then that even implied subordination should be eliminated altogether. Therefore it is necessary to make the legal forms correspond with actual fact, and that is the main purpose of adopting the Statute of Westminster. New Zealand is the only dominion so far that has not adopted it. That is an anomaly within any comity of nations—in a family I would prefer to say—and among representatives of British Governments, Parliaments, and countries. It is an anomaly that one country should be on a different basis than that of other countries. . . .

Mr. DOIDGE (Tauranga).—Sir, I must frankly admit that my objection to the measure will be based largely on grounds of sentiment. Technically, as the Prime Minister has just shown us, a case can be made for its adoption, but I submit that there must be something better than technicalities at such a time as this. The adoption of the Statute of Westminster was open to us in New Zealand sixteen years ago. In all the time since we have never felt the need for its adoption; indeed we have preferred to do without the Statute of Westminster. The reason why we did not adopt the Statute in 1932 is one which I suggest we should remember. It was because New Zealand felt that its adoption would mean weakening the ties of Empire. . . . Our status and our independence were recognized and accepted long before the Balfour Declaration was ever heard of, and long before the Statute of Westminster was introduced in the House of Commons. The dominions in those days all had equal status; they were subservient to no one. We in the dominions were recognized as a great community of nations before the Statute of Westminster was ever contemplated, and I submit now that, if we study the situation quietly, and judge this measure for what it is worth, we will realize that in actuality all that it represents is a legal bill of divorcement if required. . . . I cannot recall a major occasion within the past fifty years when we have suffered to any material extent as a result of not enjoying what it is now claimed we could enjoy if we were to invoke the Statute of Westminster. Never in my lifetime can I remember an occasion when the Imperial Government has interfered with our self-governing rights or sought to enforce legislation against the will of this Dominion. . . . All that the Statute does is to provide a facility for a breakaway from the Empire, if there is such a desire—and there is certainly no such desire in this country. We are proud of the granite strength of our loyalty, proud of our British heritage enshrined as it is in the British Throne. With us, loyalty to the Motherland is an instinct as deep as religion. Thrice in our lifetime we have gone to the aid of Britain in times of crises, and now the greatest crisis of all is at hand. There never has been any need to adopt the Statute of Westminster, and I suggest now, least of all, is that time at hand.

N.Z.P.D., 1947, vol. 279, pp. 531–64

127. THE ADOPTION OF THE STATUTE OF WESTMINSTER, 1947

'An Act to adopt certain Sections of the Statute of Westminster, 1931', 25 November 1947, with the text of the U.K. Statute reproduced in the schedule.

BE IT ENACTED by the General Assembly of New Zealand in Parliament assembled, and by the authority of the same, as follows: —

1. This Act may be cited as the Statute of Westminster Adoption Act, 1947.

2. Sections two, three, four, five, and six of the Act of the Parliament of the United Kingdom cited as the Statute of Westminster, 1931 (which Act is set out in the Schedule to this Act), are hereby adopted, and the adoption of the said sections shall have effect from the commencement of this Act.

3. (1) For the purposes of section four of the said Statute of Westminster, 1931, the request and consent of New Zealand to the enactment of any Act of the Parliament of the United Kingdom shall be made and given by the Parliament of New Zealand, and not otherwise.

(2) Every Act of the Parliament of the United Kingdom passed after the commencement of the Statute of Westminster, 1931, and before the commencement of this Act, that purports to apply to New Zealand, or extend to New Zealand as part of the law of New Zealand, shall be deemed so to apply and extend and to have always so applied and extended according to its tenor, notwithstanding that it may not be expressly declared in any such Act that New Zealand has requested, and consented to, the enactment thereof.

SCHEDULE
STATUTE OF WESTMINSTER, 1931 (22 GEO. V. c. 4)

An Act to give Effect to certain Resolutions passed by Imperial Conferences held in the years 1926 and 1930.

[11th December, 1931]

WHEREAS the delegates of His Majesty's Government in the United Kingdom, the Dominion of Canada, the Commonwealth of Australia, the Dominion of New Zealand, the Union of South Africa, the Irish Free State and Newfoundland, at Imperial Conferences holden at Westminster in the years of our Lord nineteen hundred and twenty-six and nineteen hundred and thirty did concur in making the declarations and resolutions set forth in the Reports of the said Conferences:

And whereas it is meet and proper to set out by way of preamble to this Act that, inasmuch as the Crown is the symbol of the free association of the members of the British Commonwealth of Nations, and as they are united by a common allegiance to the Crown, it would be in accord with the established constitutional position of all the members of the Commonwealth in relation to one another that any alteration in the law touching the Succession to the Throne or the Royal Style and Titles shall hereafter require the assent as well of the Parliaments of all the Dominions as of the Parliament of the United Kingdom:

And whereas it is in accord with the established constitutional position that no law hereafter made by the Parliament of the United Kingdom shall extend to any of the said Dominions as part of the law of that Dominion otherwise than at the request and with the consent of that Dominion:

And whereas it is necessary for the ratifying, confirming and establishing of certain of the said declarations and resolutions of the said Conferences that a law be made and enacted in due form by authority of the Parliament of the United Kingdom:

And whereas the Dominion of Canada, the Commonwealth of Australia, the Dominion of New Zealand, the Union of South Africa, the Irish Free State and Newfoundland have severally requested and consented to the submission of a measure to the Parliament of the United Kingdom for making such provision with regard to the matters aforesaid as is hereafter in this Act contained:

Now, therefore, be it enacted by the King's most Excellent Majesty by and with the advice and consent of the Lords Spiritual and Temporal, and Commons, in this present Parliament assembled, and by the authority of the same, as follows:—

1. In this Act the expression 'Dominion' means any of the following Dominions, that is to say, the Dominion of Canada, the Commonwealth of Australia, the Dominion of New Zealand, the Union of South Africa, the Irish Free State and Newfoundland.

2. (1) The Colonial Laws Validity Act, 1865, shall not apply to any law made after the commencement of this Act by the Parliament of a Dominion.

(2) No law and no provision of any law made after the commencement of this Act by the Parliament of a Dominion shall be void or inoperative on the ground that it is repugnant to the law of England, or to the provisions of any existing or future Act of Parliament of the United Kingdom, or to any order, rule or regulation made under any such Act, and the powers of the Parliament of a Dominion shall include the power to repeal or amend any such Act, order, rule or regulation in so far as the same is part of the law of the Dominion.

3. It is hereby declared and enacted that the Parliament of a

Dominion has full power to make laws having extra-territorial operation.

4. No Act of Parliament of the United Kingdom passed after the commencement of this Act shall extend, or be deemed to extend, to a Dominion as part of the law of that Dominion, unless it is expressly declared in that Act that that Dominion has requested, and consented to, the enactment thereof.

5. Without prejudice to the generality of the foregoing provisions of this Act, sections seven hundred and thirty-five and seven hundred and thirty-six of the Merchant Shipping Act, 1894, shall be construed as though reference therein to the Legislature of a British possession did not include reference to the Parliament of a Dominion.

6. Without prejudice to the generality of the foregoing provisions of this Act, section four of the Colonial Courts of Admiralty Act, 1890 (which requires certain laws to be reserved for the signification of His Majesty's pleasure or to contain a suspending clause), and so much of section seven of that Act as requires the approval of His Majesty in Council to any rules of Court for regulating the practice and procedure of a Colonial Court of Admiralty, shall cease to have effect in any Dominion as from the commencement of this Act.

7. (1) Nothing in this Act shall be deemed to apply to the repeal, amendment or alteration of the British North America Acts, 1867 to 1930, or any order, rule or regulation made thereunder.

(2) The provisions of section two of this Act shall extend to laws made by any of the Provinces of Canada and to the powers of the legislatures of such Provinces.

(3) The powers conferred by this Act upon the Parliament of Canada or upon the legislatures of the Provinces shall be restricted to the enactment of laws in relation to matters within the competence of the Parliament of Canada or of any of the legislatures of the Provinces respectively.

8. Nothing in this Act shall be deemed to confer any power to repeal or alter the Constitution or the Constitution Act of the Commonwealth of Australia or the Constitution Act of the Dominion of New Zealand otherwise than in acordance with the law existing before the commencement of this Act.

9. (1) Nothing in this Act shall be deemed to authorise the Parliament of the Commonwealth of Australia to make laws on

any matter within the authority of the States of Australia, not being a matter within the authority of the Parliament or Government of the Commonwealth of Australia.

(2) Nothing in this Act shall be deemed to require the concurrence of the Parliament or Government of the Commonwealth of Australia in any law made by the Parliament of the United Kingdom with respect to any matter within the authority of the States of Australia, not being a matter within the authority of the Parliament or Government of the Commonwealth of Australia, in any case where it would have been in accordance with the constitutional practice existing before the commencement of this Act that the Parliament of the United Kingdom should make that law without such concurrence.

(3) In the application of this Act to the Commonwealth of Australia the request and consent referred to in section four shall mean the request and consent of the Parliament and Government of the Commonwealth.

10. (1) None of the following sections of this Act, that is to say, sections two, three, four, five and six, shall extend to a Dominion to which this section applies as part of the law of that Dominion unless that section is adopted by the Parliament of the Dominion, and any Act of that Parliament adopting any section of this Act may provide that the adoption shall have effect either from the commencement of this Act or from such later date as is specified in the adopting Act.

(2) The Parliament of any such Dominion as aforesaid may at any time revoke the adoption of any section referred to in subsection (1) of this section.

(3) The Dominions to which this section applies are the Commonwealth of Australia, the Dominion of New Zealand and Newfoundland.

11. Notwithstanding anything in the Interpretation Act, 1889, the expression 'Colony' shall not, in any Act of the Parliament of the United Kingdom passed after the commencement of this Act, include a Dominion or any Province or State forming part of a Dominion.

12. This Act may be cited as the Statute of Westminster, 1931.

New Zealand Statutes, 1947, 11, George VI, no. 38, pp. 347–51

128. THE NEW ZEALAND CONSTITUTION AMENDMENT (REQUEST AND CONSENT) ACT, 1947

An Act of the U.K. Parliament is 'requested and consented to' in order to confer full power of constitutional amendment upon the New Zealand Parliament with respect to the 'entrenched' sections of the 1852 Constitution Act, 25 November 1947.

BE IT ENACTED by the General Assembly of New Zealand in Parliament assembled, and by the authority of the same, as follows:—

1. This Act may be cited as the New Zealand Constitution Amendment (Request and Consent) Act, 1947.

2. For the purposes of section four of the Statute of Westminster, 1931, as adopted by the Statute of Westminster Adoption Act, 1947, the enactment by the Parliament of the United Kingdom of an Act in the form or to the effect of the draft Bill set out in the Schedule to this Act is hereby requested and consented to. . . .

DRAFT OF A BILL

To provide for the Amendment of the Constitution of New Zealand

WHEREAS provision for the Constitution of New Zealand was made by the New Zealand Constitution Act, 1852, and the power to amend that Act conferred on the Parliament of New Zealand by the New Zealand Constitution (Amendment) Act, 1857, was subject to certain restrictions therein specified: And whereas on the twenty-fifth day of November, nineteen hundred and forty-seven, the Parliament of New Zealand, by an Act intituled the Statute of Westminster Adoption Act, 1947, adopted sections two, three, four, five, and six of the Statute of Westminster, 1931: And whereas it is provided by section eight of the said Statute of Westminster, 1931, that nothing in that Act shall be deemed to confer any power to repeal or alter the Constitution Act of New Zealand otherwise than in accordance with the law existing before the commencement of the said Statute: And whereas New Zealand has requested and consented to the enactment of this Act:

Now therefore be it enacted, &c. : —

1. It shall be lawful for the Parliament of New Zealand by any Act or Acts of that Parliament to alter, suspend, or repeal, at any

time, all or any of the provisions of the New Zealand Constitution
Act, 1852; and the New Zealand Constitution (Amendment) Act,
1857, is hereby repealed.

2. This Act may be cited as the New Zealand Constitution
(Amendment) Act, 1947.

New Zealand Statutes, 1947, 11, Geo. VI, no. 44,
pp. 377–8

129. NEW ZEALAND CITIZENSHIP, 1948

*In a careful explanatory statement during the Committee stage of
the British Nationality and New Zealand Citizenship Bill, in the
House of Representatives, 17 August 1948, the Minister of Internal
Affairs, William Edward Parry, explained that the change was made
necessary by the new Canadian citizenship law of 1947 and that
'We did not seek this freedom for ourselves'.*

. . . At present, any one who is born on British soil is a British
subject, and possesses British nationality. A British subject owes
allegiance to His Majesty the King, and any one who does not owe
that allegiance is not a British subject, but an alien. This 'common
code' of British nationality applies throughout the British
Commonwealth. . . . Frontier officers in foreign countries did not
have to worry about whether a man was an Englishman, or an
Australian, or a New Zealander, for, as soon as they saw the familiar
blue cover and the title page requesting, in the name of His Majesty,
that the bearer be allowed to pass without let or hindrance they
knew that the holder was a British subject. . . .

The breakdown of the common code is due fundamentally to the
increasingly different needs of the different Commonwealth
countries. . . . In January, 1947, the Canadian Citizenship Act
became law. It said very little about British subjects, and a great
deal about Canadian citizens. Canada had found it necessary to say
which of all the 400-odd million of His Majesty's subjects in the
world belonged to Canada, and she defined those persons as
Canadian citizens, simply adding at the end, 'A Canadian citizen
is a British subject.'

I do not wish to criticize the action of the Canadian Government in this matter. No doubt Canada had her good reasons for that. Actually, the Canadian Act has been studied very carefully, and I think it is a very fine document of its kind. We have done it the compliment of imitating several of its provisions. . . .

But the Canadian Act gave the clearest illustration of the fact that the common code had become inadequate and unworkable. If one Commonwealth country was to define, in its own way, who were its citizens, and then simply proclaim that those citizens were also British subjects, it meant that, not merely hundreds, but millions of people would be British according to the law of one Commonwealth country, and aliens according to the law of another, and, in fact, there would be no common code left. The United Kingdom called a conference of nationality experts to decide what should be done. That conference met in February, 1947. . . . The conference decided that the best thing would be to abandon the effort to conserve the common code. Instead, each country would determine for itself, and in its own way, what classes of persons were its citizens, and each country would accept the citizens of every other Commonwealth country as British subjects. Henceforth every Britisher would be not only a British subject, but a citizen of some Commonwealth country as well.

The British Nationality Act giving effect to these principles, was passed by the United Kingdom Parliament last month, and the present Bill applies similar principles to New Zealand, and follows the main lines of the United Kingdom Act. Our Bill defines what persons are regarded as New Zealand citizens, and then it goes on to state that all these New Zealand citizens are also British subjects. So we have saved the common code, in a sense, but only by giving each Commonwealth country the right to define, in its own way, what persons are British subjects. Speaking for New Zealand, I am bound to say that this action would not have been initiated by our Government at the present time. We did not seek this freedom for ourselves. . . .

. . . While we are bound to accept this new status of New Zealand citizenship, we are fully aware that if a New Zealander is travelling overseas it may be far more profitable, and desirable, for him to be able to say, 'I am a British subject' than to say, 'I am a citizen of New Zealand.' So, it will be observed that, in the title of the Bill, 'British Nationality' comes first, and 'New Zealand Citizenship' second. . . .

I should like to remind the House that while the sentimental importance of this Bill is very great, its practical, material importance is comparatively slight. That is to say, we propose to apply this new status of New Zealand citizenship only where we find it useful. . . .

Part I of the Bill deals with the new definition of a British subject: he is a person who is a citizen of some Commonwealth country, and the Commonwealth countries concerned are listed as Canada, Australia, the Union of South Africa, Newfoundland, India, Pakistan, Southern Rhodesia, Ceylon, and last, but by no means least, the United Kingdom and colonies, the last-mentioned including all the colonial territories which have not self-government. . . . Any one born in New Zealand or naturalized in New Zealand, and also any British subject who has had twelve months residence in New Zealand on the 1st January, 1949, is a New Zealand citizen. . . . One interesting point is that some of us are going to be citizens of more than one country of our Commonwealth. If we were born in England, or even if our father was born in England, the United Kingdom Act makes us citizens of the United Kingdom and colonies; and as we are now resident in New Zealand the present Bill makes us New Zealand citizens also. I do not consider that this dual citizenship will have any bad effects. . . .

. . . Henceforth, the allegiance which we British subjects in New Zealand owe to our Sovereign will be by virtue of our citizenship of New Zealand, and we in New Zealand are taking over the sole right of deciding what persons in New Zealand should bear that allegiance. The change in principle is great; the change in practice will be very slight. . . .

N.Z.P.D., 1948, vol. 281, pp. 1519–24

6

POLITICS, 1919 TO 1940

130. THE 1919 ELECTION: THE REFORM CAMPAIGN

A Reform newspaper charges the Liberals with being willing to take office with Labour support and warns voters against an alliance of Liberals and the 'Reds'.

The Liberal-Red Fed Combine

. . . Throughout the campaign the Liberal Leader and his backers have addressed themselves to the task of concealing the truth concerning the Liberal plan of bidding for office with the aid of the official Labour Party. They have ignored, even striven to suppress, the repeated declaration by Mr. H. E. Holland that the Official Labour Party intends to support Sir Joseph Ward on a no confidence motion in order to defeat the present Government, and thereafter support Sir Joseph Ward as long as it suits them. . . . Sir Joseph has repeatedly declared that he will not 'retain' office with the aid of the Labour Party. . . . But, although asked a hundred times to say whether he contemplates using the proffered assistance of the Reds in order to attain to office, Sir Joseph Ward has never denied that he does. . . .

And what is he offering as the policy he will carry out if he does succeed in becoming Prime Minister with the support of the Reds? For the most part a series of undertakings which everybody knows he neither can nor will undertake. . . . The alternative to a renewal of government by the Reform Party is government by an opportunist combination of Liberals and Reds, . . .

The Press, Christchurch, 16 December 1919, p. 8

131. THE 1919 ELECTION:
REFORM AND THE MIDDLE CLASS

An editorial from The Press *of Christchurch on election day, 17 December 1919, suggesting that the backbone of the state is the 'middle class' whose future depends on the return of the Reform Party. This class would have to pay in taxation for the 'wild-cat schemes' of either Labour or Wardism.*

The Middle Class

It is appropriate to-day, when the electors are being reminded, for the last time, of their duty, and urged to perform it, to point out that the fortunes of the day rest very largely in the hands of the middle class. This class provides the mass of 'silent voters', and the element of uncertainty in all elections. They are silent because, though the largest of all sections of the electorate, they are wholly unorganised. . . . Here and there in the general formless body, small sections have coalesced for some particular purpose, but in the main its numbers are unrelated and incapable of employing to the best purpose the great strength which their numbers give them. The community of New Zealand is peculiar in that it possesses practically no 'upper class'. Almost everyone in the Dominion works, and the so-called 'middle class' therefore includes almost everybody not enrolled in the ranks of organised labour. . . .

Extreme Labour must have some outlet for the statement of its views, and if it does not get it in the House it is extremely likely that expression will be found in some other way, even by the general strike which many regard as inevitable in a few weeks. . . .

The middle class needed sadly to be reminded of their defenceless position; they need to realise that the whole trend of Labour's policy threatens their existence as a class, that the nationalisation of land and industries, which is Labour's avowed aim, . . . not only involves the lessening of their individual opportunities, but renders them liable, as the chief tax-paying class, to meet the demands for funds to carry on the State enterprises. All the wild-cat schemes for benefiting the public which are dangled before the eyes of electors at election time, have to be paid for, in the long run, by the middle class. The welfare and prosperity of that class is bound up with the Reform Party, which makes no promises it cannot perform, and is the only party that can . . . present an effective resistance to the spendthrift and destructive programmes of Labour on the one hand, and Wardism on the other—or, as may yet happen, of the two in combination. The future of the middle class, which is the strength of the State, rests on the ability of the Reform Party to carry on, . . .

The Press, Christchurch, on election day,
17 December 1919, p. 8

132. THE 1919 ELECTION: THE LIBERAL PLATFORM

After deciding to end the wartime coalition in August 1919, Sir Joseph Ward, the Liberal leader, appealed to the electors by reminding them of the many Liberal reforms after 1890, and by offering a policy of nationalization of coal mines, collieries, ferries, hydroelectricity and a National Bank. State support for the individual was presented as a continuation of Liberalism and an alternative to the Socialism advocated by the Labour Party.

. . . Outlining his programme he mentioned the fixing of borrowing at $5\frac{1}{2}$ per cent plus taxation; a State bank; nationalisation of the coal mines . . . ; State colliers; Government ventures to be subject to taxation like any other institution; three millions to be provided for educational buildings, no attempt to build up a large permanent military force; the resumption and continuation of the cadet and Territorial systems; the complete demobilisation of the Expeditionary Force; land for settlement; land for soldier settlements; civilian land settlement; settlement on Native Lands; expansion and assistance of the dairy industry; removal of the restrictions on trade; preference within the Empire; protection against enemy trading; assistance to local industries; State control of the licensing of freezing works; the nationalisation, with oil steamers, of the ferry services; motor lorries to assist country people without railways; the establishment of water power plants with an expenditure of six millions in three years to bring hydro-electricity into general use . . . ; reform of the electoral laws so that no minority could get into power; an extension of the privileges under the Workers Compensation Act; workers' homes; provision for soldiers and their dependents; provision for maimed soldiers; help for the prospecting of mines and minerals; further assistance to old age pensioners, widows and orphans; the further extension under certain conditions of the superannuation system; extension of the National

Provident Fund; the better treatment of the lower paid branches of the railways and other public services and a carrying out to the very utmost of the conditions which would preserve the future peace of the world in terms of the League of Nations. He wanted to stand behind the British Navy on the Dominion naval policy. He was out for no local navy, but he favoured [the plan] Lord Jellicoe had outlined, namely an attachment to the British Navy for the preservation of the people in southern seas in years to come. . . .

The Lyttelton Times, Christchurch, 11 November 1919, p. 7

133. THE 1919 ELECTION:
LABOUR APPEALS TO FARMERS

An editorial appeal, which includes the rhetoric of class war but also appeals to small farmers, who should realize that their interests are different from those of the 'squatters'. Labour's appeal is to all workers, including those on the land.

The political fight goes on apace. On the part of the old parties, the parties that belong to the past, it is a sham fight; but on the part of Labor, the party of the Future, the party of Humanity, it is an earnest struggle to give expression to the hopes and aspirations of the toiling masses, who for countless ages had been condemned to be the hewers of wood and the drawers of water for the privileged classes. . . .

One of the most hopeful signs of the present Labor campaign is the support being freely given by the small farmers to the Labor candidates. Here let us say that the mistaken notion that Labor is opposed to the interests of the workers on the land, who happen to be small proprietors, has no basis in fact. The Labor Party's policy is one of justice for all workers, not excepting the man on the land, who, in a special sense, is a direct wealth-producer, and as such deserves to be given the full reward of his labor. At the present time the small farmers are more or less dominated by the large land-holders, with whom they regard their interests as being bound up, and in denouncing the evils of profiteering and high prices. *The Worker* and Labor speakers are sometimes misunderstood, and regarded as the enemy of the man on the land. Nothing could be further from the truth. Both the small farmer and the town

300

worker are victims of the unjust social system, or lack of system that obtains to-day, and should join forces to assert their political and social rights. It must be recognized that the larger number of workers in this country derive their living from the land, and work on the land, and that no political party that does not have the approval and support of the men on the land can hope to secure the reins of government. A working farmer of New Zealand, like his fellow in Australia, is beginning to realise that his interests and those of the squatter are not identical, and that his political hopes are bound up with the Labor Party, which has made an honest attempt to evolve a just land policy, which may not be perfect, but can be altered and amended as time goes on, as the majority of its members decide. Meantime, it is encouraging to see that many of the Labor candidates are farmers, men of good standing, of undoubted honesty and ability, who are securing the support of their fellow-workers to an extent that would have been impossible in pre-war days. . . .

The Maoriland Worker, 3 December 1919, p. 4

134. THE MEAT BOARD, 1922

The Prime Minister, W. F. Massey, addresses representatives of the meat producers in Wellington where, on 10 January 1922, they met to discuss the Reform Government's proposal for a meat pool. The scheme, which was embodied in the Meat Export Control Act, 1921–2, provided for a Board of Control, representing the industry, to supervise all aspects of the marketing of meat after it had entered freezing works.

The Prime Minister, . . . said . . . The Government had been watching the meat market very closely for a long time, and had come to the conclusion that the time had arrived to interfere with the object of assisting the producers of the Dominion to get into a better position and obtain more adequate prices for their frozen meat. . . . He believed that an improvement within a reasonable time could not be secured without combination. The pooling scheme provided for reducing the cost of production, the cost of shipping, and the cost of marketing, and at the same time for placing the farmer in a position to obtain a fair price for the meat he placed in the British market. . . . It had been suggested . . . that the New

Zealand Government was embarking upon a socialist enterprise. That was a remarkable charge to be brought against the present Government. The scheme had no taint of Socialism. It was co-operation. The members of the Government considered it their duty to assist the industries of the country, and particularly the primary industries, on which the prosperity of the whole Dominion depended. . . . The scheme was not going to involve the creation of another Government Department. There were enough Government Departments already. The new organisation would be a producers' organisation. The Government would expect to have a share of representation on the Board of Control and on the board to be established in Britain, and he did not think the producers would object to that, in view of the fact that the Government would be supporting the scheme financially. . . . In conclusion, the Prime Minister said that an important part of the work of the Board of Control and the board proposed to be established in Britain would be to prevent an over-supply of New Zealand meat reaching the market in particular months. There was no intention of doing anything to increase prices unfairly or improperly in the British market; but gluts were not fair the the producers, and the Government wished to see that the supply of meat was regulated in a reasonable manner.

> *The Dominion*, Wellington, 11 January 1922,
> p. 6

135. LABOUR APPEALS TO LIBERALS AND PROGRESSIVES, 1922

Advertisement by the Labour candidate in the Timaru electorate, which argues that Labour has taken over the 'progressive mantle' from the Liberals and that Massey and the Reform Party are the successors of the pre-1890 'Tories'.

The 'Reformers' of to-day are but the lineal descendants of the Tories of 1890. Remember the soup kitchens? Can the leopard change its spots?

The People have suffered the Muddling of Massey for 10 long years. The time is ripe for change.

THE LABOUR PARTY
ARE
THE TRUE LIBERALS . . .
BEWARE OF CAPITALIST PROPAGANDA

THE PROGRESSIVES OF TIMARU, of whatever persuasion, would ASK THE ELECTORS TO DISCARD THE PROPAGANDA which is being industriously circulated through the Press. The Electors should cast all this aside and think out the problems for themselves.

They should consider the great issues that are at stake.

They should reflect upon the deplorable condition into which the Dominion's finances have been plunged as a result of incompetent 'management.'

DO NOT BE MISLED by Bolshevik nonsense. The Labour Party of Timaru is comprised of people like yourselves, who place the interests of all the people above the interests of the class.

PROGRESSIVES, WORKERS, LIBERALS

This is no time for a 'Lie Down and Wait and See' Policy as advocated by the Reform Candidate. . . .

Timaru Post, 6 December 1922, p. 6

136. THE DAIRY BOARD, 1923

Following the model of the Meat Control Board of 1922, which was accepted by the meat industry, the Massey Government went ahead with the creation of a Dairy Board, with similar powers, in 1923. Although the majority of dairy producers approved the scheme, there was considerable opposition as shown from some of the evidence given to the Agricultural and Pastoral Industries and Stock Committee.

EBENEEZER MAXWELL examined. (No. 1.)

1. *The Chairman.*] Whom do you represent, Mr. Maxwell?—I have here letters from various factories authorizing me to represent them before this Committee: they are the Brooklands Co-operative Dairy Factory, Kahui Factory, Newell Road Factory. . . . We oppose the Dairy-produce Control Bill on the principle (1) that it is an arbitrary interference with our rights and liberties, and (2) that the primary producers have just the same rights as any manufacturer or trader to market his goods as he chooses. . . . Further, we oppose the measure because the revolutionary and communistic powers sought would in themselves and by precedent constitute a grave menace to the welfare of the community, and also because the placing of such great, arbitrary, unlimited, and unfettered powers

in the hands of a few men is improper and undesirable from every point of view. The Board would represent a gigantic monopoly. . . .

J. B. MacEwan examined. (No. 11.)

1. *The Chairman.*] Whom do you represent?—I represent the proprietary factories, and I wish to give some evidence as an exporter and as a merchant. . . .

. . . If we are at war, or possibly if an industry gets into a bad state, for many reasons we say that possibly the Government or the House would be justified in taking a hand in it until it is well established again, and then quietly withdrawing. . . .

A.J.H.R., 1923, I–10A, pp. 1 and 41

137. REPEAL OF INCOME TAX ON FARMERS, 1923

The Prime Minister, William F. Massey, defends the Land and Income Tax Bill in the House of Representatives, 14 August 1923, and the Leader of the Labour Party, H. E. Holland argues that the bill will help not the working farmer but a few wealthy landowners.

The Right Hon. Mr. Massey (Prime Minister) said,— . . . But I have a very clear recollection of what took place when agricultural land was made subject to income-tax as well as land-tax; that was in the year 1916 or 1917, and there was very strong opposition to it. . . . the members of the agricultural community were advised by myself and other Ministers that the tax was a war-tax and that it was not intended to be permanent. . . . There is another objection to the income-tax on land, and the objection holds good to-day: Farmers are not accountants, and few of them do much in the way of book-keeping. The farmer looks to his bank pass-book and to his cheque-book, and he also has his accounts with the stock and station agents with whom he does business. From these sources he generally manages to form a fairly accurate idea of what his financial position is. The matter, however, is very different when it becomes necessary for him to send in his return to the Land and Income Tax Department: he is then in trouble at once, because the furnishing of the return requires a knowledge of the Act, which is somewhat technical. . . .

. . . I think we have now arrived at the stage when an alteration should be made. The average amount collected by way of income-tax from farmers is something like £200,000 per annum. . . .

Mr. HOLLAND (Buller).— . . .

Now, it is quite an illusion to think that the *bona fida* farmer is going to get any material benefit out of this legislation which is proposed. . . . It is argued over and over again that the existing legislation was the result of war-time finance, and that war conditions have now gone. Members who have argued that way have lost sight of the fact that the war debt is with us, and has yet to be paid. It ought to be paid by the people whose property was defended, if by anybody at all. Sir, I want to deal with the statement that this Bill is intended to relieve the farmer, and I shall endeavour to show how fallacious that idea is. . . .

We have about 600,000 adults in the Dominion, and of that number some 450,000 have no land whatever. There are about 150,000 adults who may be classed as landowners, if you include every owner of a quarter-acre section. Of the 150,000, 65,000 own less than 1 acre each. Less than 55,000 of our landowners pay land-tax. Of the 55,000 who pay land-tax only 4,602 pay income-tax. So that out of the 150,000 people who own land in this country only 4,602 have been liable to pay income-tax, according to the latest returns presented to us from the Department. What do the Government members say to that? Of the 55,000 land-tax payers there are more than 50,000 who do not pay income-tax. Among this 50,000 are the vast majority of the working-farmers to whom this legislation is supposed to be capable of affording relief. The average working-farmer does not have sufficient income to bring him within the operations of the income-tax. As a matter of fact, there are nearly 100,000 landowners in this country who do not pay land-tax because they have not got sufficient land. . . . Now, Sir, I will put it in another way: There are six landowners with incomes exceeding £10,000, whose average tax is £3,503. 10s. The Government proposes to make a present to such of these six as are country landowners of £3,503. 10s. each. If a man has an assessable income of £10,000, he has no need to complain if he is called upon to pay taxation to the extent of £3,503. 10s., for, after all, as has been said on the floor of this House over and over again, it is not what you take from a man that counts, but what you leave him, and in such a case he is left with quite sufficient to live upon comfortably. Then, there are six landowners whose incomes range from £7,000 to

£10,000, their average tax being £2,152. 4s.; 47 landowners whose incomes range from £4,000 to £7,000, average tax £570. 7s.; 55 land owners whose incomes range from £3,000 to £4,000, average tax £452. 14s.; 142 landowners whose incomes range from £2,000 to £3,000, average tax £216. 10s.; 161 landowners whose incomes range from £1,500 to £2,000, average tax £118. 2s.; 474 landowners whose incomes range from £1,000 to £1,500, average tax £70 8s.; 208 landowners whose incomes range from £950 to £1,000, average tax £50. 7s.; 151 landowners whose incomes range from £850 to £950, average tax £32. 11s.; 301 landowners whose incomes range from £750 to £850, average tax £31. 5s.; 484 landowners whose incomes range from £650 to £750, average tax, £19. 15s. 6d.; 2,567 land-owners whose incomes are under £650, average tax £6. 18s. The total tax assessed is £221,886. 10s. 11d. Now, Sir, I submit that if there are working-farmers among this very small number of land-owners who pay income-tax in New Zealand—and I suppose there are some working-farmers amongst them—they will be included in the 2,567, and they will benefit on an average to the extent of £6. 18s. 10d. Who wants relief to the extent of £6. 18s. 10d. if he has an assessable income for the purpose of this law of from £500 to £650? . . . The case I want to make is that this law is not going to benefit the working-farmers whom the Government claim it is designed to benefit. It is ridiculous to claim that this law is going to give relief to the *bona fide* farmers. It is not going to do anything of the sort. It is going to give relief to a handful of big landowners—to the land profiteers of this country. . . .

The Right Hon. Mr. MASSEY (Prime Minister).

. . . There is one way of making things easy and simple for the man on the land, and that is by the way proposed in the Bill—by wiping out the income-tax altogether, and then there will be no returns to make up. . . . The money that is taken from the man on the land in the way of taxation is his wages fund. If you take that money away he is not able to provide employment. If, on the other hand, you give him the chance of spending it by improving his property, it makes a difference to the labour-market straight away. If we can only do what the Government have in view—that is, provide for a further reduction of taxation this session—we shall have done more to bring about normal prosperity than anything that has been done up to the present. . . .

N.Z.P.D., 1923, vol. 202, pp. 28–9, 49–51, 71

138. THE 1925 ELECTION:
THE COATES CAMPAIGN

Although he had built up a formidable reputation as Minister of Public Works and Railways, J. Gordon Coates, the Reform leader after Massey's death in May 1925, was a rather colourless speaker. The excerpt is from his speech in the Theatre Royal, Christchurch, 13 October 1925, which was also the first Dominion-wide political broadcast.

. . . Dealing with the land policy of the Dominion, Mr Coates said that the man in the city and the man in the country both depended almost entirely on the exportable value of New Zealand products, all of which came from the man of the land. It was essential that there should be co-operation between the man in the city and the man in the country. One could not live without the other. It should not be forgotten that the farmer worked long hours and that his job was seldom done. Many farmers could come into the towns in their motor-cars, but a good many others could not afford cars. Farming was 'not all beer and skittles'. Every farmer wanted to own his own property, and this was true even if he had a 999 years' lease. He would like to state that New Zealand would never have reached its present position had it not been for the mortgagee. Someone had to lend money and the Government had to see that the producer got it at the cheapest rate to make possible the progress of our essential industries.

A lot had been heard about land aggregation, and he would like to give an assurance that if the Reform Party were again returned to power it would do its utmost to prevent aggregation. . . .

The Press, Christchurch, 14 October 1925, p. 11

139. THE 1925 ELECTION:
THE COATES CAMPAIGN

Advertisements used in the new mass-appeal Reform campaign included (a) a letter to 'Jack' the plain citizen who wanted one 'national' party, (b) an appeal to the Women of New Zealand, with a picture of a middle class family sitting in front of the fireplace, with a warning that Labour-Socialists endangered their security, and (c) an eve-of-poll appeal to 'Diggers' to fight again for New Zealand.

(a) Dear Jack,

You say that you wish to see the two old parties abolished, or merged to form one national party.

Well and good, old man—but do you realise the logical and most direct way of attaining the 'one national party'?

You'd agree that Coates is the only man in sight to lead a 'national' government to any real achievement.

Very well; then let us all get behind Coates and put him in his proper place—at the head of a strong Coates parliament. Give him a big enough majority to enable him to choose the strongest possible colleagues for his ministry.

Thats the direct and simple road to the end that 'Nationalist' and 'Fusionists' are seeking!

Support a Coates man—secure a Coates majority—and you'll have a strong national government that will deserve and justify the support of all sane and progressive elements in the Dominion. . . .

The Press, Christchurch, 21 October 1925, p. 13

(b)   WOMEN OF NEW ZEALAND
Safeguard your Hearths and Homes

Nothing counts for more in the welfare of a nation than the home life of its people. . . .

You are now being asked to overthrow the conditions of government which have led by steady progressive steps to New Zealand's present enviable position.

WILL YOU TAKE THAT RISK?

Will you risk the security of your Home Life; the security of your employment or your husband's employment; the security of your future and your family's future? That is a plain issue for you to consider when you cast your vote at the coming election. The present Prime Minister is neither a hardshell Tory nor a 'Capitalist', nor any of these political bogeys sometimes invented to scare the simple-minded and unthinking. He is simply a young New Zealander who has shown exceptional administrative ability, constructive capacity and driving force. . . .

BEWARE THE SITUATION IS SERIOUS

Do not underrate the gravity of the present political situation. The Labour-Socialist Party is powerfully organised. It aims at securing control of the country's affairs and its efforts are being

308

assisted by vote-splitting due to National-Liberal and Country Party candidates contesting seats.

Your only safe vote—safe in the sense that it offers you assurance of sound Government and settled conditions of progress—is a vote pledged to support Mr Coates. . . .

If you love New Zealand Vote for Sound Government — Security — Progress. Vote Coates. For COATES and SAFETY.

The Press, 31 October 1925, p. 5

(c) . . . The election is important because the choice lies between sound and stable government, imbued with true British ideals, and Socialistic or sectional government. . . .

But does any New Zealander desire to see New Zealand governed in the interests of one section of the community to the exclusion or neglect of all other sections? I trust not. . . .

This is a glorious country, with a wonderful future. The best country in the world deserves the best Government its people can give it. . . .

I have outlined schemes for the development of the country's resources . . . and for the running of New Zealand on business lines.

Essential points from the policy are: Sound and prudent finance; thorough examination into incidence of taxation; closer settlement of occupied and unoccupied lands by purchase and subdivision; extension of scientific agricultural education; investigation into farmers' land banks; the well-being of the State and the Empire; support of the League of Nations; encouragement of secondary industries and the suppression of trusts; selective immigration; organisation to be strengthened; more houses and fewer slums; increased compensation benefits, investigation of a universal pension scheme, and aid to parents with large families; modernised methods of education; extension of public health policy; establishment of a Local Government Board, national safety and progressive development. . . .

There is no room in Parliament for men without decisive views. The country is entitled to know where every candidate stands. . . .

To my comrades, 'the Diggers', I say: 'We are going over the top on Wednesday, and once again the fight is for New Zealand. . . .'

The Press, 3 November 1925, p. 11

140. THE LABOUR PARTY AND LAND POLICY, 1927

Report of a Special Committee appointed by the 1926 annual conference, and presented to the 1927 conference by Michael Savage, who said Labour's 1925 policy of land nationalization and usehold tenure could not be operated without taking full control of the banking system.

LAND

Public Ownership of Land being the only ultimate remedy for the present chaos and muddle the Party's Platform provides: —

1. Conservation of all State and Publically owned lands.
2. Full recognition of owners interest in all land including tenure, right of sale, transfer and bequest.
3. Compensation for Improvements on Leasehold Lands.
4. A graduated tax on unimproved land values.
5. Acquisition (compulsory where necessary) of areas of land suitable for closer settlement and town planning.
6. TENURE OF ACQUIRED LAND
   The tenure of acquired land to be perpetual lease conditional on occupancy and use with periodic revaluations.
7. State provision of all facilities for the transfer of land.
8. Maximum assistance to organisations of producers for Co-operative Production, Purchasing, Shipping, Marketing and Credit.
9. Extension of agricultural education including the provision of research facilities to find means of bringing land to its fullest productive use.
10. The securing of an adequate supply of fertilisers at the lowest possible cost to the farmers.
11. Development and settlement of unoccupied land by most advantageous methods.
12. (*a*) Adjustment of taxation on land in business areas to prevent exploitation and to secure Community values for the people.
    (*b*) The application of the 'Betterment Principle' of land values which have been increased by public works or other community enterprise.

The Land Policy and Finance and Credit Policy of the Party are interwoven and we recommend that the following Clauses be included in the Platform:

FINANCE AND CREDIT

1. A State Bank to act as a Central Bank with full control of note issue.

2. Extension of the State Advances Office to provide all credit necessary for:—

(*a*) Primary production including loans to Co-operative Dairy Companies for the assistance of supplies in the purchase of fertilisers, equipment or stock.

(*b*) House Building.

> *New Zealand Labour Party, 1927 Annual Conference Papers*, Report of Land Policy Committee (1926–7)

141. THE 1928 ELECTION:
WARD AND THE SEVENTY MILLION LOAN

Sir Joseph Ward, the former Liberal Premier, explained the nature and policy of the United Party in a speech in Auckland Town Hall, on 16 October 1928. Ward announced that the Dominion needed to borrow for development, and pledged himself to borrow seventy million pounds. Although the New Zealand Herald *and other observers reported that Ward said he would borrow this in twelve months, the Auckland correspondent of the Liberal* Lyllelton Times *says the sum was to be spread over eight to ten years.*

. . . The United Party comprises members of all former parties in this country. There is no need for any of the different sections to change their political creed so long as they conform to the intentions of the United Party to stand in the general interest of the whole of the people of the Dominion. I am still a Liberal. . . .

Any one who has studied the financial history of the Dominion must recognize that if we are to progress at a reasonable pace there must be a departure from the present policy, which each year is bringing about a condition of chaos, that if perpetuated, will, sooner or later, result in either a deadlock or a curtailment of public requirements in the Dominion that would be detrimental, not only to the development of the country as a whole but the people in the towns and cities. . . .

The plain fact is that a system of providing some millions more money for loans for people on land is a pressing need. . . .

My proposal is that we should take steps to have money for advancing chiefly to settlers on the land, and a portion for workers' homes, of from six million to eight million per annum, by the issue of Government bonds at 4½ per cent interest, saleable at £95 per £100. Further, that we should put an end to the construction of any new short lines of railways in any portion of the Dominion and that we lay down, definitely, by Act of Parliament, what, for convenience, I term 'authorised long lines of railways' in both Islands. . . .

I propose, therefore, to raise £70,000,000 spread over eight to ten years for the purpose of providing £60,000,000 to lend to settlers on their landed interests and £10,000,000 for the completion of the main railway lines of the Dominion. . . .

> From the Auckland Correspondent, 16 October, *The Lytteleton Times,* 17 October 1928, p. 9

142. THE AUCKLAND RIOT, 1932

On 14 April 1932 postal workers, protesting about wage cuts, and unemployed workers marched to a meeting at the Town Hall. As the hall could accommodate only a fraction of the crowd the police had to intervene, and fighting and looting broke out. In his speech on the second reading of the Public Safety Conservation Bill, 19 April 1932, John A. Lee, Member for New Lynn tries to convey the atmosphere on Queen Street.

. . . I want to say first of all that the significant feature of the disturbance that occurred in Auckland lies in just this: that there was absolutely no premeditation about it. That shows the extraordinary explosiveness of the public mind at the present moment. I walked in the procession that marched to the Town Hall. As a matter of fact I think I was in the first four, and a more orderly assembly of citizens I never saw in my life. First the Civil servants and thousands of other citizens; later organized groups of unemployed men all from their respective divisional areas, all in orderly column of four, all carrying banners. A most orderly, and, I want to say, a most heartrending sight. Of course it is easy to be wise in retrospect, but it is obvious that the demonstration as planned was successful beyond the dreams of any one who planned it, and suddenly, with all the inflammable material about, twenty thousand people found themselves trying to get into a hall that would only accommodate four thousand. Of course in two or three moments there was disorder. I know the difficulties of the police at that moment; I know the hall was very rapidly crowded; I know the guardians of the law did a duty to the people inside the hall; but I realized for the first time—although it had been obvious to any man that an explosion would come—what an explosive sentiment was then abroad. There were these chaps—and I challenge contradiction—this orderly army of unemployed marching up Queen Street, as they marched down it years ago to go to the Great War. They were cheered then as they marched. Here were the same fellows again not being cheered, and there was remarkable order; remarkable determination this time; and, as evidence of the hunger, let me say they reminded me of nothing so much as a lean group of soldiers coming out of the trenches after a long time. They were pale; they were hungry. I have seen very few stout men among our unemployed; and they were poorly clad. When the meeting in the Town Hall, such as it was, was over, I walked out into Queen Street; and I think it is necessary that we should understand this, if we are going to handle this situation aright. It cannot be handled by the baton, but only by an intelligent policy that will organize, not the martial forces, but the moral forces of the State. I walked down Queen Street, and there was glass crashing on every side; and nobody was concerned. The average citizen was quite happy about it. . . . There was a carnival spirit abroad. Nobody seemed a trifle concerned. There is no doubt at all about it that for the time being everybody had lost completely any desire to do anything to maintain law and order; and I suggest that that was because of the spirit of bitterness and hostility to the Government which has grown up. We cannot establish a peaceful State upon a spirit of bitterness and hostility. . . . I saw young men and young women breaking windows and removing goods; and we may console ourselves with the suggestion that they were only young hoodlums. I believe, on the whole, the elderly section of the unemployed were round the Town Hall. But we have ten thousand young men and young women leaving school every year, and we are doing nothing for them. They are moving about from place to place, unemployed, and are becoming bitter and discontented. It almost seems, indeed, as if it was our policy not to turn them into citizens who would help to bring about an integration of all the valuable forces of the State, but to turn them into disgruntled explosive elements. These young folk, growing up jobless, are becoming a hard-bitten generation; and we are not going to solve any problem by batoning them, although at times, when riot

313

POLITICS, 1919 TO 1940

occurs, it may be necessary to take swift and severe steps. Only
a reversal of our policy is going to achieve the desired result. It is
the Government that is to blame. I firmly believe that. . . .

N.Z.P.D., 1932, vol. 232, p. 178

143. THE PUBLIC SAFETY CONSERVATION BILL, 1932

*The Prime Minister George W. Forbes defends the emergency
public safety measure introduced into Parliament after the Auckland riot. Speaking during the second reading of the Bill on 19
April 1932, the Premier stressed the need to protect 'peaceful citizens' against 'the lawless minority', and is continually interrupted
by Labour Members.*

The Right Hon. Mr. FORBES (Prime Minister).—Sir, I must say
that I have been considerably surprised at the amount of opposition
to this Bill, the object of which is to provide better protection for
our citizens. One would have thought that, in view of the damage
recently done by a lawless mob in Auckland, there would have been
no two opinions about the necessity of strengthening the hands of
the Government and those in control of affairs in the cities in obviat-
ing a repetition of such occurrences. I do not know whether the
members of the Labour party realize the position they are taking
up. It would appear that wherever there are forces of disorder they
seem to consider it their duty to champion those forces. Surely the
owners of shops are entitled to every protection. And our
determination is that there shall be no repetition of the Auckland
outbreak. . . . We are told that the measure has for its object the
batoning of the workers into doing things they do not wish to do.
    Mr. PARRY.—So it is.
    The Right Hon. Mr. FORBES.—The honourable gentleman knows
perfectly well that it is merely a measure of protection for peaceful citizens. If the honourable member for Auckland Central stands
for what occurred in Auckland then I can understand the attitude
he is adopting, but the Government is determined to afford protection to the citizens of this country. It has been said, and, I think,
correctly, that the rioting in Auckland was not done by the unemployed, but by the lawless minority who were bent on destruction.
Surely no member of the Labour party will claim that such people
should be allowed freedom to commit the crimes with impunity. . . .

Opponents to the measure have said it will apply to the holding of political meetings. All sorts of wild and extravagant statements have been made by those who oppose the Bill. And Government members have been criticized for not remaining in their seats and listening to these statements. Is it any wonder? . . . If honourable members knew anything of mob psychology they would know that if large concourses of people are brought together, and their minds are excited by inflammatory speeches, it is only looking for trouble. . . .

Mr. FRASER.—I suppose any speech criticising the Government is inflammatory. . . .

The Right Hon. Mr. FORBES . . . I cannot understand why there should be so much objection raised to a Bill that is designed for the purpose of giving protection to innocent citizens. Does the Labour party want those people to be left unprotected? Does it want to leave them to the violence of the mob? . . .

Mr. H. E. HOLLAND.—You have got all the powers you require. . . .

The Right Hon. Mr. FORBES . . . As I have said, I have looked at the reports of speeches made by Labour members, and I have noticed no attempt whatever to let the public know that the Government is not the crowd of villains it is being painted, that its members have just as much sympathy with the people who are out of employment as have the members of the Labour party themselves.

MR. SEMPLE.—Who is going to be the judge of fair criticism? . . .

N.Z.P.D., 1932, vol. 232, pp. 227–31

144. COATES AND THE FOUNDATIONS OF RECOVERY

As Minister for Unemployment from 1931 and Minister of Finance 1933-5, J. Gordon Coates was the leading minister of the Forbes Coalition. Dr. W. B. Sutch, who joined his staff as a twenty-six-year-old economist in 1933, recalls the pragmatic approach to problems which led Coates to the creation of the Reserve Bank, internal debt conversion, foreign exchange adjustment, and other economic measures which laid the foundations of recovery.

. . . If New Zealand should, at some future time, shed its colonial characteristics and become an independent nation making its own judgments; and if historians should interest themselves in the search for the beginnings of this process, they may well fix on the year 1928. In that year, the Prime Minister, J. G. Coates called at Parliament Buildings, in Wellington, the first of an unprecedented series of economic conferences. This was the National Industrial Conference, which met on 27 March 1928.

Among the five or six dozen men who attended were delegates from employers' groups or organisations: the Manufacturers' Federation, the Farmers' Union, Chambers of Commerce; shipowners', dairy farmers' and bankers' organisations. There were representatives of organised labour, parliamentarians, heads of department and a group of people who had not until that time been sought after by governments. These were the economists, professors or lecturers in the universities or agricultural colleges— . . .

The main problem that the National Industrial Conference was required to consider was unemployment, a problem from which New Zealand was—even before the great depression—suffering 'in its most acute form'. . . .

The Conference defined some problems and suggested some solutions: on unemployment the recommendation was that the government should provide from the Consolidated Fund the money and work necessary to cope with the situation, and that an unemployment committee be set up. But the Conference failed to agree on proposals for unemployment insurance; it further disagreed on whether the system of arbitration of awards and conditions should remain compulsory—the workers preferred it as it was and the employers wished to abolish it.

The conclusions seem meagre, but a milestone had been passed. The employers, farmers, Chambers of Commerce and manufacturers of New Zealand had agreed that the care of the unemployed was a function of the State, and Coates had been given his mandate to work something out. . . .

. . . In the years 1933 to 1935, I occupied with others Room 92, adjoining Coates's own office. Round the walls we had large and detailed graphs depicting changes in the prices of wool, fat lambs, butter and cheese, the marriage rate and the birth rate. Whenever an M.P. visited Room 92 we would draw his attention to the graphs and ask for his guess as to where it would end. Invariably it was taken for granted that New Zealand's population had reached its peak, especially as the Government Statistician's figures indicated that the country was not reproducing its numbers. . . .

Coates consistently sought the advice of three members of his staff, all economists, all under forty years of age, . . .

Coates was a man who liked to listen to advice and preferred it to be offered collectively. A major problem might be given to one of his economic assistants but, when the results were discussed in front of Coates, he would have the others in—as well of course as any departmental official who might be involved. Park and Ashwin of Treasury usually attended, also P. D. N. Verschaffelt, Chairman of the Public Service Commission, who had one of the finest minds and broadest judgments of any New Zealand civil servant of this century. The views that were put forward were frequently quite mixed ones, and Coates would listen quietly while we all argued. On occasions he would ask a shrewd question or steer the discussion into an area it had not covered. When he had heard enough and had made up his mind, he would stop the discussion, record his decision and then go on to the next point.

Coates had the fierce loyalty of his staff. This was not only because of his democratic, friendly personal attributes but also because of the care he took in exploring all aspects of a problem and giving weight to them all before he reached his decisions. They were not decisions reached on political grounds: the political decisions would, of course, be made in Cabinet or Caucus or elsewhere. . . .

Up to 1933, the government had held to the traditional view that it must balance the budget at all costs. Coates's own view was very different. He considered that it would be quite possible to inject purchasing power into the community by using the credit of the government with the banks. This view, of course, was heartily endorsed by the majority of New Zealanders, but it was not possible for Coates to go to the public and say what the real problem was. Mr Forbes, the Prime Minister, had repeatedly closed the question in his response to many requests for such clear action by simply saying, 'Where is the money to come from?' . . .

In 1934, . . . Coates had an enormous volume of work. . . . The activity in his office was intense. Campbell, myself and later Belshaw from his own staff, Park and Ashwin of Treasury, and Verschaffelt, Public Service Commisioner, all worked severally and jointly to define principles, get directions from Coates, check with the Law Draftsman, discuss matters with representative groups, draft explanatory pamphlets, prepare speech notes and work out the organisational aspect consequent on the legislation. At 10.30 in the evening we would have tea and sandwiches and more discussions. At midnight Coates would come through to our room (Room 92) and say, 'Why don't you chaps call it a day?' And so the work was moved.

Looking back on those days, we seemed to have assumed that it was the normal order of things that the Prime Minister, Forbes, and his mentor, Masters of the Upper House, should go for their daily walk in the sun to the Wellington Botanical Gardens; normal that, in the evenings, Masters would read newspapers and Forbes historical biographies. And at some stage during the week Coates would tell Forbes 'and his cobber, Masters' how the reconstruction and development were coming along and what Cabinet decisions would be required. . . .

> From a paper 'Foundations for an Independent Economic Policy, 1928–35', in W. B. Sutch, *Colony or Nation?*, Sydney University Press, 1966, pp. 46–50 (by courtesy of Dr. W. B. Sutch)

145. 'LABOUR HAS A PLAN': THE LABOUR PARTY MANIFESTO, 1935

From the platform first adopted at the annual conference in 1933 and reaffirmed in the following year. John A. Lee claimed that he wrote the entire manifesto. On J. T. Paul's copy of the pamphlet, now in the Turnbull Library, there is a pencilled comment: 'John A. Lee. His new Testament.'

. . . The Policy is idealistic. It visions New Zealand as the country where the plenty of the machine age shall assure to all the rich life in goods and leisure that the genius and natural resources of our country make possible. The Policy is practicable, for the committee had profound knowledge of social trends and of New Zealand conditions. To build the ideal Social State with the available material is the purpose of the Labour Party. This Policy is no essay in metaphysics but an outline of what can be done, of what must be done if New Zealand is to cease being the devastated territory it has become under the Forbes–Coates administration. The Policy was made in New Zealand by New Zealand citizens with a lifetime study of New Zealand problems. The cruel policy of the National Government came from abroad. . . .

THE PURPOSE OF PRODUCTION

The purpose of all production, primary and secondary, is to supply the social and economic requirements of the people, and the duty of the State is to organise productive and distributive agencies in order to utilise the natural resources for this purpose. . . .

CREDIT BASIS

Overseas prices and conditions cannot any longer be allowed to dictate New Zealand's living standards. By proper planning of production, with control of marketing and finance, New Zealand can establish her own living standard. The basis of all credit and currency must be production (goods and services). . . .

UNEMPLOYMENT

The workers to-day unemployed are our fellow-citizens who are out of work through no fault of their own. They are entitled to employment at a living wage. Failing such employment they should be paid a sustenance wage sufficient to provide the necessaries of life for them and their dependents. The conditions and pay of the men on relief works are a standing disgrace to the Dominion. The existing degrading system should be abolished at the earliest possible moment. The Party will organise productive development work for all who are able to do it, including present relief workers, unemployed women, and the youth who are leaving our schools. Pending organisation of employment, the Party will immediately increase the present rates of pay for relief work.

GUARANTEED PRICES

Guaranteed prices, organised employment in primary and secondary industries, with a vigorous public works policy, local and national at wages and salaries based on national production, will ensure to the farmer on the land, the worker in industry, and all others who render social service, an income that will maintain a standard of living to which the people of the Dominion are entitled. The ruinous policy of deflation and bankruptcy has been consistently opposed by the Labour Movement, . . .

BANKING, CREDIT AND CURRENCY

Immediate control by the State of the entire banking system. The State to be the sole authority for the issue of credit and currency. Provision of credit and currency to ensure production and distribution of the commodities which are required and which can be economically produced in the Dominion, with guaranteed prices, wages and salaries.

Labour asserts that the sovereign power to issue money should be in the hands of the people. . . .

To-day private bankers have the right to issue pieces of paper which constitute a lien on the goods of the community. This is nothing other than the power to confiscate the goods of all the people to the extent of the credit created. Money has no value except that it is a title to the means of life. Each penny of bank created credit is stolen from the community. . . .

Labour will insist that money becomes an instrument of distribution, an aid to production, an honest measurement of values, not a means to distress and dispossession. In a sane distributive system, of which a State Bank is the key, lies the way to a golden age.

MORTGAGES

Conservation of present holders' interests in land and homes by readjustment of all mortgages on a basis of average prices for the past seven years.

No clause in the programme is of greater importance than this. To-day thousands of tenants are caretakers of sufferance. If a Labour Government guaranteed prices but omitted to protect existing tenants in arrears, wholesale evictions would take place at the moment at which home-building and farming again became remunerative; and the same is true of borrowers being carried by the banks. . . .

OVERSEAS MARKETING AND GUARANTEED PRICES

Guaranteed prices for primary products. Negotiated agreements with Great Britain and other countries for marketing of primary products, with reciprocal contracts for the import of those classes of commodities which cannot be economically produced in the Dominion. . . . Labour will guarantee internal prices for primary production. A pound of butter, a pound of meat, the clip of a sheep have always the same human value; why not the same price value? . . . Labour will contract to take from Britain, after debt commitments have been met, goods to the full value of our export surplus. We cannot take any more unless we borrow, and that contract of exchange will apply also to other countries. Haphazardness, glut and famine will be replaced by planning and orderly marketing. . . .

INTERNAL MARKETING

Promotion of agreements between the various control boards, other associations of primary producers, and distributors' and consumers' organisations to ensure orderly marketing at guaranteed prices of the primary products required for consumption in the Dominion.

Labour does not aim at dragooning or abolishing producers' organisations. . . . To-day the spectacular stands between the farmer and the consumer, and the flow of produce is interrupted by artificial gluts and shortages to the disadvantage of both. . . .

SECONDARY INDUSTRIES

Fostering of secondary industries so as to ensure the production of those commodities which can be economically produced in the Dominion, thus providing employment for our own people, with the resultant increase in the internal demand for our primary and secondary products, with less dependency on the fluctuating and glutted overseas markets.

Any great increase in the purchasing power of the people must inevitably foster secondary industry, and until the purchasing power of the people is increased no tariff policy will avail. . . .When incomes are high enough we will have no fear of imports. . . . The road to industrial advancement is enhanced social spending.

EMPLOYMENT

Organisation of productive and development work on the following lines: Land development and settlement; completion of necessary public works; construction of backblocks roads: secondary and main highways; assistance to local authorities to undertake approved works; financial assistance in the development of secondary industries. . . .

. . . Labour would use work-saving machinery and not the shovel and the wheelbarrow in its development policy, for Labour is not afraid of the age of leisure. The Conservative is afraid of leisure for the working man. If the working man travels, as does the foreign tourist, and sees New Zealand, he will be less inclined to surrender its privileges to the few. . . .

A Labour Government will develop public works not to yield a financial profit or to keep the maximum number of men sweating, but to create the best asset with the least output of energy. Labour will give sanity to the machine age.

HOURS AND WAGES

(1) Utilisation of mechanical inventions, new processes, and research knowledge. (2) Immediate reduction in the hours of labour, in order to employ a greater number of workers in industry to meet the displacement of labour by machinery. (3) Guaranteed wages and salaries in accord with national production. . . . To-day the Government says, 'What is the least upon which a family can exist?' Labour says, 'What is the most in goods and culture and leisure the State can yield to its every member?' . . .

CONCLUSION

This statement is not a complete statement of Labour's intentions, but only an outline of the direction in which Labour's policy will move. It commences with a realisation of the need of socially controlling the financial system. To control industry is to control the body, to control the financial system is to control the nerve system that operates all. Labour will stand or fall by its ability to control the financial system. There can be no progress until the banking and money system is in the hands of the people. . . . New Zealand, with its temperate and sub-tropical zones, with its potential water power, its timber, coal and iron resources, its fisheries, its holiday resorts, can be made the centre of a new civilisation. Under Forbes–Coates we 'follow Britain' to intensifying misery. Under the Labour Government we shall use our own physical resources and apply the progressive genius that has been dormant in these past decades and erect the new Social State that will once again cause New Zealand to inspire the world. We shall determine New Zealand's standard of life by what New Zealand produces and not by an overseas price level. Human welfare and not financial profit shall be our goal.

This Policy was made in New Zealand by New Zealand citizens who know New Zealand conditions. It is not exotic, but native to our problems.

> *'Labour Has a Plan'*, Propaganda Pamphlet no. 3. The Labour Book Room, Wellington, 1935

146. THE NATIONAL PARTY OPPOSES SOCIALISM, 1938

Although the Coalition Government 1931–5 included both United (formerly Liberal) and Reform members, the party organizations did not fuse until the formation of the National Political Federation in 1935. After the election defeat by Labour, the New Zealand National Party was formed in May 1936 as a mass organization of all those who were opposed to Labour. The party leader, Adam Hamilton, introduced the 1938 party manifesto by claiming that the National Party would restore British freedom and save democracy from the 'menace of Socialism'.

'In the days of our fathers, New Zealand was known as a land of opportunity'. . . . Today, under the pervading influence of Socialism, opportunity for young men of enterprise no longer exists.

'We give to the people of the Dominion an assurance of hope for the future. We promise them a restoration of personal freedom in their work and in their leisure, and we promise to maintain the highest standard of family life as the only sound basis for the future of society.

'The issue before the people of the Dominion is simple and clear-cut'. . . . 'In less than a hundred years men of enterprise and vision have developed New Zealand to such an extent that we enjoy a standard of living unequalled elsewhere in the world. Now, during the last three years, there has arisen the menace of Socialism—the direct antithesis of all the virtues which have raised us to nationhood.

'There is not an individual in New Zealand today who is free from the menace of Socialism. Under the principles which actuate Labour legislators, the State must stand supreme and the urge for supremacy must inevitably be carried to the point where the freedom of the individual vanishes. That is the road which we are travelling today, and in our opinion, it leads downhill to national destruction.

'We have, then, the issue of British Democracy as against Socialism, but arising in part out of this there is the fundamental issue of race preservation which can only be based on family life. Socialism seeks to replace the family by the State, and in doing so it ignores a matter of basic loyalties. Family traditions and the family spirit have been of supreme importance in shaping the character of the British race and, if family loyalties and responsibilities are allowed to die, the race will die with them.

'On economic grounds alone we cannot afford to have a declining population. This generation has no right to mortgage the wealth and production of future generations without ensuring that the next generation will be numerically strong enough to carry the load.

'If youth is to be asked to pay the heavy taxes for the support of the older generation the result must be delayed marriage and fewer children. Far from taxing young people the National Party stands for letting them have full and easy finance for building their own homes—not merely for renting State owned houses. We will give all State tenants the right to freehold tenure and, in addition, we are prepared to grant loans of £100 to young couples for the purchase of furniture, the advance to be reduced with the birth of each child of the marriage until it is cancelled out at the birth of the third child. Family allowances will also be provided at the rate of 4s. a week in respect of each child over the second.

'We regard this question of race preservation as something transcending the mere mechanics of politics, and we are prepared to base our whole policy on the strengthening of family life. Complementary to this factor, we will legislate, throughout on a basis of freedom, opportunity, and justice for the individual.

'This will probably be the first occasion in the political history of New Zealand when an election will be fought on broad questions of principle'. 'To make the fight one of principles is certainly the aim of the National Party, because we are convinced that no people of British stock are prepared to throw away their birthright of democracy for the rigid fetters of the Socialist State. . . .

MANIFESTO OF THE NEW ZEALAND NATIONAL PARTY

We seek to arouse a deeper interest in the Government of our country. New Zealand is now an independent member of the Empire with close upon a century's life behind her, and must accept the full responsibility of Nationhood. . . .

As a Party, we aim at being truly National in character, representing all sections of the community—farmers, manufacturers, wage-earners, business and professional men—and we shall govern in National as distinct from sectional or class interests. We recognise no class distinctions in the people of this virile young nation. . . .

PRIVATE ENTERPRISE

Labour stands for the subjection of industry and the supremacy of the State. The National Party, on the contrary, stands for private enterprise and the greatest freedom for the individual to develop his own resources and his own initiative. . . .

THE FARMER
Primary production is the foundation industry of New Zealand and is entitled to a standard of reward comparable with other industries. . . .

LAND SETTLEMENT
New Zealand's export wealth comes almost entirely from primary products. The various types of farming offer one of the best avenues for establishing many of our people in suitable homes and permanent occupations.

To this end, we will pursue a vigorous land settlement policy, . . .

MANUFACTURING INDUSTRIES
In the field of manufacturing industries we see the most likely and fruitful field for increasing national production, enlarging the national income available to the people, absorbing our surplus man-power. . . .

In a country with a relatively small population, a larger ratio of consumption of New Zealand-produced goods is essential to efficient and economical production.

POLICY IN REGARD TO INDUSTRY
We will give industry the greatest amount of freedom from State interference and dictation, by limiting Government regulation to the prevention of abuses inimical to the public interest.

THE SMALL TRADER   THE SMALL FARMER
THE SMALL SHOPKEEPER
Recognising that New Zealand's prosperity and development have been largely built up by small traders, small farmers, small manufacturers, and small shopkeepers, we will do everything possible to ensure their prosperity and freedom from Ministerial dictatorship and interference.

The National Party is opposed to monopolistic control of any section of trade or industry. . . .

HOUSING
We will approach the housing problem from the standpoint that a home owned is far better than a house rented. . . .

SOCIAL SECURITY
On becoming the Government, the National Party will not operate the recently passed Social Security Act, but will provide all pensions in existence prior to the passing of the Act. . . .

HEALTH SCHEME

The National Party will provide a full and complete health service without charge, to that section of the community that is unable to provide such service for itself. . . .

SUPERANNUATION

The National Party strongly supports the principle of National Superannuation, but holds that the funds should be administered as a separate trust entirely independent of ordinary Government finances. . . .

REDUCTION IN TAXATION

The National Party will, wherever possible, reduce the taxation burden of the people. . . .

FUNDAMENTAL DIFFERENCE

The are fundamental differences between the two contending parties. On the one hand, the Labour Party is out to break down and destroy the existing economic order, and substitute in its place a system based on the philosophy of unadulterated, revolutionary Socialism, with State ownership of property and of industry and trade, and direction of its operations by the workers themselves. They seek to destroy private investment in industry by taxing it of existence and removing all incentive to invest money in industry.

On the other hand, the National Party believes in the present system of private enterprise and seeks to develop it in accordance with the philosophy of personal freedom, initiative, thrift and private ownership of all property with the right of investments to earn a reasonable return commensurate with the nature of the investment and the risk involved.

N.Z. National Party, cyclostyled leaflet, 1938

147. NATIONAL HEALTH AND SUPERANNUATION SERVICES PROPOSED

The Report of a Select Committee of Parliament under the Chairmanship of Arnold H. Nordmeyer, which considered the Labour Government's proposals for a National Health Service and a National Superannuation Service, 19 May 1938.

PART I.—HEALTH PROPOSALS

. . . 9. The Committee will report first on the proposals of the Government concerning health services. These are : —

(1) To provide at the inception of the scheme—

(*a*) A universal general practitioner service free to all members of the community requiring medical attention.

(*b*) Free hospital or sanatorium treatment for all.

(*c*) Free mental hospital care and treatment for the mentally afflicted.

(*d*) Free medicines.

(*e*) Free maternity treatment, including the cost of maintenance in a maternity home.

(2) To provide later, 'when the organization and finances are available,' the following additional services—

(*a*) Anaesthetic.

(*b*) Laboratory and radiology.

(*c*) Specialist and consultant.

(*d*) Massage and physio-therapy.

(*e*) Transport service to and from hospital.

(*f*) Dental benefit.

(*g*) Optical benefit.

(3) To institute a free home nursing and domestic help service 'when the necessary staff has been trained to make such a proposal practicable.'

(4) To embark upon an extended education campaign for the promotion of health and the prevention of disease. . . .

GENERAL PRACTITIONER SERVICE

(*a*) A Universal General Practitioner Service
free to all Members of the Community
requiring Medical Attention

11. This proposal met with opposition from the representatives of the New Zealand Branch of the British Medical Association. The objections of the association were mainly based on the following grounds : —

(i) That there is no need for a universal service while many people are able to pay for their own doctor and will prefer to do so.

We consider, however, that few people can with certainty claim that they will always be able to pay for their own medical services. Even if they could establish their claim, this is no more an argument against a universal service than is the suggestion that because a man can afford to pay for his child's schooling, education should not be freely available to all. This, indeed, is not a purely medical question. . . .

(ii) That the development of friendly societies and the growth of our public hospital system renders unnecessary a scheme of the extent proposed.

While we appreciate the very good work that has been done over a long period by the friendly societies, we cannot agree that the existence of a friendly-society service fully meets the needs of the people. Statistics show that the friendly-society movement covers only about one-fifth of the people of the Dominion. . . .

(iii) That the proposal will lead to a deterioration of the standard of medical service.

We cannot believe that this is likely to occur. . . .

We would also point out that the doctor working for a small salary with nothing to gain but the satisfaction that comes from the knowledge of having done a job well, has frequently given us many of the progressive discoveries in medicine. Among these are the discoveries of antisepsis and asepsis, those who gave us prevention in diphtheria, typhus, and typhoid fever, the effective treatment of diabetes, and a host of other advances in medical science.

Another suggestion is that there will be no incentive to progress if the doctor is not paid by each individual patient.

Such an attitude is not justified in view of the outstanding contributions made to medical science by the permanent army and navy medical corps, the work of the university personnel who are usually on salary, and the activities of salaried public-health officials. It would perhaps be more fair to say that the good man works well provided his conditions of work are reasonably satisfactory without regard to the manner in which he is renumerated . . .

14. We believe that the medical scheme should develop along the lines of our education system—be freely available to all whatever their rank, station, or income. If there are people in the community who prefer to make other arrangements for themselves—as they are in the educational world—they are entirely free to do so. . . .

SUPPLEMENTARY SERVICES

38. We make the following recommendations concerning the services which the Government indicated it did not propose to make available at the inception of the scheme, but to add from time to time 'when the organization and finances are available.' . . .

(f) DENTAL BENEFIT

49. While the Government's proposals do not indicate when it is intended to establish a dental benefit, the Committee heard evidence from the New Zealand Dental Association and from the Director, Dental Division, Health Department. We have been greatly impressed with the need for greater care in connection with the treatment of teeth in the comparatively young. It was good to have definite evidence that the present school dental clinic system is meeting a need in the community and that the quality of the work is exceedingly high. We would recommend to the Government that the most suitable way of meeting the dental needs of the people will be to extend the dental clinic system, until ultimately all children of school age shall be included. . . .

(g) OPTICAL BENEFITS

50. No direct evidence was furnished to this Committee concerning the proposed optical benefit. A perusal of the evidence submitted to the Preliminary Investigation Commitee indicates that the New Zealand Institute of Opticians would be prepared to assist the Government in every way to develop a service of this type. We would emphasize, however, that it is not desirable that an optical service should be commenced until such time as the services of qualified ophthalmologists are available under the Social Security Scheme. . . .

PREVENTIVE MEDICINE
AN EXTENDED EDUCATION CAMPAIGN FOR THE PROMOTION OF HEALTH AND PREVENTION OF DISEASE

54. Many witnesses before the Committee emphasized the need for greater attention to the promotion of health and the prevention of disease than is given at the present time. The representatives of the B.M.A. and other medical men were emphatic that environmental conditions play an important part in the building-up of a healthy body. . . .

56. We feel that a great deal of illness in the community can be prevented. It is important, therefore, that the Government's efforts should not only be directed to the curing of disease, but to the promotion of health. We therefore recommend that a sum be set aside for education in the principles of health and healthy living. We believe that a great deal of medical attention and hospital care will not be necessary if the people are taught to pay due care to the promotion of healthy conditions of body and mind. . . .

PART II.—NATIONAL SUPERANNUATION AND SOCIAL SECURITY BENEFITS

The proposals of the Government concerning the above are:—

Invalidity Benefits

61. (a) That a payment of 30s. per week be made to invalids when certified as permanently unfit for employment, with supplementary payments to the wife and each dependent child of the invalid of 10s. per week, with a maximum benefit of £4 per week; this benefit to supersede the existing pension of 20s. a week.

Sickness Benefit

(b) That sickness benefit of appropriate amounts be paid to men and women during periods when they are prevented from earning a livelihood by reason of sickness or accident: provision to be made for the payment of this benefit to the members of friendly societies through those societies. . . .

Disability Benefit

(c) That disability benefits be made available for persons who cannot qualify for invalidity, sickness or sustenance benefit or State superannuation, but who are otherwise physically or mentally disabled from earning a livelihood.

Sustenance Benefits

(d) That sustenance benefits be paid to persons who are capable of, and available for, work, but for whom work cannot be found: that the rates of benefit be 20s. plus, if married, 15s. for wife with 5s. for each dependent child, in lieu of the present rate of 4s.

Widowed Mothers' Benefits

(e) That a social-security benefit be paid to widowed mothers at the rate of 25s. per week and 10s. per week for each dependent child: the benefit to continue until the child reaches the age of sixteen years (instead of fifteen years as at present), and, in special circumstances, until the age of eighteen years, so long as the child is still at school: this to replace the existing widow's pension of 20s. per week. Wives of inmates of mental hospitals to qualify as at present, and deserted wives with dependent children.

Widows' Benefits

(f) That widows' benefits be payable—

(i) At any age to a widow who has previously drawn a widowed

330

mother's benefit and whose youngest child has reached the age at which the benefit ceased:

(ii) To a widow who has not previously drawn a widowed mother's benefit—

(a) If she was widowed before age fifty and has been married for not less than fifteen years, the benefit to be payable from age fifty;

(b) If she has been widowed after age fifty and has been married for not less than five years the benefit to be payable from the date of commencement of widowhood.

Orphans' Benefits

(g) That orphans' benefits be payable to relatives or guardians who have been approved as foster-parents at the rate of 15s. per week in respect of orphans under the age of sixteen years.

Family Allowance

(h) That the family allowance be paid at the rate of 4s. per week in respect of the third and subsequent children: the maximum allowable income to be £5 per week, plus the allowance (instead of the present provision of £4 per week plus the allowance); the allowance to continue to be payable in respect of eligible children until they reach the age of sixteen years.

Miner's Phthisis

(i) That superannuation at the rate of 30s. per week be paid to miners suffering from Miner's phthisis, with a supplementary benefit of 10s. for the wife and 10s. for each dependent child up to age sixteen; to supersede the present miner's pension of 25s. per week.

War Veterans and War Pensions

(j) That war veterans' allowances be paid at the rate of 25s. per week for the veteran, plus 15s. per week for his dependent wife and 5s. per week for each dependent child up to the age of sixteen years, the maximum pension to be increased from £2. 15s. to £3. 10s. per week.

State Superannuation

(k) That State superannuation be payable at the rate of 30s. per week on the attainment of sixty years, with the qualifications set out in the present legislation: the superannuation benefit not to be reduced so long as the income of the superannuitant, if a single person, or the joint income of a married couple (in addition to superannuation) does not exceed £1 per week; this will supersede the existing old-age pension of 22s. 6d. per week. . . .

SOCIAL-SECURITY BENEFITS

... it is beyond dispute that the citizens of this country have a fixed determination to provide so far as is reasonably possible for those who are unable to support themselves by reason of age, sickness, status, or other disability. Not only is this found to be a fact, but it is also clear that from time to time as the community has found itself able to meet the cost, the pensions provided for those who have been unfortunate have been steadily increased in order to make them as nearly sufficient as possible for the normal needs of the beneficiaries. It is quite clear to the Committee that public opinion in the Dominion requires that the normal Christian attitude of life of helping those in need, whatever the cause of their need, should be carried on into the community life, enabling the joint resources of the people to be applied for assisting in banishing distress and want. . . .

64. The social security benefits proposed by the Government are a logical development of the social services that have been a feature of our legislation for many decades and represent the embodiment of the public conscience as to the community's responsibilities for those who have been deprived of the means of fending for themselves. . . .

PART III.—FINANCE

115. The Government in its proposals has suggested that the cost of the scheme should be borne by a contribution of 1s. in the pound on all salary, wages, and other income, a registration levy of £1 per head per annum, and a subsidy from the Consolidated Fund to meet the difference between the produce of the contributions and levy and the total cost.

116. In his report placed before the Committee the Actuary estimated that the total cost of the benefits under the Government's proposals, including administration expenses, would be £17,850,000. The national income on which contributions would be levied was estimated in 1939–40 at £150,000,000 yielding a return from contributions of £7,500,000, to which would be added the produce of the registration levy on the present basis—namely, £500,000. This calculation would leave a sum of £9,850,000 to be found from the Consolidated Fund, an increase of £2,355,000 over the expenditure on present social services estimated to amount to £7,495,000 at the close of the financial year in 1938–39. . . .

118. The principle of social security insurance is one that is well established throughout the world, and practically every scheme in Europe and America has as its basis the payment of a premium by way of contribution from the beneficiary. This principle was readily accepted by the citizens of this Dominion in respect of unemployment, and contributions have been paid by vast numbers of citizens who, while covered against the risk, were most unlikely to be placed in the position of claiming benefits. A perusal of the schemes in operation in most of the countries overseas indicates that a flat contribution, with no variation according to the amount of wages or other income, is the course most generally adopted. This has the effect of throwing a greater proportionate burden on the low-income group, and, owing to the necessity for keeping the amount of contribution within the means of that group, the total funds so raised are necessarily restricted. The inevitable result is to keep the benefits made available down to extremely low amounts in many cases, and certainly well below the amounts which the citizens of this country regard as the minimum requirements of persons who would qualify for such benefits. In many countries the expedient has been adopted of levying a contribution on the employer, who, in effect, is required to subsidize payments by his employees. While there is no doubt that industry should bear its share in providing for those who are unable to fend for themselves, the Committee considers that the proposed method of levying the contribution assessed on a percentage of the income of every individual, augmented by a State subsidy which is found by general taxation, is a much more efficient and a much fairer way of raising the necessary funds. . . .

NATIONAL PRODUCTION

120. A certain amount of evidence was tendered to the Committee, the effect of which was an endeavour to create the impression that the cost of the scheme would be beyond the resources of the Dominion.

121. It was obviously overlooked by many of the witnesses that the effect of the scheme is simply to provide a more equitable distribution of the national income. No part whatever of the expenditure under the scheme will cease to be available for consumption of foods available in the Dominion's markets. On the contrary, the Committee feels certain that the effect of such redistribution will be a definite stimulus to production in the Dominion, particularly

for those goods which the Dominion itself produces, and should tend to cause the expansion of the primary and secondary production of the Dominion. . . .

122. We are confident on the evidence of past years that it is within the capacity of the Dominion to extend production sufficiently to carry out the scheme, and we believe that it may well be found that it has made a large contribution towards a more rapid development of the country. . . .

A.J.H.R., 1938, I–6, pp. 6–12, 17–18

148. THE ECONOMY UNDER THE LABOUR GOVERNMENT

From the Budget debate, 21 July 1938, when the Leader of the Opposition, Adam Hamilton, charged that improving conditions came from rising commodity prices, for which the Labour Government could not take credit; in fact the Government through its 'Socialism' stifled business. Michael Savage, the Prime Minister, replied that the returning prosperity was being taken into people's homes and that Christianity required men to be their 'brother's keeper'.

. . . The Hon. Mr. HAMILTON (Leader of the Opposition).—Sir, those who listened last night to the Minister of Finance must have felt a keen sense of disappointment that the overburdened taxpayer was to receive no relief. I am sure that for a long time he has been looking for some measure of relief, but the final Budget of this Parliament has now been delivered and there is no relief from taxation, which is still at its very peak. The Budget, although it may be orthodox, undoubtedly adopts a very soft-pedalling attitude. The real objective of the Government is not mentioned. It opens with a *résumé* of New Zealand's economic position and throughout takes credit to the Government for our present prosperity. That is a common attitude of the Government. It seems to be taking to itself almost the whole credit for New Zealand's present prosperity and side by side with that seems to blame the previous Government for all the difficulties of the depression period. This prosperity does not, however, lie to the credit of the Government, but, firstly, to increased overseas prices for our produce and, secondly, to the great industry and initiative of our farmers and business people. It is they who have made the prosperity of the last few years in spite of the

334

Government we have in office. The Government claims that by increased taxation it is beneficially redistributing the national income, but alongside this must be placed the penalties and disadvantages placed on both our primary and manufacturing industries. There may have been some redistribution that has brought some benefits, but alongside that must be placed the debits which, when properly tabulated, will far outweigh the benefits. In spite of added difficulties, production has increased, though to-day there are signs of further difficulties and of reduced production. I say emphatically that previous Governments who laid the foundation for New Zealand's economy have more right than, or at least, as much right, to claim credit for the last two years of prosperity as the Labour Government has. The present Government struck a fortunate period, coming into office as it did when prices were rising and there was a plentiful supply of money. . . . This Government took over the ship of State in good trim and on an even keel; but it has overloaded it with top-hamper—increased taxation and permanent commitments. At the first fall in commodity prices, over which the Minister of Finance admits he has no control, the ship of State might be in rough water, and the next stage would lead to further increased taxation to save the ship, and industry might be taxed out of its ability to compete in the overseas market. That is a stage we are already at. There is nothing in the Budget for our manufacturers but pious platitudes. Embarrassed by high costs, regimentation, and State competition we are forced to the conclusion that the policy of the Government is to push out interest payments in connection with industry, and absorb all the profits of industry in wages. . . .

Every day the issues are becoming clearer and clearer, and they are on these lines: Is New Zealand to scrap the present economic system, and to switch over to State Socialism? I, for one, say definitely, 'No.' And the people of the country say, 'No.' Are private enterprise, private ownership of land, British freedom and liberty to be replaced by Government ownership and Government dictatorship? We on this side say, 'No.'

The Hon. Mr. FRASER.—And we on this side say, 'No.'

The Hon. Mr. HAMILTON.—Is the British individual to become merely a slave of the State? We say 'No.'

The Hon. Mr. FRASER.—We say 'No,' too.

The Hon. Mr. HAMILTON.—Will Socialism be tolerated in this, 'God's Own Country?' We say, 'No,' and the electors say, 'No.'

Can industry be best managed by private enterprise or by the State? We on this side say, 'By private enterprise generally—with the qualification'—

The Hon. Mr. PARRY.—No qualifications.

The Hon. Mr. HAMILTON.—I have always said that the management of the Post Office is quite a useful State function; but that does not mean that all enterprises can be best operated in that way. . . .

The Right Hon. Mr. SAVAGE.— . . . the picture to-day is better than it has ever been since I have been in the country, and that is quite a long time. As I have said before, we have had over eighty years of self-government in New Zealand, and this Government is expected to clean up the accumulated mess of seventy-seven years in three years.

Mr. POLSON.—Have all other Governments been bad?

The Right Hon. Mr. SAVAGE.—We have had some good triers, I admit—men like Sir George Grey, men like Ballance and Seddon; and there has always been the same group sitting opposite such men, saying the same things about them as they are now saying about this Government. Will anybody tell me, in fact, that they did not say stronger things about Seddon than they do about Savage? Why, I am an angel alongside of Seddon. According to our opponents, I am not a bad fellow; it is all these chaps alongside me who are wrong. Opposition speakers say I am quite a good chap, but it is the people who are supporting me who are wrong. But I know the voters will not swallow that. We on this side of the House stand for the same programme, and we will swim together. We will not sink. I admit that there may be faults in certain things that are done by this Government. There are always faults in any structure; but I claim that the foundation we are laying is sound.

An Hon. Member.—Oh!

The Right Hon. Mr. SAVAGE.—That is a very empty sound, is it not, Mr. Speaker, that comes from the Opposition? However, we will leave it at that. We can afford to be generous because we are going with the tide. The tide of prosperity is with us, and we are helping it along. We are taking it to the people's homes; and the tide of prosperity might very easily pass the homes of the people by unless some Government took it to them. However, I am thankful that it has come to my lot to be associated with the Government that has done what has been done up to now, and that will do bigger things in the days to come. I am not going back on it. We have not gone half of the journey. The leader of the Opposition will quote that. He will be able to say that that means Socialism. I do not care what 'ism' it means. The people have not got anything like what they are entitled to have, and they are going to get it; and that includes pensioners, wage-earners, farmers, manufacturers—every one who is rendering a useful service to society. And we get them in places other than the ranks of labour. I find them everywhere— in the Courts, in the pulpits, in all walks of life—men and women, too, who are giving magnificent service. I raise my hat to all of them, and I want to see them getting a better deal; and they are going to get a better deal. I never felt more confident in my life than I feel to-night. Talk about courage! It does not need any courage to do what we are doing. It only needs the desire to do justice. We are not going to do any running. If that means courage, we are courageous. I do not know that I ought to say more. I do not think there is anything left that is worth saying. I am sure that if our friends opposite come back on to the Treasury benches they will have one cure for everything—namely, to take up our belts, to reduce costs. But they cannot reduce costs without reducing some one's income. I want to know whose income they are going to start on. They have got to start on some one's income, because one man's costs are another man's income. There is no getting away from that. The honourable gentlemen want to put the clock back. I want to know why people should not have decent wages, why they should not have decent pensions in the evening of their days, or when they are invalided. What is there more valuable in our Christianity than to be our brother's keepers in reality? What is the use of talking about it, unless we practise it in our everyday likes? I hope there is no one on the Opposition benches who thinks that I am doing this for the sake of getting rich. I am sure I shall never get rich. I have not any desire to get rich. I have no desire to see any one else get very rich. I want to see people have security, though. I want to see humanity secure against poverty, secure in illness or old age. . . .

N.Z.P.D., 1938, vol. 251, pp. 630–1, 635, 639, 648–9

149. THE SOCIAL SECURITY BILL, 1938

Speeches in the House of Representatives, 16 August 1938, at the conclusion of the Second Reading of the Bill, by Adam Hamilton, leader of the Opposition, who argued that national health and superannuation services were unnecessary, and by the Prime Minister, Michael Savage.

The Hon. Mr. HAMILTON.— . . . We have in New Zealand to-day a people enjoying a standard of health of which we can justly be proud, although there is ample room for improvement. It is all very well for the Minister to talk of what we ought to have, and what we might do. Let him just look at what has been done, and what we are experiencing—namely, a people enjoying a standard of health which we can justly be proud of; also a first-class medical service, notwithstanding any criticism the Government may offer; also a first-class hospital service, which is free to people who cannot afford to pay, a wonderful service, and, I venture to say, a much better service than we will ever get under the Minister's scheme. I would ask the Minister what action the Government proposes to take if the doctors do not join in. It is not compulsory for them to join; it is quite optional. If they do not join in, what course is the Minister going to adopt? These services have all been provided by previous Governments, and extended from time to time as conditions have warranted and circumstances have permitted. The Government would have us believe that nothing had been done until it appeared on the scene. In actual fact, as far as national health service and superannuation are concerned, this Government has done absolutely nothing. What we have has been provided by previous Governments; and the present Government will complete its term of office without any practical results with regard to either of those two important planks in the Prime Minister's pamphlet. I am not going to say there is not a health problem; there may be, and no doubt is, a problem; and we will always have problems. It is the duty of the Government to consider them as they come up, and to deal with them; but it is not the job of the Government to try to break down everything that has been done in the past; not the Government's duty to revolutionize things and start off on some new and uncharted sea that might cause a wreck later. The subject of superannuation is not new in New Zealand. . . . but this Government has brushed aside and ignored all the experience gained along those lines, and it starts off with its grandiose scheme of universal superannuation, which may not be desired and may not be required by many people who are in existing schemes. . . . Provision by way of pensions for aged people and other classes have always been a feature of New Zealand public life. There is nothing new in pensions; but in this Bill the word 'pensions' is discarded, and the word 'benefits' takes its place. I wonder if the pensioners will welcome that change. In my judgment, 'pension' is quite a good name, and is better than 'State benefits.' The health section of the Government scheme is, in my judgment, just another step towards the Government's objective of socialization. . . . Despite what honourable gentlemen opposite may say, or try to laugh off, this objective is seen throughout the bulk of their legislation. Here we see another attempt—a very drastic attempt, too—to socialize a very important section of our people. This step is being taken under the guise of public health. But there is nothing to show that there is any need for a universal health service. The Minister, in all his lengthy speech, did not prove that there was a need in New Zealand for a universal health service. The bulk of the people can quite easily make their own provision, and there is no benefit in socializing the medical profession for the purpose of making a national health service. I think most of us are prepared to make our own arrangements with our own doctors. Most of the people can do so, and would prefer to do so, for there is something personal about a doctor and sickness. . . .

. . . There is no demand for a universal service—nothing to convince an unbiased observer that the Government is not making this a political issue, and has not got a political bias rather than a desire to do its best by the medical profession and the people. The profession does not want it; most of the people do not want it. It is just a political stunt—merely the socialization of the doctors. Without any doubt whatever, the Labour party's policy is to take from the people the freedom and liberty which we on this side say is their traditional right and heritage—the freedom to move as widely as possible, according to their own tastes and desires, instead of being dominated by the State. The Labour party believes that a Government—or at least, a Socialist Government—can order the everyday lives of the people much more efficiently than the individuals concerned. We disagree with that philosophy; and that constitutes one of the fundamental differences between us and the Labour party. They want the State to expand until it dominates the whole of our private lives. We say that the State should keep out and give the people the right to live their own lives in their own way. The Government does not want to see any of the people making their own arrangements for security in old age and sickness, for the reason that, under a system of State Socialism, the individual must take his directions from the State. The Government insists on having its finger in almost everybody's private pie, for the sake of its scheme. I say that virile New-Zealanders will not stand, and are not going to stand, for this expansion of State domination and the curbing of private individual freedom. . . .

The Right Hon. Mr. SAVAGE.—The people of New Zealand need certain benefits, they need certain security; and I suggest there is only one way to get them, and that is to combine to do it for themselves. This Bill lays the foundation for that. . . .

The Government has a responsibility here. I think the medical profession will help to do the job. I think I know medical men and I feel sure that they will do the job, and I am sure that the Government will meet its responsibility to the medical profession. That means that we have to provide decent conditions for them. We do not want to socialize the medical profession. . . .

I do not care about phrases; I want to get service from the medical profession for the community, and it does not matter what that service is called—Socialism or any other 'ism'—it is just a collective effort on the part of the people of the country to safeguard themselves against ill health and other things, and I am not a bit particular about names. I would not argue about that for one second. We want the medical profession to be free, freer than it is to-day. We want the doctors to be paid for the service they give, and they never have been paid for the service they have given in the past. Some people have to pay merely because they are able to pay, and they are required to pay for those who cannot pay at all. That is an undesirable state of affairs. If they all get together the medical profession can be made one of the most efficient and humanitarian units in the community. I know that it is a humiliation to meet ones medical advisor and yet not be able to meet his bill. Many people know that better than I. . . .

. . . The leader of the Opposition says also that sickness cannot be treated on a mass-regimentation basis. Why, it is treated on a mass-regimentation basis to-day. What about the community wards in our public hospitals? I wish we could have a private ward for everybody. However, we have the communal system to-day in our public hospitals. It is only by mass action that we can get the best results. We see that everywhere, whether it be in industry, in war, or in other directions. Now, here is another gem from the leader of the Opposition—that the world's economic system is made up of trade cycles, and they will go on. Any one would think from that statement that trade cycles are just a natural force, like the sun, the moon, or the stars. Trade cycles are made by man; I would say that they are not necessarily a part of the world's economic system, but are in part the result of the people's inability to consume the things that they are producing. They keep on producing and accumulating until such time as the machine has to stop, or until we have used up the accumulation of goods. Then somebody gets a telescope, has a look at the sun, and say, 'Yes, there are spots there; this is another trade cycle.' One would think we were living in a vast mental hospital, instead of in a modern age.

. . . Then, the honourable gentleman said that the people can look after themselves better than the State can look after them. That sounds almost like anarchy. We have the State looking after the interests of the people in many ways. We have control of education, defence, law and order, and a thousand and one other services, because we can do the job better in a collective or co-operative way than it could be done by individuals. . . .

N.Z.P.D., 1938, vol. 252, pp. 338–9, 417–20

150. THE SOCIAL SECURITY ACT, 1938

The preamble and the health service sections of the Social Security Act of 1938, which came into operation on 1 April 1939. Previous legislation concerning pensions and unemployment relief was superseded and the term 'benefit' was used in the place of 'pension'.

AN ACT to provide for the Payment of Superannuation Benefits and of other Benefits designed to safeguard the People of New Zealand from Disabilities arising from Age, Sickness, Widowhood, Orphanhood, Unemployment, or other Exceptional Conditions; to provide a System whereby Medical and Hospital Treatment will be made available to Persons requiring such

Treatment; and, further, to provide such other Benefits as may be necessary to maintain and promote the Health and General Welfare of the Community.

[*14 September, 1938.*

BE IT ENACTED . . .

Medical Benefits

85. (1) For the purposes of this Part of this Act the expression 'medical benefits' means and includes all proper and necessary services of medical practitioners other than those services involving the application of special skill and experience of a degree or kind that general medical practitioners as a class cannot reasonably be expected to possess. . . .

86. (1) The Minister, in consultation with the appropriate Committee, shall fix the terms and conditions subject to which the persons entitled to medical benefits under this Part of this Act may claim such benefits, and also the terms and conditions subject to which those benefits will be provided by medical practitioners who signify their willingness to provide such benefits.

(2) The terms and conditions so fixed shall operate as an offer of a contract of service to every registered medical practitioner who is for the time being resident in New Zealand.

(3) Every registered medical practitioner who signifies in the prescribed manner his willingness to provide medical benefits in accordance with the terms and conditions so fixed shall be deemed to have thereby completed a contract of service with the Minister.

(4) Any medical practitioner who has entered into a contract of service in accordance with this section may terminate the contract by giving to the Minister not less than three months' notice in writing of his intention so to do, or by giving such shorter notice as the Minister may in any case accept.

87. (1) Every person who is entitled to claim medical benefits in accordance with this Part of this Act shall, with the concurrence of the medical practitioner concerned, have the right, in the prescribed form and manner and at the prescribed times, to select the medical practitioner by whom he desires the services included in such medical benefits to be given (being a medical practitioner who has entered into a contract of service with the Minister). . . .

88. (1) It shall be the duty of every medical practitioner who has entered into a contract of service for the purposes of this Part of this Act to render, to the best of his knowledge, skill, and ability,

all proper and necessary medical, surgical, and other services that
may be required of him under the contract by any person who is
for the time being entitled to claim such services, either for himself or for any other person. . . .

> *New Zealand Statutes*, 1938, 2 Geo. VI, no. 7,
> pp. 65, 115–16

151. THE RADICAL ATTACK ON ORTHODOX FINANCE

*Part of a letter by John A. Lee circulated to members of the Labour
Party in 1938, for which Lee was censured by the party's Annual
Conference in 1939. Lee charges the Minister of Finance, Walter
Nash, with failing to fulfil the financial promises of the 1935 platform. He argues that Nash's cautious finance, designed to help loan
conversion negotiations in London, keeps New Zealand under the
overseas 'Money Power'. He calls for exchange control and use of
the Reserve Bank to divert surplus funds from imports to manufacturing in New Zealand.*

. . . I am alarmed at the present evidence of indecision, vacillation
and drift which is apparent within the Party. I am concerned for
the future welfare of the Labour Party, not for its right to exist as an
entity returning Members to Parliament as caretakers of a capitalist
system, but for its right to exist as a driving force effecting fundamental changes in the 'boom and burst' capitalist system. I am
fearful that at any moment a statement may be made that we are
going to increase the internal interest rate, which to me, would be
a betrayal of a major order, especially after emerging victoriously
from an election in which the people defeated Money Power.

As I write, exchange control has occurred, but to every intelligent
person it must be obvious that control arrives two years in arrear,
after finance has looted the London Cash Box. To everyone it must
be obvious that exchange control has arrived now not as a positive
virtue for the purpose of safeguarding the future of the working
class party in this country by preventing gangster finance from
raiding our external exchanges, but that it has at long last been
implemented because the raid has rendered the sterling cash box
empty, and exchange control is the only alternative to default. . . .

. . . It was apparent that we could not leave high local incomes
without action to ensure that these incomes were used:

1. To sustain local industry to its maximum productivity.

2. To enable New Zealand to consume its sterling surplus after we had ear-marked sufficient exchange for debt services. . . .

Early in 1937 I wrote a propaganda pamphlet, 'Money Power for the People,' in which I expressed on Page 12, the following:—

'In terms of the original Act, the Reserve Bank was given complete control over the ownership of sterling exchange (London funds) subject to the necessity of making exchange available, under certain conditions, on demand. . . . This power is of vital importance as it arms the Government with power to control those internal movements of gangster finance capital that can occur in times of political emergency and that can do grave harm to a country's industries, that can raid a country's external credit. . . .'

My pamphlet written in 1937 and probably by some members of the Party thought to be too aggressive, because it reiterated the policy upon which we won our mandate in 1935, was only representative of Caucus. The Party pushed for exchange control and for local industrial development until it became dangerous to push any further for those things on account of each finance movement in Caucus being met with irritation, by threats of resignation, and by suggestions that those who wanted to do the right thing to give effect to our principles were being disloyal to the Party. . . .

And so to-day we are dealing with effects because we refused to deal with causes; indeed, those who wanted to deal with causes were treated as children and disloyalists. Implemented two years ago, exchange control could have been introduced with a light rein. Now, it will have to be introduced with a savage curbed bit. The political goodwill associated with doing things willingly and in time was sacrificed through vacillation and drift. The control which would have safeguarded a sterling nest-egg against our London refunding obligation, enabling us to meet banking hostility, becomes a control to prevent a default, and with the cupboard so bare that Labour may be driven to pay the British money-lender's price for re-funding the £17,000,000 loan. And yet we pretend that we have been faithful trustees of the Labour Movement with the interests of the voters at heart. . . .

MORE DEBT

We took over the Reserve Bank to free Labour development from capitalist debt, but showed our lack of faith in Labour's policy by paying £6. 5s. for a £5 share and by paying with 4 per cent. debentures instead of buying out the shares with Reserve Bank currency, a far more generous treatment in the first session than Mr. Nash proposed for the old-age pensioner.

We did the same thing, of course, with the Mortgage Corporation, paying a premium of 1/3 on each 10/- share or alternatively issuing 4 per cent. stock for share and premium. We should have retired both forms of share with Reserve Bank currency.

The first important financial transaction conducted by the Reserve Bank was the re-funding of our loan. It will be remembered that we agreed to borrow new money at $3\frac{1}{4}$ per cent. and to refund at $3\frac{1}{4}$ per cent. . . .

I was then of the opinion and am still that we should have used the powers of the Reserve Bank to wipe out most of the indebtedness although exchange control would have been necessary to prevent the raiding of sterling exchanges. We should have at least compelled the refunding at a much lower interest rate. When this was suggested in Caucus, we had all the capitalist arguments advanced against the proposal by Mr. Nash. Such an action, he said, would mean inflation; as if people with sufficient incomes and investment surpluses eat twice as much goods and buy twice as much clothing when they cannot buy bonds at a high rate. Actually, the rate of borrowing on account of our forcing money into circulation would have declined immensely. Investment surpluses are spent on the production of capitalist goods, not consumables, hence indeed the whole basis of the socialist attack on capitalism, i.e. too much capital goods, too little consumption, hence the undistributed surplus leading to unemployment crises. But Mr. Nash sets aside the whole nature of the capitalist crisis and pretends that investment surpluses will become consumer income if socialism tries to find its way out of the debt system. If we are always to be daunted by the inflation bogey, debt is with us forever. . . .

To me, refunding the whole loan at $3\frac{1}{4}$ per cent. rate of interest inherited from the Coalition Government was a complete betrayal of our promises to the people. But worse was to come. After agreeing to refund at $3\frac{1}{2}$ per cent. and on the eve of Mr. Nash's departure for London, Caucus was called hastily together and without previous warning Mr. Nash moved a resolution that $3\frac{1}{2}$ per cent. be the rate for our refunding obligations. I had the honour, with others, to oppose that resolution verbally and by vote, although I had just received my appointment as Under-Secretary in Charge of Housing.

Fifty per cent. of the Caucus voted against the $\frac{1}{4}$ per cent. increase. We were told at that Caucus that the alteration was necessary to create a good atmosphere for Mr. Nash in London, that is, that Labour has to be good. . . .

It was only in arrear of the decision to increase the refunding rate to $3\frac{1}{2}$ per cent. that the real inwardness of the increase was understood. Only after Mr. Nash's departure did the news start to filter through that the Reserve Bank Board, then composed of anti-Labour Directors, were whooping with joy for they had carried a resolution that $3\frac{1}{2}$ per cent. instead of $3\frac{1}{4}$ per cent. be the underwriting rate for our loan. This decision of the Reserve Bank Board was not communicated to Caucus. It is doubtful if it were communicated to all members of Cabinet, although it must have been communicated to some members of Cabinet. Thus, at the first challenge of conservative finance Labour retreated, allegedly to make an easier London atmosphere for Mr. Nash, although what London gave us for our surrender I have yet to ascertain.

With the low rate of interest, say $2\frac{1}{2}$ per cent., and exchange control to prevent the raiding of sterling, we would have forced funds into the development of New Zealand Industries. . . .

CALLING UP OF OVERDRAFTS

And now to-day we are caught again dealing with effects because we refused to alter causes. The unchecked transfer of funds to capitalism to London has undermined the present legal basis for bank advances. We are about to ask New Zealand industry to expand, and while we are calling for expansion scores of solvent businesses are having the screw put upon them and are being asked to reduce their overdrafts. Where this restriction applies to imports, it should have been applied long since. Where it applies to local woollen mills, etc., which are being asked to expand, it is wicked and does not conform to Labour's principles. Carried far enough, it will cause a rise in unemployment of the crisis order, and maybe a spectacular bankruptcy or two. . . .

To perpetuate the borrowing process is to sell the people of New Zealand. To increase the internal interest rate instead of positively reducing the internal interest rate is to sell the people of New Zealand. . . .

The letter, circulated in late 1938, as published in the pamphlet, *A Letter Which Every New Zealander Should Read*, 1939

152. THE LEE AFFAIR, 1939–40

From John A. Lee's notorious attack on Michael Savage, the Prime Minister, entitled 'Psycho-Pathology in Politics', which appeared in Tomorrow, *6 December 1939, when Savage was dying of cancer.*

Let us blame the novelist rather than the politician, for recently I have become interested in the problem of pathology in politics. McLaurin long ago in his Post Mortem and Mere Mortals, drew attention to the way in which the fate of Nations and Parties has been affected by physical illness in a statesman causing mental unbalance and ill-health; and it is really astounding, even in modern politics, how often the fate of a political party is determined by the physical illness and resultant pathology of a leader, rather than by other considerations. Megalomania, and what McLaurin calls psychasthenia, are by-products of democratic leadership not infrequently. Democracy is the best of systems, not because it in-evitably produces the best leader (history demonstrates freakish exceptions) but because it at least offers a means, short of blood-shed, of getting rid of a discredited leader. . . .

A few men suddenly find themselves elevated to the position of high priests of a new cult even in spite of themselves. They develop followings which for the time being come to accept them as infallible for in them ideas are incarnate. And because the people cannot peer into the workings of every mind of what might be termed its political priestly caste, cannot, indeed, know to what extent the in-ward thoughts of the legislator coincide with his outward pretence, the personality of the leader tends to become something almost mystically reverenced. If the party of the people does much that is in the interests of the people, the leader can become mighty in prestige. Even if he has actually and privately been opposing all that his party has been doing, he is judged on the public performance of his party and not on his private opinions. The leader can be the one man out of step if the party appears to be going the right way.

Hence, gradually a leader can become, for a moment, more important than the whole of his party. And if in this moment the leader is a willing instrument of policy, this fact can achieve much that is good, for good becomes the leader's personality; but if, on the contrary, the leader is a person trying privately to resist most that his party is compelling him toward and that his party promised, a fantastic situation is created, wherein the chief opponent of party policy derives most prestige from the deeds he opposes. In such a circumstance a monstrous situation exists wherein the chief wrecker is best revered.

The Case of Woodrow Wilson

A recurring problem in political pathology is the problem of the leader who has become venerated throughout his country and who suddenly goes physically and then mentally sick. . . . Woodrow Wilson was a great figure, who gave utterance to some magnificent principles far more easy to talk about than to live for. Right at the pinnacle of his career and when the recognised leader of his party and the rallying point of much radical opinion throughout the world, Woodrow Wilson became severely ill physically. The result of physical illness was reflected in mental illness.

It was easy for his party to talk about physical sickness. It was ungentlemanly to refer to the mental sickness. And so Woodrow Wilson, apparently a democrat and the leader of radicalism, became an autocrat of the worst type. . . . How could his party handle a problem of this sort? It frankly could not. The radical-turned-pathological autocrat destroyed his own prestige and destroyed his party, while 'yes' men kept up the stream of flattery until the very end. . . .

And Ramsey MacDonald

Great Britain had a similar problem in Ramsay MacDonald. Ramsay mouthed radical platitudes about democracy, about socialism. As he grew old, his utterances grew more and more platitudinous, all rarified air and no physical content. He became a master of nebulous generality. He surrounded himself with toadies who fawned and flattered so that they might get what the great man had to hand out. . . . The pathological state of Ramsay MacDonald must have been apparent to many people in his party long before he dragged the party down to its grave and caused the worst Government in a century to be established in Great Britain. But to talk about Ramsay MacDonald's physical illness was respectable. . . . To have referred to his pathological state would have been an outrage, would have been ungentlemanly, would have been considered disloyalty to the party. To have dealt with this problem honestly at the commencement might have saved the workers of Great Britain from the crash that occurred later. The party crashed while the official Labour Press was servile to a dead but as yet unburied legend.

In New Zealand, the pathological ancient is not unknown. I was present in the House of Parliament when the Rt. Hon. W. F. Massey was breaking up. Massey did not become a pathological case. Massey's body rather than his mind abdicated. I think he was mentally responsible right to his concluding hours in politics as have been most of our premiers.

Sir Joseph Ward's case was different. Sir Joseph was obviously mentally sick as a result of physical illness. Here again, we had the problem associated with the decline and fall of Woodrow Wilson and Ramsay MacDonald. Sir Joseph had moments of extraordinary lucidity, alternating with moments wherein physical illness made it difficult for him to understand any political issue. And yet the unwritten convention safeguarded Sir Joseph. No one inside or outside his party must open fire on the Red Cross. . . .

. . . A party cannot live on its past leadership and its present pathology. A man sick physically and mentally excites sympathy but never adds to political strength. Youth is recruited by the promise of to-morrow, not by the odour of the sickroom.

Politicians, after all, are only human beings, subject to the normal run of human ailments. . . .

Politics and pathology. The novelist in me has studied politics since 1922 and I find this problem, among others, of absorbing interest. The average man seems to get old and possess his faculties unto the last, although even when he does his mind can be too much derived from yesterday, too little patterned by contemporaneity. An odd politician becomes physically, becomes mentally sick, and while he is physically and mentally sick sycophants pour flattery upon him. Like a child who will only play if he gets his own way, he stays in the sickroom as a way of escape from problems. He becomes vain of mind and short of temper, and believes that everybody who crosses his path has demoniac attributes. Wherever this problem of what I call pathology in politics occurred, except that the party managed to cut off the diseased limb, it went down to crashing defeat. For if when the blind lead the blind both fall into the ditch, when the physically and mentally sick lead the radical, radicalism falls into the ditch. Politics are a battlefield as is war, if words and ideals and not bayonets are the barbs. There is no instance yet recorded in history of a party winning a people by carrying a leader on a sick-bed in front, by asking to-morrow to grow reverent at the odour of iodine. Nevertheless, history seems not

349

to have discovered a suitable technique for the immediate retirement of pathological democrats. Too frequently they pull their parties with them into the grave, for they have come to believe a mystic something resides in their flesh and that with the death of their generation all hope must be abandoned. The vanity of old men going down hill is not lessened by the laughter of modern spirits. Men gone pathological do not understand that spring leaf is as eternal as death.

Sometimes the novelist in me says take time off and deal with some of these problems of all times in a novel. But the socialist politician will not give the novelist time. . . .

Tomorrow, Wellington, 1939, 6(3): 75–7

153. THE DEMOCRATIC LABOUR PARTY, 1940

After he was expelled from the Labour Party in April 1940, because of his attack on the dying Savage, Lee formed the Democratic Labour Party, which advocated complete control of finance and credit and also called for industrialization. The party contested fifty-two electorates in the 1943 election, but secured no seats. In this early pamphlet Lee appeals to those who want to see industrial development and those who wish to improve family and cultural life.

Democratic Labour and Industry

New Zealander! (I say New Zealander for to-day well over 90 per cent of our audience is New Zealand born . . .) the time has arrived for you to take an active interest in governing your country. . . . The terrific spurt given to prodution by modern machine methods must reverse our old political standards. We live on the eve of an age of abundance, and our political philosophy is governed by the economics of scarcity. . . . We want your aid to free New Zealand's National, Local Body and industrial development from the system of debt finance. For decades the industrialist, the small business man, the farmer, the home builder, has allied himself with the system of finance which enslaves him. . . . The Democratic Labour Party is the only party in New Zealand which says the debt system must end before it ends the prosperity of the people, before it produces another depression. . . .

. . . I have placed on record in Parliament particulars of a £77,000 loan raised in 1860. On the £77,000 we had paid, up till 1939, £278,000 in simple interest, and we still owe the £77,000. . . . Compound interest increases the debt to such proportions that we can no longer pay the interest. We borrow to pay the interest, increasing the burden of debt. For instance, since 1901 we have borrowed £133,000,000 in London while paying in interest £145,700,000. If a business man had to apply the same principles to his own business as are applied to the Nation's accounts he would revolt against the stupidities of the system in a few minutes. . . . Democratic Labour aims at starting New Zealand off with a new money system, making money the slave instead of the master of industry. . . .

New Zealand must develop her industries and occupy her country speedily or perish. We have our part to play in the future history of the Pacific. Too long we have been content to allow our industries to develop haphazardly. The Nation must plan and drive. A rich future is ours when we care to reach out toward it. In an age of power we have more power close to the seaboard than any country our size in the world. . . . We must manufacture in New Zealand or know frustration.

Democratic Labour and the Home

Democratic Labour believes that there should be immediate recognition of the service the mother gives to the Nation. . . . The mother should receive an allowance for each child and every child, and that regardless of the income of herself or her husband. . . . The State Advances Corporation should be made the Housing Branch of the Reserve Bank and . . . funds should be made available to Local Bodies for slum clearance at lower rates than at present. . . . We also believe that the State Advances Corporation's present lending rate to private house builders is not the lowest possible. . . .

Wanted, universal superannuation regardless of income at an age to be fixed. . . . Democratic Labour would spend more of the radio revenues on art and artists, give musical scholarships to boys and girls, would take an interest in the provision of abundant recreational facilities. Democratic Labour would see to it that education really was available for bright children from the kindergarten to the university. . . . We would recognise the aristocracy of intellect. . . .

We stand for the free association of people in cultural, in religious, in trade union organisations, . . . but we are against that form of 'Bossism' which has recently developed within one or two organisations.

The two old parties have their roots in the past. Both lack an inspiring vision of the future of New Zealand. . . . We are a new group, we are being reinforced by people dissatisfied with existing parties. *We truckle to no vested interests.* . . . We fight for New Zealand. We ask you to help us.

> Pamphlet by John A. Lee, *The Democratic Labour Party, In Business and the Home.* Wellington, 1940

7

THE DIPLOMACY OF A SMALL STATE

---

154. LABOUR AND FOREIGN POLICY, 1919

At the Fourth annual conference of the New Zealand Labour Party in July 1919, sub-committee consisting of Holland, Fraser, Semple, and Bell considered the Versailles peace terms. The conference adopted a 'Manifesto dealing with the peace terms and international situation'.

1. The peace terms do not represent the voice of the people. Labour has had no part in making the treaty. No Parliament has had a voice, and the people have not been consulted. Only the ruling class representatives of the five Great Powers in the war alliance have a deciding vote in the matter, and it is not to be wondered at that the treaty violates almost every principle that Labor holds sacred as well as every principle that the Allies claimed to stand for in the war. In the whole treaty there is not a single word about the preservation of popular liberties and the mis-named League of Nations is representative of Governments and not of peoples, and would seem to have been designed for the purpose mainly of protecting the trading interests of the Allied capitalists.

2. The great power of the league . . . is vested in the executive council and the secretariat of officials which it appoints. The composition of the executive council is the most damning feature of the document. It installs a perpetual autocracy of the foreign Ministers (or their nominees) of the five Great Allied Powers. . . . Now, the council is nothing more or less than the existing war alliance. . . .

3. The terms of the peace settlement make for war, and not for peace. They violate almost all of President Wilson's 14 points, the acceptance of which by both the Germans and the Allies was responsible for the armistice. . . . They bear the evidence of a compromise influenced by Capitalism and Imperialism. . . . It is a peace

with vengeance instead of a peace with security. . . . The terms raise more dangers than they lay, and scatter dragons' teeth across Europe, opening up hopeless vendettas and leaving the Germans no longer hope but revenge.

4. . . . Generally speaking, the terms have been formulated from the viewpoint of the international trader.

5. The terms of the indemnity will make it inevitable that the British markets will be flooded with German-made goods, with the accompanying danger of our own workers standing idle and unemployed. . . .

6. We were constantly told that the war was being fought to end militarism, but the terms impose on Germany alone the obligation to abolish conscription. Militarism is more firmly established in all the Allied countries. . . .

7. The compulsory handing over of peoples and territories to foreign dominations, as, for example, in the case of the coal mining population of the Saar Valley, abrogates every principle of self-determination. . . . Although at every election the Saar Valley miners voted for Social Democracy and against the Kaiser and militarism, they are now to be placed in bondage for the sins committed by Kaiserdom.

8. The terms transfer the Chinese province of Shantung from German domination to Japanese domination. This has already resulted in . . . the development of a situation pregnant with the possibility of another disastrous war in the East.

9. The Conference declares in favor of self-determination for Ireland, Egypt, India, and all subject peoples, self-determination meaning the right of the people to determine by the vote of the adult population their own form of government.

10. The Conference of the New Zealand Labour Party joins with the workers of Europe in general, and Britain, France, and Italy in particular, in demanding the withdrawal of Allied troops from Russia, Hungary, and all the Socialist republics. . . .

11. We declare unreservedly in favor of the lifting of the blockade which is being operated against the Russian people, inflicting misery, hunger, and death on many thousands of children, women and men. . . .

12. Finally, we declare our firm conviction that the world can never be made safe for humanity while Capitalism, with its adjuncts of Imperialism and militarism, remains. It is, therefore, the duty of

the workers to unite, industrially and politically, in all countries for the purpose of superseding Capitalism with industrial democracy, which is Socialism, and forming not a league of nations, but a league of peoples, with an international unity which will make warfare not only unnecessary, but altogether impossible.

The Maoriland Worker, 16 July, 1919, p. 5

155. CITIZEN ARMY OR UNARMED NATION, 1919?

At its annual conference in 1919 the Labour Party adopted a policy of ending wartime defence laws and creating a volunteer citizen army. In the debate on an amendment proposing the abolition of all military training, Peter Fraser drew a distinction between 'pacifism and Socialism' and Walter Nash declared that the unarmed nation would be 'impregnable'.

Defence
8. (*a*) The repeal of the Defence Act and the Military Service Act. The repeal of all provisions in the War Regulations Act and its amendments that interfere with our civil and industrial liberties.

   (*b*) A citizen army on a voluntary basis, with standard wages while on duty.

Peace
9. The industrial and political unity of all countries, for the purpose of superseding capitalism by industrial democracy and of forming, not a League of Nations, but a League of Peoples. . . .

Mr. N. Bell moved the minority report, asking for the repeal of subclause (*b*) of clause 8. . . . He said that if they stood sincerely for peace they should prepare for peace by abolishing all military training whatsoever. . . .

Mr. P. Fraser supported the majority report. They must distinguish between mere pacifism and Socialism. The choice had to be made between armed resistance or passive resistance to possible enemies of the working class or a working-class State. If the majority of the party advocated passive resistance then let them adopt the minority report, but let there be no misunderstanding of the position. . . . Mr. W. Nash supported the minority report, which stated in unmistakable unequivocal terms the party's opposition to militarism in all its forms. They should not tamper with this side of State

355

THE DIPLOMACY OF A SMALL STATE

activity at all. They should boldly proclaim their faith in peace and live up to their profession of faith. He believed that an unarmed nation would be an impregnable nation.

Majority report carried, 5 July 1919. Reported
in The Maoriland Worker, 6 August 1919, p. 5

156. COLLECTIVE SECURITY AND THE LEAGUE OF NATIONS

Speech by Walter Nash in the King's Theatre, 16 September 1935.

'THE LABOUR PARTY is solidly behind the idea of collective security. This can best be achieved through adherence to the Covenant of the League of Nations. The Articles of the Covenant, while guaranteeing the territorial integrity of the members of the League, also contain provisions for the amendment of existing treaties whose continuance may endanger the peace of the world. In supporting the Covenant the Labour Party feels that those nations that carry out their undertakings can be completely effective without firing a single shot.'

The above statement summarizing the attitude of the New Zealand Labour Party towards the present international situation was made . . . by Mr. Walter Nash, M.P., National President of the Party, when addressing an audience on the Italo-Ethiopian situation, which he declared constituted the gravest situation in the history of the League of Nations.

Mr. Nash drew a vivid word picture of the losses of the nations in the Great War, and said that the abolition of war was dependent on justice internally as well as externally. The security of the world demanded understanding and co-operation between the nations commercially, and the best way to secure that was for each country to make conditions all that they should be for its people. When the people of one country came into the enjoyment of all that Nature and science had provided for them they should be prepared to help others to improve their standard of living, and he suggested that the proposals of the Labour Party would help to bring about that state of affairs. . . .

Mr. Nash also made the suggestion that a peace ballot should be taken in New Zealand for the purpose of showing that the people of New Zealand were in favour of international disputes being settled by the League of Nations instead of by force of arms. Such a ballot, he considered, would be of great value at the present time when the League needed every support, because, if the authority of the League could be enforced, much more than the avoidance of an Italo-Ethiopian war would depend on it.

The failure of the League at the present time would mean a continuance of the old order which had always meant the domination of the weak by the strong.

When war broke out the first thing it killed was truth, said Mr. Nash, and already a murmuring of what would be done in the event of war had commenced in one part of the Dominion.

NO BRAGGING AND SHOUTING
'If we have got to go to war let us go because we are sad and not because we glory in war,' said Mr. Nash. In the past war had been made possible because the emotions of the people were stirred. If war became necessary it was to be hoped the people of New Zealand would not go into it shouting and cheering but because it was necessary to save the world for the future. . . .

Mr. Nash . . . then traced the progress of the dispute between Italy and Abyssinia. Unless the other nations took steps that had never been taken before Italy would go on with her programme and that could only be carried out by conquest. As a member of the League of Nations, Abyssinia was on a par with New Zealand, and Italy's demands could be likened to the demands of a foreign Power that wanted to build a railway from Gisborne to Wellington and control all the land to the west of that line.

The Covenant of the League of Nations was the finest thing that had ever been signed for the peace of the world, Mr. Nash said. The trouble was that it had not been kept in the past, but the nations were now proposing to keep it and if they did a certain thing would have to be done. . . .

In conclusion, Mr. Nash said the Labour Party was working towards rational and reasonable agreement between the nations. New Zealand was a nation and had signed the Covenant as such. New Zealand belonged to the British Commonwealth of Nations, but was a unit in it and not a satellite behind any other unit in it. The Labour Party in New Zealand would do all that it could to uphold the Covenant of the League of Nations. . . .

It was no use talking of abolishing war unless there was justice between the nations and justice within the nations themselves. That would not come about until the countries were ruled by the people themselves. 'I know that is coming,' he said. (Applause.) 'I believe that whilst we are a small nation we can make a contribution to the world's wellbeing, but it depends on you. The Government of a country can write its laws, but the people must stand behind the Government. You will have a chance in November or December to keep the old order or try something new.'

> Report of meeting from *The New Zealand Worker*, 25 September 1935, p. 1

157. UNIVERSAL COLLECTIVE SECURITY—
THE REFORM OF THE LEAGUE OF NATIONS

The Prime Minister, Michael Joseph Savage—memorandum to the Secretary-General, 16 July 1936.

'Prime Minister's Office, Wellington, N.Z., 16th July, 1936
'SIR,—

'In accordance with the resolution of the Assembly of the League on the 4th July, 1936, and anticipating the formal request from the Council (as is necessary in the circumstances of New Zealand if the proposals of the New Zealand Government are to be received by the Secretary-General before the 1st September next), I have the honour to forward herewith an expression of the views of the New Zealand Government on the Covenant of the League of Nations:—

'(1) We believe in the first place that there is no material fault in the existing provisions of the Covenant and that the difficulties that have arisen, and that may arise in the future, are due to the method and the extent of its operation.
'(2) We believe that the Covenant has never yet been fully applied and that it cannot be characterized as an ineffective instrument until it has been so applied.
'(3) We are prepared to reaffirm with the utmost solemnity our continued acceptance of the Covenant as it stands.
'(4) We believe, nevertheless, that the Covenant is capable of amendment, which should take the form of strengthening rather than weakening its provisions.

'(5) We are prepared to accept, in principle, the provisions proposed for the Geneva Protocol of 1924 as one method of strengthening the Covenant as it exists.

'(6) We are prepared to take our collective share in the application, against any future aggressor, of the full economic sanctions contemplated by Article 16, and we are prepared, to the extent of our power, to join in the collective application of force against any future aggressor.

'(7) We believe that the sanctions contemplated by the present Covenant will be ineffective in the future as they have been in the past—

'(1) Unless they are made immediate and automatic:

'(2) Unless economic sanctions take the form of the complete boycott contemplated by Article 16:

'(3) Unless any sanctions that may be applied are supported by the certainty that the Members of the League applying the sanctions are able and, if necessary, prepared to use force against force.

'(8) It is our belief that the Covenant as it is, or in a strengthened form, would in itself be sufficient to prevent war if the world realized that the nations undertaking to apply the Covenant actually would do so in fact.

'(9) We are prepared to agree to the institution of an international force under the control of the League or to the allocation to the League of a definite proportion of the armed forces of its Members to the extent, if desired, of the whole of those forces—land, sea, and air.

'(10) We consider that there can be no certainty of the complete and automatic operation of the Covenant unless the Governments of all Members of the League are supported, in their determination to apply it, by the declared approval of their peoples.

'(11) We propose, therefore, that all the Members of the League, and as many non-Members as may be persuaded to adopt this course, should hold immediately a national plebiscite with the object of taking the opinion of their peoples on the following points—

'(1) Whether they are prepared to join automatically and immediately in the sanctions contemplated by

359

Article 16 of the Covenant against any aggressor nation nominated as such by the Council or the Assembly:

'(2) Whether in such case the armed forces of their country (or such proportion as may previously have been fixed by the League) should be immediately and automatically placed at the complete disposal of the League for that purpose.

'(12) We do not accept the desirability of regional pacts, but, if Members of the League generally approve of such pacts, we should be prepared to support a collective system in which all Members of the League, while accepting the immediate and universal application of the economic sanctions contemplated by Article 16, nevertheless, if they desired to do so, restricted to defined areas their undertaking to use force.

'(13) In such a case we consider that the question of the use of force in defined areas should also be made the subject of national plebiscites.

'(14) We believe it improper to enforce a system of preventing war without at the same time setting up adequate machinery for the ventilation and, if possible, rectification of international grievances, and we would support the establishment of an acceptable tribunal for that purpose.

'(15) We believe that the Peace Treaties of the Great War carried within themselves the germs of future conflicts. We realize the enormous (but not insuperable) difficulties of reconsidering the status established by those Treaties and for our part we are prepared in the most genuine and broadminded spirit to join in such a reconsideration.

'(16) As a first step we are prepared to agree to a proposal that the Covenant of the League should be separated from these Peace Treaties.

'(17) For any general reconsideration of the Peace Treaties we should wish to see all the nations of the world, whether Members of the League or not, invited to take part.

'(18) We should wish also to see all the nations of the world, whether Members of the League or not, invited to take part in the consideration of the terms and the application of the Covenant, or of any other universal method of collective security that may be proposed in its stead.

'(19) We realize the important effect of economic conditions on the peace of the world and we should wish, also, that a world-wide survey of such conditions should be undertaken at the same time.

'(20) We feel that the peoples of the world, as distinct from their Governments, should be afforded every possible facility for following the transactions of the League, and that all appropriate League discussions and decisions should accordingly be broadcast by short-wave radio.

'(21) Finally, although we believe that a collective peace system that is not supported by all the nations of the world is better than no collective system at all, yet we are convinced that no such system can be entirely satisfactory until it is universal and that every proper effort should be made to that end.

'I have the honour to be,
'Sir,
'Your obedient servant,
'M. J. SAVAGE, Prime Minister.'

When forwarding the above memorandum to the Secretary-General of the League of Nations it was stated in a further memorandum that if these proposals were not considered immediately practicable the New Zealand Government would not demur to consideration of progress by stages or to alternative proposals.

A.J.H.R., 1936, A–5ᴬ, pp. 2–3

158. THE LEAGUE AND THE SPANISH CIVIL WAR

William Joseph Jordan's speech to the League of Nations Council, 28 May 1937.

'I am sure we all feel the responsibility of the position in which we find ourselves at this table of the Council of the League of Nations. We have made a definite pledge with a purpose. The eyes of the world are on the Council at this time. Whatever the matter in dispute may be, whatever the cause of the conflict, the people of the world are shocked at the dreadful happenings in Spain, and the situation at the present time surely calls for some action.

'When it was announced in the papers of the world that the
League was to meet this week, prayers went up from millions of
people for the success of our deliberations. I am sure that the
members of the Council are conscious of the responsibility which
falls upon them by being here and having to deal with this matter.

'As it is a function of the League to safeguard the lives of people,
to maintain peace, and to uphold lawful and constitutional Governments against invasion and the violence of outside Powers, it is
now undoubtedly time that some decision in the Spanish situation
was taken if the League is going to act at all in the matter. . . .

'Authoritative evidence which has been made public recently
shows that the military forces of outside Powers are operating in
Spain. Is it the determination of those Powers to operate in opposition to the fundamental principles which the League was established
to uphold? We have before us the report of the Spanish Government,
which contains one hundred documents, alleging that at least one
outside Power has a fully equipped army in Spain committing acts
of aggression not only against the people of Spain, but also against
the political independence of that country, and submitting weighty
evidence in support of the allegations. Do we question the authen-
ticity of these documents? If not, the evidence which they furnish
must be received and treated with the utmost gravity by the Council.

'There is no need to detail independent reports which show what
is happening in Spain. I will merely mention a report published by
four prominent women in the United Kingdom, three of them
members of Parliament, and also the report of a representative
religious delegation. Some of the foremost of the Christian men
and women of the United Kingdom visited Spain recently for the
purpose of obtaining first-hand knowledge, and any one who reads
these and other reports must agree that what is going on in Spain
to-day is one of the most flagrant challenges to the authority of the
League which has occurred in its history.

'On the other hand, we have received a copy of a statement by
General Franco charging the elected Government with being supporters of anarchy and crime, but submitting no evidence in support
of the statement. From this table last December the question was
asked, What case is there from these people who claim that the
election in Spain was irregular? The question was asked, Why do
they not come forward and make a statement? How can the League
Council be expected to know the details and how can these people

be respected by the Council if they fight and kill the citizens of one of the League members, and at the same time withhold from us evidence of what they say is the cause of the trouble?

'Whatever the political views of the elected Spanish Government may be, is there any justification for the invasion of Spain by an outside Power? The only action taken so far by any power associated with the League appears to be the imposition of an embargo which has handicapped the Government and strengthened the hands of its aggressors.

'What is the Council definitely going to do? We have heard a speech on the prospects of success of the work of the Non-intervention Committee. We are informed that a report was presented last Wednesday. We have heard that the Governments of Europe cannot be satisfied that the objectives of the Non-intervention Committee have been realized until the last foreigner has been withdrawn and until that unhappy country has been allowed to settle her own destinies in her own way. It has been said that the main purpose of this meeting of the Council is to uphold and endorse the work of the Non-intervention Committee, to emphasize our wish for the early withdrawal of all foreign nationals from Spain, and ourselves to determine to do all in our power to facilitate the result. That sentiment is shared by all the members of the Council. We pray for the success of the Non-intervention Committee and we are determined to do all in our power to facilitate the result, but when we say we will do all in our power I ask the question, What action, if any, is being taken? In other words, are we making progress? I hope we are.

'The representative of His Majesty's Government in the United Kingdom says that Spain should be allowed to settle her own destinies in her own way. The representative of France said, *inter alia,* that the Spanish people are no longer sole masters of their own destiny. So we come back to the point we have in mind, the welfare and independence of the people of Spain. This does not mean acres, cities, and harbours, but the welfare of the people—men, women, and children. The people are our concern: they are their own concern.

'We would fain ask that a committee of the Council be set up to act forthwith, but we have been assured that the Non-intervention Committee will go beyond the matter of non-intervention: it has been said that the Governments of Europe cannot be satisfied until the last foreigner has been withdrawn from Spain, and until that unhappy country has been allowed to settle her own destinies in her own way.

'Could we then from this Council table ask the Non-intervention Committee definitely to extend its powers? Could we ask that the Non-intervention Committee, while endeavouring to secure the cessation of hostilities by the withdrawal of foreign combatants forthwith, in accordance with the hope so admirably expressed here, should also endeavour to restore peace and good order, and then have again a democratic expression of opinion by the Spanish people?

'I repeat that the future welfare of the Spanish people is their own concern and, speaking as a democrat, I express the wish that the desires of the Spanish people should be consulted. Would it be within the power of the Council to operate directly, or through the Non-intervention Committee so that, the cessation of hostilities having been achieved, the people of Spain could be assured of their own form of Government and that for a while the League might offer to assist in order that peace may be restored the more quickly? Having secured the cessation of hostilities and the withdrawal of foreign combatants, could it not be left to the people of Spain to decide? That is to say, could there not be a consultation with the people, whose business it is?

'Surely we all agree that this matter could better be settled by reason than by guns. We should like a direct approach to those concerned asking that they cease hostilities, because only by reason and not by force can peace be maintained. The earth is being menaced by the danger of an attempt to govern by force. The only satisfactory form of Government is a Government elected by the people—when a Government occupies its position at the request of the governed.

'Surely there is ingenuity enough in the League of Nations, and sincerity and ability enough among the peoples of Spain, for such a proposal to be put into operation. If we cannot do this, we cannot do something bigger. If, however, the people of Spain could be consulted, when once the horror of war has been removed, there would be some hope of happiness, peace and security for their lives and homes.'

A.J.H.R., 1937–8, A–5B, pp. 32–3

159. NEW ZEALAND'S WAR AIMS, 1939

Broadcast by the Prime Minister, Michael Joseph Savage, 5 September 1939.

... It is not my purpose tonight to state at length the issues involved in the conflict that has now begun, but I should like to tell you in a few sentences just how I see them.

The war on which we are entering may be a long one, demanding from us heavy and continuous sacrifice. It is essential that we realize from the beginning that our cause is worth the sacrifice. I believe in all sincerity that it is.

None of us has any hatred of the German people. For the old culture of the Germans, their songs, their poetry and their music, we have nothing but admiration and affection. We believe that there are many millions of German people who want to live in peace and quietness as we do, threatening no one and seeking to dominate no one. But we know, alas! that such a way of life is despised and rejected by the men who have seized and hold power in Germany. We know that those men have done and are doing incalculable harm to the true interests of their country; and that they are wasting and destroying the intellectual, artistic, moral and spiritual resources that their people have built up throughout the centuries. In doing this they have, for the time being, cowed the spirit of a vast number of their best people. Their work of destruction they have already carried into other countries; and, despite denials, now intend to carry into Poland. If they succeed there they will next attempt the overthrow of France and Britain. Let us make no mistake about that. Of course they repudiate any such intention, but, fortunately for the world, we know now, what it has taken us a long time to learn, that their promises are worthless, are made only to gain an advantage for the time being and are broken as soon as that advantage has been secured. Not a moment too soon have Britain and France taken up arms against so faithless and unscrupulous an adversary.

The fight on which we are now engaged is one whose issue concerns all the nations of the world, whether as yet they realize it or not. We are fighting a doctrine that springs from a contempt of human nature—a doctrine that government is the affair only of a self-elected élite who, without consulting the people, may irrevocably determine what the people shall do and shall not do. The masses are to be used as instruments of power in the hands of their masters. They are to be given slogans and directed towards this or that objective approved by those masters. But never are they to be treated as free men, as individual and responsible souls. The individual man is submerged and forgotten—the intrinsic worthiness of his personality contemptuously ignored. Freedom of action and expression is denied to him. Dissent or criticism is brutally suppressed. These are a few of the incidents of the Nazi philosophy that is seeking to thrust itself everywhere over Europe today and the rest of the world tomorrow.

Nazism is militant and insatiable paganism. In its short but terrible history it has caused incalculable suffering. If permitted to continue, it will spread misery and desolation throughout the world. It cannot be appeased or conciliated. Either it or civilization must disappear. To destroy it, but not the great nation which it has so cruelly cheated, is the task of those who have taken up arms against Nazism. May God prosper those arms.

I am satisfied that nowhere will the issue be more clearly understood than in New Zealand—where for almost a century, behind the sure shield of Britain, we have enjoyed and cherished freedom and self-government. Both with gratitude for the past, and with confidence in the future, we range ourselves without fear beside Britain. Where she goes, we go, where she stands, we stand. We are only a small and a young nation, but we are one and all a band of brothers, and we march forward with a union of hearts and wills to a common destiny.

Documents and Speeches on British Commonwealth Affairs 1931–1952, ed. N. Mansergh, vol. i, Oxford, 1953, pp. 489–91

160. GENERAL FREYBERG'S 'CHARTER', 1940

Extract from the instructions of Michael Savage, the Prime Minister, to the General Officer Commanding the Second New Zealand Expeditionary Force, 5 January 1940.

The General Officer Commanding will act in accordance with the instructions he receives from the Commander-in-Chief under whose command he is serving, subject only to the requirements of His Majesty's Government in New Zealand. He will, in addition to powers appearing in any relevant Statute or Regulations, be vested with the following powers:

(*a*) In the case of sufficiently grave emergency or in special circumstances, of which he must be the sole judge, to make decisions as to the employment of the 2nd New Zealand Expeditionary Force, and to communicate such decisions directly to the New Zealand Government, notwithstanding that in the absence of that extraordinary cause such communication would not be in accordance with the normal channels of communication. . . .

> *Documents relating to New Zealand's Participation in the Second World War, 1939–45,* vol. i, Wellington, 1949, pp. 31–2

161. TURNING TO THE UNITED STATES FOR PROTECTION

Telegram from the Secretary of State for Dominions Affairs, London, to the High Commissioner for the United Kingdom, Wellington, 13 June 1940, and a telegram in reply from the Governor-General of New Zealand, 15 June 1940.

(*a*) 13 June 1940
. . . 8. 'In the unlikely event of Japan, in spite of the restraining influence of the United States of America, taking the opportunity to alter the *status quo* in the Far East, we should be faced with a naval situation in which, without the assistance of France, we should not have sufficient forces to meet the combined German and Italian navies in European waters and the Japanese fleet in the Far East. In the circumstances envisaged, it is most improbable that we could send adequate reinforcements to the Far East. We should therefore have to rely on the United States of America to safeguard our interests there. . . .'

(*b*)   15 June 1940
Following for Prime Minister from my Prime Minister:

1. There is one aspect of your most secret telegram Circular Z.106 of 14 June to the High Commissioner for the United Kingdom in New Zealand to which His Majesty's Government in New Zealand wish especially to refer. In this telegram a departure is made from the understanding, reinforced by repeated and most

explicit assurances, that a strong British fleet would be available to, and would, proceed to Singapore should the circumstances so require, even if this involved the abandonment of British interests in the Mediterranean. His Majesty's Government in New Zealand do not in any way demur to this decision (which they have always regarded as a possibility) if, as they assume, it is necessary in order to safeguard the position in the central and critical theatre of war, and they are quite prepared to accept the risks which they recognise are inevitable if the most effective use is to be made of Commonwealth naval forces. At the same time His Majesty's Government in New Zealand must observe that the undertaking to dispatch an adequate fleet to Singapore, if required, formed the basis of the whole of this Dominion's defence preparations. They assume that this undertaking will again be made operative as soon as circumstances may allow, and they would most earnestly request that the whole situation should be reviewed if the position in the Far East should become threatening.

2. In the hope of strengthening the security of the Pacific and of reinforcing the representations already made to President Roosevelt on behalf of the Allies, H.M. Government in New Zealand feel that it would be advantageous if they were at once to send to Washington a Minister of the Crown on special mission and if H.M. Government in United Kingdom see no objection they would propose to dispatch a Minister accordingly. If H.M. Government in United Kingdom concur H.M. Government in New Zealand would be grateful if they would immediately make the necessary approaches to United States Government with a view to ascertaining at the earliest possible moment whether such a special mission would be agreeable to that Government. Ends.

> *Documents Relating to New Zealand's Participation in the Second World War, 1939–45,* vol. iii, pp. 206–7. (Paragraph 2, which is not quoted in full in this book, is printed here by permission of the Ministry of Foreign Affairs, Wellington.)

162. THE CANBERRA PACT

Australian–New Zealand Agreement, made in Canberra 21 January 1944. (The New Zealand signatories are Peter Fraser, Frederick Jones, Patrick Charles Webb, Carl August Berendsen.)

HIS MAJESTY'S Government in the Commonwealth of Australia and His Majesty's Government in the Dominion of New Zealand (hereinafter referred to as 'the two Governments') . . . having met in conference at Canberra from the 17th to the 21st January, 1944, and desiring to maintain and strengthen the close and cordial relations between the two Governments, do hereby enter into this agreement.

DEFINITION OF OBJECTIVES OF
AUSTRALIAN–NEW ZEALAND CO-OPERATION

1. The two Governments agree that, as a preliminary, provision shall be made for fuller exchange of information regarding both the views of each Government and the facts in the possession of either bearing on matters of common interest.

2. The two Governments give mutual assurances that, on matters which appear to be of common concern, each Government will, so far as possible, be made acquainted with the mind of the other before views are expressed elsewhere by either.

3. In furtherance of the above provisions with respect to exchange of views and information, the two Governments agree that there shall be the maximum degree of unity in the presentation, elsewhere, of the views of the two countries.

4. The two Governments agree to adopt an expeditious and continuous means of consultation by which each will obtain directly the opinions of the other.

5. The two Governments agree to act together in matters of common concern in the South-west and South Pacific areas.

6. So far as compatible with the existence of separate military commands, the two Governments agree to co-ordinate their efforts for the purpose of prosecuting the war to a successful conclusion.

ARMISTICE AND SUBSEQUENT ARRANGEMENTS

7. The two Governments declare that they have vital interests in all preparations for any armistice ending the present hostilities or any part thereof, and also in arrangements subsequent to any such armistice, and agree that their interests should be protected by representation at the highest level on all armistice planning and executive bodies.

8. The two Governments are in agreement that the final peace settlement should be made in respect of all our enemies after hostilities with all of them are concluded.

9. Subject to the last two preceding clauses, the two Governments will seek agreement with each other on the terms of any armistice to be concluded.

10. The two Governments declare that they should actively participate in any armistice commission to be set up.

11. His Majesty's Government in the Commonwealth of Australia shall set up in Australia, and His Majesty's Government in the Dominion of New Zealand shall set up in New Zealand, armistice and post-hostilities planning committees, and shall arrange for the work of those committees to be co-ordinated in order to give effect to the views of the respective Governments.

12. The two Governments will collaborate generally with regard to the location of machinery set up under international organizations, such as the United Nations Relief and Rehabilitation Administration, and, in particular, with regard to the location of the Far Eastern Committee of that Administration.

SECURITY AND DEFENCE

13. The two Governments agree that, within the framework of a general system of world security, a regional zone of defence comprising the South-west and South Pacific areas shall be established and that this zone should be based on Australia and New Zealand, stretching through the arc of islands north and north-east of Australia, to Western Samoa and the Cook Islands.

14. The two Governments regard it as a matter of cardinal importance that they should both be associated not only in the membership, but also in the planning and establishment, of the general international organization referred to in the Moscow Declaration of October, 1943, which organization is based on the principle of the sovereign equality of all peace-loving states and open to membership by all such states, large or small, for the maintenance of international peace and security.

15. Pending the re-establishment of law and order and inauguration of a system of general security, the two Governments hereby declare their vital interest in the action on behalf of the community of nations contemplated in Article 5 of the Moscow Declaration of October, 1943. For that purpose it is agreed that it would be proper for Australia and New Zealand to assume full responsibility for policing or sharing in policing such areas in the South-west and South Pacific as may from time to time be agreed upon.

16. The two Governments accept as a recognized principle of international practice that the construction and use, in time of war, by any power of naval, military, or air installations, in any territory under the sovereignty or control of another power does not, in itself, afford any basis for territorial claims or rights of sovereignty or control after the conclusion of hostilities.

CIVIL AVIATION

17. The two Governments agree that the regulation of all air transport services should be subject to the terms of a convention which will supersede the Convention relating to the Regulation of Aerial Navigation.

18. The two Governments declare that the air services using the international air trunk routes should be operated by an international air transport authority.

19. The two Governments support the principles that—
   (a) Full control of the international air trunk routes and the ownership of all aircraft and ancillary equipment should be vested in the international air transport authority;
   (b) The international air trunk routes should themselves be specified in the international agreement referred to in the next succeeding clause.

20. The two Governments agree that the creation of the international air transport authority should be effected by an international agreement.

21. Within the framework of the system set up under any such international agreement the two Governments support—
   (a) The right of each country to conduct all air transport services within its own national jurisdiction, including its own contiguous territories, subject only to agreed international requirements regarding safety, facilities, landing and transit rights for international services and exchange of mails;
   (b) The right of Australia and New Zealand to utilize to the fullest extent their productive capacity in respect of aircraft and raw materials for the production of aircraft; and
   (c) The right of Australia and New Zealand to use a fair proportion of their own personnel, agencies, and materials in operating and maintaining international air trunk routes.

22. In the event of failure to obtain a satisfactory international agreement to establish and govern the use of international air trunk routes, the two Governments will support a system of air trunk routes controlled and operated by Governments of the British Commonwealth of Nations under government ownership.

23. The two Governments will act jointly in support of the above-mentioned principles with respect to civil aviation, and each will inform the other of its existing interests and commitments, as a basis of advancing the policy herein agreed upon.

DEPENDENCIES AND TERRITORIES

24. Following the procedure adopted at the Conference which has just concluded, the two Governments will regularly exchange information and views in regard to all developments in or affecting the islands of the Pacific.

25. The two Governments take note of the intention of the Australian Government to resume administration at the earliest possible moment of those parts of its territories which have not yet been reoccupied.

26. The two Governments declare that the interim administration and ultimate disposal of enemy territories in the Pacific are of vital importance to Australia and New Zealand, and that any such disposal should be effected only with their agreement and as part of a general Pacific settlement.

27. The two Governments declare that no change in the sovereignty or system of control of any of the islands of the Pacific should be effected except as a result of an agreement to which they are parties or in the terms of which they have both concurred.

WELFARE AND ADVANCEMENT OF NATIVE PEOPLES OF THE PACIFIC

28. The two Governments declare that, in applying the principles of the Atlantic Charter to the Pacific, the doctrine of 'trusteeship' (already applicable in the case of the mandated territories of which the two Governments are mandatory powers) is applicable in broad principle to all colonial territories in the Pacific and elsewhere, and that the main purpose of the trust is the welfare of the native peoples and their social, economic, and political development.

29. The two Governments agree that the future of the various territories of the Pacific and the welfare of their inhabitants cannot be successfully promoted without a greater measure of collaboration between the numerous authorities concerned in their control, and that such collaboration is particularly desirable in regard to health services and communications, matters of native education, anthropological investigation, assistance in native production, and material development generally.

30. The two Governments agree to promote the establishment, at the earliest possible date, of a regional organization with advisory powers, which could be called the South Seas Regional Commission, and on which, in addition to representatives of Australia and New Zealand, there might be accredited representatives of the Governments of the United Kingdom and the United States of America, and of the French Committee of National Liberation.

31. The two Governments agree that it shall be the function of such South Seas Regional Commission as may be established to secure a common policy on social, economic, and political development directed towards the advancement and well-being of the native peoples themselves, and that in particular the Commission shall—

(a) Recommend arrangements for the participation of natives in administration in increasing measure with a view to promoting the ultimate attainment of self-government in the form most suited to the circumstances of the native peoples concerned;

(b) Recommend arrangements for material development, including production, finance, communications, and marketing;

(c) Recommend arrangements for co-ordination of health and medical services and education;

(d) Recommend arrangements for maintenance and improvement of standards of native welfare in regard to labour conditions and social services;

(e) Recommend arrangements for collaboration in economic, social, medical, and anthropological research; and

(f) Make and publish periodical reviews of progress towards the development of self-governing institutions in the islands of the Pacific and in the improvement of standards of living, conditions of work, education, health, and general welfare.

MIGRATION

32. In the peace settlement or other negotiations the two Governments will accord one another full support in maintaining the accepted principle that every Government has the right to control immigration and emigration in regard to all territories within its jurisdiction.

33. The two Governments will collaborate, exchange full information, and render full assistance to one another in all matters concerning migration to their respective territories.

INTERNATIONAL CONFERENCE RELATING TO THE SOUTH-WEST AND SOUTH PACIFIC

34. The two Governments agree that, as soon as practicable, there should be a frank exchange of views on the problems of security, post-war development, and native welfare between properly-accredited representatives of the Governments with existing territorial interests in the South-west Pacific area or in the South Pacific area, or in both—namely, in addition to the two Governments, His Majesty's Government in the United Kingdom, the Government of the United States of America, the Government of the Netherlands, the French Committee of National Liberation, and the Government of Portugal—and His Majesty's Government in the Commonwealth of Australia should take the necessary steps to call a conference of the Governments concerned.

PERMANENT MACHINERY FOR COLLABORATION AND CO-OPERATION BETWEEN AUSTRALIA AND NEW ZEALAND

35. The two Governments agree that—

(a) Their co-operation for defence should be developed by—

(i) Continuous consultation in all defence matters of mutual interest;

(ii) The organization, equipment, training, and exercising of the armed forces under a common doctrine;

(iii) Joint planning;

(iv) Interchange of staff; and

(v) The co-ordination of policy for the production of munitions, aircraft and supply items, and for shipping, to ensure the greatest possible degree of mutual aid consistent with the maintenance of the policy of self-sufficiency in local production;

(*b*) Collaboration in external policy on all matters affecting the peace, welfare, and good government of the Pacific should be secured through the exchange of information and frequent ministerial consultation;

(*c*) The development of comerce between Australia and New Zealand and their industrial development should be pursued by consultation and in agreed cases by joint planning;

(*d*) There should be co-operation in achieving full employment in Australia and New Zealand and the highest standards of social security both within their borders and throughout the islands of the Pacific and other territories for which they may jointly or severally be wholly or partly responsible; and

(*e*) There should be co-operation in encouraging missionary work and all other activities directed towards the improvement of the welfare of the native peoples in the islands and territories of the Pacific.

36. The two Governments declare their desire to have the adherence to the objectives set out in the last preceding clause of any other Government having or controlling territories in the Pacific.

37. The two Governments agree that the methods to be used for carrying out the provisions of clause 35 of this Agreement and of other provisions of this Agreement shall be consultation, exchange of information, and, where applicable, joint planning. They further agree that such methods shall include—

(*a*) Conferences of Ministers of State to be held alternately in Canberra and Wellington, it being the aim of the two Governments that these conferences be held at least twice a year;

(*b*) Conferences of departmental officers and technical experts;

(*c*) Meetings of standing inter-governmental committees on such subjects as are agreed to by the two Governments;

(*d*) The fullest use of the status and functions of the High Commissioner of the Commonwealth of Australia in New Zealand and of the High Commissioner of the Dominion of New Zealand in Australia;

(*e*) Regular exchange of information;

(*f*) Exchange of officers; and

(*g*) The development of institutions in either country serving the common purposes of both.

PERMANENT SECRETARIAT

38. In order to ensure continuous collaboration on the lines set out in this agreement and to facilitate the carrying-out of the duties and functions involved, the two Governments agree that a permanent secretariat shall be established in Australia and in New Zealand.

39. The secretariat shall be known as the Australian–New Zealand Affairs Secretariat, and shall consist of a secretariat of the like name to be set up in Australia and a secretariat of the like name to be set up in New Zealand, each under the control of the Ministry of External Affairs in the country concerned.

40. The functions of the Secretariat shall be—

(*a*) To take the initiative in ensuring that effect is given to the provisions of this agreement;

(*b*) To make arrangements as the occasion arises for the holding of conferences or meetings;

(*c*) To carry out the directions of those conferences in regard to further consultation, exchange of information, or the examination of particular questions;

(*d*) To co-ordinate all forms of collaboration between the two Governments;

(*e*) To raise for joint discussion and action such other matters as may seem from day to day to require attention by the two Governments; and

(*f*) Generally to provide for more frequent and regular exchanges of information and views, those exchanges between the two Governments to take place normally through the respective High Commissioners.

41. His Majesty's Government in the Commonwealth of Australia and His Majesty's Government in the Dominion of New Zealand each shall nominate an officer or officers from the staff of their respective High Commissioners to act in closest collaboration with the Secretariat in which they shall be accorded full access to all relevant sources of information.

42. In each country the Minister of State for External Affairs and the Resident High Commissioner shall have joint responsibility for the effective functioning of the Secretariat.

RATIFICATION AND TITLE OF AGREEMENT

43. This agreement is subject to ratification by the respective Governments and shall come into force as soon as both Governments have ratified the agreement and have notified each other accordingly. It is intended that such notification will take place as soon as possible after the signing of this agreement.

44. This agreement shall be known as the Australian–New Zealand Agreement 1944.

Dated this 21st day of January, 1944.

Signed on behalf of His Majesty's Government in the Dominion of New Zealand— . . .

A.J.H.R., 1944, A–4, pp. 1–4

163. THE CANBERRA PACT, 1944

The Prime Minister, Peter Fraser, speaks in the House of Representatives, 29 March 1944.

. . . Although both countries cordially agreed to closer collaboration and the utmost co-operation, I want to emphasize that it is distinctly understood that there is no sinking or subordinating of one to the other, or discarding the opinions of either country. Collaboration? Yes. Co-operation? Yes. Unity where unity can be achieved, but, where unity of opinion cannot be achieved, then there shall be a friendly agreement to differ. That is the position. Neither country is subordinated to the other. . . .

. . . In regard to the post-hostilities period, the Governments of both countries feel that it is only right that we should express vital interest in possible armistice and armistice terms. While we realize the greatness of the United Nations, the greatness of the United Kingdom, of the United States of America, our great ally, of Russia, our other great ally, and of China, which has endured so much, throughout the whole of the negotiations in connection with the Agreement, neither New Zealand nor Australia had any enlarged opinion of its own capacity, its status, or its power. While there is nothing of the humbleness of the Uriah Heep type about either Government or their peoples, we have a sense of responsibility, and there is a realization that without the co-operation and help of our larger allies we and our ideals and efforts will be stultified. Therefore, there is nothing in the way of seeking to differ from, or quarrel with, the other United Nations. On the contrary, the Agreement makes the widest possible provision for the greatest measure of co-operation. In fact, all the nations of the Pacific are invited to express their willingess to co-operate with us; but we do say that if an Agreement is signed in Cairo, in Teheran, or in Moscow, then such Agreement affects us, and ultimately our countries should have the right to express opinions in connection with them. . . . I am not prepared, and neither are the people of New Zealand nor the people and Government of Australia prepared, to apologize for our existence. We have given of our resources. Our young men have given their lives or suffered sickness and wounds, trials and tribulations, and our people generally, in both countries, have rallied to the war effort. Therefore, we are entitled to be heard in peace as in war. . . .

N.Z.P.D., 1944, vol. 264, pp. 794–5, 798

164. UNIVERSAL COLLECTIVE SECURITY— AMENDMENTS TO THE UNITED NATIONS CHARTER, 1945

The Prime Minister, Peter Fraser, speaks at the plenary session of the San Francisco Conference, 3 May 1945.

. . . The Dumbarton Oaks proposals, which we value and for which we are grateful, are not sacrosanct. The four great powers which have convened the Conference have not adopted a take it or leave it attitude. In that broad and generous atmosphere engendered by the speeches of the representatives of the sponsoring powers, we can set ourselves to the great and sacred task entrusted to us. If we fail, we betray all mankind. If we succeed, we prevent future generations from being plunged again into the horrors, bloodshed, suffering, destruction, and devastation of war. We will have saved the world. . . .

'New Zealand in common with all the other United Nations places the utmost emphasis on the need for an effective international organisation to maintain peace and security. We have studied the Dumbarton Oaks proposals with special care, and accept these proposals, deficient as they are in certain particulars, as the basis on which the organisation should be built. . . .

'The two main deficiencies in the Dumbarton Oaks plan, as we see them, are the absence of any definite pledges on the part of members of the world organisation to protect one another against external aggression, and the disproportionate role that is allotted to the small powers.

'There is in the Dumbarton Oaks plan no clear statement that the security of the individual members of the organisation is the objective, and no embodiment of the stirring claim of the Atlantic Charter that the peace we aim at is one which will afford to all nations the means of dwelling in safety within their own boundaries, and which will afford an assurance that all the men in all the lands may live out their lives in freedom from fear and want. New Zealand would wish that in the Charter we are about to draft there should be placed in the core of the undertakings which members will assume the unequivocal pledge to resist all acts of external aggression against any member of the organisation. . . .

'The peoples of the world deserve to know—they have the right to know—what rule of conduct is to guide their assembled representatives in deliberating on every critical phase of the relationship between nations. . . . They should have an international rule of conduct set before them clearly and simply, and in the opinion of the New Zealand Government this can be done only by the universal pledge by each and every nation that all acts of aggression will be resisted. . . .

'The second major deficiency we see in the Dumbarton Oaks proposals is the excessive authority conferred on the great powers. We fully realise that the primary condition for the success of the organisation is that the more powerful nations should remain united in support of it, and we realise also that no security programme is worth pursuing unless it commands the adherence of the great powers. We feel, however, that the part the smaller nations may take in the framing of the decisions of the world organisation could without loss of security be enlarged. . . .

. . . I do not for a moment overlook the fact that the great powers must have inevitably a predominant voice on matters which call for the use of armed force, but clearly there will be difficulty in the way of accepting a proposal under which the great powers retain for themselves the right to say in every important case whether the organisation shall act or not, and whether they themselves shall be bound or not, and are at the same time vested with the right to deny to the smaller powers not only a vote but a voice in these matters.

'In our view the power of the Assembly should therefore be so wide as to give that body the right to consider any matter within the sphere of international relations. The Security Council would have its specific powers, but the powers of discussion and recommendation of the Assembly should not be constitutionally limited. We would also propose that when sanctions are called for by the Security Council the endorsement by the Assembly should normally be required and all members should be bound by the Assembly's decision. . . .

'As I stated at the outset of my remarks, the maintenance of peace is the paramount problem that confronts us. This is a moral problem and not merely a mechanical one to be solved by procedures, however carefully devised and comprehensive in their nature. The failure of the League of Nations—one of the noblest conceptions in the history of mankind—was a moral failure on the part of individual members and was not due to any fundamental defect of the machinery of the League. The League of Nations failed because its members would not perform what they undertook to perform. It failed because of the recession that took place in public morality in the face of the rising tide of Fascism and Nazism. It failed because the rule of expediency replaced that of moral principles.

'I would therefore stress that, unless in the future we have the moral rectitude and determination to stand by our engagements and principles, then the procedure laid down in this new organisation will avail us nothing; the suffering and sacrifices our peoples have endured will avail us nothing. . . .

> *N.Z. and the San Francisco Conference,*
> Department of External Affairs Publication,
> no. 10, 1945

165. THE AMENDMENTS PROPOSED BY NEW ZEALAND

Insertions shown in italics *and deletions in* ~~erasure type~~ *proposed by New Zealand to the Dumbarton Oaks draft for the U.N. Charter.*

CHAPTER I.—PURPOSES

1. To maintain international peace and security *and to preserve as against external aggression the territorial integrity and political*

independence of every member of the Organization; and to that end to take effective collective measures for the prevention and removal of threats to the peace and the suppression of acts of aggression or other breaches of the peace, and to bring about by peaceful means the adjustment or settlement of international disputes which may lead to a breach of the peace.

CHAPTER II.—PRINCIPLES

[New paragraphs, 1A, 2A, 4A, proposed]

1A. *All members of the Organization solemnly reaffirm and pledge themselves to the principles of the Atlantic Charter of 14 August 1941 and the United Nations Declaration of 1 January 1942.*

2A. *All members of the Organization undertake to preserve, protect and promote human rights and fundamental freedoms, and in particular the rights of freedom from want, freedom from fear, freedom of speech and freedom of worship.*

4A. *All members of the Organization undertake collectively to resist every act of aggression against any member.*

CHAPTER IV.—PRINCIPAL ORGANS

[New paragraph, (*b* i) proposed]

(*b* i) *An Economic and Social Council.*

CHAPTER V.—THE GENERAL ASSEMBLY

B. *Functions and Powers*

[New paragraph, *o.* 1, proposed]

o. 1. The General Assembly shall have the right to consider any matter within the sphere of international relations.

1. *In particular* the General Assembly should have the right to consider the general principles of co-operation in the maintenance of international peace and security including the principles governing disarmament and the regulation of armaments; to discuss any questions relating to the maintenance of international peace and security brought before it by any member or members of the Organization or by the Security Council; and to make recommendations with regard to any such principles or questions. Any such questions on which action is necessary should be referred to the Security Council by the General Assembly either before or after discussion. The General Assembly should not on its own initiative make recommendations on any matter relating to the maintenance of

~~international peace and security which is being dealt with by the Security Council.~~

2. The General Assembly should be empowered to admit new members to the Organization. ~~upon the recommendation of the Security Council.~~

3. The General Assembly should, upon the recommendations of the Security Council, be empowered to suspend from the exercise of any rights or privileges of membership any member of the Organization against which preventive or enforcement action shall have been taken by the Security Council *or which in any way shall have violated the obligations of membership.* The exercise of the rights and privileges thus suspended may be restored by the decision *of the General Assembly upon recommendation* of the Security Council. The General Assembly should be empowered upon the recommendation of the Security Council to expel from the Organization any member of the Organization which persistently violates the principles contained in the Charter.

CHAPTER VI.—THE SECURITY COUNCIL

A. *Composition*

The Security Council should consist of one representative of each of eleven members of the Organization. Representatives of the United States, the United Kingdom of Great Britain and Northern Ireland, the Union of Soviet Socialist Republics, the Republic of China, and in due course, France should have permanent seats. The General Assembly should elect six States to fill the non-permanent seats. *Unless the General Assembly otherwise decides* these six States should be elected for a term of two years, three retiring each year, *and* they should not be immediately eligible for re-election. In the first election of the non-permanent members three should be chosen by the General Assembly for one-year terms and three for two-year terms.

CHAPTER VIII.—ARRANGEMENTS FOR THE MAINTENANCE OF INTERNATIONAL PEACE AND SECURITY, INCLUDING THE PREVENTION AND SUPPRESSION OF AGGRESSION.

(b) Determination of Threats to the Peace or Acts of Aggression, and Action with respect thereto

[New paragraph, 4A, proposed]

4A. (a) A decision of the Security Council involving the application of the measures contemplated in paragraphs (3) and (4) of

Chapter VIII, Section (b), shall require the concurring vote of the General Assembly, deciding by a simple majority.

(b) Nevertheless, in any case which, in the opinion of the Security Council, is of extreme urgency the Security Council may decide to apply such measures forthwith without the concurring vote of the General Assembly but in every such case it shall forthwith report its decision to the General Assembly.

(c) Every decision made in accordance with subparagraphs (a) and (b) of this paragraph shall be binding on all members of the Organization.

5. In order that all members of the Organization should contribute to the maintenance of international peace and security, they should undertake to make available to the Security Council, on its call and in accordance with a special agreement or agreements concluded ~~among themselves~~ *with it,* armed forces, facilities and assistance necessary for the purpose of maintaining international peace and security. Such agreement or agreements should govern the numbers and types of forces and the nature of the facilities and assistance to be provided. The special agreement or agreements should be negotiated as soon as possible, and should in each case be subject to approval by the Security Council and to ratification by the signatory States in accordance with their constitutional processes.

C. REGIONAL ARRANGEMENTS

1. Nothing in the Charter should preclude the existence of regional arrangements or agencies for dealing with such matters relating to the maintenance of international peace and security as are appropriate for regional action, provided such arrangements or agencies and their activities ~~are consistent with the purposes and principles of the Organization~~ *are approved by the Organization as being consistent with its purposes and principles.* The Security Council should encourage settlement of local disputes through such regional arrangements or by such regional agencies, either on the initiative of the States concerned or by reference from the Security Council.

CHAPTER IX.—ARRANGEMENTS FOR INTERNATIONAL ECONOMIC AND SOCIAL CO-OPERATION

B. *Composition and Voting*

Unless the General Assembly otherwise decides the following provisions will be in force:—

The Economic and Social Council should consist of representatives of eighteen members of the Organization. The States to be represented for this purpose should be elected by the General Assembly for terms of three years. Each such State should have one representative, who should have one vote. Decisions of the Economic and Social Council should be taken by simple majority vote of those present and voting.

D. *Organization and Procedure*

~~1. The Economic and Social Council should set up an Economic Commission, a Social Commission, and such other Commissions as may be required. These Commissions should consist of experts. There should be a permanent staff which should constitute a part of the Secretariat of the Organization.~~

~~2. The Economic and Social Council should make suitable arrangements for representatives of the specialized organizations or agencies to participate without vote in its deliberations and in those of the commissions established by it.~~

~~3. The Economic and Social Council should adopt its own rules of procedure and the method of selecting its president.~~

The Economic and Social Council may set up such subordinate bodies and make such arrangements concerning its organization and procedure as it may decide. World Organizations concerned with industry, agriculture, labour, and other subjects within the competence of the Economic and Social Council, including the International Labour Organization, and such specialized Organizations or Agencies as may be brought into relationship with the Organization, shall be represented, where appropriate, on the subordinate bodies which the Economic and Social Council may set up.

Chapter X.—The Secretariat

4. The responsibilities of the Secretary-General and staff of the Organization shall be exclusively international in character. They shall not seek or receive instructions in regard to the discharge of such responsibilities from any authority external to the Organization and shall avoid any action which might prejudice their position as international officials. The members of the Organization undertake fully to respect the international character of the responsibilities of the Secretary-General and staff and not to seek to influence any of their nationals in the discharge of such responsibilities.

5. *In appointing the staff the Secretary-General shall, subject to the paramount importance of securing the highest standards of efficiency and of technical competence, pay due regard to the importance of selecting staff recruited on as wide a geographical basis as possible.*

> United Nations Conference on International Organization, Department of External Affairs, Wellington, 1945, pp. 164-7

166. THE ANZAM DEFENCE ARRANGEMENTS

Shortly after the 1939-45 war, the United Kingdom, Australian, and New Zealand Governments made an 'arrangement' for consultation and co-operation for the defence of their interests in the South-East Asian area. No formal document was drawn up and very little information was published, but the following account was given by a New Zealand contributor to The Round Table *in a symposium of views of the Commonwealth in 1960.*

. . . An informal defence arrangement, known as ANZAM, enables the Australian, New Zealand and United Kingdom Governments to prepare plans for the defence of their interests in South-East Asia. ANZAM had its beginnings in 1946. Its headquarters are in Canberra and use is made of the Higher Australian defence organization, with the participation of United Kingdom and New Zealand staffs. New Zealand's major decision to station forces oversea in peacetime was taken within the ANZAM framework. In 1955 the three partners agreed on the value of having forces immediately available for 'fire brigade' operations, and they created a Commonwealth Far East Strategic Reserve to which all three countries contributed ground, air and naval units. While the primary rôle of this force is to constitute a mobile reserve available to meet any international emergency in the area, the three governments agreed in 1957, at the request of the newly created Malayan Government, to allow their forces to assist the Malayans in operations against the Communist terrorists in the Federation. The three governments still maintain these forces.

ANZAM has been called a Commonwealth defence arrangement, but the stationing of New Zealand troops in Malaya reflects, in part, traditional associations with the United Kingdom, since assistance in the external defence of Malaya is regarded as primarily a United Kingdom responsibility. On the other hand, New Zealand's contribution to the Strategic Reserve must also be seen as a contribution to the broader international obligations assumed by New Zealand for collective defence in the area. . . .

'A New Zealand View. A Changing Defence Pattern', *The Round Table*, London, 1960, no. 200, p. 359

167. THE ANZUS ALLIANCE

Collective Defence Treaty between Australia, New Zealand, and the United States, made in San Francisco, 1 September 1951. (New Zealand signatory, C. A. Berendsen.)

The Parties to this Treaty,

Reaffirming their faith in the purposes and principles of the Charter of the United Nations and their desire to live in peace with all peoples and all Governments, and desiring to strengthen the fabric of peace in the Pacific Area,

Noting that the United States already has arrangements pursuant to which its armed forces are stationed in the Philippines, and has armed forces and administrative responsibilities in the Ryukyus, and upon the coming into force of the Japanese Peace Treaty may also station armed forces in and about Japan to assist in the preservation of peace and security in the Japan area,

Recognizing that Australia and New Zealand as members of the British Commonwealth of Nations have military obligations outside as well as within the Pacific Area,

Desiring to declare publicly and formally their sense of unity, so that no potential aggressor could be under the illusion that any of them stand alone in the Pacific Area, and

Desiring further to coordinate their efforts for collective defense for the preservation of peace and security pending the development of a more comprehensive system of regional security in the Pacific Area,

Therefore declare and agree as follows:

Article I

The Parties undertake, as set forth in the Charter of the United Nations, to settle any international disputes in which they may be involved by peaceful means in such a manner that international peace and security and justice are not endangered and to refrain in their international relations from the threat or use of force in any manner inconsistent with the purposes of the United Nations.

Article II
In order more effectively to achieve the objective of this Treaty the Parties separately and jointly by means of continuous and effective self-help and mutual aid will maintain and develop their individual and collective capacity to resist armed attack.

Article III
The Parties will consult together whenever in the opinion of any of them the territorial integrity, political independence or security of any of the Parties is threatened in the Pacific.

Article IV
Each Party recognizes that an armed attack in the Pacific Area on any of the Parties would be dangerous to its own peace and safety and declares that it would act to meet the common danger in accordance with its constitutional processes.

Any such armed attack and all measures taken as a result thereof shall be immediately reported to the Security Council of the United Nations. Such measures shall be terminated when the Security Council has taken the measures necessary to restore and maintain international peace and security.

Article V
For the purpose of Article IV, an armed attack on any of the Parties is deemed to include an armed attack on the metropolitan territory of any of the Parties, or on the island territories under its jurisdiction in the Pacific or on its armed forces, public vessels or aircraft in the Pacific.

Article VI
This Treaty does not affect and shall not be interpreted as affecting in any way the rights and obligations of the Parties under the Charter of the United Nations or the responsibility of the United Nations for the maintenance of international peace and security.

Article VII
The Parties hereby establish a Council, consisting of their Foreign Ministers or their Deputies, to consider matters concerning the

implementation of this Treaty. The Council should be so organized as to be able to meet at any time.

Article VIII

Pending the development of a more comprehensive system of regional security in the Pacific Area and the development by the United Nations of more effective means to maintain international peace and security, the Council, established by Article VII, is authorized to maintain a consultative relationship with States, Regional Organizations, Associations of States or other authorities in the Pacific Area in a position to further the purposes of this Treaty and to contribute to the security of that Area.

Article IX

This Treaty shall be ratified by the Parties in accordance with their respective constitutional processes. The instruments of ratification shall be deposited as soon as possible with the Government of Australia, which will notify each of the other signatories of such deposit. The Treaty shall enter into force as soon as the ratifications of the signatories have been deposited.

Article X

This Treaty shall remain in force indefinitely. Any Party may cease to be a member of the Council established by Article VII one year after notice has been given to the Government of Australia, which will inform the Governments of the other Parties of the deposit of such notice.

Article XI

This Treaty in the English language shall be deposited in the archives of the Government of Australia. Duly certified copies thereof will be transmitted by that Government to the Governments of each of the other signatories.

A.J.H.R. 1952, A–13

168. SEATO

South-East Asia Collective Defence Treaty, the 'Understanding' of the United States and the Manila Protocol, signed 8 September 1954. (New Zealand signatory, T. Clifton Webb.)

The Parties to this Treaty,

Recognizing the sovereign equality of all the Parties,

Reiterating their faith in the purposes and principles set forth in the Charter of the United Nations and their desire to live in peace with all peoples and all Governments,

Reaffirming that, in accordance with the Charter of the United Nations, they uphold the principle of equal rights and self-determination of peoples, and declaring that they will earnestly strive by every peaceful means to promote self-government and to secure the independence of all countries whose peoples desire it and are able to undertake its responsibilities,

Desiring to strengthen the fabric of peace and freedom and to uphold the principles of democracy, individual liberty and the rule of law, and to promote the economic well-being and development of all peoples in the treaty area,

Intending to declare publicly and formally their sense of unity, so that any potential aggressor will appreciate that the Parties stand together in the area, and

Desiring further to coordinate their efforts for collective defense for the preservation of peace and security,

Therefore agree as follows:

Article I

The Parties undertake, as set forth in the Charter of the United Nations, to settle any international disputes in which they may be involved by peaceful means in such a manner that international peace and security and justice are not endangered, and to refrain in their international relations from the threat or use of force in any manner inconsistent with the purposes of the United Nations.

Article II

In order more effectively to achieve the objectives of this Treaty, the Parties, separately and jointly by means of continuous and effective self-help and mutual aid will maintain and develop their individual and collective capacity to resist armed attack and to prevent and counter subversive activities directed from without against their territorial integrity and political stability.

Article III

The Parties undertake to strengthen their free institutions and to cooperate with one another in the further development of economic measures, including technical assistance, designed both to promote economic progress and social well-being and to further the individual and collective efforts of governments towards these ends.

Article IV

1. Each Party recognizes that aggression by means of armed attack in the treaty area against any of the Parties or against any State or territory which the Parties by unanimous agreement may hereinafter designate, would endanger its own peace and safety, and agrees that it will in that event act to meet the common danger in accordance with its constitutional processes. Measures taken under this paragraph shall be immediately reported to the Security Council of the United Nations.

2. If, in the opinion of any of the Parties, the inviolability or the integrity of the territory or the sovereignty or political independence of any Party in the treaty area or of any other State or territory to which the provisions of paragraph 1 of this Article from time to time apply is threatened in any way other than by armed attack or is affected or threatened by any fact or situation which might endanger the peace of the area, the Parties shall consult immediately in order to agree on the measures which should be taken for the common defense.

3. It is understood that no action on the territory of any State designated by unanimous agreement under paragraph 1 of this Article or on any territory so designated shall be taken except at the invitation or with the consent of the government concerned.

Article V

The Parties hereby establish a Council, on which each of them shall be represented, to consider matters concerning the implementation of this Treaty. The Council shall provide for consultation with regard to military and any other planning as the situation obtaining in the treaty area may from time to time require. The Council shall be so organized as to be able to meet at any time.

Article VI

This Treaty does not affect and shall not be interpreted as affecting in any way the rights and obligations of any of the Parties under the Charter of the United Nations or the responsibility of the United Nations for the maintenance of international peace and security. Each Party declares that none of the international engagements now in force between it and any other of the Parties or any third party is in conflict with the provisions of this Treaty, and undertakes not to enter into any international engagement in conflict with this Treaty.

Article VII
Any other State in a position to further the objectives of this Treaty and to contribute to the security of the area may, by unanimous agreement of the Parties, be invited to accede to this Treaty. Any State so invited may become a Party to the Treaty by depositing its instrument of accession with the Government of the Republic of the Philippines. The Government of the Republic of the Philippines shall inform each of the Parties of the deposit of each such instrument of accession.

Article VIII
As used in this Treaty, the 'treaty area' is the general area of Southeast Asia, including also the entire territories of the Asian Parties, and the general area of the Southwest Pacific not including the Pacific area north of 21 degrees 30 minutes north latitude. The Parties may, by unanimous agreement, amend this Article to include within the treaty area the territory of any State acceding to this Treaty in accordance with Article VII or otherwise to change the treaty area.

Article IX
1. This Treaty shall be deposited in the archives of the Government of the Republic of the Philippines. Duly certified copies thereof shall be transmitted by that government to the other signatories.
2. The Treaty shall be ratified and its provisions carried out by the Parties in accordance with their respective constitutional processes. The instruments of ratification shall be deposited as soon as possible with the Government of the Republic of the Philippines, which shall notify all of the other signatories of such deposit.
3. The Treaty shall enter into force between the States which have ratified it as soon as the instruments of ratification of a majority of the signatories shall have been deposited, and shall come into effect with respect to each other State on the date of the deposit of its instrument of ratification.

Article X
This Treaty shall remain in force indefinitely, but any Party may cease to be a Party one year after its notice of denunciation has been given to the Government of the Republic of the Philippines, which shall inform the Governments of the other Parties of the deposit of each notice of denunciation.

Article XI

The English text of this Treaty is binding on the Parties, but when the Parties have agreed to the French text thereof and have so notified the Government of the Republic of the Philippines, the French text shall be equally authentic and binding on the Parties.

UNDERSTANDING OF THE UNITED STATES OF AMERICA

The United States of America in executing the present Treaty does so with the understanding that its recognition of the effect of aggression and armed attack and its agreement with reference thereto in Article IV, paragraph 1, apply only to communist aggression but affirms that in the event of other aggression or armed attack it will consult under the provisions of Article IV, paragraph 2.

PROTOCOL TO THE SOUTH-EAST ASIA COLLECTIVE DEFENCE TREATY
DESIGNATION OF STATES AND TERRITORY AS TO WHICH PROVISIONS OF ARTICLE IV AND ARTICLE III ARE TO BE APPLICABLE

The Parties to the Southeast Asia Collective Defense Treaty unanimously designate for the purposes of Article IV of the Treaty the States of Cambodia and Laos and the free territory under the jurisdiction of the State of Vietnam.

The Parties further agree that the above-mentioned states and territory shall be eligible in respect of the economic measures contemplated by Article III.

This Protocol shall enter into force simultaneously with the coming into force of the Treaty.

A.J.H.R., 1954, A–12, pp. 3–7

169. FORWARD DEFENCE— FROM THE MIDDLE EAST TO MALAYA, 1955

The Prime Minister, Sidney Holland speaks in the House of Representatives, 24 March 1955 on his return from the Commonwealth Prime Ministers' conference which discussed nuclear weapons and the formation of a Commonwealth Far East Strategic Reserve in Malaya.

... I find it is good to be back in one's own country after having seen so much of what is going on in other parts of the world. I repeat that it is good to be back in the country one belongs to. I was born here, and I think I understand our country. It is good to be face to face again with the old problems that existed down the years, and my trip abroad has made me appreciate more than ever the good fortune that is ours, and at the same time realize the great responsibility that is ours to ensure that the way of life that our forebears have passed on to us, the British way of life, is preserved intact so that we may hand it down to those who follow. ...

Civilization is today at the crossroads. It is threatened by international communism. Without that threat the world could, through the inventions of modern science, go on to greater heights, and the way of life now enjoyed by millions of people could be enjoyed by many more millions. I believe that without the threat of international communism the world could go on to greater progress and prosperity. We who live in this God-blessed country must all admit that there are many millions of people who lack sufficient food and sufficient clothing. All of us must strive to ensure that what we have available to us continues to be available to us. We must strive to see that the seeds of communism are not sown in other countries that may bring about our own downfall. We must all continue our work to help those people. The work that has already been done by New Zealand—not by the Government, but by New Zealand herself, out of her own resources—is bearing rich fruit in the world today.

There can be no finer conception of our duty to the world than that we should spare some of our own prosperity for distribution to other countries so that their peoples might have a fuller life than would otherwise be the case. That is our bounden duty. ...

... British policy is to work for peace, and we share that policy. Britain has forces spread round the world, and I would be less than appreciative of what Britain is doing were I not to pay my tribute to what Britain has done. We can never calculate what this has been for countries such as ours which, from their own resources, are quite incapable of defending themselves. ...

In the two previous conferences it has been my privilege to attend I suggested that it did not seem realistic that we should have our defence commitments in the Middle East when the problems of the

THE DIPLOMACY OF A SMALL STATE

area in whose defence we would be likely to be employed were so much nearer our own back door. The advice we had then ... was that because of problems in the Suez Canal area the time was not ripe for making a shift. It is not for me to pit my amateur knowledge of military matters against that of a field-marshal, so we cheerfully and gladly accepted [the C.I.G.S.'s] advice at that time. However, the position has now changed, and we are now being asked to consider whether we should switch our defence commitments from the Middle East. We have been engaged in two wars there. . . . It is almost with a feeling of regret that we leave our old battlegrounds in France and North Africa.

I say with great seriousness that we as a country can no longer operate and function as though we were observers of a world situation, quite content to call our men up and train them once war has broken out, and in the meantime leaving a great deal of the burden of maintaining peace to the Mother Country. Today, because of her exertions in the last war, Britain is hard pressed. She has her forces spread around the world, and I believe we must lend a hand and play our part. What we should do is a matter of judgment, but I believe every honourable Member would support me when I say that New Zealand is willing and anxious to play her part and to relieve to the best of her ability the disproportionate share of the burden that Britain is bearing at present.

If people will consult a map they will realize that the troubled area in the world—from Korea, to Japan, Formosa, Indo-China, Indonesia—is a succession of steps in the direction of New Zealand, and about the last place we can make a stand without coming into our own territory is Malaya. So the Government asked me to stop in Malaya, . . . have a look at the situation, and bring back recommendations about what was the best thing to do in the light of the advice I had been receiving in London. Whatever plans we have . . . we must try to do two things. First of all we must earn the help and support of other people if the security of this country is to be assured. We must earn the support of Britain by pulling our weight in the British boat. That is a British thing to do. We have always done it, and now Britain has spoken to us, and we have consulted her, and she have given us a plan that I believe is within our reach and our capacity. Not only must we justify help from Britain by being prepared to pull our weight in the British boat, but also we must earn the active support of the United States by demonstrating to her that we are prepared to play our part in our own defence. . . .

I believe that the emphasis in world affairs is shifting from Europe into the Pacific because we have been so strong in Europe, and the Russians acknowledge strength and scorn weakness. I believe that whoever wins Germany wins Western Europe, and that whoever wins Japan has a jolly good chance of winning the Pacific. We ought to think of what we can do for that country. I do not say that we can do anything, but we should at least study the things that we might do, and if we do study them we may be able to do something. We cannot have 86,000,000 Japanese locked up in that little island and refuse to trade with them. There are things they can supply that we need, and I hope that at some future conference we can give further consideration to the problem of Japan. We might hold out the right hand of fellowship and let the Japanese know that we want their friendship and are prepared to do something about it. . . .

We should never for one moment forget that if we go to war everything we have in the world is at stake. War may descend upon us, but we will never seek it, of course. When we enter into fresh obligations we must not overlook our existing obligation to the Mother Country to produce foodstuffs in ever increasing quantities. In our enthusiasm we must be careful that we do not weaken our economy or our ability to carry out that particular obligation. We must bear in mind that we have a comparatively small population with which we must continue to produce food in large quantities, and at the same time discharge our defence obligations.

In reply to my question as to how we could help the United Kingdom in the light of the changed strategy brought about by the hydrogen bomb, we were asked to revise our programme and to switch our existing commitments from the Middle East to the Pacific. By this means we can shorten our communication lines, and from every point of view the change is to be commended. That change was recommended by the United Kingdom Government. I am free to say that that Government will cancel the Middle East commitments so far as they concern us, and will then ask us if we will agree to shift our commitments to the Pacific area. I have recommended to the Government that that course be adopted. That change will involve obligations, and it would be unwise for me to go into them in detail as to the extent of the forces that will be available in the event of a global war. I have recommended raising one infantry division with accompanying armour, artillery, and the other ancillary units. . . .

. . . Because of the greatly increased importance of South-East Asia and because of the changed situation in international affairs, I think it is necessary that New Zealand should have closer links with that part of the world. All of us would acknowledge gratefully what Britain has done for us up to the present in this matter of representation. She has maintained very large and expensive establishments which have provided us with all the information Britain gets, and we have been charged nothing whatever for it.

I think the time has come when we are sufficiently grown up to undertake a little of our own diplomatic work, working alongside the United Kingdom. The Minister of Defence and I have therefore recommended to Cabinet that New Zealand have representation in that area. What will be the quality of our representation has not yet been decided, except that it will be good. We do not know yet whether we shall have an Ambassador or a Commissioner. There are certain forms to be observed in having a British representative in another British country. One does not have an Ambassador in such a case. In the case of a foreign country, however, we could have ambassadorial representation. The question has arisen as to whether we should have diplomatic representation or trading representation. While in Bangkok, the Minister of External Affairs, with the full approval of our Government, agreed that we should play our part and be a member of the SEATO Committee, which has its headquarters in Bangkok. We think at the moment that we should have our headquarters in Singapore, but have a special representative seconded for duty in Bangkok to enable us to carry out the undertaking given by the Minister of External Affairs that we would be represented on the SEATO Committee. . . .

We have been invited to undertake this time a very special duty, and that is to form what you might term a cold war front in Malaya, the idea being to ensure that an enemy that wants to indulge in infiltration and subversion is going to be stopped before he gets here. We are going to help Britain draw that line in a British country. We cannot go into anybody else's country to do it, and if you have a look at the map you will see that Malaya is the last place where we can do it. In Korea our men have brought great distinction to our country. As an old artilleryman, I suppose I take natural pride in the fact that a regiment of artillerymen was selected to do that service in Korea. In this instance, we are not being asked for the same service because of the change in the type of warfare, type of training, and type of campaigning. . . .

N.Z.P.D., 1955, vol. 305, pp. 11–26

170. THE SUEZ CRISIS, 1956

The Prime Minister, Sidney Holland speaks in the House of Representatives, 7 August 1956.

. . . Not one word was said about it at the [Commonwealth] Conference. There was no thought of this crisis developing. Today I think we are facing a grave crisis with grave possibilities. It is characteristic of the world political scene that a crisis arises almost overnight, without any warning, and a matter of hours alters the whole outlook of nations towards events and towards policy. . . . I was asked for our immediate reaction, and I at one cabled the Right Hon. Mr. Holyoake and the Cabinet what I had been told and suggested the answer that we should send. I was able to tell Sir Anthony Eden and Mr. Selwyn Lloyd that Britain could count on New Zealand standing by her through thick and thin. I am sure the House will applaud that announcement, as I am sure that we will not allow these people to get away with this. It was a very great man who coined the sentence, 'Where Britain stands, we stand'. I have said many times that we on this side of the House adopt that. I believe that that is the mood of the people of New Zealand. Where Britain stands, we stand; where she goes, we go, in good times and bad. . . .

. . . The Suez Canal is vital to Britain, and Britain is vital to New Zealand. Where she is in difficulty, we are in difficulty, and the Western world is in difficulty if Britain is not to have a free flow of her ships through this vital international waterway. . . .

. . . I am confident that the United Kingdom Government's decision to call a conference to see if some ways and means can be found of settling this problem peacefully is a right one. I do not think it is unfair to anybody to say there are some nations in the world that appreciate a show of strength, and in the problems of Cyprus and these other places I am sure the British have taken the proper course in their assembling of certain forces. I am confident, too, that New Zealand and her people will support the decision to stand as partners with the United Kingdom in this problem. The natural question arises, What does our support involve? I am not prepared at this stage to go further than to say that that means exactly what it says. . . .

N.Z.P.D., 1956, vol. 309, pp. 889–90

171. A MILITARY CONTRIBUTION IN VIETNAM, 1965

The Prime Minister, Keith Jacka Holyoake speaks in the House of Representatives, 28 May 1965.

Sir, I move, *That this House, conscious of the threat to free peoples everywhere posed by the armed Communist campaign, directed, supported, and supplied from North Vietnam, to overthrow the Republic of Vietnam, reaffirms its belief in the principle of collective security; recognises that the defence of the Republic of Vietnam cannot at the present time be carried out by the United Nations or any force drawn from a group of nations acceptable to the parties involved in the struggle; commends the Government's decision to contribute an artillery unit to assist in the defence of the Republic of Vietnam; supports the search for a negotiated settlement in Vietnam which would uphold the rights of the people of South Vietnam; and supports the initiative of the United States Government in offering $1,000 million for an expanded cooperative economic programme for South-East Asia.*

The Government's decision in this matter is perhaps the most significant taken, in this sphere at least, by any Government in New Zealand since 1950, when we made a decision very similar to this to assist South Korea in its efforts to defend itself against Communist aggression from the north. The circumstances are very similar, and, extraordinarily enough, the offer of armed forces from New Zealand is almost the same except that we sent a considerably larger artillery unit to Korea than we propose to send to South Vietnam. I remind the House that when I went to the SEATO conference in Manila last year I called at Saigon on my way home, and the Prime Minister of South Vietnam asked me for military assistance under the South-East Asia Treaty Organisation. After some discussion he suggested that the best form of assistance would be military engineers for reconstruction. The Government of New Zealand decided to do that, and we gave that assistance. I have today laid upon the table of the House copies of letters which have passed between the present Prime Minister of South Vietnam and myself, and the Prime Minister of South Vietnam has now asked for combatant military aid. The question, of course, is whether we should respond to that call for aid. The Government has decided, as it has a constitutional responsibility to do, to respond to that call. Briefly I would remind members, if they need reminding, of a classic example in our time when a country called in vain for aid. I refer to Czechoslovakia. Many of us, unwisely as history has shown, were willing to follow the fatal path of appeasement in the hope that that would be the solution, but the holocaust of World War II was the result. We realised then—and I hope we have not forgotten the terribleness—that we cannot escape that kind of cataclysm by turning away from our duty to oppose aggression wherever it occurs before it is too late. . . .

The critical issue, and naturally the one which deeply concerns the Government, members of Parliament, and everyone in the country, is why it should be necessary to make a military contribution in Vietnam. Most of the reasons have been stated. Only a few days ago I made a statement to the country on radio and television and in the newspapers, but I suppose I should restate to the House and the country the fundamental facts upon which the Government has made its decision. They come under seven heads. The first is that the Government must be always concerned with the security of the people of New Zealand, both short term and long term. I underline those words 'both short term and long term'. The second fact that confronted us was that New Zealand's first line of defence is in South-East Asia. This has been recognised, accepted, and acted upon by successive Governments in New Zealand. We have entered into treaties to that end, and they have been continued by successive Governments. The third fact is that the war in Vietnam is not a civil war or a popular uprising, as some people would claim. It is ruthless Communist aggression directed and supplied by Communist North Vietnam and openly encouraged, supported and partly supplied by Communist China. The fourth fact is that the South Vietnamese are fighting for their freedom and liberty. They have half a million men in their army and local defence forces fighting against Communist aggression. The fifth fact is that events in Vietnam threaten New Zealand just as much as events in Malaysia, and indeed at this stage probably more so. The sixth fact is that the New Zealand Government has a fervent wish to bring about a peaceful settlement which will guarantee the territorial integrity of South Vietnam and of the neighbouring countries in that area. The seventh and final act upon which the Government made its decision was that until North Vietnam and its instrument, the Vietcong forces, discontinued their aggression, and gave evidence of their readiness to enter into negotiations and to accept a peaceful settlement, the independence of the people of South Vietnam must be safeguarded. It cannot be safeguarded with words. At present it can be done only by military means. There is no other way of safeguarding the freedom and liberty of South Vietnam. . . .

. . . I am bound to say that, with their usual facility for twisting the meaning of words, the Communists have called this, as they have called so many other similar forays, a war of national liberation. It is a very nice-sounding term, but it is simply naked aggression. It is simply an attempt to impose by force one more Communist dictatorship upon another country in Asia—in this case South Vietnam. It has been said that, because of its commitment to defend Malaysia, New Zealand should not diffuse its military effort by sending troops to Vietnam as well. The decision to help Vietnam in the way I have announced, by sending an artillery battery, will not reduce our ability to maintain our force in Malaysia. We have not been asked at any time for artillery forces in Malaysia, and at this moment I cannot see a role for them. In any case it is being quite blind to realities if we conveniently divide South-East Asia into separate packets and say we will help here but not there.

It is often said that peace is indivisible. It is certainly indivisible in this area, which is under attack from a number of points. . . .

Another point I wish to make is that the Government's decision conforms to our treaty obligations. I have not time to go into detail, but only a few weeks ago members will have read that the SEATO Council, meeting in London, urged that the member States should continue, and, consistent with their commitments elsewhere, should increase, their efforts in South Vietnam. Surely that is clear enough. The Government's decision is also in accord with the Charter of the United Nations, which recognises the right of members to take collective action for self-defence. This can be spelt out by other speakers in greater detail. I want to say here that in the light of our treaty obligations, in the light of our obligations to the United Nations, and in the light particularly of the failure of the United Nations peacekeeping efforts, this Government, and I believe the people of New Zealand, will not shrink from their responsibilities. We must, I believe, range ourselves with our American and Australian allies. . . .

. . . A vote in favour of this motion means, quite apart from the protection of our own New Zealand interests, that we are still concerned about the fate of small countries threatened by aggression. It means that we believe in the right of all men to choose their own form of government, free from external interference. A vote for this motion also means that we are prepared to back up our beliefs with action. A vote against this motion would mean paying lip service to these principles and that we are not prepared to defend them. It would be saying that we leave the defence of these principles to others. This Government is determined to demonstrate that we are prepared to act in defence of our principles.

N.Z.P.D., 1965, vol. 342, pp. 7–11

172. COLLECTIVE SECURITY IN SOUTH-EAST ASIA

The Review of Defence Policy, *1966, which outlined the chief objectives of defence policy and the general method of approaching them. A threat to the stability of South-East Asia, by Communist China acting as an 'exporter of revolution' is outlined and New Zealand's role accepted. In return, home security is also placed fundamentally upon collective defence arrangements.*

GENERAL BASIS OF DEFENCE PLANNING

. . . 6. The present *Review* is based on the belief that the New Zealand people, while supporting international efforts towards disarmament and the settlement of outstanding East–West differences by negotiation wherever possible, will continue to reject 'neutralism' or 'isolationism' as an acceptable basis of national policy. From the time it started to take an active interest in international affairs New Zealand has striven to uphold what it believes to be right, and to oppose—at times at great sacrifice—what it believes to be wrong. To seek now to stand aside from the great issues that confront us would be foreign to our character and tradition, and dangerous to our long-term security. Post-war Governments have accepted that New Zealand must be concerned with the security and stability of South-East Asia, that there is a Communist threat to this area, and that the best way of countering the threat is through collective defence arrangements. Although we cannot ignore the steadily growing danger of proliferation of nuclear weapons, and modern means of delivering them, among countries which may not be well-disposed towards Western interests, the Government believes that its decision not to acquire a military nuclear capability reflects the will of the New Zealand people.

7. The creation and maintenance of defence forces and a defence potential in New Zealand are related to support of broad national objectives. Some of these objectives are relatively fixed because they reflect unchanging basic factors (our resources, our geographical remoteness, our dependence on overseas trade), but others are the products of history or circumstances and need to be reconsidered from time to time. The more substantial objectives in relation to national security include:

(a) To preserve the security, national interests and independence of New Zealand, and the island territories for which it is responsible:

(b) To help maintain the stability and security of New Zealand's allies and other friendly countries:

(c) To provide material backing to New Zealand political efforts to preserve peace and to make collective defence, whether through the United Nations or through regional arrangements, as effective as possible, thereby increasing the security of New Zealand:

(d) To establish a claim upon our major allies for consultation, a voice in important decisions, and in the last resort, and most importantly, military assistance and protection in time of need. This requires New Zealand to demonstrate willingness to make an appropriate degree of national defensive effort, and willingness and ability to assist our allies in matters affecting *their* national interests.

8. Specifically, the size and nature of the New Zealand forces should be related to the following missions:

(a) Maintaining an ability to deploy in the area immediately around New Zealand and in the South Pacific, forces to deal with situations affecting New Zealand's interests for which our allies would expect New Zealand to assume primary responsibility:

(b) Contributing to the protection of sea and air communications vital to New Zealand:

(c) Maintaining an ability to contribute in time of war to the fullest extent possible towards the collective defence of the friendly countries of the areas of primary strategic importance to New Zealand:

(d) Contributing forces as appropriate to assist the United Nations, our partners in defence arrangements, and other friendly countries, in situations short of large-scale hostilities where the presence or use of restricted forces is required:

(e) Contributing to the general deterrent effect of Western forces in keeping the peace and/or preventing escalation. . . .

13. The strategic assessment undertaken in the course of preparing this review makes it clear that South-East Asia will continue to be a disturbed and unstable area up to 1970, and indeed throughout the seventies. Attempts to expand by force the area of Communist influence or control in South-East Asia represent a threat to New Zealand's national interests. This threat does not stem from a direct menace to New Zealand's own territory by Communist Chinese forces, at this time at least, but from Communist China's active role, as the 'exporter of revolution' throughout the area. There is likely to be a general slow deterioration in stability and security over the period which could lead to increasing New Zealand involvement in the military as well as the political problems of the area. In certain situations, such as the massive confrontation between Communist and Western supported forces in South Vietnam, it is possible that hostilities involving New Zealand and her allies could be on a scale requiring a major effort on our part. . . .

HOME DEFENCE

15. The defence of New Zealand itself in the most unlikely event of invasion or nuclear missile attack could not be ensured by New Zealand's own efforts, and our security rests fundamentally on the collective defence arrangements in which New Zealand participates. Nevertheless, New Zealand must continue to make some basic provisions for its own defence against any possible threats.

The presence in New Zealand of forces whose primary task is to fight abroad will provide some continuing ability to deal with situations arising in the immediate area of New Zealand. Any requirements for home defence can be met within present defence arrangements. The main provisions likely to be required for defence of the New Zealand area to 1970 are surveillance and the maintenance or establishment of anti-submarine and mine-clearing capabilities. . . .

A.J.H.R., 1966, A–8, pp. 5–6, 8–9

173. BRITAIN'S WITHDRAWAL FROM EAST OF SUEZ

The announcement that Britain would withdraw its forces from East of Suez, except Hong Kong, by 1971, was seen by Keith Holyoake, in his Report of the Department of External Affairs, 31 March 1968, as a time for reconsidering foreign policy. Relations with Australia and the United States are given greater significance.

. . . Britain's impending withdrawal marks for New Zealand a time for reappraisal of its international position, almost as profound as that made necessary by the fall of Singapore in 1942. It makes necessary a searching re-examination of New Zealand's policies in South-East Asia, so many of which have depended for their full effect on their being carried out in close association with Britain. It gives new emphasis to the trend towards closer relations and co-operation with Australia that has become so conspicuous and essential a feature of our recent international activity. It increases the importance of New Zealand's relationship with the United States. And it changes the perspective within which the broad pattern of New Zealand's continuing ties with Britain must now be examined.

It is impossible, at this point, to indicate what the outcome will be of this far reaching appraisal. I am satisfied that the policies which New Zealand has pursued in South-East Asia during the past 20 years have not only been soundly based but at every point (with the exception of Vietnam where opinion has been more divided) have had the support and approval of the vast majority of New Zealanders. I have no doubt that these policies served New Zealand's interests well and I am in no way convinced that the alternatives of non-alignment or a self serving neutrality would at any point in that period have been a valid, realistic, or honourable response to the situations with which New Zealand was confronted. Whatever directions our future policies may take (and clearly these will be affected by the British decision) the principles which have underlain our varied activities in South-East Asia stand still as sound guidelines to the future.

Of our future relations with Australia, I would say simply that closer association between us is inevitable and welcome. We enjoy the advantages of long-standing friendship, similar backgrounds, and a record of shared endeavour; the foundations of understanding and co-operation between us are as favourable as could be found between any two countries on earth. There are many fields in which we both have much to gain from working together and in the past year leaders of both countries have declared their determination to do so. This is all that the situation confronting us requires.

I expect our relations with the United States also to assume new range and meaning. With the reduction of Britain's presence and influence in South-East Asia and the Pacific region, the ANZUS Pact has even greater significance for New Zealand than before, and the need increases for wider contact and understanding with the United States. This is not a prospect over which we need hesitate. The United States is a great power and New Zealand is a small one. But our relations have always rested securely on the basis of the sovereign equality between us. . . .

A.J.H.R., 1968, A–1, p. 5

174. AN ANZAC FORCE IN SINGAPORE AND MALAYSIA AFTER 1971

On 25 February 1969 Keith Holyoake, the Prime Minister, and John Gorton, the Australian Prime Minister, announced that an ANZAC force would remain stationed in Malaysia and Singapore after the British withdrawal scheduled for 1971. In an address to the New Zealand Institute of International Affairs on 6 March 1969, Holyoake gave some of the reasons for this decision and rejected recently mooted alternative policies.

. . . I want to talk today about our national security policy, the broad range of national activities designed to promote and protect the security, stability, and well-being of New Zealand.

In the past too many people have ignored the issues and pretended that there was no problem. They have been content because they believed that New Zealand was tagging along behind Britain and that this was the obvious—the 'loyal'—thing to do. This attitude is clearly irrelevant today, and has been irrelevant for years. . . .

An analysis of our national security policy must begin with some geography and some history. For 100 years, New Zealand's relationship with Britain enabled us to evade the full implications of our geographical position. But, more recently, as the relationship has changed we have had to come to terms with geography. New Zealand does not consist of a few islands somewhere off the coast of Britain. We look north on to the Pacific Ocean. We have many important goals—of national policy—a life of satisfaction and expanding opportunity for our people, greater trade, and so on. But our first concern must be security because it is on this that the achievement of our other goals directly depends. We are concerned with the security of our nation, of the region in which we live, and of the world at large.

. . . What we have done in South-east Asia has involved a broad national effort; it has been developed over a comparatively long period of our history; it has been imposed by the logic of our national situation; and it has so far served us well. . . . In the new situation emerging today, will our basic policies continue to be sound and in the national interest? . . .

In the short term, we still foresee no direct threat of attack in the area immediately around New Zealand and we believe that, if we and others follow sound policies in the Pacific Islands, there need be no instability there that will cause tension or difficulty. Moreover, looking to the longer term, provided reasonably sound conditions can be created in East Asia, we see no reason to believe that there will be any direct threat to New Zealand independent of a threat to other countries in the region. . . .

In East Asia one great problem is the role of Communist China: . . .

It is in South-east Asia, divided and with some vulnerable weakness, that there may be room for an enlargement of area of influence. Any trend of this sort would pose a long term threat to Australia, and to New Zealand. In the short term, it would carry the danger of instability and of hostilities.

It is for these reasons that our defence interest has come to be focused primarily on South-east Asia.

. . . The basic approach behind our consideration of what forces from any service we should have in the area after 1971 has been the belief that we have an interest and a role. The main argument in favour of the deployment of forces forward—the ready availability of trained and acclimatised forces for 'fire brigade' action—is still valid and will remain valid for as far ahead as we need foresee. . . .

For these reasons I believe that a policy of collective defence and of defence cooperation makes good sense and deserves our support.

Some disagree and set forward several, quite different, objections.

One argument is that it is quite unnecessary. We hear people say: 'Communist China isn't expansionist; besides it doesn't matter what happens in South-east Asia, we'll be all right; certainly, we shouldn't face any direct threat for a few years, so let's keep our heads down and hope to be ignored.' I don't find this convincing. . . .

Another argument is that it is 'immoral' to 'choose' someone else's territory in which to defend oneself. We never have and never shall. We did not 'choose'. . . . The question was not whether we chose to defend ourselves in other people's territory rather than our own, but whether we chose to ignore an attack on others. I don't see anything very moral about deciding that we will ignore what happens to others in the hope that it won't matter to us.

Another argument is that our defence policy should consist solely of aid and trade, that aid and trade are the best form of defence. It is argued that we shall store up goodwill for New Zealand and attack the real root of security problems. . . . Aid alone is not constructive defence: it is valuable in its own right, but it is not defence.

Some have advocated a policy of non-alignment or neutralism: a policy of remaining free from defence obligations. But, if we are free of defence obligations to others, others are free of defence obligations to us. . . . We have felt the need of friends before and we may again. Moreover, we do not see any wisdom in trying to huddle down in Fortress New Zealand or even Fortress Australasia and ignore the rest of the world. To me, it makes greater sense to take a part in helping shape events. . . . Neutralism or non-alignment as a policy suits some countries whose background and position are different from our own: but we are not a Switzerland or a Sweden. I do not want to see a Swiss or Swedish policy for New Zealand. I want to see a New Zealand policy.

Others want a qualified alignment. What that means, I'm not sure. I suspect it means they welcome a United States obligation to us, but don't want to have any obligation in return. They really want a one-sided ANZUS Treaty, a free ride, with the right to criticise the driver. If you want to criticise the driver, you need to pay your share of the costs of the journey.

Others have suggested we should look to the United Nations for our defence and devote all our support to it. New Zealand is second to none in its support for the United Nations. But there is no point in pretending that the Organisation can do things that in fact it cannot, or arguing that we can help build the United Nations into an effective security body by renouncing our readiness to help others in case of need. . . .

Some have voiced concern that, by joining collective defence arrangements, we lost our independence or our independent judgement, that we are inevitably 'committed' by other people's actions. . . . I must say I find it odd that some people, in the one breath, can dismiss the ANZUS or Manila treaty as useless because it doesn't really commit the United States to help us and objectionable because it commits us inescapably. . . . A good ally is not subservient: he has judgement and a voice, and uses them; but he is also prepared to take up his share of the burden. Our voice can be all the more effective by having an accepted place with our close friends, rather than sitting on the side lines. To take our share of the burden does not diminish our national independence: it is a mark of independent policy. . . .

. . . The main policy lines are clear. In our judgement, the logic of our position points to a policy of defence cooperation and of a readiness to play a part in South-east Asia. New Zealand—indeed Australia and New Zealand together—cannot take the British role in South-east Asia. There is no reason why we should. We can take a New Zealand role. It will be one of close cooperation with countries in the area and with countries interested in the security of the area. We are not writing a blank cheque guarantee for other people's security, but we are prepared to make a contribution to regional security. . . .

The Dominion, Wellington, 7 March 1969, pp. 15–18

8

SOME POLITICAL LANDMARKS
SINCE 1940

---

175. THE NATIONAL PARTY'S 1943 PLATFORM

The New Zealand National Party's programme for post-war social improvement. Although it lays emphasis on the role of 'competitive free enterprise' as against 'state interference' and bureaucracy, the party called for progressive policies and accepted many aspects of the welfare state.

The New Zealand National Party . . .

is a nation-wide political organisation offering the people of New Zealand the only practical alternative to the present Socialist Government. . . .

HOUSING

Since the true basis of national life is happy family life in the people's own homes, the National Party focuses its whole policy on the objectives of the greatest possible number of people having homes of their own. A housing plan surpassing in magnitude and type anything hitherto attempted in New Zealand is envisaged. . . .

—25,000 extra men to be employed in full-time employment for ten years building homes for the people.

—Restoration of private house building.

—The freehold for everyone who wants it, but rental houses for those who prefer that method.

—90% of the cost, and 100% if necessary, in the case of servicemen, found by the Government, in co-operation with Building Societies and local bodies. . . .

—State tenants to have the right to acquire the Freehold.

—Entirely new scheme of training house builders. . . .

—State mortgages to provide for regular payments of principal. . . .

TRADE AND COMMERCE

New Zealand's highly-developed system of trade and commerce

functions best when given the greatest measure of freedom from State interference. . . .
—Competitive free enterprise to be restored.
—Liberty of the subject to be reinstated. Bureaucratic dictation to cease.

INDUSTRIAL RELATIONS

There can be no real progress in industry without harmony, goodwill and understanding between the employer, with his capital and organisation, on the one hand, and the worker, with his skill and craftsmanship on the other. Fair play must be the keynote of industrial relations, the interests of the workers and the employer being inseparable. The workers' right to collective bargaining, and the legitimate need for industrial unions of employers and workers, are fully recognised.
—Profit-sharing and schemes of co-partnership, payment by results, co-operation and other systems to increase efficiency and workers' pay, to be promted and encouraged. . . .
—Compulsory Arbitration to be re-introduced.
—Workers' Compensation laws to be brought up-to-date.
—Compulsory or voluntary unionism to be decided by secret ballot of workers.
—Compulsory levies on union members for party political purposes to be made unlawful.
—Paid holidays for workers.
—Preference for unionists. . . .

THE PRIMARY PRODUCER

To maintain and improve New Zealand's standard of living, we must have a large population of successful, free and independent farmers. The conditions of life, and financial returns from farming. for farm workers as well as farm owners, must compare favourably with other occupations.
—Producer-control of production and marketing in co-operation with Government.
—Guaranteed minimum prices for farm produce, with ceiling prices determined by the producers themselves.
—Maintenance reserves to remove taxation injustices.
—Scientific and financial assistance in establishing new primary industries.
—Overseas Trade Commissioners to promote sales. . . .

MANUFACTURING INDUSTRIES

New Zealand factories and workmen have shown themselves adaptable and capable of producing a wide variety of goods. As the principal means of absorbing our manpower, manufacturing must be fully supported and encouraged. Natural resources must be developed and our climate, soil, and water-power utilised for increased production.

—Full protection against low living standard countries.

—Preference for N.Z.-made goods.

—Bureau of scientific co-operation.

—Special encouragement in establishing industries using New Zealand materials.

—Freedom from State interference. . . .

LAND SETTLEMENT

. . . Isolation must be reduced to a minimum and up-to-date educational, health, postal and transport services must be made available. In settling people on the land, the guiding principle must be settlement at the productive value and no more. . . .

—Settlers will be placed under the supervision of local Advisory Committees, composed of practical farmers.

—They will be given the option of either Freehold or Leasehold. . . .

—Any costs of development above the productive value will become a charge on the community as a whole, and not on the individual farmer. The aim will be to stabilise land values at prices based on productive values. . . .

—Roads, electric power, transport, education and health services will be considered essential to the actual development work, and not left till after the settlers are in possession. . . .

THE MOTHERS OF CHILDREN

The National Party has a special appreciation of the important part played in the national life by the mothers of our children, and will expand our social services to aid the nation's mothers.

The causes that result in small families must as far as possible be removed. Amongst the chief of these is the difficulty of obtaining suitable help in the home.

—Home help training centres to be established.

—Corps of trained home helpers to be organised.

—Special assistance during sickness, holidays, and confinement.

—Work saving appliances to be free of duty, surtax, etc.

—Cheap electricity for the home and special aid in reticulating remote districts.

—Improved telephone, medical, educational, travel and mail services.

—Cheap train services to towns.

—Boarding allowances to be liberalised.

—Kindergartens and creches to be extended.

—Plunket Society to be further assisted to help the child more adequately from birth to school age, when it will be transferred to care of School Medical Service. . . .

COST OF LIVING

The cost of living is unreasonably high and essential goods are in unnecessarily short supply. To correct this, decisive measures are necessary.

—Internal Marketing Department to be abolished.

—Freedom for the small trader.

—Goods the public want, not what the Government decides.

—Competition, which means lower prices and better quality. . . .

PUBLIC WORKS

Public Works are essential for future development but should not be used merely as 'relief' jobs. Construction of roads and other means of communication must precede other development.

—More hydro-electric power stations.

—Completion of unfinished railway lines.

—Irrigation in suitable districts. . . .

EDUCATION

The nation's greatest asset is its children, who must be given every opportunity to develop their talents. Emphasis will be laid on the development of the moral qualities which are the basis of good citizenship.

—Free education from kindergarten to University.

—Equal facilities for Maori and pakeha, with separate Native schools where required in predominantly Maori centres of population.

—Medical examination of each child twice a year, an X-ray examination at least once a year, and corrective treatment for any weakness disclosed.

—Free education for servicemen and women during and after the war.

—National scholarships and bursaries, supplementing provision already made.

—Specialist teachers in games and physical training.

—Health camps and hostels in approved localities to accommodate all children who require corrective treatment.

—Unification of controlling bodies.

—Right of appeal against non-appointments to be given to teachers.

—Adequate boarding allowances for children obliged to attend school away from home.

—School leaving age to be raised.

—Love of country and Empire to be fostered among school children. . . .

QUESTIONS OF THE DAY

Social Security: All existing benefits will be continued, and anomalies and injustices will be removed.

Wages: The National Party pledges itself not to cut wages or pensions.

Unionism: The workers themselves will decide whether unionism shall be compulsory or voluntary.

Parliament: Outside domination of Parliament shall cease.

Freedom for M.P.'s: Every National Party Member of Parliament shall be free to vote on every question according to his consciece.

> *Election Manifesto,* New Zealand National Party, 1943

176. THE NATIONAL PARTY'S 1943 PLATFORM

Favourable editorial comment on the new National programme in the Christchurch Press, *30 August 1943, which stresses the central role of the proposed housing improvements.*

. . . In summary, the policy declares every citizen's right to steady, useful, well paid work in good conditions; accepts the task of renovating the avoidable causes of want in unemployment and sickness; and upholds the idea of a community whose free wellbeing shall be based on the prosperity and health of the family unit. These are broad principles and general aims. . . .

To begin with, the elector's attention should be directed to two or three prominent planks. First, the National Party offers a housing policy of courageous scope, calling for the addition of 25,000 workers to the building trade during a 10-year period and for training schemes that will recruit this skilled labour force. It should not be overlooked that this plan is designed to make full co-operative use of the resources of private enterprise, from the builder to the building society; to encourage ownership, while serving the demand for rental houses also; and to be vigorously developed not only in urban but in rural areas. This is a link, second, with the National Party's scheme for rural development, and a vital link. The decision to bring rural standards in housing, social services, and public utilities to a level of advantage fairly comparable with those of the towns is a wise and timely one. The future of primary production in New Zealand depends as much on social as on economic policy in rural communities. The economic measures will fail, or fall short, unless the social ones support and complete them: a fact which the National Party recognises, not merely in this general decision to correct the disparity which is the prime cause of urban drift, but in the form of the settlement plans, for servicemen and others.

Housing, again, in the third place is linked with the party's various projects to strengthen family life and ease its burdens. It is essential . . . to abolish the squalid conditions in which too many New Zealanders are obliged to live. There must be slum clearance. There must be decent homes for all. But 'for all' is a phrase that looks forward to a greater population and to the conditions which will produce and maintain it in security. Housing policy, therefore, falls into place in plans to 'remove the economic causes of a low birthrate', to relieve wives and mothers by organising a trained domestic service corps, to ease the financial burdens of the family, to extend the kindergarten and creche system, and to bring every child, from the pre-natal to the final school stage, under continuous and effective medical care. . . .

. . . The National Party is to be congratulated on asserting its claim to lead the Dominion in a new, broad-fronted social advance. It was bound to suffer still from the reaction of 1935, until it found the courage of a faith more active and more productive than mere antagonism to bureaucratic socialism, less open to practical contradiction than the mere protest against the overthrow of old, rugged individualism and initiative. . . .

The Press, Christchurch, 30 August 1943, p. 4

177. MAORI SOCIAL AND ECONOMIC ADVANCEMENT ACT, 1945

Although the Labour Party formed an alliance with Wiremu Ratana in 1935 and by 1943 the four Maori seats in Parliament were held by Ratana–Labour members, little change could be made in government policies because of the urgency of depression, and then wartime problems. In 1945 a comprehensive Act reorganized the Maori Councils and repealed the 1900 Act and seven subsequent pieces of legislation.

An Act to make provision for the social and economic advancement and the promotion and maintenance of the health and general well-being of the Maori community. [*7 December 1945.*]

. . . 4. Welfare Officers.—For the purposes of this Act there shall from time to time be appointed as officers of the Public Service (whether as permanent or temporary officers) . . . a Controller and such Welfare Officers as may be necessary. . . .

5. General duties of Controller and Welfare Officers.—(1) It shall be the duty of the Controller to advise and assist the Tribal Executives and the Tribal Committees. . . .

Tribal Executives

6. Tribal districts.—(1) The Governor-General may from time to time by Proclamation declare any part or parts of New Zealand to be a tribal district. . . .

7. Tribal Executive Committees.—(1) In every tribal district there shall be a Tribal Executive Committee (hereinafter referred to as a Tribal Executive). . . .

8. Constitution of Tribal Executives.—(1) Every Tribal Executive shall consist of—

(*a*) Two representatives of each Tribal Committee (as hereinafter constituted under this Act) within the tribal district, who shall be appointed by the Minister upon the recommendation of the Tribal Committees of which they are members (hereinafter referred to as elected members):

(*b*) A Welfare Officer who shall be appointed as a member by the Minister. . . .

11. Maori Wardens.—(1) For the purposes of this Act the Minister may from time to time appoint as Maori Wardens for the whole or any part of a tribal district one or more persons who shall be Maoris. . . .

12. General functions of Tribal Executives.—The general functions of a Tribal Executive shall be, in relation to the Maoris within its district,—

(a) To promote, encourage, guide, and assist members of the Maori race,—

(i) To conserve, improve, advance, and maintain their physical, economic, industrial, educational, social, moral, and spiritual well-being;

(ii) To assume and maintain self-dependence, thrift, pride of race, and such conduct as will be conducive to their general health and economic well-being;

(iii) To accept and maintain the full rights, privileges, and responsibilities of citizenship;

(iv) To apply and maintain the maximum possible efficiency and responsibility in their local self-government and undertakings; and

(v) To preserve, revive, and maintain the teaching of Maori arts, crafts, language, genealogy, and history in order to perpetuate Maori culture:

(c) To collaborate with and assist the Education Department and any educational institutions in the vocational guidance and training of Maori children:

(d) To co-operate with and assist all State Departments, local bodies, associations, institutions, clubs, trustees of [Maori] reservations, incorporated or unincorporated bodies, or any person or persons in connection with any matter or question arising out of or pertaining to the well-being of the Maori race or any member thereof:

(g) To make such recommendations to the Minister on any matter affecting the well-being of the Maori race as it shall deem fit. . . .

District Conference

13. District Conference.—(1) Where it appears to the Minister that any matter or question affecting or relating to the well-being of any tribe or allied tribes, or affecting or relating to the exercise of the powers and authorities conferred by this Act ought to be the subject of consideration or review by two or more Tribal Executives, he may require such Tribal Executives to appoint one or more delegates to meet in conference. . . .

Tribal Committees
14. Tribal Committee areas.—(1) The Minister may from time to time, by notice published in the *Gazette*, declare any part or parts of a tribal district to be a Tribal Committee area.

15. Tribal Committees.—(1) In every Tribal Committee area there shall be a Tribal Committee which shall consist of—

(a) Not less than five and not more than eleven persons (hereinafter referred to as elected members) who shall be representative of the tribes or tribal groups within the Tribal Committee area and who shall be elected every two years at a general meeting of the Maori residents within such area held for the purpose:

(b) A Welfare Officer who shall be appointed as a member by the Minister. . . .

19. General functions of Tribal Committees.—(1) A Tribal Committee shall have the same general functions as a Tribal Executive appointed under this Act, save so far as those functions are functions which can be performed by a Tribal Executive only. . . .

21. Maori villages.—(1) A Tribal Committee may, from time to time, define the boundaries of any kainga, village, or pa situated within the Tribal Committee area, and declare the kainga, village, or pa to be a Maori village for the purposes of this Act. . . .

32. Powers as to water and sanitation.—(1) A Tribal Executive may within any part of its district establish, install, carry out, and administer any scheme of works having for its object the supply of water or the provision of sanitation for Maoris, and, if the Tribal Executive thinks fit, for such other persons as can be conveniently supplied. . . .

34. Subject matter of bylaws.—A Tribal Executive may from time to time make in relation to its district such bylaws as it thinks fit for all or any of the following purposes: . . .

[the health and personal convenience and comfort of Maoris, cleansing of dwellings, preventing and abating nuisances, prevention of trespass by cattle, horses, sheep, protection of Maori meeting houses, protection of recreation grounds, licensing of billiard rooms, prevention of gambling, regulating the sale of goods, regulation and control of Maori meetings, regulating traffic, protection of Maori burial grounds.]

39. Prevention of drunkenness.—A Maori Warden may at any

reasonable time enter any licensed premises . . . and warn the licensee or any servant of the licensee to abstain from selling or supplying liquor to any Maori who in the opinion of the Warden is in a state of intoxication, or is violent, quarrelsome, or disorderly, or is likely to become so, whether intoxicated or not, and if the licensee or any servant of the licensee thereafter on the same day supplies liquor to the Maori, the licensee, and, if the servant had been warned by the Warden, the servant, shall be liable to a fine not exceeding twenty pounds. . . .

40. Maori may be ordered to leave hotel.—(1) A Maori Warden may at any reasonable time enter any licensed premises. . . . and order any Maori who in the opinion of the Warden is intoxicated or partly intoxicated, or is violent, quarrelsome, or disorderly, whether intoxicated or not, to leave the premises. . . .

43. Manufacture of liquor in Maori villages.—Any person, whether a Maori or not, who, in any Maori village, manufactures any intoxicating liquor commits an offence and shall be liable to a fine not exceeding twenty-five pounds or to imprisonment for a term not exceeding one month. . . .

47. Imposition of penalties by Tribal Committees.—(1) Subject to any direction to the contrary by the Tribal Executive for the district, it shall be the duty of each Tribal Committee to investigate all breaches of any bylaws under this Act committed in the Maori village or villages in the Tribal Committee area.

(2) If a Committee is satisfied that any such breach . . . has been committed, it may authorize proceedings to be taken in a summary manner under the Justices of the Peace Act 1927 in respect of the offence or it may, in its discretion, impose on the offender a penalty in respect thereof of such amount as it thinks fit, not exceeding the maximum penalty prescribed by or under this Act or a sum of five pounds, whichever is the less. . . .

New Zealand Statutes, 1945, no. 43, 9 Geo. VI,
pp. 379–402

178. THE NATIONAL PARTY AND PRIVATE ENTERPRISE

In 1946, in an illustrated pamphlet, S. G. Holland the party leader outlines 'his philosophy that modern industry is in effect a partnership between the employer and the worker'. He warns of the danger *of inflation, illustrating his point with pictures of German postage stamps in the 1930s with face values of millions of marks.*

TODAY there are two competing philosophies: Socialism on the one hand and private enterprise on the other. . . .

The socialist thinks that more goods will be produced by using his methods, i.e., State control, import restrictions, licensed industries, commandeer of produce, very high taxation; by destroying initiative and incentive, by destroying the profit system, by wiping out competitors of the State; by licenses, coupons, rationing and constant filling in of forms, permits for nearly everything, AND BY BRIBING THE TAX-PAYERS WITH THEIR OWN MONEY in the shape of State payments; by wiping out competition at every turn and by establishing monopolies, and finally by shorter hours for more pay. They believe the more civil servants you have the better. . . .

Thousands and thousands of people are now realising that these things cannot continue indefinitely. Thousands of people are aware of where complete National Socialism led Germany and the world to. Thousands of people know that social security, a very worthy thing in itself, can only continue out of the earnings of the people. Thousands of people cheerfully gave up their freedom to help win the war, but they don't want these restrictions, this loss of freedom, this constant dictation by the State, this constant increase in the cost of living, this steadily growing burden of taxation. . . .

It is perhaps only natural, but it is very, very true that the more people run to the Government for this and that, the more will the Government want to run us. Thousands of workers realise that their welfare depends on steady, worth-while creative employment, and they know that if taxation is going to take all the employer's profit, then the boss will not be bothered expanding and giving more employment and more wages.

With these thoughts in mind, many thousands of people, including many who were hard hit during the depression and turned towards Labour, seeking any port in a storm, are now satisfied that Labour and its socialistic doctrine will not give them what they want. They see, as the only alternative, the National Party, practically a brand new team since the depression days. . . .

New Zealand's economy is following a vicious circle. . . . Mr. Holland shows how heavy taxation is giving the worker a sense of frustration. . . .

The Scene: A New Zealand boot and shoe factory.

Working Hours: 44 per week.

Average Wages: £5. 10s. per week (2s. 6d. per hour).

Output per week: 1000 pairs.

Average Retail Price: 25s. per pair.

THE UNION SECRETARY: We are applying for a 40-hour week.

THE WORKER: That will reduce my wages by 10s. per week (four hours at 2s. 6d.).

SECRETARY: We have told the Government wages must not be reduced.

WORKER: That sounds fine.

One Month Later:
The works foreman reports to the general manager:
Factory output: 909 pairs per week.
Wages the same.
Overhead the same.
Costs up 10 per cent.
Price Tribunal authorises increase.
Retail price now 27s. 6d. per pair.

The worker's wife requires shoes for the children. She has the same money in her husband's pay envelope. Prices are up 10 per cent—she is worse off. To pay for the children's shoes the increased cost must come from something else she wanted.

WORKER TO UNION SECRETARY:
'Look here, by wife says she is worse off—same amount of money but higher living costs.'

SECRETARY TO WORKER: 'My wife says the same, so we are going for a new award and more wages.'
And so the vicious circle goes on.

THE PUBLIC: When is this crazy thing going to stop?

ANSWER: When we have profit-sharing, which gives more goods and shorter hours, and lower taxes to provide incentive for more work.

But wait. There's a nigger in the woodpile. Just as it is unreasonable to expect the worker to work harder and produce more if the 'boss' is to get all the benefits, it is equally unreasonable to expect the worker to work harder and earn more if Mr. Nash is going to take too large a share in taxes. . . .

> S. G. Holland, *Talking Things Over*, New Zealand National Party pamphlet, 1946, pp. 6–7, 29

179. STABILIZATION IN PEACETIME

In December 1942, after various attempts to prevent inflation, the Government introduced a comprehensive stabilization scheme to hold down all prices, farm returns and costs, transport charges and costs, wages, and rent. A Stabilization Commission was established and the keystone of the whole operation was the 'Wartime Prices Index'. New Zealand stabilized its economy more successfully than its major allies, but by 1948 socialists argued that it merely maintained the status quo *in a capitalist economy.*

No one will deny that unrest is widespread throughout New Zealand.

FARMERS have ceased to vote for the Government which rescued them from certain ruin;

MANUFACTURERS, whose very existence has been the result of the Government policy of import control, join in the opposition.

TRADERS AND SHOPKEEPERS do likewise, despite the fact that the Government money policy has, until this year, enabled them to sell all the goods which they can lay their hands upon.

But among the 550,000 WAGE AND SALARY EARNERS, unrest is the most marked. Real wages reached their peak in 1938. Since then, total money wages have risen at the most by 80 per cent. It is widely believed that prices have overtaken and outstripped them. Going hand in hand with the confusion among the workers has been the gradual loss of vitality in the Labour Party itself.

No policy, in a single field, is responsible for this state of affairs, but the keystone of all the policies is STABILIZATION.

SOCIALISM

Broadly, Socialism implies the social ownership and control of the significant means of production as distinct from their private ownership. . . .

THE CLASS STRUGGLE

The class struggle is an over-riding fact. It is the fight waged between social classes to better their respective economic and social positions—a struggle in which all classes co-operate and compete one with another at the one time. Labour co-operates with capital to produce goods and services—Labour fights with capital to wrest a larger share of the product.

The struggle of the workers for socialism is part of the class struggle. . . .

STABILIZATION

Critical war time circumstances made some such policy as Stabilization vitally necessary. Had it not been introduced, not only would our war effort have been undermined but anarchy arising from the inevitable price crisis would have resulted. Nevertheless, economic stabilization does mean the buttressing of the existing forms of economic and social organization—whether these are just or unjust. Technically, the policy of stabilization is aimed at the most efficient operation of existing institutions—not at changing them. . . . What has to be decided is whether the policy of economic regulation is strengthening capitalism or promoting progress to Socialism. . . .

. . . Clearly, the worker's slice of the cake is dwindling.

To sum up the money income position of the workers:

Of the total of aggregate private incomes, £185 m. in 1939, the wage and salary earners received £109 millions. In 1947/8 their share by the most liberal estimate is £200 m. out of a total of £360 million.

Even on this estimate, the workers' share in 1939 was 59 per cent. as compared with only 56 per cent. today.

Putting it another way, the wage and salary earners have achieved an aggregate increase of 80 per cent., whereas the propertied classes have gone ahead by 110 per cent. . . .

THE FINAL SCORE

Here is the final score:—

(1) Stabilisation has entrenched and extended the ownership of wealth—land, money, shares, factories, capital—by the three propertied classes, the farmers, manufacturers and traders;

(2) Stabilisation has enabled the scales of money income to be tipped in favour of the three propertied classes as against wage and salary earners and pensioners;

(3) Stabilisation has enabled the scales of *real income* to be tipped violently in favour of the propertied classes at the expense of the workers;

(4) Stabilisation has involved policy retreats from planned marketing (e.g., The Dairy Commission) and the abandonment of subsidies;

(5) Stabilisation has proved itself a conservative policy, the negation of a real Labour policy. . . .

IV. WHAT MUST BE DONE

EMERGENCY MEASURES

These, five in number, are all designed to give immediate relief to wage and salary earners and pensioners. They are:—

(1) Legislate for a further substantial general wage increase to restore the 1939 purchasing power of wage and salary earners and at the same time combat the incipient domestic trade recession which is a reflection of the declining real purchasing power of the workers.

(2) Institute a deliberate profit control policy to ensure that manufacturers and traders filch none of the purchasing power conferred on the workers by the general wage increase.

(3) Ease the burden of income tax on the breadliner and the family man by lifting the exemption maximum from £200 to £300, thus further influencing purchasing power in favour of the wage and salary earners. . . .

(4) Appreciate the N.Z. pound to parity or near parity with sterling (and in future maintain at least the current exchange relationship to the dollar), thereby obliging the farmers to draw on their stabilisation reserves to maintain farm incomes.
. . .

(5) Do something drastic about housing (a) by fixing maximum rentals for rooms of different kinds, having regard to class of room, floor space and quality; (b) by fixing maximum rentals for furniture per room and per house; and (c) by confining state house tenancies to breadliner wage and salary earners and pensioners. . . .

MID-RANGE MEASURES

These, still ignoring schemes of an Utopian Socialist kind, include measures which a socialistically-minded Government could and should at least embark upon within the next two or three years. . . .

(6) Reverse the trend towards large-scale private accumulation of wealth (a) by revising the tax system so as to put a steeply graduated tax on personal wealth . . . as well as on income. . . .

(7) Set out consciously to combine the manpower, material and money resources of the country. . . .

(8) Limit net profits to a percentage of the shareholder's equity. . . .

(9) Control investment. . . .

(10) Pursue a definite policy of control of land use and land ownership. . . .

(11) Initiate a concrete industrial policy aimed at eliminating inefficient backyard manufactories. . . .

(12) Rationalise distribution by the development of state wholesaling, using Public Import Corporations, and by the encouragement of retail co-operatives. . . .

(13) Socialize finance by nationalizing remaining banks and financial houses. . . .

(14) Extend social services and social security benefits on the basis of doing more for those who need it and less for those who don't. . . .

(15) Inasmuch as the foundation of Socialism is the sovereignty of the organized society in question over the use of its own human, material and financial resources, repudiate Bretton Woods and I.T.O. both of which are schemes aiming at the integration of all countries into a single world production, trading and financial system dominated by capitalist market forces. A capitalist free trade world renders Socialist planning in a single country futile. . . .

> *Stabilization or Socialization? A Controversy between a Study Group and Ormond Wilson M.P. and A. M. Finlay M.P.*, New Zealand Fabian Society Pamphlet no. 1, 1948, pp. 3, 7, 22, 26–8, 40–1

180. NATIONAL SERVICE IN PEACETIME

In the later years of the Labour Government, after the 1939–45 war, fear of Communist expansion overseas made New Zealand Labour leaders increasingly alarmed. On his return from the 1948 Commonwealth Prime Ministers' Meetings in London, the Prime Minister, Peter Fraser, determined to introduce National Service in New Zealand. A report entitled 'Defence of New Zealand' was accepted by caucus on 21 May 1949, but when presented to the

Annual Conference met opposition to its National Service clause, which was amended by Fraser in favour of a referendum on compulsory National Service.

THAT the Conference approves that full provision be made by the Government for—

(1) the adequate and efficient defence of New Zealand, including the Pacific area necessary to the maintenance of the defence of New Zealand;

(2) the maximum contribution possible to the defence of the British Commonwealth with which the destiny of New Zealand is wholly and completely bound up.

TOWARDS these ends the Conference—

(3) requests the Government to use all the resources of the country, including compulsory national service, if the Government, after exploring all possibilities and alternatives, is convinced that such a measure is essential for the defence and preservation of our people, our country and our Commonwealth;

(4) considers that these proposals shall be placed on the policy platform of the Party for the General Election. . . .

[Moved by Fraser, seconded by Forsyth. An amendment immediately proposed.]

Amendment.—A. B. Grant (Christchurch Bricklayers' Union) moved, and J. Roberts (Canterbury Clothing Trades' Union) seconded:—

That Clause 3 be deleted and the following substituted: 'Reasserts its opposition to conscription in peace; and in war reasserts its support for equal conscription of wealth and manpower. . . .

After the lunch adjournment . . . the Prime Minister, [Fraser] asked leave to amend Clause (3) as follows: 'Requests that Government to use all resources of the country essential for the defence and preservation of our people, our country, and our Commonwealth, and that if the resources are not available without compulsory National Service, the Government be requested to obtain the views of the electors on the question by a referendum'.

The amendment was accepted and the previous amendment withdrawn.

New Zealand Labour Party, Report of the Thirty-third Annual Conference, Wellington, 1949, pp. 19–20

181. THE WATERFRONT STRIKE EMERGENCY REGULATIONS, 1951

Order in Council under the Public Safety Conservation Act of 1932 giving the Government very extensive emergency powers.

(a) THE EMERGENCY REGULATIONS

PURSUANT to the Public Safety Conservation Act, 1932, there being a Proclamation of Emergency now in force under that Act, His Excellency the Governor-General, acting by and with the advice and consent of the Executive Council, doth hereby make the following regulations. . . .

MINISTER MAY DECLARE STRIKES TO WHICH THESE REGULATIONS APPLY

3. If in respect of any strike the Minister is satisfied that it has caused or is likely to cause serious loss or inconvenience and that it has been brought about (whether before or after the commencement of these regulations) wholly or partly by any union or by any member or members of a union, the Minister, by notice in the *Gazette*, may require the union to end the strike within a time specified in that behalf in the notice, and may declare that if the strike is not ended within that time it shall be a strike to which these regulations apply.

OFFENCES

4. Every person commits an offence against these regulations who—

(a) Is a party to a declared strike; or

(b) Encourages or procures a declared strike or the continuance of a declared strike; or

(c) Incites any person or any class of persons or persons in general to be or to continue to be a party or parties to a declared strike; or

(d) Prints or publishes any statement, advertisement, or other matter that constitutes an offence against these regulations, or that is intended or likely to encourage, procure, incite, aid, or abet a declared strike or the continuance of a declared strike, or that is a report of any such statement made by any other person.

5. If any member of any union or of any branch of a union is a party to a declared strike every officer of the union or of that

branch shall be deemed to have encouraged or procured the continuance of the strike unless he proves that he counselled the members of the union or branch to discontinue the strike and that he did not encourage or procure the continuance of the strike or incite any person or any class of persons or persons in general to be or to continue to be a party or parties to the strike.

6. (1) Every union commits an offence against these regulations—

(a) If at any time not less than 20 per cent of the members of the union or not less than 20 per cent of the members of any branch of the union are parties to a declared strike:

(b) If any officer of the union commits an offence against these regulations.

(2) Where any union commits an offence against these regulations every officer of the union shall be deemed also to have committed the offence unless he proves that the offence occurred without his knowledge or that he did everything in his power to prevent the commission of the offence.

APPOINTMENT OF RECEIVER

7. (1) If the Minister is satisfied that any members of any union or of any branch of a union are parties to a declared strike, the Minister may appoint a Receiver of the funds of the union or branch. . . .

(4) For the purpose of exercising his functions any Receiver appointed under this regulation may from time to time—

(a) Require any person to deliver to the Receiver or as he directs any funds, books, accounts, vouchers, records, or documents of the union or branch. . . .

CONTRIBUTIONS IN AID OF STRIKE

8. Every person commits an offence against these regulations who—

(a) Makes any payment or contribution to any union while any of the members of the union or of any branch of the union are parties to a declared strike:

(b) Makes any payment or contribution to any branch of a union while any of the members of that branch are parties to a declared strike:

(c) Makes any payment or contribution to or for the benefit of any workers who are parties to a declared strike.

SUSPENSION OF ORDERS AND AWARDS

9. (1) If the Minister is satisfied that any members of any union are parties to a declared strike, the Minister may, by order in writing, suspend in whole or in part all or any of the provisions of any award, industrial agreement, or other agreement. . . .

ARMED FORCES

10. (1) The appropriate Service Board may from time to time by order authorize the temporary employment of members of the New Zealand Naval Forces, or the New Zealand Army, or the Royal New Zealand Air Force, as the case may be, in any kind of work specified in the order. . . .

CONTROL OF ADMISSION TO WHARVES

11. (1) Any constable may direct any person not to enter or remain upon any wharf or loiter in the vicinity of any entrance to a wharf. . . .

COUNSELLING STRIKE, ETC.

12. (1) Every person commits an offence against these regulations who—

(a) Compels, counsels, procures, or induces, or attempts to compel, procure, or induce, or does any act or thing that would be likely to compel, procure, or induce any other person to do any act to which this regulation applies:

(b) Attends at or near any premises or place where any other person resides or works or proposes to work for the purpose of compelling, counselling, procuring, or inducing, or for the purpose of attempting to compel, counsel, procure, or induce, or in such a manner as would be likely to compel, procure, or induce that other person to do any act to which this regulation applies:

(c) Is found by a constable attending at or near any premises or place where any other person resides or works or proposes to work, and fails to satisfy that constable that his attendance is not an offence against this regulation. . . .

THREATS

13. (1) Every person commits an offence against these regulations who uses, either orally or in writing, any threatening, intimidatory, offensive, or insulting words to another person or to the wife, child, or parent of another person for the purpose of procuring that other person to do any act to which regulation 12 hereof applies or

on account of that other person refusing or failing to do any such act.

(2) Every person who commits an offence under this regulation may be arrested without warrant by any constable. . . .

PICKETING

14. (1) Where the presence of any person on any road or street, land, premises, or place is, in the opinion of a constable, intended or likely to influence any other person—

(a) To do any act that would constitute an offence against these regulations; or

(b) To refrain from or to cease working in any employment or doing any work,—

that constable may give to the first mentioned person such oral directions as the constable considers necessary in the circumstances, including a direction to remove himself forthwith from the road or street, land, premises, or place where he then is or both a direction so to remove himself and a direction to remain at such distance from the road or street, land, premises, or place as may be specified by the constable. . . .

UNLAWFUL DISPLAY OF POSTERS, ETC.

15. (1) Every person commits an offence against these regulations who—

(a) Carries or displays, or drives or causes to be driven any vehicle carrying or displaying, or affixes in any place where it is in sight of any other person, any banner, placard, sign, or other thing which contains any words to which this regulation applies; or

(b) Writes or prints or displays, or causes to be written or printed or displayed, on any vehicle, wall, fence, erection, road, street, or footway, or otherwise within sight of any other person, any words to which this regulation applies. . . .

POWER OF ENTRY

18. Any member of the Police Force who is of or above the rank of sergeant may enter at any time, using force if necessary, and with such assistance as he may deem necessary, into or upon any land, premises, or place—

(a) In the exercise of or for the purpose of exercising any power conferred upon members of the Police Force by these regulations. . . .

429

(b) THE WATERFRONT STRIKE NOTICE 1951

Pursuant to the Waterfront Strike Emergency Regulations 1951, the Minister of Labour, being satisfied that the strike now existing in the waterfront industry has caused and is likely to cause serious loss and inconvenience and that it has been brought about by members of the New Zealand Waterside Workers' Industrial Union of Workers, hereby gives notice as follows. . . .

3. The union is hereby required to end the strike not later than 8 a.m. on Monday, the 26th day of February, 1951.

4. If the strike is not ended at or before the time specified in clause 3 hereof, it shall from that time be a strike to which the Waterfront Strike Regulations 1951 apply.

(c) THE NEW ZEALAND WATERSIDE WORKERS' UNION CANCELLATION NOTICE 1951

Whereas in respect of discontinuances of employment by members of the New Zealand Waterside Workers' Industrial Union of Workers the Minister of Labour is satisfied that the discontinuances have caused and are likely to cause serious loss and inconvenience and that they have been brought about wholly or partly by those members:

Now, therefore, pursuant to section 2 of the Industrial Conciliation and Arbitration Amendment Act, 1939, the Minister of Labour hereby gives notice as follows:—

1. (1) This notice may be cited as the New Zealand Waterside Workers' Union Cancellation Notice 1951. . . .

2. The registration of the New Zealand Waterside Workers' Industrial Union of Workers is hereby cancelled.

> New Zealand Gazette, 1951, nos. 24, 25, and 26, pp. 65–75

182. THE WATERSIDE DISPUTE, 1951

An illegal leaflet of the New Zealand Waterside Workers' Union, which charges that the waterfront dispute is a Lock-out.

WATERSIDERS CALL ON ALL WORKERS!
OUR WAGES FIGHT IS YOUR FIGHT!

The Holland Government's plans to attack the 40-hour week, drag living standards to the bread-line and smash unionism, are out in the open.

Watersiders have been locked out as a test case. If the employers can weaken this strong union they intend to pick off the rest—one by one.

Workers! The watersiders and their allies stand between you and a vicious employers' Government. Here are the facts:

Less than the Court Gave.

The Arbitration Court's decision was denounced by every union in the country including the F.O.L. Yet the shipowners final offer to the watersiders was LESS than the Court increase. They said we could live on overtime.

Since we were penalised for working long hours we offered to work 40 hours until they would re-open negotiations—and we still do. They refused to negotiate or let us work.

In Hitler's Steps

To keep our case from the public and take the next step in condition-smashing the Government brought in fascist-like emergency regulations.

But no emergency existed. We were PREVENTED from working. It's all a pretext for moving in on the workers—first us, and then you.

Intimidation Fails.

The watersiders are determined their wives and children shall receive a fair share of life's necessities.

Tens of thousands of other workers—miners and freezing-workers, seamen, hydro workers, cool store and harbour board workers—are on strike to help us defend living standards and trade union rights. Thousands more won't touch scab goods.

The issue is clear: Help us win or help Holland bring Tory misery to our fair land.

Handle No Scab Goods !

Beware Press and Radio Lies !

United We Must Win !

Dick Scott, *151 days*, Auckland, 1954, p. 22

183. THE 1951 STRIKE AND THE GENERAL ELECTION

Opening his electoral campaign with a speech in the Theatre Royal, Christchurch, on 13 August 1951, the Prime Minister, Sidney

Holland, alleged that the waterfront strike had been part of a communist conspiracy.

... I will remind you of facts that cannot be disputed. ... A group, determined, unscrupulous and powerful in the sense of their position in key industries, schemed and contrived to overthrow our system of industrial management. Many of them obviously owed no allegiance to New Zealand and were indifferent concerning Empire welfare. Many of them saw virtues in the Russian system. By clever scheming and devoted to a cause they got themselves key positions in vital industries.

Their objective was to replace the rule of law with the rule of force. With meticulous care, following the now familiar Communist pattern, they launched their demands. They believed that no Government could possibly hold out. Fortunately New Zealand had a Government which had entirely other views.

The unscrupulous wreckers received much encouragement from those who play their game and from responsible people who are neither for nor against this Communist-inspired conspiracy. Let us not forget that many countries have been overthrown because of the same carelessness to the welfare of the people.

Mr. Nash broke with the Federation of Labour rather than break with the Trade Union Congress which stood for the defiance of law and order, and for direct action and force. All that has been done can be lost if we elect a Government that is weak and is neither for nor against the conspiracy. ...

This strike has taught us some valuable lessons. Those of us behind the scenes have had our eyes opened, and we sought this earliest opportunity of coming before the people who have the opportunity of electing a Government that will govern the land.

Communism is ever so much stronger in New Zealand than any of us ever imagined. Communism is strong, powerful and determined. It it is not handled firmly it will prosper, grow and finally overthrow us. Its underground is firmly established and this strike was merely an opportunity for a try-out.

We will discharge our duty of strengthening our laws against sabotage and intimidation.

I am not drawing on my imagination when I say that the wreckers will try again if they think they have a Government which they think they can line up. Mr. Nash will say he can't be lined up ...

I believe that if Labour is elected the old waterfront leaders will be back in their old places. I believe we would see a return to the old system and the days of pay without work, and the old inefficiency. What we have won at such terrific cost would be lost. . . .

We must go ahead and complete the task. We must root out this underground of Communism from its hiding-place. . . .

The Press, Christchurch, 14 August 1951, p. 6

184. THE ELECTORAL ACT, 1956

Section 189 which restricts the repeal or amendment of six of the earlier sections except by a majority of 75 per cent of the House of Representatives or a majority in a poll of all electors. The section itself, however, could be repealed by an ordinary parliamentary majority.

. . . 189. Restriction on amendment or repeal of certain provisions—
(1) This section applies to the following provisions of this Act (hereinafter referred to as reserved provisions), namely:

(a) Section twelve, relating to the duration of the House of Representatives:

(b) Section fifteen, relating to the Representation Commission:

(c) Section sixteen, and the definition of the term 'European population' in subsection one of section two, relating to the division of New Zealand into European electorates after each census:

(d) Section seventeen, relating to the allowance for the adjustment of the quota:

(e) Subsection one of section thirty-nine, and the definition of the term 'adult' in subsection one of section two, and paragraph (e) of section ninety-nine, so far as those provisions prescribe twenty-one years as the minimum age for persons qualified to be registered as electors or to vote:

(f) Section one hundred and six, relating to the method of voting.

(2) No reserved provision shall be repealed or amended unless the proposal for the amendment or repeal—

(a) Is passed by a majority of seventy-five per cent of all the members of the House of Representatives; or (*b*) Has been carried by a majority of the valid votes cast at a poll of the electors of the European and Maori electoral districts:

Provided that this section shall not apply to the repeal of any reserved provision by a consolidating Act in which that provision is re-enacted without amendment and this section is re-enacted without amendment so as to apply to that provision as re-enacted. . . .

New Zealand Statutes, 1956, no. 107, p. 1253

185. THE 'BLACK BUDGET' 1958

In his Budget speech, 26 June 1958, the Labour Minister of Finance, Arnold Nordmeyer, increased taxes in order to reduce demand for imports, encourage local manufacturing and conserve overseas exchange, at the same time as fulfilling an election pledge to increase social security payments. The Christchurch Star-Sun *called this giving with one hand and taking with the other.*

(a) From Mr Nordmeyer's speech, 26 June 1958.

Since the last Budget 11 months ago the returns from our exports have fallen unexpectedly and considerably. This fall will, for so long as it continues, retard the phenomenal progress achieved in many productive fields since the war which ended some 13 years ago.

The object of the Government's financial and economic proposals, some of which I shall announce tonight, is to ensure that any reduction in living standards arising from lower overseas prices for our exports is spread fairly throughout the community without hardship or unemployment. If the situation which has developed internally is handled with firmness it is likely that our standard of living will remain high—not as high as it might have been if export prices had been maintained at the level of the last few years, but still higher than that enjoyed by most other countries.

Tonight's Budget will announce increases in taxation over a broad field. It will indicate the method by which, and the source from which, the guaranteed price for butterfat will be financed. It will reveal the Government's programme for implementing its election policy concerning social security and other matters. . . . The present internal situation requires some measure of restraint if inflation is to be avoided and economic stability maintained. The measure and duration of such restraint will depend upon the course of events overseas—particularly the price received for our exports.

A fundamental objective of Government policy is the maintenance of full employment. In this field New Zealand has an enviable record in the post-war years. The Government does not subscribe to the view, widely held, that full employment is not possible without inflation. Nor does it believe that a measure of unemployment is necessary for the maintenance of a healthy economy. The Government will therefore strive to ensure that the country is protected from recurrence of unemployment such as has occurred in past periods as a consequence of falling demand for our export products.

To safeguard employment it is essential that we maintain solvency in our external transactions. Disruption of local industry would be the inevitable outcome of inability to import sufficient raw materials and equipment.

It will be the Government's aim to maintain stability by avoiding both inflation and deflation. . . .

N.Z.P.D., 1968, vol. 316, pp. 276–81

(b) Unfavourable editorial comment.

Mr Nordmeyer is out to get his £100 income tax rebate back at a rate that would raise a blush to the cheek of the most blatant usurer. His taxation proposals in his first Budget are almost vindictive in their harshness—a rise in income tax of 33⅓ per cent; dearer beer, petrol, cigarettes, and cars; hire purchase restricted; higher death duties; a raid on the expansion savings of companies; taxes on dividends which mean double taxation in many cases; and farm special depreciation withdrawn.

On the other hand he intends to raise Social Security benefits; allow beneficiaries to earn more; increase the family allowance by 5s. a child a week; and increase universal superannuation.

Let it be said right away—the increases to the less fortunate members of the community will be more than eaten up by the increases in the cost of living that must come from Mr Nordmeyer's Budget. . . .

In every way, it is the little man who will have to pay the Budget bills. . . .

The 1958 Budget proves how easy it is to overcome the embarrassment of election promises. Give with one hand and take away a lot more with the other. And keep on taking it, for the Budget makes it clear that Mr Nordmeyer does not regard his new measures as temporary. . . .

The Christchurch Star-Sun, 27 June 1958, p. 2

186. MAORI AFFAIRS—THE HUNN REPORT, 1960

In an attempt to make a statistical stocktaking of Maori affairs J. K. Hunn, deputy chairman of the Public Service Commission, was appointed Acting Secretary for Maori Affairs and Maori Trustee on 18 January 1960. His report, 24 August 1960, suggested that a future policy relating to the Maoris had never been defined but that integration was occurring by a process of evolution.

RACIAL POLICY

7. What precisely is New Zealand's policy for the future of the Maori race? The answer is elusive because nowhere is it defined— neither by statute nor by resolution of the Board of Maori Affairs. Remiss as this may seem, it is probably deliberate and wise. It recognises that evolution will take its course and pay scant attention to statutory formulas. Official policy can accelerate or retard but not thwart or divert the process of self-determination. Evolution governs policy, not *vice versa*. This will be the lesson of South Africa's attempt to force a policy of apartheid on an unwilling people.

8. Evolution is clearly integrating Maori and pakeha. Consequently 'integration' is said to be the official policy whenever the question is asked. In theory, the alternatives are assimilation, integration, segregation, and symbiosis, which terms are intended to mean:

Assimilation: To become absorbed, blended, amalgamated, with complete loss of Maori culture.

Integration: To combine (not fuse) the Maori and pakeha elements to form one nation wherein Maori culture remains distinct.

Segregation: To enforce a theoretical concept of 'apartheid'. One school of thought in New Zealand advocates 'parallel development', which in essence is segregation under another name.

Symbiosis: To have two dissimilar peoples living together but as separate entities with the smaller deriving sustenance from the

436

larger (seemingly an attempt to integrate and segregate at the same time).

The Swiss (French, Italians, Germans) appear to be an integrated society; the British (Celts, Britons, Hibernians, Danes, Anglo-Saxons, Normans) are an assimilated society. In the course of centuries, Britain passed through integration to assimilation. Signs are not wanting that that may be the destiny of the two races in New Zealand in the distant future.

9. Meanwhile integration, without benefit of statutory definition, is the obvious trend and also the conventional expression of policy. Integration, as stated, implies some continuation of Maori culture. Much of it, though, has already departed and only the fittest elements (worthiest of preservation) have survived the onset of civilisation. Language, arts and crafts, and the institutions of the marae are the chief relics. Only the Maoris themselves can decide whether these features of their ancient life are, in fact, to be kept alive; and, in the final analysis, it is entirely a matter of individual choice. Every Maori who can no longer speak the language, perform the haka or poi, or take his place on the marae, makes it just so much harder for these remnants of Maori culture to be perpetuated.

10. When the first Europeans arrived in New Zealand about A.D. 1800, the Maoris were in much the same condition as the Ancient Britons at the time of the Roman invasion in 55 B.C. In the short century and a half since then, many Maoris have overtaken the pakeha lead and adopted the 1960 pattern of living in every way. A few others, the slowest moving members of the race, have probably not yet passed the 1860 mark. There is at least a century of difference between the most advanced and the most retarded Maoris in their adjustment to modern life. The Maoris today could be broadly classified in three groups:

A. A completely detribalised minority whose Maoritanga is only vestigial.
B. The main body of Maoris, pretty much at home in either society, who like to partake of both (an ambivalence, however, that causes psychological stress to some of them).
C. Another minority complacently living a backward life in primitive conditions.

The object of policy should presumably be to eliminate Group C by raising it to Group B, and to leave it to the personal choice of Group B members whether they stay there or join Group A—in other words, whether they remain 'integrated' or become 'assimilated'. But the methods of reaching this objective have to be flexible enough to cater for diverse types of case in divers ways. No single prescription can administer to the needs of a people who differ individually between such wide extremes. Variform policies are required, especially in such matters as housing; otherwise social conflict may be generated both in the individual personality and in the mixed community.

11. Here and there are Maoris who resent the pressure brought to bear on them to conform to what they regard as the pakeha mode of life. It is not, in fact, a *pakeha* but a *modern* way of life, common to advanced people (Japanese, for example)—not merely white people—in all parts of the world. Indeed some white people, everywhere, are not able to make the grade. Full realisation of this fact might induce the hesitant or reluctant Maoris to fall into line more readily.

12. The problem for the Maori people and their advisers is not one of destination or route, but of pace. That alone is problem enough because the rearguard, if left to go their own gait, soon fall behind into a world of their own that provokes all the frictions of coexistence. . . .

A.J.H.R., 1960, G–10, pp. 14–16

187. RACIAL INTEGRATION

The Hunn Report of 1960 suggested that integration of the races, however ill-defined, was 'the obvious trend and also the conventional expression of policy'. In 1962 the Department of Maori Affairs in its pamphlet Integration of Maori and Pakeha *considered the question 'What is meant by Integration?' and also suggested certain guiding principles.*

That both Maori and pakeha must, in fact, become more closely integrated has been generally accepted. This is inevitable as contacts increase. . . .

WHAT IS MEANT BY INTEGRATION

We speak of the 'integration' of Maori and pakeha as a desirable aim, but this term has been used with such a variety of meanings by different writers that it needs clear definition if it is to be of use. As used here, integration denotes a dynamic process by which

Maori and pakeha are being drawn closer together, in the physical sense of the mingling of the two populations as well as in the mental and cultural senses, where differences are gradually diminishing. Remembering that the dictionary definition of the verb 'to integrate' is 'to make whole' we regard the integration of Maori and pakeha as the making of a whole new culture by the combination and adaptation of the two pre-existing cultures. . . . If, in the past, it has been the Maori who has had to accommodate himself to pakeha values, the position has now been reached in some places where, if the boot is not on the other foot, at least both feet are shod and more pakehas are recognising the part they have to play in closing the gap between the two cultural groups.

In a more fundamental sense, integration is something that has to occur on a purely personal level. Elements of both cultures (using 'culture' in its widest sense) must be harmonised within the personality of each individual who has a foothold, however small, in both Maori and pakeha worlds. For some, this will be a major achievement; for others, a minor adjustment. Integration does not imply social uniformity, but rather a unification arrived at personally by each individual of a range of cultural elements derived from both Polynesian and European cultures.

A well integrated, racially-mixed community would be composed largely of people who have achieved a cultural balance suitable to their particular environment and the make-up of the local population. Activities would be shared by both Maori and pakeha, and participation would not be determined entirely on the basis of race but of personal interest and ability as well. The community would be tolerant of diversity and would not attach handicaps to particular cultural choices. There can be no one pattern of integration prescribed for all communities. Through tolerance and goodwill each must find a balance that suits its own situation. . . .

THE RATE OF INTEGRATION

Many different views have been expressed about the rate at which integration should proceed. Some experts have maintained that the strains of culture conflict can be eased best by slowing down the rate of change, strengthening Maori communities, and preserving Maori culture; others have urged an active educational programme to inculcate modern attitudes as quickly as possible. The various policies advocated have ranged from the one extreme of separate Maori development to that of complete assimilation into pakeha ways. Perhaps all the experts have been right to a degree as they have based their recommendations on their own experiences with groups of Maoris who are living in many different environments. They have been wrong however, if they have assumed that the one solution is applicable to all groups. A policy of integration must allow for regional and local diversity.

The view that the Maori could be completely assimilated in a short time into New Zealand's Western-type culture may have been given some credence by the fact that some individual Maoris have successfully made this change. The rare individual can, of course, detach himself from his cultural background by breaking his ties with his group. The group itself, however, naturally maintains its own culture or changes it only slowly. The Maori people as a whole cannot be expected to give up their entire Maoritanga in the process of adopting the ways of the pakeha. Integration will proceed by the two groups growing together, and Maoris will make a considerable contribution to the common culture in areas where their numerical proportion is high. . . .

GENERAL PRINCIPLES TO GUIDE INTEGRATION

In the relationship between Maori and pakeha in New Zealand the following principles might have value as a guide to action.

(1) Regardless of any racial or cultural differences, Maoris have a natural and legal right to full equality with all other New Zealanders.

(2) It is in the country's interest for all citizens to have access to the facilities which will enable each one to attain the fullest possible development of his personality. Where cultural differences handicap the Maori in the use he can make of the facilities generally available the Government will continue to provide special facilities for as long as they may be needed, and it is hoped that other organisations will do the same.

(3) While it is apparent that economic and other factors make it imperative for the majority of Maori people to become more closely associated with pakehas in many spheres of activity, any efforts of the Maori people to retain their language, to gather together for cultural or recreational purposes, and to retain their identity as Maoris should be regarded with sympathy and supported where this is appropriate.

(4) Although individuals have the right to choose their own associates, no discrimination against Maoris by any organisation which sets itself up to provide a public service should be tolerated. We should all fight against any racial distinctions in employment, accommodation, sport, or in any other field.

(5) Integration is a two-way process and the teaching of Maori history, games, and other relevant subjects, including race relations, should be encouraged in the schools, in adult education, and elsewhere by any available means. . . .

> *Integration of Maori and Pakeha*, no. 1 in
> Series of Special Studies by Dept. of Maori
> Affairs, Wellington, 1962

188. THE MAORI WELFARE ACT, 1962

Designed to amend and supercede the 1945 Act, the Maori Welfare Act (1962) made certain changes in nomenclature and definition. The Tribal Committees became 'Maori Committees', the Tribal Executives became 'Maori Executives' and the District Conferences of Tribal Executives were given a more defined role as 'District Maori Councils'. The main innovation was the provision for the New Zealand Maori Council with functions defined in Section 18.

An Act to provide for the constitution of Maori Associations, to define their powers and functions, and to consolidate and amend the Maori Social and Economic Advancement Act 1945.

[*14 December 1962*]

. . . *Maori Committees*

8. Maori Committee areas—(1) Any area which, at the commencement of this Act, is declared a Tribal Committee area under section 14 of the Maori Social and Economic Advancement Act 1945 shall be deemed to be a Maori Committee area. . . .

9. Maori Committees—(1) For the purposes of this Act there shall be a Maori Committee for every Maori Committee area constituted under section 8 of this Act.

(2) Each Maori Committee shall consist of seven members elected in accordance with this Act. . . .

SOME POLITICAL LANDMARKS SINCE 1940

Maori Executive Committees

11. Maori Executive Committee areas—(1) Any area which, at the commencement of this Act, is declared a tribal district under section 6 of the Maori Social and Economic Advancement Act 1945 shall be deemed to be a Maori Executive Committee area. . . .

District Maori Councils

14. Maori Council districts—(1) The Minister may from time to time, by notice in the *Gazette*, declare any part of New Zealand defined in the notice to be a Maori Council district for the purposes of this Act and may assign a name by which the Maori Council district shall be described and known. . . .

16. Functions of District Maori Councils—(1) Each District Maori Council shall, in relation to the Maoris within its district, have the functions conferred on the New Zealand Maori Council by subsection (1) of section 18 of this Act. . . .

New Zealand Maori Council

17. New Zealand Maori Council—(1) For the purposes of this Act there shall be a New Zealand Maori Council.

(2) The members of the New Zealand Maori Council shall consist of members appointed in accordance with this section by District Maori Councils.

(3) Each District Maori Council shall appoint three members to the New Zealand Maori Council.

(4) The members of the New Zealand Maori Council of Tribal Executives established under section 13E of the Maori Social and Economic Advancement Act 1945 in office at the commencement of this Act shall be deemed to be members of the New Zealand Maori Council.

18. General functions of the New Zealand Maori Council—(1) The general functions of the New Zealand Maori Council, in respect of all Maoris, shall be—

(a) To consider and discuss such matters as appear relevant to the social and economic advancement of the Maori race:

(b) To consider and, as far as possible, give effect to any measures that will conserve and promote harmonious and friendly relations between members of the Maori race and other members of the community:

(c) To promote, encourage, and assist Maoris—

442

(i) To conserve, improve, advance and maintain their physical, economic, industrial, educational, social, moral, and spiritual well-being;

(ii) To assume and maintain self-reliance, thrift, pride of race, and such conduct as will be conducive to their general health and economic well-being;

(iii) To accept, enjoy, and maintain the full rights, privileges, and responsibilities of New Zealand citizenship;

(iv) To apply and maintain the maximum possible efficiency and responsibility in their local self-government and undertakings; and

(v) To preserve, revive and maintain the teaching of Maori arts, crafts, language, genealogy, and history in order to perpetuate Maori culture:

(d) To collaborate with and assist State Departments and other organisations and agencies in—

(i) The placement of Maoris in industry and other forms of employment;

(ii) The education, vocational guidance, and training of Maoris;

(iii) The provision of housing and the improvement of the living conditions of Maoris;

(iv) The promotion of health and sanitation amongst the Maori people;

(v) The fostering of respect for the law and law-observance amongst the Maori people;

(vi) The prevention of excessive drinking and other undesirable forms of conduct amongst the Maori people; and

(vii) The assistance of Maoris in the solution of difficulties or personal problems.

(2) The New Zealand Maori Council shall advise and consult with District Maori Councils, Maori Executive Committees, and Maori Committees on such matters as may be referred to it by any of those bodies or as may seem necessary or desirable for the social and economic advancement of the Maori race. . . .

New Zealand Statutes, 1962, no. 133, vol. ii, pp. 893–900

189. THE MAORI AFFAIRS AMENDMENT ACT, 1967

Extracts from the long and controversial Act passed, 22 November 1967, designed to remove anomalies in certain laws relating to Maoris and Maori land, and make land available, for 'better use'.

STATUS OF MAORI LAND

... 3. Application of this Part—(1) This Part of this Act applies to Maori freehold land beneficially owned by not more than four persons for a legal and beneficial estate in fee simple. ...

6. Registrar may issue declaration of change of status—Where, upon inquiry made under section 4 of this Act, in respect of any block, the Registrar is satisfied—

(a) That the block comprises land to which this Part applies; and

(b) That there is no reason to believe that any of the owners, as disclosed by the records of the Court, is deceased; and

(c) That the land is suitable for effective use and occupation; and

(d) That a plan of the land sufficient for the purposes of registration of the order constituting the title to the land has been prepared or that a description and diagram thereof has been prepared and duly certified by the Chief Surveyor under subsection (3) of section 5 of this Act,—

the Registrar shall issue in respect of the block a declaration that the status of the land to which the declaration relates shall cease to be that of Maori land. ...

PROMOTION OF BETTER USE AND ADMINISTRATION OF MAORI LAND

16. Secretary may institute investigation of land—(1) The Secretary may, from time to time, issue instructions to officers of the Department to investigate the use and ownership of any Maori freehold land or class of Maori freehold land. ...

17. Determination by Improvement Officer of necessary action —(1) After such consultation as is conveniently practicable with the owners of the land and other interested persons or bodies, the Improvement Officer shall determine whether or not it is necessary or desirable to take action to improve the fitness of the land for effective and profitable use, or to permit the more efficient administration of the land. ...

PROVISIONS RELATING TO CONVERSION

152. Sale of vested land to lessees—The Maori Vested Lands Administration Act of 1954 is hereby further amended by inserting, after section 61, the following section:

'61A. (1) In this section the term "block" means all vested land held by the Maori Trustee upon the same trusts for one group of beneficial owners.

'(2) Subject to the provisions of this section, the Maori Trustee may sell to the lessee thereof any vested land which is subject to a new lease issued under Part II of this Act.

'(3) The Maori Trustee may, in his absolute discretion, determine that the sale under this section of the land in any specified block or group of blocks is impractical or inexpedient, and may inform a lessee of any such land that no offer for the land under this section can be entertained.

'(4) A lessee of vested land to which subsection (2) of this section relates may give notice to the Maori Trustee that he desires to acquire the freehold of the land comprised in his lease at a price to be stated in the notice, being a sum not less than the amount of the capital value of the land as determined by a special valuation to be made for the purposes of this subsection by the Valuer-General, at the expense of the lessee, not earlier than six months before the date of the notice, reduced by a sum equal to two-thirds of the amount of the value of the improvements on the land as disclosed by that valuation with the addition to such reduced sum of ten percent thereof: . . .'

> *New Zealand Statutes*, 1967, no. 124, vol. ii,
> pp. 815, 817, 823, 922.

190. SELF-GOVERNMENT FOR THE COOK ISLANDS, 1964

After being governed as an integral part of New Zealand since 1901 the Cook Islands received a new constitution after an Act of 1964 provided for self-government. The Head of State remained the Queen 'in the right of New Zealand', and the Cook Islanders remained New Zealand citizens, but they received as wide a measure of self-government as they desired and U.N. officers who observed elections in 1965 declared that the ideal of 'self-determination' was fulfilled.

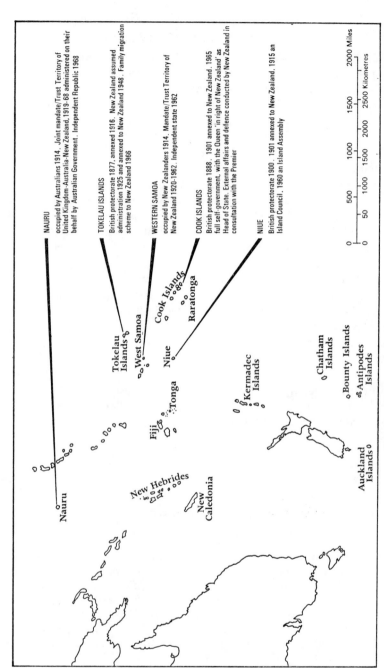

NAURU
occupied by Australians 1914 . Joint mandate/Trust Territory of
United Kingdom-Australia-New Zealand, 1919-68 administered on their
behalf by Australian Government . Independent Republic 1968

TOKELAU ISLANDS
British protectorate 1877, annexed 1916 . New Zealand assumed
administration 1925 and annexed to New Zealand 1948 . Family migration
scheme to New Zealand 1966

WESTERN SAMOA
occupied by New Zealanders 1914 . Mandate/Trust Territory of
New Zealand 1920-1962 . Independent state 1962

COOK ISLANDS
British protectorate 1888 . 1901 annexed to New Zealand. 1965
full self-government, with the Queen 'in right of New Zealand' as
Head of State. External affairs and defence conducted by New Zealand in
consultation with the Premier

NIUE
British protectorate 1900 . 1901 annexed to New Zealand. 1915 an
Island Council . 1960 an Island Assembly

Nauru

Tokelau
Islands

West Samoa

Tonga

Fiji

New Hebrides

New
Caledonia

Cook Islands
Raratonga

Niue

Kermadec
Islands

Chatham
Islands

Bounty Islands

Antipodes
Islands

Auckland
Islands

| 0 | 500 | 1000 | 1500 | 2000 Miles |

| 0 | 500 | 1000 | 1500 | 2000 | 2500 Kilometres |

MAP 8. NEW ZEALAND'S ISLAND TERRITORIES

An Act to make provision for self government by the people of the Cook Islands (other than Niue) and to provide a constitution for those islands. [**17** *November 1964.*]

. . . 3. Cook Islands to be self-governing—The Cook Islands shall be self-governing.

4. Constitution of the Cook Islands—The Constitution set out in the Schedule to this Act shall be the Constitution of the Cook Islands, and shall be the supreme law of the Cook Islands.

5. External affairs and defence—Nothing in this Act or in the Constitution shall affect the responsibilities of Her Majesty the Queen in right of New Zealand for the external affairs and defence of the Cook Islands, those responsibilities to be discharged after consultation by the Prime Minister of New Zealand with the Premier of the Cook Islands. . . .

THE CONSTITUTION OF THE COOK ISLANDS
PART I
THE GOVERNMENT OF THE COOK ISLANDS

2. The Head of State—Her Majesty the Queen in right of New Zealand shall be the Head of State of the Cook Islands. . . .

The High Commissioner of the Cook Islands

3. High Commissioner of the Cook Islands—(1) There shall be a High Commissioner of the Cook Islands, who shall be the representative of Her Majesty the Queen in the Cook Islands, and shall also be the representative of the Government of New Zealand in the Cook Islands. . . .

5. High Commissioner to act on advice—(1) Except as otherwise provided in this Constitution, the High Commissioner in the performance of his functions as the representative of Her Majesty the Queen shall act on the advice of Cabinet, the Premier, or the appropriate Minister, as the case may be. . . .

PART II
THE EXECUTIVE GOVERNMENT OF THE COOK ISLANDS

12. Executive authority—(1) The executive authority of the Cook Islands shall be vested in Her Majesty the Queen in right of New Zealand. . . .

Cabinet

13. Cabinet—(1) There shall be a Cabinet of Ministers, comprising the Premier of the Cook Islands (who shall preside over

447

Cabinet) and not fewer than three nor more than five other Ministers, which shall have the general direction and control of the executive government of the Cook Islands, and shall be collectively responsible to the Legislative Assembly. . . .

PART III

THE LEGISLATIVE GOVERNMENT OF
THE COOK ISLANDS

The Legislative Assembly

27. Legislative Assembly of the Cook Islands—(1) There shall be a Legislative Assembly to be called the Legislative Assembly of the Cook Islands.

(2) The Legislative Assembly shall consist of twenty-two members, to be elected by secret ballot under a system of universal suffrage by the electors of the following islands or groups of islands. . . .

88. Power of Governor-General to make regulations—(1) The Governor-General may from time to time, by Order in Council made at the request and with the consent of the Government of the Cook Islands, make regulations, not inconsistent with any provisions of this Constitution, for the peace, order, and good government of the Cook Islands. . . .

> Reprinted in *New Zealand Statutes*, 1966, vol. 3, pp. 2029–63

191. NAFTA, 1965

From a speech by the Minister of Overseas Trade, Mr. J. R. Marshall, in the House of Representatives on 17 August 1965 explaining the scope of the recently negotiated Free Trade Agreement with Australia. The 'Free Trade Area' was defined as the metropolitan territory of New Zealand and the States and mainland Territories of Australia. Article 4, relating to the scaling down of Import Duties is included here.

(*a*) Hon. J. R. MARSHALL (Minister of Overseas Trade)—The agreement will establish a free trade area consisting of New Zealand and Australia with the objective of a sustained and mutually beneficial expansion of trade. The 1933 trade agreement between our two countries will be deemed to form part of the new agreement and this will ensure that our future trade relations will be governed by one treaty. The free trade provisions apply to selected goods set out in a schedule to the agreement. Many of the goods included in this schedule are already duty free, and they will remain so. Where goods are at present dutiable there is provision for the phasing out of duties by stages. Where duties now exceed 10 per cent provision is made for an eight-year period of transition through which the duties would be reduced or eliminated. The commodities to which free trade conditions apply will cover some 60 per cent of the value of trade between the two countries and include some 85 per cent of our exports to Australia.

I cannot at this stage give more than a general indication of the scope and coverage of the schedule but the list includes almost all forest products—newsprint pulp; timber, rough sawn and dressed; plywood and veneers; packaging papers and boards; and other papers. It includes petroleum products, lead and zinc and other metal, copper bars and rods, fish, wool and wool tops, and some types of machinery and chemicals. Of iron and steel products only tinplate and rails are included. There is a special provision that these items may be withdrawn completely from the schedule if New Zealand should find this necessary after the establishment of its iron and steel industry. It has also been agreed to include a number of agricultural items such as wheat, oranges, dried fruits, and sugar. Members will also be interested to know that the agreement includes agricultural items of interest to our export industries such as lamb, pig-meat—including ham and bacon—cheese, frozen and dried vegetables, and strawberries. In the case of pork for processing and cheddar cheese, the arrangement is for satisfactory duty free quotas, details of which will be published with the agreement. For timber and paper products, where rates of duty vary considerably, the phasing out of duties will be accomplished in a manner which will result in the duties in the two countries being equal at each step during the transitional period. There are a number of safeguards which are intended to prevent any disruption of trade or industrial development. Provision is made for prompt and effective action where goods are dumped or subsidised by the exporting country. The agreement provides that either country may suspend its obligations in respect of products which are being imported in such increased quantities or under such conditions as to cause, or threaten to cause, serious injury to the producers of that country.

In negotiating this agreement we have recognised that both our countries are still at the stage of rapid industrial development, and that New Zealand industry in particular is at a less advanced stage than that of Australia. New industries, not at present planned or foreseen, will be established in the future in both countries; therefore, provision has been made to deal with this situation by withdrawing such items from the agreement and providing for protection to enable such industries to be established. Goods withdrawn from the schedule in this way could be protected by duties for a period of up to 12 years before the full conditions of free trade would be re-applied. In addition, in exceptional circumstances, items can be withdrawn completely from the schedule where it is necessary in the interests of the economic development of the country concerned. . . .

. . . Either country may exclude goods if their inclusion would cause or threaten to cause material injury to or hinder the establishment of industry.

A new and significant provision is the agreement to establish a joint consultative council on forest products, with the objective of achieving a mutually beneficial expansion of trade on the basis of the most efficient use of the resources of the two countries. The Australian Government raised with me the question of certain import duties where New Zealand charges higher rates against Australian goods than the lowest rates applied to other countries. Recently Australia has revised its customs tariff and has eliminated similar higher rates of duty against New Zealand goods. The New Zealand Government has agreed that where import duties levied on goods from Australia are higher than the lowest rate applicable to like goods imported from any third country it is the intention to eliminate this difference at the earliest practicable date. . . .

The Government's objectives in negotiating this agreement have been to create conditions that will lead to an increase in the value and volume of trade with Australia, to an improvement in the balance of trade, which is at present four to one against us, and to the continuing expansion and development of sound and efficient industries in New Zealand. . . .

N.Z.P.D., 1965, vol. 343, pp. 1958–60

(b)   ARTICLE 4

Import Duties

1. Subject to the provisions of Articles 6, 7, 8, and 9 of this

Agreement, each Member State shall reduce and eliminate, in accordance with the provisions of this Article, import duties on scheduled goods imported from the territory of the other Member State.

2. If, on the day immediately preceding the day on which this Article first applies to them, scheduled goods are—

    (*a*) free of import duties—they shall remain free of import duties;

    (*b*) subject to import duties not exceeding 5 per cent ad valorem or import duties of equivalent effect—they shall be and remain free of import duties from the day on which this Article first applies to them;

    (*c*) subject to import duties of more than 5 per cent but not exceeding 10 per cent ad valorem or import duties of equivalent effect—

        (i) they shall, from the day on which this Article first applies to them, be subject to import duties not exceeding 50 per cent of those payable on the day immediately preceding the day on which this Article first applies to them; and

        (ii) they shall, from the day two years after the day on which this Article first applies to them, be and remain free of import duties;

    (*d*) subject to import duties of more than 10 per cent ad valorem or import duties of equivalent effect—they shall, from each of the days listed hereunder, not be subject to import duties exceeding the percentage specified against that day of the import duties payable on the day immediately preceding the day on which this Article first applies to them:

the day on which this Article first applies to them	80 per cent
the day two years after the day on which this Article first applies to them	60 per cent
the day four years after the day on which this Article first applies to them	40 per cent
the day six years after the day on which this Article first applies to them	20 per cent

and from the day eight years after the day on which this Article first applies to them, they shall be and remain free of import duties. . . .

A.J.H.R., 1965, A–17, pp. 5–6

192. INDUSTRIALIZATION AND SURVIVAL

An appeal for industrialization by Dr. W. B. Sutch, who had served on Gordon Coates's staff in the 1930s and was Secretary for Industries and Commerce from 1951 until prematurely retired in 1965—the year he wrote the paper 'Colony or Nation? The Crisis of the Mid-1960s'.

... New Zealand must justify its existence to the world in the second half of the twentieth century. It cannot do this as a colony. Switzerland has justified her existence in Europe; New Zealand can justify itself and its contribution to economic and social equality if it can prove that its system can last. This will not happen if we continue to hug our chains. . . .

The direction last imparted to New Zealand began in 1882 when commercial refrigeration—first used by British companies in Argentina and Australia—was successfully applied to New Zealand. The production of food in the southern hemisphere could respond to the demand for food in the northern, in Great Britain especially. This development caused a change of direction, at a crucial time. By 1882, the size and clustering of the population was becoming adequate to support a broader base of manufacturing, and manufacturing skills were in fact being developed. But the discovery of refrigeration diverted activities towards grassland farming, and since then our whole economic structure and our State and private institutions have been directed primarily towards grassland farmers. Other activities have had to fit into this pattern.

The pattern has never been a healthy one. . . . In 1958, New Zealand suffered a fall in overseas funds receipts. At that time a large number of New Zealanders realised that the way out of the impasse was to embark on a policy of rapid, extensive and deep industrialisation. . . .

In 1962 came another warning. In that year, it seemed almost certain that Britain was going to join the European Economic Community, the 'Common Market'. . . .

The need for industrialisation and diversification has become not less but more acute since 1962, but not in any dramatic manner, and we in New Zealand apparently cannot make an independent decision about policy except in a time of stress. Why? It is not simply because of high material living standards, of full employment and a good climate: these are but superficial explanations.

It is rather because of our social heritage, of our patterns of thought and customary ways, and of our amiable inferiority. All of these stem from nineteenth-century colonial society. . . .

The crisis for New Zealand in the mid-1960s is not that the basis of our wealth has suddenly gone. It has not gone; and the trends that have produced the crisis have not been sudden. The crisis consists in this: the time in which we can take remedial measures is getting shorter and shorter; and the longer we delay these measures, the more the crisis deepens. Rapid and radical action is needed to readjust our economic structure and institutions to meet our new development needs. . . .

The crisis is one of time and of attitude. It lies in a failure to understand fully the fact and nature of a crisis that has already arrived; and a failure to meet it quickly enough. It is also a crisis of dependence—a 'decisive moment' for our future—colony, or nation?

> W. B. Sutch, *Colony or Nation? Economic Crises in New Zealand from the 1860s to the 1960s*. Sydney University Press, 1966, pp. 181–3 (by courtesy of Dr. W. B. Sutch)

193. THE LETTER OF INTENT TO THE IMF, 1967

Excerpts from the letter by the Minister of Finance, R. D. Muldoon, to Paul Schweitzer, Managing Director of the International Monetary Fund, 26 October 1967, requesting standby credit because falling wool prices had cut overseas earnings. It included a declaration of intent as to the domestic economic policies which would reduce imports and tighten exchange controls and credit.

. . . overseas exchange transactions on current account showed deficits of over NZ$50 million in the year to June 1965 and over NZ$100 million in 1965/66. With conditions tightening in the international capital markets, we have encountered difficulties in raising long-term loans abroad and it has, therefore, been necessary to make use of our reserve facilities, including our access to the Fund, in order to finance a considerable part of these deficits. . . .

3. The Government set out to counter the adverse movement in the balance of payments by strengthening domestic financial policy. . . .

4. The balance of payments position then, however, took a sharp turn for the worse as a result of an unexpected weakening in the overseas demand for wool. The average price for wool sold at auction in 1965/66 was nearly 35 cents per pound and the Wool Commission's support price for the 1966/67 season was set at what was expected to be the fairly conservative level of 30 cents per pound. However, with demand for wool exceptionally weak, the Wool Commission had to buy in nearly 650,000 bales in the 1966/67 season; this buying, which took place mainly in the second half of the season, represented approximately one-third of the clip and export receipts from wool fell by over NZ$60 million, or more than a quarter. The current account deficit for the year to June 1967 reached about NZ$132 million and further short-term borrowings, including a drawing under the Fund's compensatory financing facility, were arranged in order to prevent a critical fall in reserves. . . .

5. The pressure of internal demand and the price weakness for our major export product, wool, thus combined to produce a critical situation which made it impossible to continue the high rate of economic growth achieved in recent years. . . .

6. The measures taken so far in 1967 include:

(a) Fiscal and related measures

In *February* consumer subsidies on butter and flour were removed; funds for new lending by the State Advances Corporation were reduced; state house rentals were increased by 12½ percent; postal, telephone, and telegraph charges were raised from April 1967. The combined effect of these measures produced an annual saving to the budget directly or indirectly of approximately NZ$34 million. It was also announced in *February* that the Government intended to limit the rate of increase in central government expenditure in the fiscal year which began 1 April 1967. In *April* an increase in electricity charges averaging 12½ percent was announced to take effect from 1 October 1967; the increase in revenue is estimated at about NZ$12 million a year. In *May* the Government introduced a further set of measures including increases in sales taxes on motor vehicles and marine engines, increased fees for motor vehicle licensing and registration, and increased duties on motor fuels, alcoholic spirits, cigarettes, tobacco, and cigars. The additional revenue from the measures announced in May was estimated at NZ$50 million in a full year.

(b) Monetary and credit measures

In *February* hire purchase regulations were tightened for second-hand cars and light trucks, motorcycles, and all other consumer goods. In addition, the policy of credit restraint continued to be applied firmly and capital issues control was extended to all finance companies raising a sum in excess of NZ$2,000 in any year. In *May* the banks were directed to reduce their advances broadly to the level of a year ago and each customer's overdraft limit, with some exceptions, was reduced by 10 percent by July 1967.

(c) Other measures

Exchange control on current transactions was tightened in *February* in a number of respects; and the no-remittance import scheme is to be eliminated over a period so as to lessen the incentive to hold assets abroad. The import licensing schedule for the year to June 1968 provided for cuts in allocations for consumer goods and a wide range of industrial raw materials for manufacture. The list of items exempt from licensing was, however, maintained unchanged. . . .

For the 1967/68 season, the average floor price at which the Wool Commission will purchase wool on offer was reduced in July 1967 from 30 cents a pound to 25 cents a pound. On 13 October 1967, the Commission announced that the floor price to growers of 25 cents a pound. . . . In these circumstances, we hereby request the Fund to agree to a stand-by arrangement in an amount equivalent to US$87 million for a period of one year in order that we may have the assurance of adequate resources while the task of establishing equilibrium is completed in accordance with the programme outlined above. In particular, financial support from the Fund in the near future would provide support to our reserve position at a time when there is normally a sharp seasonal decline. . . .

> Reserve Bank of New Zealand, *Bulletin*,
> November 1967, pp. 192–4

194. THE NATIONAL DEVELOPMENT CONFERENCE, 1968

At the first plenary session of the Conference the report of the Targets Committee, which recommended the goal of an average economic growth rate of 4½ per cent over a decade, was discussed. In his opening speech the Prime Minister, K. J. Holyoake, accepted the idea of 'indicative planning'.

'The final programme or plan arising from this conference will not be something forced upon the people by Government action', he said. 'I want to make this point emphatically at the outset. It will emerge as a result of a genuine co-operative effort and an example of indicative planning which this Government so firmly believes in.'

Mr Holyoake listed six basic concepts around which the Government had developed its economic planning policy:

(1) The Government would consult with the people affected and would invite them to participate in the planning. Consultation and participation in such a fashion was consistent with the free-enterprise system and with parliamentary democracy.

(2) Broad objectives or targets should be set. 'We try to work out what is needed to achieve the targets, what resources are to be made available to do the job, and what arrangements are necessary to follow up the targets.'

(3) Targets should be indicative rather than imperative. 'The whole basis of indicative planning is that the guidelines are not to be regarded as a strait-jacket—they are guidelines.'

(4) Planning must be export oriented. 'Export earnings are the key to the growth of our economy the key to improving the standard of living and social standards.'

(5) Planning should take place in the context of the overall economy. 'This we believe helps to set sensible and realistic objectives which are consistent one with the other and which would not then create violent distortions within the whole economy.'

(6) Consultative planning leads naturally to the creation of continuing machinery (preferably based on existing institutions), so that progress towards the targets may be kept under review.

'I do emphasise this point that we believe we are much more likely to be successful if we build on the institutions and administrative arrangements that have grown up in New Zealand.

'What we are trying to do is indicate the best lines of growth while leaving wide elements of choice to the company, the organisation, and the individual. These three, the company, the organisation, and the individual, will take into account the inducements offered to them. For the successful attainment of the targets, there must be continued participation by the individual and continued consultation with him, but in the last resort he must make the final decisions. . . .'

Report of the Proceedings of the National Development Conference, Plenary Session, 27–9 August 1968, Wellington, 1969, p. 47

457

APPENDIX

1. POPULATION

(1) ESTIMATES OF MAORI POPULATION at the time of contact and early settlement.

1768	100,000	(Cook)	240,000	(Lewthwaite, 1950)
1817	150,000	(Nicholas)		
1834	200,000	(Williams)		
1840	100,000	(N.Z. Company)		
1849	120,000	(Grey)		
1853	60,000	(McLean)		
1857	56,049	(Census Estimate)		

Source: G. R. Lewthwaite, 'The Population of Aotearoa', *New Zealand Geographer*, 1950, 6 (1): 37. See also P. H. Buck 'The Passing of the Maori', *Trans. of the N.Z. Institute*, 1924, 55: 362–75.

(2) EARLY COLONIAL POPULATION, excluding military personnel, as given by Thomson, 1859.

1840	2,050	1846	13,274
1841	5,000	1847	14,477
1842	10,992	1848	17,166
1843	11,848	1849	19,543
1844	12,447	1850	22,108
1845	12,774		

Source: A. S. Thomson, *The Story of New Zealand: Past and Present—Savage and Civilized*, London, 1859, vol. ii, p. 329. Thomson's figures are used in early Official Year Books. Slight revisions were made by C. G. F. Simkin (ed.), *Statistics of New Zealand for the Crown Colony Period, 1840–1852* Auckland, 1954.

APPENDIX

(3) CENSUS FIGURES (A)

	European	Maori	Other races	Total
1851	26,707			
1858	59,413	56,049 (Est.)	..	115,462
1861	97,904	55,336 (Est.)	..	..
1864	171,009	..	..	..
1867	217,437	38,540 (Est.)	..	..
1871	254,928	37,520 (Est.)	..	..
1874	297,654	47,330	..	344,984
1878	412,465	45,542	..	458,007
1881	487,889	46,141	..	534,030
1886	576,524	43,927	..	620,451
1891	624,455	44,177	..	668,632
1896	701,094	42,113	..	743,207
1901	770,304	45,549	..	815,853
1906	885,995	50,309	..	936,304
1911	1,005,585	52,723	..	1,058,308
1916	1,096,228	52,997	3,204	1,149,225
1921	1,214,677	56,987	5,438	1,271,664
1926	1,344,469	63,670	6,302	1,408,139
1936	1,491,484	82,326	6,976	1,573,810
1945	1,603,554	98,744	10,678	1,702,298
1951	1,823,796	115,676	14,355	1,939,472
1956	2,036,911	137,151	20,624	2,174,062
1961	2,216,886	167,086	31,012	2,414,984
1966	2,426,352	201,159	49,408 (B)	2,676,919

Sources: A Survey of New Zealand Population, Wellington, 1960, pp. 1–3;
New Zealand Census of Population and Dwellings, 1966, vol. vii, 'Race',
Wellington, 1969, pp. 3–5; see also Buck.

Notes: Table 3

(A) *Military*: Census figures for the period before the withdrawal of British troops from New Zealand in 1870 do not include military personnel and their families, and the censuses for 1901, 1916, 1945, and subsequent years do not include persons on military service overseas.

(B) Other races at the time of the 1966 Census were as follows:

Polynesian	26,271
Chinese	10,283
Indian	6,843
Fijian	1,323
Syrian, Lebanese, and Arab	1,099
Others	3,589

460

APPENDIX

Of the two largest minority groups, the Polynesians are the faster growing, as a result both of migration into N.Z. (mainly since 1945) and natural increase, rising from 8,103 in 1956 to 26,271 in 1966, when they were made up as follows:

Samoan   11,842 (of which 6,823 were born in W. Samoa)
Cook's   8,663
Niuean   2,846
Tongan   1,389 (with balance accounted for by Hawaiians and
          Tahitians)

The Chinese population dates from the gold rushes of the 1860s and has fluctuated as follows:

1874	4,816	1926	3,374
1881	5,004	1936	2,943
1891	4,444	1945	4,940
1896	3,859	1956	6,731
1916	2,147	1966	10,283

2. IMMIGRATION, EMIGRATION, AND EXCESS OF ARRIVALS OVER DEPARTURES, 1860–1968 (A)

(in five-year periods)

Period	Arrivals	Departures	Excess arrivals over departures
1860–4	132,225	45,301	86,924
1865–9	62,561	33,493	29,268
1870–4	87,469	27,216	60,253
1875–9	103,358	30,532	72,826
1880–4	75,023	43,337	31,686
1885–9	74,987	77,403	−2,416*
1890–4	98,953	86,310	12,643
1895–9	95,051	85,349	9,702
1900–4	136,968	98,993	37,975
1905–9	191,646	144,786	46,860
1910–14	204,052	168,158	32,894
1915–19	95,836	89,045	6,791
1920–4	197,480	150,133	47,347
1925–9	196,124	165,923	30,201
1930–4	112,730	118,999	−6,269*
1935–9	173,913	163,926	9,987
1940–4	38,617	34,634	3,983
1945–9	144,269	123,550	20,719
1950–4	303,588	236,206	67,382
1955–9	388,727	337,146	51,581
1960–4	704,110	647,266	56,844
1965–8 (B)	967,959	952,115	15,844 (C)

* Excess of departures.

| 1860–1968 | Total net gain | 725,025 |

Sources: A. H. McLintock (ed.), Encyclopædia of New Zealand, Wellington, 1966, vol. ii, p. 132; Reports on Population, Migration and Building, Department of Statistics, Wellington, for years after 1964.

461

APPENDIX

Notes: Table 2

(A) Figures exclude crews, through passengers, armed forces (1914–19 and since 1939).

(B) Four-year period only.

(C) Net losses in 1967 (−1,115) and 1968 (−8,924), mainly to Australia.

Comment on Migration

There have been six periods of marked increase in the European population of New Zealand from immigration:

(i) *c.* 1846–55: organized settlement by the N.Z. Company and its associates;

(ii) the early 1860s: gold rushes in the South Island;

(iii) the 1870s: assisted immigration under the 'Vogel' schemes;

(iv) *c.* 1900–14: farming prosperity and some industrial growth;

(v) the 1920s: participation in British emigration schemes;

(vi) post-1945: industrial expansion.

New Zealand's immigrants have been, until recently, practically all Europeans, and overwhelmingly British, New Zealand virtually sharing in the policy of 'White Australia' since the 1880s. There has been significant trans-Tasman exchange of migrants, especially in the 1860s, the period *c.* 1885–93, and in the 1960s, with two periods of loss to Australia (1885–91 and 1967–8). In the last two decades there has been significant immigration of Polynesians from New Zealand's island territories.

3. THE IMPACT OF THE GOLD RUSHES OF THE 1860s

(1) EXPORT VALUE

The four most valuable items compared with total export of N.Z. produce—in £ sterling.

	Total	Wool	Gold	Gum	
1860	549,133	444,392	17,585	9,851	13,653 Potatoes
1861	1,339,241	523,728	752,657	9,888	14,301 Hewn timber
1862	2,358,020	674,226	1,591,389	11,107	24,719 Chrome ore
1863	3,342,891	830,495	2,432,479	27,026	9,869 Sawn timber
1864	3,050,634	1,070,997	1,855,830	60,590	18,102 Hewn timber
1865	3,503,421	1,141,761	2,252,689	46,060	14,061 Potatoes and onions
1866	4,396,100	1,354,152	2,897,412	70,572	17,106 Sawn timber
1867	4,479,464	1,580,608	2,724,276	77,491	22,503 Wheat
1868	4,268,762	1,516,548	2,492,793	72,493	66,644 Oats
1869	4,090,134	1,371,230	2,341,592	111,307	52,664 Oats
1870	4,544,682	1,703,944	2,163,910	175,074	132,578 Flax

(2) SETTLER POPULATION TOTALS

Total European population (C = census year, E = estimate); military and Island totals.

	Total Europeans	Military	North Island		South Island	
1860E	79,625	4,294				
1861C	99,021	7,294	41,641	42·10%	57,274	57·90%
1862E	125,812	7,302				
1863E	164.048	11,309				
1864C	172,158	11,973	65,263	37·93%	106,809	62·07%
1865E	190,607	11,105				
1866E	204,114	4,568				
1867C	218,668	1,455	79,913	36·58%	138,571	63·42%
1868E	226,618	1,192				
1869E	237,249	1,020				
1870E	248,400					

(3) VESSELS ENTERING N.Z. PORTS
First eight in order of magnitude.

	1		2		3		4		5		6		7		8	
1860	Auck	82	Dun	69	Well	49	Russ	44	Nel	44	Mang	35	Lytt	31	Inv	16
1861	Dun	256	Auck	103	Nel	45	Russ	43	Lytt	35	Well	32	Inv	30	N.P. / Mang	16 / 16
1862	Dun	395	Auck	107	Lytt	75	Bluff	67	Russ	40	Nel	44	Well	36	Mang	16
1863	Dun	496	Auck	177	Inv	136	Lytt	106	Nel	54	Well	36	Bluff	35	Russ	24
1864	Auck	362	Dun	305	Lytt	98	Nel	73	Inv	48	Well	47	Bluff	54	N.P.	26
1865	Auck	261	Dun	157	Nel	114	Hok	84	Well	57	Lytt	56	Inv	20	N.P.	19
1866	Auck	198	Hok	160	Nel	135	Dun	133	Well	90	Lytt	74	Grey	62	Bluff	31
1867	Hok	218	Dun	132	Auck	130	Nel	109	Well	98	Grey	69	Lytt	45	Bluff	45
1868	Auck	134	Dun	125	Hok	111	Nel	105	Well	92	Lytt	76	Bluff	66	Grey	53
1869	Auck	210	Dun	105	Hok	70	Lytt	70	Nel	68	Well	63	Grey	42	Bluff	42
1870	Auck	207	Dun	94	Lytt	82	Nel	70	Well	58	Hok	53	Grey	50	Russ	38

Symbols

Auck:	Auckland	Mang:	Manganui
Bluff:	Bluff	Nel:	Nelson
Dun:	Dunedin	N.P.:	New Plymouth
Grey:	Greymouth	Russ:	Russell
Hok:	Hokitika	Wang:	Wanganui
Inv:	Invercargill	Well:	Wellington
Lytt:	Lyttelton		

Source: all three tables compiled from *Statistics of New Zealand*, 1860–71.

Gold provided half the value of New Zealand's exports, contributed to the trebling of the population, caused a shift of the centres of population to the South Island, and accounted for the rise of ports such as Dunedin and Hokitika.

APPENDIX

4. EXTERNAL TRADE OF NEW ZEALAND, 1851–1969 (selected) years) (in millions of N.Z. dollars) (A)

Year B	Import c.d.v. (excluding gold and specie)	Exports (excluding gold and specie)	Wool	Frozen meat	Dairy products	Other products (selected years)
1851	·65	·17	..	..	..	..
1854	1·6	·6	·14	..	·02	..
1858	2·0	·8	·5	..	..	..
1861	4·4	1·2	1·0	..	..	..
						Gold
1864	12·1	2·6	2·1	..	..	3·7 (D)
1867	9·7	3·8	3·2	..	..	5·4
1871	7·0	5·0	3·2	[·3] (E)	·03	5·6
1874	14·5	7·5	5·7	[·2] (E)	·01	3·0
1878	15·3	9·3	6·6	[·2] (E)	·04	2·5
						Wheat
1881	13·3	9·8	5·8	·04 (F)	·03	1·5
1886	11·5	11·2	6·1	·85	·3	2·1 (G)
						Gold (cont.)
1891	11·7	17·1	8·3	2·4	·5	2·0
1896	16·5	12·8	8·8	2·5	·8	2·1
1901	20·6	22·2	7·4	4·5	2·3	3·5
1906	26·0	31·4	13·5	5·8	3·8	4·5
1911	34·1	34·3	13·0	7·0	5·6	3·6
1916	45·5	64·2	24·8	14·5	12·3	..
1921	77·7	88·4	10·4	22·3	41·0	..
1926	90·6	89·5	23·7	17·3	30·0	..
1931	48·2	68·7	11·0	17·8	30·7	..
1936	80·5	110·7	26·6	24·5	41·7	..
1941	89·4	131·3	25·2	33·2	52·6	..
1945	100·1	160·7	53·2	35·2	59·6	..
1951	375·5	494·6	256·4	50·7	124·2	..
1956	469·5	554·5	183·1	127·7	159·6	..
						Pulp, Paper, Paper Board
1961	576·4	567·4	200·7	144·3	127·1	11.7
1966	729·4	767·3	231·9	19	175·4	18.3
1969 (H)	849·6	987·5	212·6	193·1	183·0	29.0

Sources: New Zealand External Trade, 1965–6 and 1966–7, Report and Analysis, Department of Statistics, Wellington, 1968, Tables 1 and 8; New Zealand Official Year Book, 1963, p. 660; 1964, p. 651; 1969, p. 633; Monthly abstract of statistics, December 1969, p. 3; B. L. Evans, Agricultural and Pastoral Statistics of New Zealand, 1861–1954 (Wellington, 1956).

APPENDIX

Notes:

(A) Figures correct to *one* decimal place, except in case of some earlier returns.

(B) Census years chosen with the following exceptions: 1931 and 1941 added; 1969 (provisional returns); 1853–1961, calendar years; 1963 onwards, June years; .. indicates negligible return.

(C) c.d.v. = current domestic value in country of export at time of shipment.

(D) Highest gold return: 1866, 5·8.

(E) Preserved meat exports.

(F) This is 1882 return (first).

(G) This is 1883 return (highest).

(H) The 1969 figures are provisional

Comment on table

These figures amply demonstrate the importance of external trade to New Zealand. The heavy dependence on primary products for overseas earnings is also clear; they have made up *c.* 90 per cent of the total since 1919, though there has been a small but significant rise in manufactured exports recently. The long-term primacy of wool among pastoral products is qualified by cycles of low prices for this product. The revolution caused by the coming of refrigeration (1882) combined with the return of British prosperity (*c.* 1895) is shown by the rise in frozen exports. Apart from a brief Australian predominance in the 1860s, the United Kingdom has been New Zealand's great market, though its old share of *c.* 75 per cent is now falling below 40 per cent. Fluctuations in British prosperity are reflected in New Zealand's returns; this is painfully demonstrated in the early 1930s.

APPENDIX

5. REPRESENTATIVES OF THE CROWN IN NEW ZEALAND

From annexation until the Proclamation of the Colony in 1841, New Zealand was a dependency of New South Wales, with a Lieutenant-Governor under the Governor of New South Wales. Thereafter the representative of the Crown was styled Lieutenant-Governor from 1841 to 1848, Governor-in-Chief from 1848 to 1853, Governor from 1853 to 1917, and thenceforth Governor-General.

Vice-Regal Representative	Assumed Office	Retired
DEPENDENCY OF NEW SOUTH WALES		
Lieutenant-Governor		
Captain William Hobson, R.N.	30 Jan. 1840	3 May 1841
THE CROWN COLONY		
Captain William Hobson, R.N.	3 May 1841	10 Sept. 1842
Captain Robert FitzRoy, R.N.	26 Dec. 1843	17 Nov. 1845
Captain George Grey	18 Nov. 1845	31 Dec. 1847
Governor-in-Chief and Governor of New Ulster and New Munster Commission 23 Dec. 1846		
Sir George Grey, K.C.B.	1 Jan. 1848	7 Mar. 1853
THE SELF-GOVERNING COLONY		
Governor of New Zealand		
Sir George Grey, K.C.B.	7 Mar. 1853	31 Dec. 1853
Colonel Thomas Gore Browne, C.B.	6 Sept. 1855	2 Oct. 1861
Sir George Grey, K.C.B.	4 Dec. 1861	5 Feb. 1868
Sir George Ferguson Bowen, G.C.M.G.	5 Feb. 1868	19 Mar. 1873
The Right Hon. Sir James Fergusson, BART., G.C.S.I., K.C.M.G., C.I.E.	14 Jun. 1873	3 Dec. 1874
The Right Hon. the Marquess of Normanby, G.C.B., G.C.M.G., P.C.	9 Jan. 1875	21 Feb. 1879
Sir Hercules George Robert Robinson, G.C.M.G.	17 Apr. 1879	8 Sept. 1880
The Hon. Sir Arthur Hamilton Gordon, G.C.M.G.	29 Nov. 1880	23 June 1882
Lieutenant-General Sir William Francis Drummond Jervois, G.C.M.G., C.B.	20 Jan. 1883	22 Mar. 1889
The Right Hon. Earl of Onslow, G.C.M.G.	2 May 1889	24 Feb. 1892
The Right Hon. Earl of Glasgow, G.C.M.G.	7 Jun. 1892	6 Feb. 1897
The Right Hon. Earl of Ranfurly, G.C.M.G.	10 Aug. 1897	19 June 1904
The Right Hon. Baron Plunket, K.C.M.G., K.C.V.O.	20 June 1904	8 June 1910
The Right Hon. Baron Islington, G.C.M.G., G.B.E., D.S.O.	22 June 1910	2 Dec. 1912
The Right Hon. the Earl of Liverpool, G.C.B., G.C.M.G., G.B.E., M.V.O., P.C.	19 Dec. 1912	27 June 1917

Vice-Regal Representative	Assumed Office	Retired
Governor-General of New Zealand		
The Right Hon. the Earl of Liverpool, G.C.B., G.C.M.G., G.B.E., M.V.O., P.C.	28 June 1917	7 July 1920
The Right Hon. Earl Jellicoe, G.C.B., O.M., G.C.V.O.	27 Sept. 1920	26 Nov. 1924
General Sir Charles Fergusson, BART., G.C.B., G.C.M.G., D.S.O., M.V.O.	13 Dec. 1924	8 Feb. 1930
The Right Hon. Viscount Bledisloe, G.C.M.G., K.B.E., P.C.	19 Mar. 1930	15 Mar. 1935
The Right Hon. Viscount Galway, G.C.M.G., D.S.O., O.B.E., P.C.	12 Apr. 1935	3 Feb. 1941
Marshal of the Royal Air Force the Right Hon. Baron Newall, G.C.B., O.M., G.C.M.G., C.B.E., A.M.	22 Feb. 1941	19 Apr. 1946
Lieutenant-General the Right Hon. Baron Freyberg, V.C., G.C.M.G., K.C.B., K.B.E., D.S.O.	17 June 1946	15 Aug. 1952
Lieutenant-General the Right Hon. Baron Norrie, G.C.M.G., G.C.V.O., C.B., D.S.O., M.C.	2 Dec. 1952	25 July 1957
The Right Hon. Viscount Cobham, G.C.M.G., T.D.	5 Sept. 1957	13 Sept. 1962
Brigadier Sir Bernard Fergusson, G.C.M.G., G.C.V.O., D.S.O., O.B.E.	9 Nov. 1962	20 Oct. 1967
Sir Arthur Espie Porritt, BART., G.C.M.G., K.C.V.O., C.B.E.	Dec. 1967	

Sources: New Zealand Year Book; New Zealand Parliamentary Record.

6. MINISTRIES

Between the demand for responsible government in 1854 and the answer from the Colonial Office, the officer administering the government agreed to appoint four members of the General Assembly to the Executive Council. Although two attempts were made at forming such a 'mixed ministry', the experiment was short-lived. James Edward FitzGerald, leader of the first group of 'unofficials', was in fact referred to by one of his colleagues as 'Prime Minister', but he was really more like a modern 'Leader of Government Business'.

Responsible government was inaugurated in 1856 when Henry Sewell, as head of the Ministry, assumed the office of Colonial Secretary, and became the first 'Premier'. Until 1880 the Colonial Secretaryship was frequently, but not invariably, occupied by the Premier. The latter usage did not become standard for some years, and styles such as 'First Minister', occasionally 'Prime Minister' were used. The term 'Prime Minister' was adopted by Seddon towards the close of the century and appeared in the official Year Book in 1900.

Name of Ministry	Name of Premier / Prime Minister	Assumed Office	Retired
Sewell	Henry Sewell	7 May 1856	20 May 1856
Fox I	William Fox	20 May 1856	2 June 1856
Stafford I	Edward William Stafford	2 June 1856	12 July 1861
Fox II	William Fox	12 July 1861	6 Aug. 1862
Domett	Alfred Domett	6 Aug. 1862	30 Oct. 1863
Whitaker I	Frederick Whitaker	30 Oct. 1863	24 Nov. 1864
Weld	Frederick Aloysius Weld	24 Nov. 1864	16 Oct. 1865
Stafford II	Edward William Stafford	16 Oct. 1865	28 June 1869
Fox III	William Fox	28 June 1869	10 Sept. 1872
Stafford III	Edward William Stafford	10 Sept. 1872	11 Oct. 1872
Waterhouse	George Marsden Waterhouse	11 Oct. 1872	3 Mar. 1873
Fox IV	William Fox	3 Mar. 1873	8 Apr. 1873
Vogel I	Julius Vogel, C.M.G.	8 Apr. 1873	6 July 1875
Pollen	Daniel Pollen, M.L.C.	6 July 1875	15 Feb. 1876
Vogel II	Sir Julius Vogel, K.C.M.G.	15 Feb. 1876	1 Sept. 1876
Atkinson I	Harry Albert Atkinson	1 Sept. 1876	13 Sept. 1876
Atkinson II (reconstituted)	Harry Albert Atkinson	13 Sept. 1876	13 Oct. 1877
Grey	Sir George Grey, K.C.B.	15 Oct. 1877	8 Oct. 1879
Hall	John Hall	8 Oct. 1879	21 Apr. 1882
Whitaker II	Frederick Whitaker, M.L.C.	21 Apr. 1882	25 Sept. 1883
Atkinson III	Harry Albert Atkinson	25 Sept. 1883	16 Aug. 1884
Stout I	Robert Stout	16 Aug. 1884	28 Aug. 1884
Atkinson IV	Harry Albert Atkinson	28 Aug. 1884	3 Sept. 1884
Stout II	Sir Robert Stout, K.C.M.G.	3 Sept. 1884	8 Oct. 1887
Atkinson V	Sir Harry Albert Atkinson, K.C.M.G.	8 Oct. 1887	24 Jan. 1891
Ballance	John Ballance	24 Jan. 1891	27 Apr. 1893
Seddon	Right Hon. Richard John Seddon	1 May 1893	10 June 1906
Hall-Jones	William Hall-Jones	21 June 1906	6 Aug. 1906
Ward I	Right Hon. Sir Joseph George Ward, BART., K.C.M.G.	6 Aug. 1906	28 Mar. 1912
Mackenzie	Thomas Mackenzie	28 Mar. 1912	10 July 1912
Massey I	Right Hon. William Ferguson Massey	10 Jul. 1912	12 Aug. 1915
Massey II National	Right Hon. William Ferguson Massey	12 Aug. 1915	25 Aug. 1919
Massey III	Right Hon. William Ferguson Massey	25 Aug. 1919	10 May 1925
Bell	Hon. Sir Francis Henry Dillon Bell, G.C.M.G., K.C.	14 May 1925	30 May 1925
Coates	Right Hon. Joseph Gordon Coates, M.C.	30 May 1925	10 Dec. 1928
Ward II	Right Hon. Sir Joseph George Ward, BART., G.C.M	10 Dec. 1928	28 May 1930
Forbes I	Right Hon. George William Forbes	28 May 1930	22 Sept. 1931
Forbes II Coalition	Right Hon. George William Forbes	22 Sept. 1931	6 Dec. 1935

APPENDIX

Name of Ministry	Name of Premier / Prime Minister	Assumed office	Retired
Savage	Right Hon. Michael Joseph Savage	6 Dec. 1935	27 Mar. 1940
Fraser I	Hon. Peter Fraser	1 Apr. 1940	30 Apr. 1940
Fraser II	Right Hon. Peter Fraser, C.H.	30 Apr. 1940	13 Dec. 1949
Holland	Right Hon. Sir Sidney George Holland, G.C.B., C.H.	13 Dec. 1949	26 Sept. 1957
Holyoake I	Right Hon. Keith Jacka Holyoake	26 Sept. 1957	12 Dec. 1957
Nash	Right Hon. Walter Nash, C.H.	12 Dec. 1957	12 Dec. 1960
Holyoake II	Right Hon. Keith Jacka Holyoake	12 Dec. 1960	

Sources: *New Zealand Year Book; New Zealand Parliamentary Record.*

7. DISTRIBUTION OF PARLIAMENTARY ELECTORATES

The table illustrates the brief period of South Island predominance and its gradual decline in the twentieth century. By the Electoral Amendment Act of 1965 the number of South Island European seats was fixed as a quota of twenty-five.

Selected Elections	No. of Seats			
	N. Is.	S. Is.	Maori	Total
1853	23	14	..	37
1861	29	24	..	53
1862	29	28	..	57
1866	29	41	..	70
1867	29	43	4	76
1871	30	44	4	78
1875	34	50	4	88
1881	36	55	4	95
1890	31	39	4	74
1896	34	36	4	74
1902	38	38	4	80
1908	41	35	4	80
1925	46	30	4	80
1938	48	28	4	80
1946	49	27	4	80
1969	55	25	4	84

Source: *New Zealand Parliamentary Record*, (ed.) G. H. Scholefield, Wellington, 1950, p. 90.

INDEX

Australasian Naval Agreement, 1887, 252–4

Australia, Wakefield and the theory of 'sufficient price', 1–3; Wakefield and the 'frontier' of New South Wales, 3–4; Hobson's instructions, 10–17; pastoralism in New Zealand compared, 27; squatters in Canterbury, 32–3, 39; Charter of 1840 for separate colony, 54–7; early colonial trade, 72; responsible government, 84; borrowing, 190–1; Maritime Strike, 198–9; naval defence, 239, 245–8; trade negotiations, 250–2; naval subsidies, 252–4; Naval Station limits, 254; Federation Commission, 265–9; Statute of Westminster, 288–92; citizenship, 296; working farmers, 301; Canberra Pact, 368–78; ANZAM, 385–6; ANZUS, 386–8; SEATO, 388–92; Vietnam military co-operation, 398–401; Britain's withdrawal from East of Suez, 404–5; Malaysia–Singapore commitment 1969, 405–8; NAFTA, 448–51

Australia, New Zealand, Free Trade Area, 448–51

Australian–New Zealand Affairs Secretariat, 376

Australian–New Zealand Agreement (1944), 368–78

Australian Naval Station, Limits of, 254

Autonomy, 276–8

Avon, River, 33

Balance of Payments crisis (1967), 453–5

Balfour Committee (1926), 276–8, 285, 287–8

Ballance, John, Calls for Liberal Party, 182–5; 1890 Election address, 201–3; tax proposals, 204–5; Liberal, 224–5; H. E. Holland refers, 233; Savage refers, 336; date as Premier, 468

Ballot, Land, Nelson (1841), 21–3

Bangkok, 396

Bartley, T. H., 36

Bay of Islands, 6, 115

Bell, Sir Francis Henry Dillon, 273–5, 468

Bell, Francis Dillon, 250–2, 273–5

Bell, N. M., 353, 355

Belshaw, Dr. H., 317

Benefits, see Social Security

Berendsen, Carl August, 368, 386

Betterment Principle, 310

Bills, see Statutes; Native Rights Bill

Black Budget (1958), 434–5

Bledisloe, Governor-General Viscount, 467

Bluff, 463

Board of Control, meat export, 301–2

Board of Conciliation, 210–11

Board of Maori Affairs, 436

Borough Councils, 57

Borrowing, Public, Vogel's 1870 public works and immigration speech, 42–51; 1856 Compact, 99–105; Britain as 'mortgagee', 190–1; 1890 Election, 200–3; Advances to Settlers, 207–8; Reform policy, 222; Liberal 1919 platform, 299; Liberal 1928 platform, 311; Labour 1935 policy, 320; Lee's attack on Labour finance, 343–6; 350–2; from I.M.F., 453–5

Boundaries, Colonial Charter, 1840, 54–7

Bowen, Governor Sir George, 234–8, 466

Boxer uprising, 265

Braddon, Sir E. N. C., 259

Bramston, John, 244, 255

Bretton Woods, 424

Britain, Adoption of Statute of Westminster, 284–92; Afghanistan, 250; annexation, 3–18; ANZAM, 385–6 assimilated Society, 437; Australasian Naval Agreement (1887), 252–4; Balfour definition (1926), 276–8; Boxer uprising, 265; Citizenship laws, 294–6; Colonial Conference (1897), 259–60; Constitutional amendment, 293–4; Crown colony rule, 54–63; defence against aggression, 236–8; demand for food, 452; Division in 1914–18 War, 273–5; 'Dominion', Title of, 269–70; Dreadnought, 272–3; expeditionary forces, 250, 260–5, 273–4, 397–8; Far East Strategic Reserve, 392–7; German War (1939), 284–5, 365–6; Gov. Gordon, 240–4; Gov. Jervois, 245–

473

Manganui (Monganui), Port of, 463
Manila Pact, 388–92
Manila Protocol, 392
Manufacturers' Federation, 316
Manufacturers, Federation Commission; 267–8; Lee policy, 346, 350; 'Labour has a Plan', 321; 1943 National platform, 411; Dr. W. B. Sutch, 452–3
Manukau Harbour, 18
Maori Affairs Amendment Act (1967), 444–6
Maori Committees, 170, 415–18, 441–3
Maori Council, New Zealand, 441–3
Maori Councils, 1900 Act, 168–70; Land Councils, 170–4; 1945 Act, 415–18; 1962 Act, 441–3
Maori Electorates, 469
Maori Executives, 441–3
Maori King, Election of Potatau I, 125–31; Gorst's view, 133–4; Grey's 1861 visit to Waikato, 146–53; Tawhiao's Constitution, 165–8; Pomare's view, 175; attitude to Ratana, 178; withdrawal of British troops, 235
Maori Land courts, 155–8, 162
Maori Parliament, Movement for, 162–5
Maori Population, Estimates of, 459
Maori religious leaders, Te Whiti, 158–62; Tawhiao, 165–8; Rua, 175–8; Ratana, 178–9; 415
Maori Social and Economic Advancement Act (1945), 415–18
Maori Trustee, 436, 444–6
Maori Vested Lands Administration Act (1954), 446
Maori Villages, Committees, 417
Maori Wardens, 415–18
Maori Wars, see Anglo-Maori Wars
Maori Welfare Act, 1962, 441–3
Maoriland Worker, The, 300–1
Maoris, United Tribes of New Zealand, 6; Stephen's priorities, 8–10; Hobson's instructions, 10–17; attitude of Earl Grey and 1846 Constitution, 60–1; Gov. Grey, 65; military and economic skills, 70–1; entire fusion, 71; 1852 Act, 81, 82–3; Maori affairs reserved, 92–3, 121–2; reservation ended, 108–11; Treaty of Waitangi, 115–19, map

of tribal regions, 116; Colonial Office and Hone Heke's resistance, 119–20; Fenton's idea of model farms, 122–4; the King movement, 125–34; Fox's policy, 141–3; Runanga scheme, 144–6; Grey's 1861 visit to Waikato, 146–53; confiscation policy, 153–4; Te Whiti's community at Parihaka, 158–62; Maori parliament movement, 162–4; Tawhiao's constitution, 165–8; the 1900 Acts, 168–74; Pomare predicts integration, 174–5; Rua, 175–8; Ratana, 178–9; withdrawal of British troops, 234–6; one quarter of battalion offered in 1885, 250; Federation Commission, 268; Maori Social and Economic Welfare Act, 1945, 415–18; Hunn Report, 436–8; Integration policy, 438–4; Maori Welfare Act, 1962, 441–3; Maori Affairs Amendment Act, 1967, 444–6
Maoritanga, 437, 440
Maritime Strike (1890), 198–9, 200, 204
Marlborough, Early pastoralism, 26–8; map, 74; land settlement, 206
Marshall, J. R., 448–50
Marx and Marxism, 193, 227
Massey, William Ferguson, Freehold tenure, 216–19; Prime Minister, 224–6; H. E. Holland attacks, 227; Naval defence, 270; Meat Board, 301–2; Dairy Board, 303–4; repeal income tax on farmers, 304–6; J. A. Lee, 349; dates as Prime Minister, 468
Maungapohatu, 175–8
Maxwell, Ebenezer, 303–4
Meat Export Control Board, 301–2
Medical benefits, 342–3
Merchant Shipping Acts, 291
Middle East, 393–5, 397–8
Middle Island, the 1840 Charter, 54
Military forces, Colonial, not available 1840, 18; Hone Heke's resistance, 119–20; self-reliance, 109–11; withdrawal of British garrison, 234–6; see also Defence
Military settlements, 153–4
Millar, John Andrew, 196–7
Mills, W. T., 228

INDEX

PRINTED IN GREAT BRITAIN
AT THE UNIVERSITY PRESS, OXFORD
BY VIVIAN RIDLER
PRINTER TO THE UNIVERSITY